PRAGMATIC STEPS FOR GLOBAL SECURITY

NATIONAL PERSPECTIVES ON NUCLEAR DISARMAMENT

EDITED BY:
Barry M. Blechman
Alexander K. Bollfrass

March 2010

The Henry L. Stimson Center
1111 19th Street, NW   12th Floor   Washington, DC 20036
phone: 202-223-5956   fax: 202-238-9604   www.stimson.org

TABLE OF CONTENTS

PREFACE

I am pleased to present *National Perspectives on Nuclear Disarmament*, the final Stimson publication in a series addressing obstacles to the elimination of nuclear weapons. The Stimson project on nuclear security, *Unblocking the Road to Zero*, has explored the practical dimensions of this critical 21st century debate, identifying both political and technical obstacles that could block the road to "zero" and outlining how each of these could be addressed.

Led by Stimson's co-founder and Distinguished Fellow Dr. Barry Blechman, the project provides useful analyses that can help US and world leaders make the elimination of nuclear weapons a realistic and viable option. This volume is a compendium of a previously-published six-part series of country assessments. It follows the release of *Elements of a Nuclear Disarmament Treaty*, a volume on the technical issues of governance, verification, and enforcement of a disarmament regime.

The authors of each chapter in this book are leading authorities on the factors influencing their subject governments' nuclear decision-making and are well positioned to predict those nations' reactions to the disarmament scenarios they have been asked to evaluate. Most chapters were written by knowledgeable nationals of each country. The result is an honest appraisal of the geo-political obstacles to global disarmament that sheds light on the nuclear decision-making mechanisms of key nuclear countries and bypasses the platitudes exchanged by diplomats in public forums.

The *Unblocking the Road to Zero* series makes an important contribution to the renewed debate about how to rid the world of the dangers of nuclear weapons. It frames nuclear disarmament as a realistic, strategically sound goal for the world, rather than an idealistic vision and distant pursuit. This enduring strategic issue has been a central concern of the Stimson Center since its founding twenty years ago. I hope that this new publication will provide insights and pragmatic ideas to facilitate wise policymaking, in keeping with Stimson tradition.

Sincerely,

Ellen Laipson
President and CEO
The Stimson Center

INTRODUCTION

Barry M. Blechman and Alexander K. Bollfrass

In September 2009, the 15 members of the UN Security Council, including the five declared nuclear weapon states, unanimously pledged, "to create the conditions for a world without nuclear weapons." The road to nuclear disarmament will no doubt be long and arduous, but its feasibility does not depend upon scientific discoveries or the invention of new technologies; it hinges strictly upon governments' willingness to embark upon it.[*]

During 2009, Stimson's *Unblocking the Road to Zero* project reviewed advanced nuclear nations' degrees of resistance to the idea of negotiated, multilateral nuclear disarmament. The results show that with serious effort, hard work, compensating security arrangements, and a measure of luck, nuclear disarmament a viable endeavor.

The nine governments with nuclear weapons would all need to consent to a disarmament process, but the achievement of a *concurrent* consensus would not be necessary. They each would have to agree on incremental and reciprocal steps at appropriate junctures. The nations with the largest arsenals could begin the disarmament process. As they dismantled weapons, pressures would grow for others to join.   Concurrently, negotiations could be held to resolve the security concerns motivating some states to acquire nuclear weapons, and also to place tighter controls on civilian nuclear materials and facilities so that they could not be diverted for weapon programs in a disarmed world. The approach taken must be tailored to each nuclear power individually.

United States and Russia: No matter how one envisions the initiation of nuclear disarmament or its timeframe, it is certain that the US and Russia – which jointly own more than 95 percent of the world's nuclear weapons – must take the lead. Although talks for a treaty to reduce their nuclear arsenals are underway, the START agreement that should emerge later this year will only be a modest, initial bilateral step toward the ultimate goal. The next round of negotiations must address shorter range weapons and reserve warheads, as well. As Dmitri Trenin points out in his essay, before it will make truly deep nuclear cuts, Russia must overcome its sense of inferiority in conventional forces, particularly in its relationship with NATO. For its part, the US must become convinced that Russia no longer seeks to reassert control or undue influence over states that formerly were members of the

---

[*] Technical obstacles to nuclear disarmament and how they might be overcome are explored at length in Barry M. Blechman and Alexander K. Bollfrass (eds.), *Elements of a Nuclear Disarmament Treaty* (Stimson, 2010).

Soviet Union or the Warsaw Pact. In both countries, presidential leadership for nuclear disarmament must be impressed upon key institutional players. The two countries must come to terms about the relationship between nuclear reductions and the deployment of missile defenses, either accepting limitations on missile defenses or working cooperatively to develop multinational defenses.

France and the United Kingdom: America's NATO allies currently have contrasting views regarding their nuclear arms' utility. As described by Lawrence Freedman, British mainstream political debate has moved closer to considering unilateral disarmament to avoid diverting resources from its strained war-fighting capacity. Bruno Tertrais stresses that France has been far more resistant to the idea, although it is worth noting that France has recently joined the ranks of countries with former national security leaders publicly calling for disarmament. Both Freedman and Tertrais conclude that if the US and Russia made significant progress toward deep reductions in their own arsenals, these two US allies would find it difficult to resist joining multilateral negotiations with the goal of eliminating nuclear weapons from all nations.

China and India: The similarities in these emerging global powers' approach on nuclear weapons are notable. Both have been satisfied so far with surprisingly modest nuclear postures and only the slow modernization of their forces, and both espouse support for far-reaching disarmament objectives. But as Rajesh Basrur points out for India, and Pan Zhenqiang to China, the path for a broad dialogue on nuclear elimination among all of the major nuclear powers will only be cleared if the US and Russia first make deep cuts.

Pakistan and Israel: These two countries are paired as both see their nuclear arsenals as offsetting opponents' actual or potential conventional military advantages. Thus, the two countries will likely require concrete security guarantees to join the disarmament process. Both Feroz Khan, in the case of Pakistan, and Shlomo Brom, in the case of Israel, argue that dedicated US leadership and the support of the other great powers would be required to reduce the existential threats perceived by these two nations. Giving them the confidence to join in multilateral reductions, in particular, would require the resolution, with credible guarantees by all relevant parties, of two of the world's most intractable conflicts. Between them, Israel likely poses the greater challenge.

Iran and North Korea: Skirting the boundaries between weapon- and non-weapon states are the countries whose nuclear misbehaviors have dominated headlines in recent years. Both Iran and North Korea have pursued nuclear programs beyond the boundaries of the Nonproliferation Treaty. Leon Sigal and Joel Wit note that although North Korea has made clear its intention to remain a nuclear-weapon state, it is conceivable that over time, a wide-ranging program to resolve Pyongyang's security concerns and to ensure its economic development could put it on a new course. Anoush Ehteshami stresses that Iran's ambitions are less clear. Iranian leaders maintain that their nuclear activities are restricted to civilian purposes, although the revelation in late 2009 of a secret enrichment facility gives lie to this statement. Again, addressing underlying geo-political tensions in Iran's neighborhood might provide sufficient incentives to persuade it to dedicate its nuclear program to verifiably peaceful purposes.

Non-weapon states: Several non-weapon states with advanced nuclear technologies, such as Brazil, must lead the effort to guarantee that procedures and organizations are in place to ensure that civilian nuclear facilities, particularly enrichment and reprocessing facilities, could not be quickly or covertly diverted to weapon purposes in a disarmed world. Marcos C. de Azambuja discusses this for the case of Brazil. Another important group of non-weapon states are the thirty countries covered by the United States' extended nuclear deterrent. Fears have been raised that a disarming United States could change the security calculus for these states, such as Japan, discussed by Matake Kamiya, or Turkey, discussed by Henri J. Barkey. This strategic shift could potentially prompt them to seek their own nuclear arms. Both groups of non-weapon states need to be engaged early to shape future non-nuclear security assurances and to develop restrictions on the most proliferation-prone technologies.

Support for nuclear disarmament is spreading and deepening across the globe. The Security Council's resolution was an important step, but merely a symbolic one. Real progress can only be made by grounding the process in an understanding of key governments' views of the roles nuclear weapons play in their defense policies, not simply their vague rhetorical promises.

A Brazilian Perspective on Nuclear Disarmament

Marcos C. de Azambuja[*]

Brazil enjoys a comfortable geopolitical situation. Its policy concerns and priorities should always be seen against this backdrop. Brazil identifies no actual or potential rivals or adversaries in South America or in the South Atlantic basin. Further south, the Antarctic may be the most peaceful and well regulated region in the world. Even the Malvinas/Falklands conflict in 1982 was an isolated episode that did not alter the fact that, compared with other areas of the globe, the American shore of the South Atlantic remains a quiet and largely uneventful strategic backwater.

This peaceful prospect can be understood from an even wider perspective. The southern hemisphere is free from weapons of mass destruction, being entirely covered by treaties establishing nuclear-free zones. It is not the stage for any major international confrontation—be it ethnic, religious, territorial, ideological, or primarily economic and commercial—in which weapons of mass destruction or nuclear deterrence could play a significant role. This has been true for nearly 20 years, since South Africa dismantled its nuclear program in 1990–91 after it became unnecessary when, with the abolition of apartheid, South Africa no longer felt threatened by its neighbors. Indeed, South Africa became the friend and loose partner of those same neighbors.

South America thus presents a paradox: its states have shown a significant degree of domestic volatility since independence, but they have been able to keep up a tradition of restraint and peaceful relations with each other. The political map of South America has remained essentially unchanged for over a century and a half; the last war among neighbors to result in significant territorial changes took place in the second half of the nineteenth century. The more recent and limited conflicts between Paraguay and Bolivia (1931–1935) and between Peru and Ecuador (1941) illustrate the trend of border permanence. It is striking to note how infrequently, in the last 60 years, questions relating to South America have been brought to the attention of the UN Security Council as matters of grave and urgent concern to the international community.[†]

---

[*] Marcos C. de Azambuja is vice president of the Brazilian Center for International Relations. The views expressed in this chapter are his and do not necessarily represent those of the Center.
[†] On the paradox between the domestic turbulence and international stability of the South American region, see Kalevi Jaakko Holsti, *The State, War, and the State of War* (New York: Cambridge University Press, 1996), 154.

LIMITS TO BRAZIL'S NUCLEAR AMBITIONS

It was easy and almost natural, therefore, for Latin America to become the first inhabited nuclear-weapon-free zone in the world.[‡] The immediate impulse to ban such weapons in the region sprang from the Cuban missile crisis in October 1962. For a few frantic days, diplomats sought a way in New York to provide the Soviet Union with a face-saving excuse for withdrawing the weapons it had placed, or was in the process of placing, on the island and to recall the Russian ships that were headed toward Havana. The first UN resolution proposing the denuclearization of Latin America was introduced in those perilous days by Brazil, seeking as its immediate goal to defuse what was certainly the Cold War's moment of greatest global risk. The Brazilian initiative did not ultimately play a role in the solution of the Cuban crisis—a different way was found to secure the Soviet withdrawal and guarantee Cuba's protection from invasion—but that draft resolution was the starting point of a process that would lead to the 1972 signing in Mexico City of the Treaty of Tlatelolco, which denuclearized Latin America.[1]

The rare pursuit of nuclear military capabilities in Latin America and the Caribbean has been either an extension of extraregional conflicts or an expression of the desire to attain greater international influence and prestige by joining the global group of nuclear-weapon states. Real or potential threats to the security of the aspiring nuclear-weapon state from any other regional actor were negligible or nonexistent. Nor were targets for attack identified.

In other words, the nuclear aspirations of Latin American nations have been more symbolic than strategic. Because of this lack of grounding in real security concerns, military nuclear programs never obtained real national support or funding and, when an appropriate moment arrived, they were relatively easy to discredit and dismantle. Only four countries in the whole of Latin America could have pursued nuclear military programs with any credibility: Cuba, Mexico, Brazil, and Argentina.

Cuba's nuclear project did not spring from its own scientific and technological capabilities or strategic needs, but from its close strategic alliance with the Soviet Union, which for a number of reasons wished to install nuclear weapons in Cuba with delivery systems for them that would threaten the United States. The agreement reached between the United States and the USSR in 1962 ended that project.

Mexico had the economic and technological capacity to develop a military nuclear program, but its proximity to and relationship with the United States made this option a nonstarter. Mexico from the beginning has consistently presented itself as

---

[‡] All weapons are banned from Antarctica, which is inhabited only by researchers.

the great promoter of Latin American nuclear disarmament. Today, it hosts the Agency for the Prohibition of Nuclear Weapons in Latin America and the Caribbean, which was created to ensure adherence to the Latin American Treaty for Non-Proliferation of Nuclear Weapons, known as the Treaty of Tlatelolco.[2]

Thus, only two countries in the region would have been able to sustain to some degree a nuclear arms race: Brazil and Argentina. Even in these two countries, motives for nuclear rivalry were tenuous. More than seeking to threaten one another, each country sought to enhance its position on the world scene. Moreover, their leaders believed that, if the programs proved successful, they would gain additional legitimacy for their largely unpopular military regimes.[3]

Under those military regimes, for the better part of the 1960s, 1970s, and early 1980s, both countries kept alive a rivalry that, in one way or another, had endured since their independence early in the nineteenth century. With the return of civilian rule and democracy to both countries more or less at the same time in the later 1980s, one of the priorities of their newly elected civilian leaders was to get rid of what were then euphemistically called "parallel nuclear programs." In particular, they each wished to differentiate military and civilian nuclear activities. The latter were fully compatible with the principles and objectives of the Treaty of Tlatelolco and were maintained in compliance with the full scope of safeguards established by the International Atomic Energy Agency (IAEA).

Even when the two military regimes were at the height of their power, the rivalry between them was largely rhetorical and never really threatened to get out of control. The military leaders of both countries were on the same side of the Cold War, were staunchly anticommunist, and shared similar doctrines of national security. Moreover, there were no conflicting territorial claims between them, as there were in the more serious disputes between Chile and Argentina over the Beagle Channel and Patagonia. The only substantial clash of interests between Buenos Aires and Brasilia was over use of the water resources of the Paraná River, a matter that was largely resolved with the building of the Itaipu hydroelectric project by Brazil and Paraguay, followed downstream a few years later by the Yacireta dam, in which Argentina and Paraguay were partners.

Brazil under President José Sarney and Argentina under President Raul Alfonsin undertook largely symmetrical efforts in the late 1980s to dismantle their countries' military nuclear programs. They also set in motion a confidence-building process that led to the so-called Quadripartite Agreement, signed in Vienna in 1991 by Argentina, Brazil, the IAEA, and the Argentine Brazilian Agency of Accounting and Control of Nuclear Materials. The process of defusing the apparent competition between military-controlled nuclear programs took about six years—from the signing of the Declaration of Foz do Iguaçu in 1985 to the conclusion of the Quadripartite Agreement in 1991.[4] The confidence-building process is still active today.

This work was reinforced by progress in economic relationships between the two countries. Beginning in earnest in 1991 with signature of the Treaty of Asunción, and running parallel with the dismantling of nuclear and missile programs, the two states began to build MERCOSUR (Mercado Comum do Sul), a regional trade agreement. This growing economic relationship played a major role in replacing a sterile relationship, based to a large extent on mistrust and rivalry, with one in which cooperation and trust are essential components. Soon it became incongruous that two countries working to establish not only a free trade zone but also a common market and a close political union should preserve projects and attitudes that no longer corresponded to the realities of their relationship. Key sectors in both countries promoted MERCOSUR, not only because of its intrinsic commercial and economic merits, but also because it was seen as an antidote to attitudes that had been rendered obsolete by the end of the Cold War, the triumph of democracy on the continent, and ever closer physical and economic integration between the two neighbors.

During this same period, the Treaty of Tlatelolco finally came fully into force, with all countries within its geographical perimeter but Cuba subscribing to it,[§] as well as outside powers that accepted limitations on their deployment of nuclear forces within the zone. In 1994, Brazil fully accepted the obligations of the Treaty of Tlatelolco, but it took three years more for Brazil to join the Nuclear Non-Proliferation Treaty (NPT). Brazilian reservations about the NPT are major and deeply rooted in the national mindset. Brazilians assume that sooner or later—preferably sooner—Brazil will emerge as a major power and that nothing should be done that limits or jeopardizes its expectations or hinders its access to that status. Given that the NPT identifies two classes of states—the five declared nuclear-weapon states and the rest, who are all non-nuclear-weapon states—Brazil was reluctant to accept its grouping into the latter category.[5]

Developments in the last 15 years have strengthened Brazil's self-confidence. Its membership in the group of emerging powers along with China, India, and Russia has added a new dimension to a pervasive feeling in some sectors that by joining the NPT, Brazil had fulfilled its responsibilities for nonproliferation and that it should not give up the possibility of developing and acquiring civilian nuclear technologies allowed by the treaty. A concern that has been frequently and emphatically expressed is that Brazil signed the NPT without any real negotiation or

---

[§] Cuba finally joined the Treaty of Tlatelolco in 2002.

compensation. Brazilians by and large view the NPT as discriminatory and profoundly flawed. The results—or more precisely the lack of results—of the most recent NPT review conferences in 2000 and 2005, and the long paralysis of multilateral disarmament initiatives in Geneva and New York, reinforced the conviction held in many quarters in Brazil that the nuclear powers have not lived up to their pledges to promote meaningful negotiations toward nuclear disarmament and have failed to fulfill their commitments under Articles V and VI of the NPT. More broadly, many Brazilians believe that the policy of the nuclear-weapon states is, in fact, to impose more constraints and extract further concessions from the non-nuclear powers while failing to accomplish—or even to try to accomplish—what was expected from them when the NPT bargain was struck.

From a Brazilian perspective, the 2010 NPT Review Conference will be a test of whether the attitude of the nuclear powers has become more flexible and constructive or whether the impasses of the two most recent reviews will prevail. The results of the preparatory conference held at the United Nations in New York from May 4 to 15, 2009 suggest that the prospects for the 2010 NPT Review Conference are much brighter than the results of the previous two reviews. A new mood is easy to identify and this change in attitude and expectations has already been reflected in the Committee on Disarmament in Geneva, where after long years of virtual paralysis there is now an agreed agenda that will allow that body to begin productive work.

The Prague speech by President Obama in April 2009 has to be seen as a landmark. While expressing his long-term vision for a nuclear-weapons-free world, the President suggested a road map of practical steps beginning with a new US-Russia arms control treaty to replace the current START agreement that expires on December 5th. Among other goals, President Obama announced that his administration will work towards American ratification of the Comprehensive Test-ban Treaty and that he plans to convene a Global Summit on Nuclear Security in 2010. The joint statement by Presidents Obama and Russian President Medvedev of April 1st expressing their joint commitment to eliminating nuclear weapons is equally relevant. In short, after a long period of neglect, disarmament issues are back on the agenda and even if progress is difficult and slow, there is an encouraging prospect for the long run.

These renewed prospects aside, and despite Brazilian concern about the discriminatory nature of the NPT, Brazil is unlikely to go back on its commitment to nonproliferation. That commitment was entered into by a legitimate government, acting in good faith after a mature weighing of options, and will be honored by future Brazilian governments. Brazil, after all, is bound not to develop nuclear weapons by a many-tiered arrangement. First of all, it has treaty obligations with

Argentina and the IAEA and cannot ignore the cooperative nature of ABACC (the Brazilian-Argentine Agency for Accounting and Control of Nuclear Materials) and MERCOSUR. It must also uphold its regional commitments under the Treaty of Tlatelolco and comply, on a global scale, with the NPT. Furthermore, the Brazilian Constitution in Articles 21 and 177 expressly prohibits the pursuit of non-peaceful uses of atomic energy. And, as important as all these cumulative legal obligations and constraints are, the central fact remains that Brazil has always lacked the military motivation to develop weapons of mass destruction and only ever did so half-heartedly—tempted not by defensive or aggressive security goals but by a desire not to renounce certain scientific and technological gains and the prestige and major-power status that it associates with them.

While there is a lingering feeling of regret, among sectors of the military establishment and in some nationalistic groups, that Brazil failed to develop nuclear weapons and delivery systems during the more than 40 years when it was free to do so, this sentiment is in fact residual and nostalgic and limited in its rhetoric and militancy to groups that remain to a greater or lesser degree attached to the objectives and values of the largely discredited military regime.

BRAZIL'S CIVILIAN NUCLEAR GOALS

Brazil's commitment to the nonproliferation regime thus appears irrevocable unless circumstances change dramatically. But its determination to go forward with its long-established and successful uranium enrichment program is no less firm. To the Brazilian government, scientific establishment, and broad segments of public opinion, the trade-off that the country made is clear. Brazil joined the NPT with the explicit understanding that nuclear activities allowed under the treaty would be pursued. Brazil already has the fifth or sixth largest uranium reserves in the world, and a substantial part of its territory remains to be prospected.[6] It also has an ambitious and long-standing program to master the complete nuclear fuel cycle, plans to build several more nuclear power plants besides the two already in operation, and seeks to develop nuclear-powered naval turbines. Brazil has no intention to abandon any of these projects.

Currently, the Brazilian government is reluctant to adhere to the IAEA's Additional Protocol for more intrusive safeguards. The president of Brazil's Nuclear Energy Commission has claimed to be "studying the thing" for several years, and says Brazil's reluctance is based on "issues about other countries' compliance with the traditional NPT. For example, about disarmament."[7] Even so, there is arguably no major substantive obstacle to its eventual adherence; the timing of such a move, however, will depend on a favorable negotiating environment. Brazil is unlikely to take any additional steps with regard to the NPT or to make further concessions, such as adhering to the Additional Protocol, in the absence of meaningful concessions from the nuclear-weapon states. Moreover, should the United States (or the nuclear-weapon states collectively) put pressure on Brazil to abandon its nuclear projects, including enrichment, there would be a very robust, probably insurmountable, resistance.

Brazil's earlier attempts to develop a largely autonomous nuclear capacity have been costly and marked, more often than not, by disappointment and failure. The most glaring example of this was the German-Brazilian Nuclear Agreement, which was signed in 1975 and operated fully for 10 years. The original agreement called for a vast transfer of technology and also had a very important industrial component as it envisaged, in the short and medium term, the construction in Brazil of eight nuclear power plants. Not only would this agreement have benefited Brazil, but it would have provided a great boost to German industry and technology.

But the agreement raised major international resistance, especially from the United States, and both Germany and Brazil were under considerable pressure to revoke or at least to modify the agreement. Thus, the enrichment process, which was originally to be based on the well-tested centrifuge technology, was modified in favor of the so-called "jet nozzle" approach, an experimental alternative which up until now has not produced economically viable results.

In support of the agreement, and in pursuit of somewhat grandiose nationalistic objectives, the Brazilian government spent an enormous amount of money setting up facilities subsidiary to its NUCLEBRAS (Empresas Nucleares Brasileiras S.A.) agency. These facilities proved to be over-sized and later had to be scaled down so that they could be utilized at all, albeit in a modified way. [8]

A modified version of the agreement still exists, but its scope has been sharply scaled down, and the current version is not only devoid of any objectionable provisions, but is also very strong in its environmental focus.

The agreement with Germany came near the end of the military phase in Brazilian politics and at a moment when two decades of accelerating economic growth were faltering, primarily because of the first oil shock of 1973–74. It became obvious to Brazil at that time that it would be extremely difficult to find reputable external help for its nuclear projects as long as the country remained outside the NPT and while some activities were still being carried out with military objectives. NUCLEBRAS, the Brazilian agency responsible for coordinating efforts in the nuclear field, was designed to act as the counterpart for Brazil's German partners. It has since been replaced by new agencies under the supervision of the Ministry of Science and Technology. NUCLEBRAS had many of the characteristics of the Brazilian institutions of that period. It was too big, too heavy in its administrative structure, and rather weak in the qualifications of its scientists. Its recruiting methods lacked transparency. It was essentially unconcerned about costs and largely insensitive to social and environmental concerns.

Despite these shortcomings, NUCLEBRAS was a turning point in the history of Brazilian nuclear development, and many of its personnel remain active in Brazilian nuclear projects, particularly in Brazilian Nuclear Industries (Industrias Nucleares Brasileiras or INB), based primarily in Resende, a city halfway between Rio and São Paulo. Some other units function in different parts of Brazil, but most derive from NUCLEBRAS as well. Besides the cluster of plants and other units assembled around and under INB, uranium enrichment takes place under naval supervision in the Aramar center in Iperó in the state of São Paulo.[9]

Today, three separate ministries have jurisdiction over the Brazilian nuclear program: the Ministry of Science and Technology; the Ministry of Mines and Energy, which oversees the National Commission for Nuclear Energy and INB; and the Ministry of the Environment, with the Brazilian Institute of Environment and Renewable Natural Resources as its executive agency. Nuclear policies in their broadest scope fall under the supervision of the president's office, and the Ministry of External Relations has an influential role on issues with international implications.

There are deep divisions within Brazil about what nuclear policies the country should follow. A substantial number of environmentally oriented NGOs oppose the construction of more nuclear plants and express concern about the safety and environmental impact of those already in operation. They also express anxiety about the final disposal of nuclear waste. Some Brazilian nuclear physicists also have indicated their misgivings about plans to expand Brazil's nuclear capabilities. There are divisions within the scientific community on virtually every aspect of the current program and on its future expansion.

Some experts believe that Brazil should further develop its hydroelectric capabilities, move forward with biofuel projects, explore the inland and offshore reserves of oil and natural gas that are continuing to be discovered, and utilize wind and solar energy in a much more robust way. They argue that nuclear energy is particularly expensive to develop and hazardous to the environment, and that Brazil has a range of less costly and less risky alternatives at its disposal. Although their numbers are not negligible, they remain a minority.[**]

[**] The Brazilian Association for the Advancement of Science frequently reports in its periodical, *Jornal da Ciência,* on the divisions within the Brazilian government regarding the further development of nuclear power. Generally, the Ministry of Science and Technology and the president's staff are in favor of an expanded program, while the Ministry of Mines and Energy and the Ministry of the Environment oppose it. But even within each agency opinions are divided. Opponents of expansion cite economic factors, saying Brazil can produce cheaper energy in other ways,

The majority of the Brazilian scientific and administrative establishment, on the other hand, supports the completion of Angra 3, a partially built nuclear plant.[††]

Plans to build six or eight new nuclear plants over the next few years fluctuate according to the rate of growth of the Brazilian economy, the cost of oil in the international market, and the ability of Brazilian reservoirs to supply enough water to existing hydroelectric turbines during years of low rainfall. These and other variables interact in many complex equations. Until the fourth quarter of 2008, before the current global credit crunch and financial crisis had fully settled in, projections indicated the need to go forward with a vigorous nuclear program. Since then, however, projections have changed drastically and the case to move forward in the short term appears far less compelling.

In September 2008, Brazil and Argentina signed an agreement to set up a binational nuclear enterprise—operating within the guidelines of the Nuclear Suppliers Group, of which Brazil and Argentina are both members—that will enrich uranium, produce radiological medical supplies, develop new applications for agriculture, and design and construct research reactors. The agreement is the result of work by the Binational Committee on Nuclear Energy, a body that was set up to move nuclear cooperation between Argentina and Brazil forward from the early arrangements in the 1980s. The latter were primarily designed to generate trust and transparency; the new projects are geared to respond to the present and future nuclear needs of South America.

It is estimated that beyond the projected expansion of existing nuclear facilities in Argentina and Brazil, new plants will also be built over the next few years in Chile, Uruguay, Peru, and Venezuela. 10 The hope is that the new binational venture will be able to bid competitively to supply these future plants with equipment, technology, and fuel, and thus become an effective player in a field for which impressive growth and substantial profits are projected in the coming years. Although the situations are not exactly the same, one potential model is the URENCO Group in Europe.

---

and argue that nuclear power poses inherent ecological risks. Proponents argue that nuclear power is a clean source of energy and that Brazil has the technology to produce it and an abundant fuel supply.

[††] Angra 3 is expected to begin operation in late 2013. After prolonged discussions, the National Commission on Nuclear Energy, the Brazilian Institute for the Environment, and the municipal authorities of Angra dos Reis have agreed to restart construction of the plant, for which the site and the foundation already exist, as well as nearly 50 percent of the equipment, which was bought quite a few years ago from the Siemens group and has been stored at considerable expense. Angra 3 will have the same generating capacity as Angra 2—1,350 megawatts. See "Angra 3 pode abrir caminhos para novas usinas atômicas no país," *Problemas Brasileiros,* January 10, 2008.

BRAZILIAN VIEWS ON DISARMAMENT

Brazilians cannot identify any grounds for optimism on the prospects for significant progress by the nuclear-weapon states toward arms control and nuclear disarmament. In the Brazilian assessment, the years immediately following the end of the Cold War provided a favorable environment for progress on a number of stalemated negotiating fronts, but that window of opportunity was not used. Today, with Russia reasserting its power, an ambitious and vigorous China more active on the world stage, and India and Pakistan as new players, the nuclear weapons game appears more complicated than ever. Furthermore, with the rise of international terrorism, preventing Iran from carrying out its weapon plans appears to be the only urgent and realistic goal now being pursued. Even this rather limited goal may be beyond reach unless intense negotiations are soon set in motion. However, even if Iran is not prevented from acquiring a military nuclear capability (either by creative diplomacy or by preemptive military attacks from the United States or Israel), Brazil is not likely to withdraw from its NPT commitments.

Brazil does not see the adoption of a treaty to eliminate all nuclear weapons on a global scale as a realistic goal. Brazilian leaders are even doubtful that gradual and modest steps in that direction will be taken in the foreseeable future. The prevailing opinion in Brazil is that the nuclear-weapon states are satisfied with the indefinite extension of the NPT and would rather tackle one by one the specific national cases that threaten the integrity and stability of that instrument, rather than to set in motion the vast and extremely complex machinery of disarmament negotiations. This case-by-case approach appears to have worked so far with Libya and it is hoped that combined and sustained pressure against Iran and North Korea might succeed in finally convincing these countries to stop short of acquiring a nuclear weapon capability or to dismantle its small arsenal, respectively. It is not easy to identify other countries that might seek to develop nuclear weapons in the short term. But the possibility that extremist groups could acquire nuclear weapons poses an entirely different set of questions and many additional difficulties.

Brazilian experts do not anticipate complete nuclear disarmament. While they do not expect a new nuclear arms race, they do not see any political, economic, or scientific indication that any of the nuclear powers is prepared to contemplate a radical global solution such as disarmament. Brazil's conviction is that, rather than the complete elimination of nuclear arsenals, all serious efforts should be focused on an accommodation that essentially respects and manages the status quo and perhaps places limits on weapon development and expansion based on what is possible to achieve given the prevailing political and strategic realities.

If, nonetheless, the complete elimination of nuclear weapons—with all the immense strategic changes that this would entail—were to be accomplished, Brazil's options would obviously have to be reconsidered. Under a disarmament regime, there would likely be a limited number of suppliers of enriched uranium—perhaps one or two each in Europe, the Americas, Asia, and the Middle East—operating under the licensing and control of a global authority. Brazil would likely try to become one of these suppliers and the leading partner in any Latin American arrangement that emerged from such a dramatically changed environment.

Although I doubt that this scenario could become reality in the foreseeable future, if substantive progress were nonetheless made toward this objective, Brazil could be counted on to be a leader in the negotiations, just as it has been since the creation of the Eighteen Nations Disarmament Committee in 1962, from which the current Conference on Disarmament evolved. Brazil made important contributions to the three special sessions that the United Nations dedicated to disarmament in 1978, 1982, and 1988, and will do so again if a fourth session is convened.

In short, Brazil and Latin America will not develop nuclear weapons and will remain active and constructive partners in the establishment of a world safe from weapons of mass destruction. Not even if undesirable developments were to occur in other parts of the world would Brazil or its neighbors be tempted to enter a nuclear arms race that they have wisely avoided so far. But Brazil is equally unlikely to give up its goal of being a key player in the important nuclear fuel market. There are virtually no limits to what Brazil would do to reassure others of its transparency and good faith in these areas, and I believe Brazilian leaders could accept a global authority regulating this field. What Brazil would not accept is to be left out of the highly selective and profitable club of nuclear fuel suppliers, to which it feels fully entitled to belong.

Endnotes

[1] Atomic Archive, *Latin America Nuclear Free Zone Treaty (1967)*, www.atomicarchive.com/Treaties/Treaty5.shtml; Arms Control Association, *Latin America Nuclear Weapons Free Zone Treaty (Treaty of Tlatelolco)*, www.armscontrol.org/documents/tlatelolco.

[2] Embajador Alfonso Garcia Robles, *México y el Desarme,* vol. 4, *Política Exterior de Mexico—175 Años de Historia,* ed. Secretaría de Relaciones Exteriores (1985).

[3] David Albright and Kevin O'Neill, "Argentine-Brazilian Nuclear Rapprochement" (summary of the seminar "Argentina and Brazil: The Latin American Nuclear Rapprochement," sponsored by the Shalheveth Freier Center for Peace, Science and Technology and the Institute for Science and International Security, May 16, 1996), www.isis-online.org/publications/israel96/exsum.html.

[4] Everton Vieira Vargas, "Atomos na Integração: a aproximação Brasil Argentina no campo nuclear e a construção do MERCOSUL," *Revista Brasileira de Política Internacional* 40 (January–June 1997).

[5] Jorge Castañeda de la Rosa, *La No Proliferación de armas nucleares en el orden universal* (Mexico: El Colegio de Mexico, 1969).

[6] Industrias Nucleares do Brasil, *Reserves—Brazil and World,* www.inb.gov.br/inb_eng/WebForms/Interna2.aspx?secao_id=48.

[7] Miles A. Pomper and William Huntington, "Interview with Odair Gonçalves, President of Brazil's Nuclear Energy Commission," *Arms Control Association*, September 28, 2005, www.armscontrol.org/interviews/20050928_Goncalves.asp.

[8] Christian Lohbauer, *Brasil-Alemanha fases de uma parceria, 1964–1999* (São Paulo, SP, Brasil: Konrad-Adenauer-Stiftung, 2000).

[9] Programa Nuclear Brasileiro INB, Senado Federal Agosto de 2007, Ciclo do Combustível Nuclear, Audiência Pública (senado.gov.br. AP 20070809-INB). [This is the record of a hearing in the Brazilian senate.]

[10] "Argentina, Brazil to Team Up on Nuclear Power," *ABC News*, February 23, 2008, www.abc.net.au/news/stories/2008/02/23/2170606.htm?site=news (accessed July 28, 2009); Geraldo Lino, "Acordo nuclear Brasil-Argentina: grande passo na integração regional," *Alerta em Rede*, September 2, 2008, www.alerta.inf.br/integracao/1377.html; Pedro Aguiar, "Brasil e Argentina saem na frente," *Revista Brasil Nuclear* 14, no. 34.

CHINA'S NUCLEAR STRATEGY IN A CHANGING WORLD STRATEGIC SITUATION

Major General Pan Zhenqiang (Retired)

Since it first demonstrated nuclear weapons capability in 1964, China has followed a unique nuclear policy and doctrine. China's nuclear forces are intended for only one purpose: to retaliate following a nuclear attack. Any state contemplating a nuclear strike against China must calculate the risk of nuclear retaliation and the resulting devastating loss the attacker would suffer. This prospect would hopefully deter the attacker. If one were to affix a description to China's nuclear strategy, it is perhaps best described as "purely defensive in nature."[1]

To further understand this definition, it is essential to distinguish "deterrence effects" from "deterrence strategy." It is certainly correct to say that China's nuclear strategy has the effect of deterring nuclear attacks, but it is not correct to suggest that China pursues a strategy of nuclear deterrence as do other nuclear weapon states. Any military strategy that is designed to attain military and security objectives through the use of military assets has a deterrent effect. In the Western sense, nuclear forces, like conventional military assets, constitute a legitimate, usable part of military capabilities in a military conflict or war. During the Cold War years, nuclear weapons were conceived—especially by the United States and NATO—as a means of compensating for the deficiencies of their conventional forces vis-à-vis the Soviet Union and its allies in the Warsaw Pact. Thus, the US and NATO deterrence strategy included the pledge that if NATO were losing a war with the Soviet Union, the alliance would be willing to make first use of nuclear weapons to prevent defeat.

Nuclear weapons were also conceived by both nuclear superpowers as essential instruments to help achieve political aims: either to intimidate other countries or control their allies by extending their "nuclear umbrella" in the form of extended deterrence. The nuclear strategies of the United Kingdom and France also had strong political motivations. By becoming a nuclear state, the UK evidently hoped to reach a more equitable status in its special relations with Washington, while France apparently wished to be recognized as a relevant world power through its nuclear status. Both countries seemed also to conceive of their nuclear weapons as trip-wires to ensure that the United States would not leave them alone in a possible major military conflict with the Soviet Union in Europe.

China makes none of these calculations and shares none of these objectives in its nuclear strategy. In this sense, it can be argued that China is *not* a nuclear weapon state in the traditional Western sense.

Strategically and politically, China has offered an unconditional pledge that it would not be the first to use nuclear weapons (NFU). This pledge constitutes the very quintessence of China's nuclear strategy, and has continued from the beginning of its nuclear age. The NFU pledge has not only reflected the nature and mission of China's nuclear forces, but also determines the size, configuration, readiness, and pace of development of China's nuclear forces. The NFU policy is further developed in a second pledge of equal importance. China has vowed not to use or threaten to use nuclear weapons against any non-nuclear weapon states under any circumstance. This commitment of unconditional negative nuclear assurances extends logically to Beijing's active support for establishing nuclear-free zones in various regions, and for China's subsequent willingness to undertake all necessary obligations in accord with the provisions of such nuclear-free zones.

Many Western analysts dismiss China's pledge of NFU as unverifiable and empty talk. But this skepticism is reminiscent of the typical Western mind-set of evaluating China's strategic intentions through the traditional Western way of thinking and behavior. Although the pledge of NFU indeed cannot be technologically verified, China's nuclear posture, which is based on NFU, can easily be discerned and through its evaluation, the pledge fully verified.

In an operational sense, since China's strategic objective is solely to deter a nuclear attack, the means to that end do not require a large nuclear arsenal. Maintaining a capability to destroy a few big cities in retaliation should be enough to frustrate any opponent considering a nuclear strike against China. Thus, China's focus is on maintaining a small, but credible, retaliatory force. This means an adequate number of warheads to ensure the survivability of at least some portion of its force after absorbing a preemptive strike from anywhere. The operational needs of China's sole goal of nuclear deterrence also requires a reasonable degree of alertness on Beijing's part to prepare for dealing with any contingencies, but not necessarily keeping its nuclear forces on hair-trigger alert. Since the only mission would be a counter-attack after a nuclear attack, and since it might usually take days to determine whether a real nuclear attack had actually occurred on its soil and who was responsible, there is no need for China to prematurely mate its warheads with the missiles, aircraft, or submarines that would deliver them. Furthermore, because Beijing's sole nuclear mission is to retaliate against cities, known as a "counter-value mission," the NFU makes it unnecessary to seek a nuclear war-fighting capability, or to develop nuclear weapons for non-strategic uses.

All of these limitations on the necessary capabilities of its nuclear forces enable China to avoid engaging in arms races with other nuclear weapon powers, and to exercise great restraint in the building up of its nuclear force. Thus, to claim that the NFU pledge is unverifiable is groundless. Also, the pledge is reflected in the slow and narrow evolution of Chinese nuclear forces and can be verified by observing the lack of rapid development in those forces   China's nuclear forces have been, and continue to be, modernized, but only to keep pace with the change of times; modernization has never been a major priority on Beijing's national agenda.[*]

EVOLUTION OF CHINA'S NUCLEAR DOCTRINE AND STRATEGY

First and foremost, China has always harbored a dialectical attitude towards nuclear weapons. True, Mao Zedong, who made all the important decisions regarding China's acquisition of nuclear weapons, as well as the design of its nuclear strategy, had a famous saying that atom bombs are but paper tigers. To understand it, however, one must put the remark in context. Mao made the comment in 1946 when the US was the only power with atom bombs, had actually used them on an enemy state in the previous year, and was brandishing them as a trump card in its post-war strategy for the confrontation with the Soviet Union, then allied with Mao's China. Mao used the metaphor to highlight his contempt for the US ambition to exploit the power of nuclear weapons for political objectives. The statement also reflected Mao's firm belief that it is human factors, rather than sophisticated weapons, that eventually decide the outcome of war. On the other hand, Mao and his colleagues in China's inner decision-making circle had a very sober-minded calculation about the devastating effects of nuclear weapons as weapons of mass destruction. They believed that these weapons were inhumane, posed a threat against all humanity, and should be completely eliminated and totally prohibited.

Pending that outcome, however, and faced with grave military threats from the United States in the 1950s, Chinese leaders perceived that they had no alternative

---

[*] Some US specialists note, for example, that China, unlike the United States or Russia, has taken extraordinarily long periods of time to field new weapon systems. They stress that, "China has not pursued these programs on a 'crash' basis and in many instances the weapons were obsolete when they were finally deployed. Even after initial deployment, China's build-up of additional forces has been slow. It is true that the Chinese have been working on improving their missiles and submarines for the past 15 to 20 years, but the pace of modernization grinds on and each annual Pentagon projection pushes the operational dates further into the future." See, for example, Hans M. Kristensen, Robert S. Norris, Matthew F. Mckinzie, *Chinese Nuclear Forces and U.S. Nuclear War Planning*, (Washington, DC: Federation of American Scientists/Natural Resources Defense Council, September 2006), page 3.

to ensure China's security but to develop their own atom bombs. As Zhou Enlai, the chief executor of China's nuclear programs then put it,

Had we not had nuclear weapons, the imperialists would have used them. China developed nuclear weapons in order to resist nuclear blackmail and counter nuclear threats. It is after all for the purpose of halting the hands at the trigger of the bombs that China must have its own nuclear bombs.

Mao echoed the view by stressing on one occasion that, "In today's world, if we are not to be bullied by others, this thing is indispensable."[2] The remarks succinctly pointed out not only the defensive nature of China's nuclear programs, but also the fact that Beijing perceived that it had no choice but to develop its nuclear capability because of the environment in which it found itself.[†]

Second, China's nuclear strategy has almost solely been affected by the nuclear capabilities, nuclear strategies, and nuclear doctrines of the two nuclear superpowers, the US in particular. Looking in retrospect at the Cold War, it is no exaggeration to say that China was the only country to have become the near-target of potential nuclear strikes by the United States and the Soviet Union (and sometimes even by both at the same time) on occasions either before China had developed nuclear weapons or when its nuclear weapon programs were in the embryonic phase. Even after the Cold War had ended, China still remained on the list of Washington's potential nuclear strikes in its war planning. China's nuclear posture has always reflected the threat posed to it by the United States' nuclear strategy. Since the early 1990s, for example, Washington's development of missile defense systems has been one of the crucial factors shaping China's efforts to upgrade its nuclear arsenal. Similarly, despite its expressed desire to see the complete elimination of nuclear weapons and its willingness to undertake concrete steps toward that end, China remains extremely cautious about joining the disarmament process and renouncing its small nuclear arsenal so long as the threats from the United States' nuclear capabilities persist. One telling example is China's attitude towards the Comprehensive Test Ban Treaty (CTBT). Both the US and China had played a proactive role in facilitating the conclusion of the treaty, and both became signatory states the very first day that the treaty was open to signature in 1996. But the US Senate refused to ratify the Treaty in 2000, and China consequently has also yet to ratify. The only plausible

---

[†] As the decision-making process that led to the development of nuclear weapons is still top-secret in China, there are few official documents available in that respect. However, many articles and memoirs by leading officials or specialists involved in the process of China's bomb-building have recently been published, which provide valuable clues to the thinking, although fragmented, of the then-leadership of China towards the development of nuclear weapons. See, for example, Jin Zhongji, *Biography of Zhou Enlai* (Beijing; The Central Publishing House of Historical Documents, 1994); Li Qi, *Memories n Those Years with Zhou Enlai* (Beijing: The Central Publishing House of Historical Documents, 1994). Both volumes are in Chinese; the quotes are translated by the author.

explanation of why Beijing is delaying ratification is its concern about the US reticence toward the comprehensive ban on testing.

Third, there are many reasons why China does not equate the use of nuclear weapons with the use of conventional weapons. It can partially be explained by Beijing's repugnance of using this category of inhumane weapons, as well as Beijing's self-confidence in its ability to win a conventional war without utilizing nuclear weapons, based on its long-term historical experience in past military conflicts and wars. China has no ambition to expand beyond its current borders. If a major war were to take place, putting China's core interests at stake, it would be the result of an invasion of its territory. This was the familiar pattern of war in the lives of leaders like Mao Zedong and Zhou Enlai, who had spent almost the best parts of their life coping with these kinds of threats. Thanks to the vast territory and large population of China, they believed that the Chinese people would surely prevail over any powerful invading enemy by luring it in and "drowning" it in the sea of people in a protracted conventional war. Thus, as long as the use of nuclear weapons is prevented, China has no fear in fighting a conventional war with any other state.

Last, but not least, Beijing may also have made a pragmatic calculation in insisting on a defensive nuclear posture from the very beginning. Given the lag between the United States' and Soviet Union's development of nuclear weapons and China's development of the bomb, the resulting discrepancies between China and the two nuclear superpowers in terms of both numbers of weapons and level of technological sophistication, and both nuclear superpowers' strong suspicion about Beijing's strategic intentions with its newly emerged nuclear assets, China may have been keenly aware that either the US or the Soviet Union (or both) may well have harbored an impulse to launch a "surgical strike" to eliminate China's infant nuclear capability before it became a real threat to them. The "No First Use" pledge was likely designed as a signal of reassurance to the world community that China's new nuclear capability posed no threat to any other country. Keeping its nuclear posture in low profile did seem to work in allaying the suspicion and misgivings of the two superpowers and maintaining world stability. It should be noted that this success was also due to the peculiar international environment during the Cold War. The United States and the Soviet Union were so tightly locked in their scramble for military supremacy and world domination that both of them seemed to quietly accept the "legitimacy" of China's small nuclear arsenal as long as Beijing's emerging nuclear weapons did not upset the international structure and the balance of forces between them.

THE CONTEMPORARY SITUATION

Of course, all the elements discussed above that underlay the evolution of China's nuclear strategy and doctrine are not static. In fact, they have been constantly evolving, particularly in the post-Cold War era. The international strategic situation has seen dramatic changes in recent years, which appear to give rise to a fundamentally new international environment, in which the role of nuclear weapons needs to be reevaluated. There are both positive and negative changes affecting China.

On the positive side, the end of the Cold War indicated the end of nuclear confrontation between the United States and the former Soviet Union. The possibility of a large scale nuclear war among the major nuclear powers has become increasingly remote. As a result, the arsenals of the nuclear weapon states—other than China, according to Western estimates—have been reduced in number. In particular, the United States and Russia—the nuclear successor of the disintegrated Soviet Union—have each reduced the number of their nuclear weapons in a dramatic way. Altogether, the number of US and Russian nuclear warheads has been reduced from roughly 50,000 in 1990 to perhaps 25,000 in 2008.[3] One has good reason to expect that the two major nuclear powers may continue the process of deep cuts, either through a new or extended bilateral agreement or unilaterally. A number of significant international treaties in the field of arms control, disarmament, and nonproliferation were also concluded in the first decade after the Cold War ended. In the nuclear realm, the most significant among them are the indefinite and unconditional extension of the Non-Proliferation Treaty (NPT) in 1995 and the conclusion of the CTBT in 1996. Although the latter has not yet officially entered into force, all five nuclear weapon states recognized by the NPT have observed a moratorium on testing since the Treaty was concluded. The five nuclear weapon states have also refrained from producing additional fissile materials. The overwhelming majority of the non-nuclear weapon states also continue to adhere to the NPT, although they resent the apparent indifference of the nuclear weapon states on following through with their responsibility to meaningfully disarm, as stated in Article VI of the Treaty. With the rapid development of science and high-technology, the international community has also registered substantial progress in monitoring and verifying adherence to treaties, thus contributing greatly to the insurance of treaty compliance by member states, and strengthening the international nonproliferation regime.

On the negative side, however, new uncertainties seem to be arising in the global security situation. The international community is now facing four chief challenges: nuclear multipolarity among the older nuclear-armed states, proliferation to new states and potentially to non-state groups, strategically relevant technological advances, and the deadlock in international arms control, disarmament, and nonproliferation diplomacy.

These problems were first demonstrated in the growing complexity and unpredictability of the world nuclear architecture. During the Cold War, labeled as central weapons, nuclear weapons seem to be largely the luxury of major powers. Because of their enormous destructive power, striving for nuclear superiority seemed to become a central theme of the US-Soviet confrontation. But also because of this destructive potential, actual use of these weapons seemed to have been deterred by the two sides' huge arsenals, and they seldom were considered to be a central element in regional security arrangements, except in Europe, where the two major military blocks were set to confront one another with both conventional and nuclear armaments. The world's nuclear architecture was then a fairly simple and relatively stable, bipolar configuration, with the British and French nuclear forces perceived as supplements to the US force in NATO. Only China was an exception, staying outside the bipolar structure with its independent nuclear force. But China's capability was so small, and with the self-imposed restraining discipline in its nuclear strategy, the two major powers apparently thought they could afford to ignore it as long as Beijing remained limited in its nuclear posture.

The end of the Cold War has fundamentally changed the nuclear security architecture. Today, although the world nuclear system continues to remain bipolar, since the two nuclear superpowers—the United States and Russia—continue to own more than 95 percent of the world's total nuclear weapons, the architecture has become increasingly less stable with the fast weakening of Russia in terms of its comprehensive strength, and the more assertive attitude of the United States under former President George W. Bush as the world's only superpower. Washington is evidently not content with the remaining relics of the bipolar architecture in the nuclear field. When George W. Bush became the US president in 2000, the administration seemed particularly intent on remolding the world into a unipolar structure by taking advantage of the collapse of the Soviet Union, on the one hand, and the emergence of new military technologies on the other. The US moves triggered a vehement reaction by Moscow, and a renewed nuclear competition, if not a nuclear arms race, seemed to be starting. At the same time, Washington shifted much of its attention to China. With the fast economic development of China, the US seemed to no longer take Beijing for granted. As China began to modernize its nuclear forces, a debate began in Washington as to the extent to which China's nuclear arsenal could pose a threat to US security, and how Washington should engage with China in the future. In short, the nuclear architecture among the NPT's five nuclear weapon states seems to have begun experiencing a reshaping of relative capabilities. Whether or not this trend continues under the new Obama Administration remains to be seen.

The issue has been further compounded by a new risk of the proliferation of nuclear weapons. It has chiefly found expression in two forms. One is the acquisition of nuclear weapons by regional powers. In addition to the five nuclear weapon states recognized by the NPT, India, Israel, and Pakistan have now become *de-facto* nuclear weapon states. With a nuclear test in 2006, North Korea has apparently also announced a nuclear weapons capability, although Pyongyang has committed itself to dismantling this production capability thanks to progress in the Six Party Talks.[4] Iran also may soon acquire the capability of manufacturing nuclear bombs through its program to produce highly enriched uranium, allegedly for peaceful purposes. Iran's case, in particular, reflects a dilemma facing the international nonproliferation regime. Tehran claims, with legitimate justification perhaps, that it is fully entitled to the peaceful use of nuclear energy in accordance with the provisions of the NPT. Yet there is no clear line of demarcation between nuclear technologies used for peaceful or for military purposes. Given sufficient time, Iran is almost sure to obtain the necessary technologies, expertise, and nuclear materials for the manufacturing of nuclear bombs through operation of its nuclear reactors. Thus, the risk is that reactors used for allegedly peaceful purposes could be a well-disguised form of proliferation of nuclear weapons. And Iran is not alone in raising this type of proliferation danger. With increasing demands for energy and the threat of climate change resulting from the consumption of hydrocarbon fuels, more and more non-nuclear weapon states are exploring peaceful nuclear programs as recipes for sustained economic development. Like in Iran's case, the surging expansion of nuclear industry would inevitably be accompanied by a growing risk of proliferation of nuclear weapon capabilities to more countries. The world community is yet to find an effective approach to this newly emerging challenge.

A second rising risk associated with nuclear proliferation is the emerging role of non-state actors, organizations who could be both a new source, as well as the potential users, of nuclear materials, technologies, and know-how. The international community is facing a rising danger of a nuclear bomb, a crude nuclear explosive device, or even a conventional explosive device made of radioactive materials (dirty bomb) falling into the hands of such malevolent non-state actors as international terrorists or organized crime gangs. The scenario in which such a device explodes in a big city, be it New York, Paris, or Beijing, killing hundreds of thousands of innocent people, is not a far-fetched fiction-story. Documents have already been discovered in caves occupied by Al-Qaida operatives in Afghanistan showing that these terrorists were studying how to manufacture a dirty bomb. Although there is no evidence to prove to what extent they had been successful, the discovery of the interest itself was enough to alert the world that this danger cannot be ignored. This is a new threat indeed, as the international nonproliferation regime has so far only been dealing with the behavior of nation-states.

The third challenge that has influenced the world strategic situation is the emergence of new dimensions of nuclear weapon capabilities thanks to the rapid development of science and technology, particularly in the military field. Beginning 1990, the US believed that it might be feasible to build effective defenses against nuclear-armed missiles and aircraft. It is well known that the two major nuclear powers in the Cold War were able to achieve strategic stability mainly through a two-part negotiated arrangement that allowed development of strategic offensive forces (within certain limits) while banning the deployment of strategic defensive forces. The rationale was based on the concept of Mutual Assured Destruction (MAD): By prohibiting defenses, the arrangement ensured that both sides retained the capability to survive an attack and wipe out the other side in retaliation. This situation was believed to be effective in preventing nuclear war, as neither side dared to launch a preventive nuclear strike, since it could be certain that the attack would lead to retaliation by the other side and bring about its virtual self-destruction. From a technical point of view, the situation was allowed to prevail because both the US and the Soviet Union were restricted in their actual capability of doing otherwise – effective defenses against the large offensive forces deployed by each side were technically impossible and economically prohibitive. During President Ronald Reagan's administration, Washington explored developing effective missile defenses through the Strategic Defense Initiative (SDI, or Star Wars), but the effort soon ended in failure, because of the immaturity of prevailing technologies.

Interest in building defenses against smaller missile forces was reborn in Washington at the end of the 1990s and gained greater momentum with the inauguration of George W. Bush. This new interest was fueled both by concerns about the development of missile systems by nations hostile to the United States, like North Korea, and by the availability of new military technologies. To facilitate the development and deployment of these systems, the Bush Administration announced in December 2001 its intention to withdraw from the 1972 ABM Treaty, following the mandatory one-year delay required by the Treaty. The Treaty had long served as the pillar underlying strategic stability in the Cold War, and the US withdrawal thus opened the way for a re-ignition of arms races in both offensive and defensive weapon systems.

The George W. Bush Administration also attempted to exploit new military technologies to develop nuclear weapons with special enhanced effects, including, for example, "improved earth penetrating weapons...and warheads that reduce collateral damage," such as low-yield nuclear weapons that – in principle–would be more likely to be used in a conventional war.[5] These weapons are smaller, more accurate, and intended to be used specifically to destroy targets like deeply-buried underground command posts or weapon storage facilities allegedly with less collateral damage to civilians. If they had been developed, nuclear weapons might have been able to perform some of the military missions that are usually done by conventional weapons, although there is much debate about this point. So there seems to be much uncertainty in the future prospect for weapons with a lower threshold of usability. The good news is that the US Congress refused to appropriate the funds requested for these purposes for two consecutive years and the Obama Administration has pledged not to develop these weapons. On the other hand, continued development of science and technology may soon offer great incentives for new military capabilities.

In addition to these attempted changes to US defensive and offensive capabilities, the George W. Bush Administration highlighted a fundamental shift in the US nuclear doctrine, chiefly through its 2001 Nuclear Posture Review (NPR), part of which was revealed in early 2002. What is most noteworthy in the document is the emphasis on the establishment of a new triad, composed of 1) offensive strike systems (both nuclear and non-nuclear); 2) both active and passive defenses; and 3) a revitalized nuclear infrastructure that can maintain a reliable nuclear stockpile and provide new capabilities in a timely fashion to meet emerging threats.[6] All these were said to be aimed at reducing the US dependence on nuclear weapons and improve its ability to deter attack in the face of new actors proliferating weapons of mass destruction (WMD). Many observers, however, believed that the Bush Administration had actually envisaged the use of nuclear weapons in a much wider range of circumstances than before, with a particular emphasis on tactical uses. If that is the case, such an emphasis in a declaratory policy has not been seen since the days of flexible response forty or so years ago, when tactical nuclear weapons were deployed in Europe and elsewhere.

The George W. Bush Administration's more aggressive nuclear force posture set a dangerous precedent that other nuclear weapon states may try to emulate or counter. Modernization of nuclear force continues to be a priority in some nations' agendas and efforts to upgrade some nuclear arsenals have been sped up. The Russians, in particular, vowed to invest more heavily to modernize its strategic forces, which they believe to be the most significant national instrument of defense, allowing them to compete with the Americans militarily and to restore their former nuclear superpower status. Moscow even backed off further from its previous "no first use" policy, stressing that since its conventional military capabilities had been greatly reduced, it would be ready to use nuclear weapons in any conventional war to protect its core interests. Except for China, today all the other four NPT-acknowledged nuclear weapon states claim they are ready to be the first to use nuclear weapons if their security situation requires it. The NPT-declared nuclear weapon states, other than China, believe that their nuclear weapons play an indispensable role in maintaining security or for other political purposes.

Against this backdrop, comes the fourth challenge to the world community: the virtual deadlock in multilateral efforts for nuclear arms control, disarmament, and nonproliferation. This deadlock is the result of many factors, but not the least is increasing tensions between the nuclear and non-nuclear weapon states. The continuing reliance of nuclear weapon states on nuclear weapons has angered many non-weapon states. During the Review Conference of the NPT in 1995, a heated debate erupted between nuclear weapon states and non-nuclear weapon states as to whether the NPT should be indefinitely and unconditionally extended. It was only after the nuclear weapon states reiterated their pledge to honor their commitment to nuclear disarmament that non-nuclear weapon states agreed to accept the indefinite extension of the treaty. In the 2000 review conference, under heavy pressure from non-weapon states, the verbal commitment of nuclear weapon states was further crystallized into 13 practical steps that they were expected to take at the earliest date possible.[‡] Most of these steps, however, have been ignored by the nuclear weapon states. The US even openly declared that it would find no way to honor these obligations.[§] The tension between nuclear weapon states and non-weapon states has thus been exacerbated. The major sticking point in the confrontation seems to be diametrically opposing positions between the two sides concerning the priority steps toward nuclear disarmament. Non-nuclear weapon states contend that if nuclear weapon states continue to insist on the legitimate role of nuclear weapons, upgrade their nuclear arsenals, and even threaten the use of these weapons against non-weapon states, they must expect that these weapons will proliferate. In their view, the central issue is how rapidly the nuclear weapon states undertake their responsibility to disarm. Nuclear weapon states, on the other hand, seem to be horrified by the prospect of nuclear weapons falling into the wrong hands. They insist that as long as there is potential for nuclear weapons to proliferate to other countries, or even non-state actors, weapon states have to keep nuclear arsenals for their own security. They struggle with what measures to take to strengthen the international nonproliferation regime so as to create more favorable conditions for controlling

---

[‡] For the details of these steps, see "2000 NPT review Conference Final Document", Arms Control, New York, June 2000. http://www.armscontrol.org/act/2000_06/docjun.

[§] J. Sherwood McGinnis, "Article VI of the NPT," May 1, 2003. McGinnis said, "We made clear last year that the United States no longer supports all 13 steps."

proliferation and thus for nuclear disarmament. Even among nuclear weapon states there is also a debate as to when and how the lesser nuclear weapon states should join the major nuclear powers in the process of nuclear disarmament. The contradiction among nuclear weapon states, as well as the tension between these countries and non-nuclear weapon states, has resulted in the virtual paralysis of all the meaningful international negotiations for nuclear arms control, disarmament, and nonproliferation.

This virtual deadlock in multilateral negotiations existed throughout the eight year tenure of the George W. Bush Administration. But the promise of a new administration seemed to herald a dramatic change. It started with two essays which appeared in the *Wall Street Journal* in January 2007 and January 2008, respectively, by four former eminent US officials. In the two essays, they called on the United States to renounce the nuclear deterrence strategy and take the leadership role in helping to create a nuclear-free world. They also offered a set of concrete steps to be taken by the international community, which they believe would lead to genuine nuclear disarmament.[7] Observers were greatly surprised; not really because of the views expressed, but because of the authors themselves. The four are all unexpected disarmament advocates, not only for the national security decision-making circle of the United States while they served their country, but their past as staunch Cold-War warriors, advocating reliance on nuclear deterrence for the United States throughout their careers. The fundamental shift of their perspective thus carries special significance. Furthermore, the four US officials were not alone. Behind them followed a long list of well-known, prestigious former high-ranking officials, specialists and scholars, who expressed their support by signing the two articles. Many governments, as well as NGOs in Western countries, are taking steps to echo their views. Various suggestions have been made in an attempt to translate new understanding into specific actions for the purpose of achieving a nuclear-free world. Together, they initiated a dynamic campaign that had not been seen for years, alerting the world about the practical danger of nuclear weapons and calling for meaningful steps toward the elimination of all nuclear weapons.

The new vision, of course, is not without opposition. There are still many people in Washington and other world capitals that question the value or feasibility of a nuclear-free world, and argue that the US and other nations risk undermining their security interests without the deterrent protection of nuclear weapons. In the meantime, a large number of non-nuclear weapon states are electing to be silent, indicating their strong skepticism about the motivation of the newly rising enthusiasm within Western countries about the idea of a nuclear-free world. They wonder if this campaign is not merely another episode of sporadic interest from the Western countries for nuclear disarmament, one that will fade away before long. They seem particularly interested in watching the first year of Obama's presidency. Will he be able to overcome the resistance of the opposition, embrace the idea of global zero, and work out meaningful, concrete steps to that end?

The prospect remains uncertain. However, one should not underestimate the significance of the dynamics of the initiative underway. Behind the vision, there seems a more realistic and sober-minded re-examination by a growing number of elites in the United States and other countries of the continued existence of nuclear weapons and whether they are really in the best interest of global security. The reasons for growing doubts about continuing reliance on nuclear weapons globally are two-fold: 1) "With nuclear weapons more widely available, deterrence is decreasingly effective and increasingly hazardous;" and 2) There is a very real possibility that, "the deadliest weapons ever invented could fall into dangerous hands." Under the circumstances, "the US soon will be compelled to enter a new nuclear era that will be more precarious, psychologically disorienting, and economically even more costly than was Cold War deterrence." In short, nuclear weapons today have become a security problem – not a solution. [8]

There may be another reason that the authors touched on, but did not elaborate. By holding high the banner of nuclear disarmament, nuclear weapon states like the United States would reoccupy the moral high ground. This would be particularly important when Washington is coming under increasing pressure from the non-nuclear weapons states to implement their disarmament commitments and have not been able to show tangible progress in that respect.

IMPLICATIONS FOR CHINA'S NUCLEAR STRATEGY AND DISARMAMENT POSTURE

Emerging trends in the world strategic situation no doubt have profound influence on China's nuclear strategy and its position towards nuclear disarmament, as well. The implications can be summarized as follows.

Despite the reduction of the two major nuclear powers' arsenals by more than one-half, the current world nuclear architecture remains a smaller version of its Cold War structure in Beijing's perspective. The US and Russia continue to maintain the preponderance of nuclear weapons with the other powers each having relatively small arsenals. To China, the main nuclear threat seems increasingly to come from the US ambition to strengthen its nuclear eminence and the uncertain strategic intention towards Beijing's small nuclear retaliatory force suggested by its efforts to deploy missile defense forces.

The emergence of regional nuclear powers, particularly on China's periphery, has no doubt complicated China's threat perceptions, as well as its contingency preparations. However, Beijing may address this as a proliferation issue, rather than the appearance of new strategic threats that would demand Beijing to fundamentally change its strategic focus. In Beijing's perspective, it is almost inconceivable to imagine a major conventional war leading to a future nuclear exchange with India, Pakistan, the DPRK, or any other nuclear-armed developing country. Japan may be a different story, however. But a nuclear Japan would certainly pose as many, if not more, strategic challenges to the United States as to China. Why should China be particularly worried if the United States is not? This assessment does not suggest, of course, that China would welcome regional nuclear proliferation. What is worthy of note in Beijing's view is that since regional proliferation affects the security of all the other regional states, it can best be solved through the concerted efforts of all the countries concerned, preferably within a regional framework, similar to the one taking place with the Six-Party Talks for the DPRK's nuclear issue. To put it another way, although regional nuclear proliferation is a serious problem from Beijing's perspective, it can hardly distract China from its major concern over the practical threat from the United States – because it is that country that still seriously prepares for a nuclear strike in a possible military conflict against China.

If the US were to renew its efforts to upgrade the quality of its nuclear forces (offensive and defensive), and with the prospect of the US acquisition of new military capabilities in space, Beijing may feel increasingly less confident in the reliability of its small nuclear forces for retaliation. Imagine the military pressure from the US that Beijing may well be confronted with: A numerically reduced but upgraded precision-guided offensive nuclear capability; a robust missile defense system; some offensive capability in space, like an anti-satellite capability; and a more aggressive preemptive nuclear doctrine. All these are backed up by powerful conventional capabilities and the potential resurging capabilities of a nuclear infrastructure that had been rebuilt even after drastic reductions to the size of the arsenal. Under the circumstances, Beijing may need to answer two critical questions: 1) Will China continue to maintain an absolute self-defensive nuclear posture?; and 2) if the answer to the first question is yes, what should China do to ensure the reliability and effectiveness of its retaliatory nuclear force in the future?

Despite these confrontational aspects of the relations among nuclear weapon states, there is a bright side to the evolution of the world strategic situation—the growing, overlapping interests among these countries to deal with their common problems that no one power or group of powers can address single-handedly. Common interests give rise to a growing need for international cooperation.

Sino-American relations are perhaps a particularly good case-in-point. Despite the fact that the two countries are so discrepant in terms of their nuclear capability, and so divergent in their perspectives with regard to the role of nuclear weapons, they often seem to find that cooperation, rather than confrontation, serves their best interests. Both hope to build a new nuclear world order, for example, that can ensure sustained international security and stability. Efforts to that end would include closer cooperation, particularly in the field of the nonproliferation of nuclear weapons. It is precisely in this spirit that China has become a valuable constructive partner of the United States in the international effort to solve the regional nuclear crisis on the Korean Peninsula, as well as the fight against international terrorism. Furthermore, both capitals also seem to be keenly aware of the significance of maintaining strategic stability between the two sides. Indeed, nuclear stability could well become an inherent part of the overall China-US relationship in the future. On the other hand, as long as the overall relationship remains good, there is a propitious political basis for strategic stability, based on strengthened confidence and trust in each other. The two countries would then be able to keep their nuclear weapons as a background issue in their relationship. The key to the success of this process will be sincere political will on both sides, with an adequate sense of sensitivity over the core security interests of the other side. China should continue to maintain a defensive nuclear posture, exercise self-restraint, and refrain from taking provocative measures to challenge the US core interests, while the US has to make sure that further developments in its nuclear posture do not threaten the credibility of Beijing's small nuclear retaliatory force.

Against this backdrop, it is extremely unlikely that China will fundamentally change its nuclear posture and nuclear strategy. Continuity will continue to characterize its self-defensive nuclear posture. As China's Defense White Paper in 2006 put it:

> China's nuclear strategy is subject to the state's nuclear policy and military strategy. Its fundamental goal is to deter other countries from using or threatening to use nuclear weapons against China. China remains firmly committed to the policy of no first use of nuclear weapons at any time and under any circumstances. It unconditionally undertakes not to use or threaten to use nuclear weapons against non-nuclear-weapon states or nuclear-weapon-free zones, and stands for the comprehensive prohibition and complete elimination of nuclear weapons. China upholds the principles of counterattack in self-defense and limited development of nuclear weapons, and aims at building a lean and effective nuclear force capable of meeting national security needs. It endeavors to ensure the security and reliability of its nuclear weapons

and maintains a credible nuclear deterrent force. China's nuclear force is under the direct command of the Central Military Commission (CMC). China exercises great restraint in developing its nuclear force. It has never entered into and will never enter into a nuclear arms race with any other country.[9]

Within this policy framework, Beijing will advance the evolution of its nuclear strategy in the future with a two-pronged approach.

First, Beijing will continue to modernize its nuclear forces in modest ways. With the backing of its economic development and scientific and technological achievements, China will accelerate its weaponry and equipment modernization drive mainly by relying on its own efforts. The aim is to build a streamlined and effective strategic force with both nuclear and conventional capabilities. The major initiatives would include quickening steps to raise the informational level of its weapon systems, building an agile and efficient operational command and control system, and increasing capabilities of land-based, strategic, nuclear counter-strikes and precision-strikes with conventional missiles, among others. In other words, China may only continue to respond to the implications for its security in spite of what the other nuclear weapon states, the US in particular, are doing. If we look at the US missile defense programs, for example, for all the official reassurance that they are not intended against China, Beijing believes that these systems are chiefly meant to neutralize China's nuclear force provided technology permits.[10] Under the circumstances, China has no other alternative than to quicken the pace and scope of its modernization drive, including increasing the number of its warheads and building more mobile intercontinental-range ballistic missiles (ICBMs). This is perhaps the main reason explaining why China seems still to strive to expand its nuclear force, albeit in a small way, while other nuclear weapon states are reducing the number of their nuclear warheads, according to the Western reports.

Second, China will take measures to enhance international cooperation, to build up a world nuclear order which is conducive to world peace, security, and stability, as well as to China's own interests. These measures will mostly include efforts to maintain nuclear stability among nuclear weapon states, to strengthen the international nuclear nonproliferation regime, and to create necessary conditions to reactivate progress in multilateral negotiations for nuclear arms control and disarmament.

It is in this context that the initiative launched by the Western political elites for a nuclear-free world may well fit into Beijing's long-sought objective of the complete prohibition and thorough destruction of nuclear weapons. One might recall that on October 16, 1964, the very day that China exploded its first atomic bomb, the Chinese government issued the following statement:

> [China] proposes to the governments of the world that a summit conference of all the countries of the world be convened to discuss the question of the compete prohibition and thorough destruction of the nuclear weapons, and that as the first step, the summit conference conclude an agreement to the effect that the nuclear powers and those countries which may soon become nuclear powers undertake not to use nuclear weapons either against non-nuclear countries and nuclear–free zones or against each other.[11]

This was indeed the first-ever proposal from a nuclear weapon state calling for not only the building of a nuclear-free world, but also a practical and effective approach to that end. China has put forward on numerous occasions similar views and proposals on the issue, and has never given up the objective of a nuclear-free world. In light of this consistent position, it can be envisioned that Beijing would welcome the proposal by the four eminent politicians from the United States to renounce reliance on nuclear deterrence and make concerted efforts for a nuclear-free world. China may be proactive in joining international efforts to explore what steps should be taken that might lead to this lofty goal. The devils, however, are in the details, particularly when people are trying to define a realistic roadmap towards the goal of global zero.

Two major challenges may arise that could hinder China in joining in the process of nuclear disarmament in the future.

The first is that China is only a weak nuclear power. As such, China must decide on the circumstances in which it would be ready to join the US and Russia in the process of disarmament. This could prove to be a complicated issue. Since China always maintains that it would participate in this process only when the United States and Russia seriously implement their special responsibility, the particularly pertinent question is what level of reductions by the two major nuclear powers could induce China to join in the process. Some Western specialists have suggested deep-cuts by the two states to a level on the order of 1,000 or 800 warheads in each of their nuclear arsenals may be an indicative point that would require China's involvement in further disarmament. But, from China's perspective, although numerical reductions are certainly one essential part of nuclear disarmament, it alone cannot reduce the nuclear threat that China is faced with today. Thus, what matters more to China is the reduction of threat, rather than the reduction in number of nuclear weapons by the United States and

Russia, in order to produce a truly propitious environment for all the nuclear weapon states to join these two major powers for further nuclear disarmament.

In this connection, it might be in order to recall a proposal entitled, "Proposal on Essential Measures for an Immediate Halt to the Arms Race and for Disarmament," put forward by the Chinese Delegation at the Second Special Session of the UN General Assembly on Disarmament (SSOD II) in 1982, which highlighted systematically the guidelines, as well as specific measures, to be taken for nuclear disarmament. On the basic principles for nuclear disarmament, the Chinese proposal set forward six points:

1. Efforts for disarmament cannot be separated from those for the maintenance of international security. They must be combined with those for the maintenance of world peace and security. In order to create a favorable climate and conditions for disarmament and to achieve real progress in this field, it is essential to uphold the Charter of the United Nations and the norms of international relations. No country is permitted to seek any form of hegemony anywhere in the world. The use or threat of force against the sovereignty and territorial integrity of any state should be strictly prohibited.

2. The two superpowers should take the lead in reducing their armaments. They possess the greatest nuclear and conventional arsenals and their rivalry and arms race are menacing international peace and security, hence they bear the primary responsibility for disarmament and should be the first to reduce their armaments. After they have substantially cut back their armaments, the other nuclear states and militarily significant states should join them and reduce their armaments according to a reasonable proportion and procedure.

3. Nuclear disarmament should be carried out in conjunction with conventional disarmament. It is certainly important to take effective measures to achieve the objective of nuclear disarmament in view of the grave threat to mankind posed by nuclear war, but one should not overlook the fact that conventional arms are used in committing aggression against or otherwise threatening other countries. Only a combination of measures for both nuclear and conventional disarmament can help reduce the danger of war. Simultaneously with nuclear and conventional disarmament, all other types of weapons of mass destruction should be banned.

4. Small and medium-sized countries are all entitled to take what measures they deem necessary to maintain their defense capabilities for resisting aggression and safeguarding their independence. The measures and steps decided at different stages of disarmament must not prejudice or endanger the independence, sovereignty and security of any state.

5. Disarmament agreements should provide for strict and effective international verification.

6. All states may participate in the settlement of disarmament issues on an equal footing. As disarmament has a bearing upon the security and interests of all states, big or small, nuclear or non-nuclear, militarily strong or weak, every state is entitled to participate on an equal footing in the deliberations and negotiations on this matter and in supervising the implementation of the agreements reached.[12]

In the spirit of the above said principles, the proposal also suggested the following four essential measures for an immediate halt to the arms race and for disarmament:

1. An agreement should be reached by all the nuclear states not to use nuclear weapons. Pending such an agreement, each nuclear state should, without attaching any condition, undertake not to use nuclear weapons against non-nuclear states and nuclear-weapon-free zones, and not to be the first to use such weapons against each other at any time and under any circumstances.

2. The Soviet Union and the United States should stop testing, improving or manufacturing nuclear weapons and should reduce by 50 percent all types of their nuclear weapons and means of delivery.

3. After that, all other nuclear states should also stop testing, improving or manufacturing nuclear weapons and should reduce their respective nuclear arsenals according to an agreed proportion and procedure.

4. Conventional disarmament should be effected simultaneously with nuclear disarmament. As a first step, all states should undertake not to use conventional armaments for intervention or aggression against and military occupation of any country.[13]

A careful look at these basic principles and specific measures suggests they constitute a comprehensive, as well as operational, roadmap for the task of nuclear disarmament. Obviously, what China hoped the two major nuclear powers would do included, at least: 1) a dramatic change of their nuclear doctrines pending complete nuclear disarmament; that is, adoption of a commitment to NFU; 2) drastic quantitative reductions in their nuclear arsenals; 3) stopping qualitative improvements of nuclear weapons (like testing, improving, or manufacturing new nuclear weapons); and, 4) other vital disarmament measures that would greatly facilitate nuclear disarmament like conventional disarmament, etc.

In the meantime, this proposal did not put China on the sidelines as an indifferent onlooker. In the speech by the then-Foreign Minister Huang Hua to introduce this proposal at the session, he pledged that China would be a constructive participant and be ready to undertake its due share of responsibility in the process of nuclear disarmament. He solemnly announced that:

If the two superpowers take the lead in halting the testing, improving or manufacturing of nuclear weapons and in reducing their nuclear weapons by 50 per cent, the Chinese Government is ready to join all other nuclear states in undertaking to stop the development and production of nuclear weapons and to further reduce and ultimately destroy them altogether.[14]

Over 26 years have passed since China's proposal, yet the two major nuclear powers still failed to meet completely the demands contained in the proposal so as to create the essential condition for all the nuclear weapon states to join the process of nuclear disarmament. Much has changed in the strategic situation since then, and China's specific proposal may become obsolete in the new and different strategic environment. But the guiding principles for the matter of nuclear disarmament in the proposal remain valid, and would still provide inspiration for the condition in which China would be ready to participate in the process of nuclear disarmament and the realization of a nuclear-free world.

The second challenge is that China must also overcome a conceptual ambivalence towards the role of nuclear weapons in order to get ready to participate in the process of disarmament in the future. As noted above, China has always held a dialectic view of nuclear weapons—it has a strong repugnance towards these particularly devastating weapons of mass destruction. At the same time, it must keep and upgrade them to ensure its national security. With the passage of time, this dialectical view has developed into ambivalent feelings towards nuclear weapons. Like other nuclear weapon states, China had also adopted measures to modernize its nuclear capability. This modernization process had started in the early 1960s in the form of the projects dubbed as "two-bombs, one-satellite"– meaning developing an atom bomb, a hydrogen bomb, and a man-made satellite. It has proved to be a symbol of the nation's spirit of developing its national defense science and technology chiefly through self-reliance, despite its initially backward economic and technological conditions. It has become the pride of the whole Chinese nation that China can achieve whatever the Western powers have achieved and may do it better.

As Deng Xiaoping once put it:

> It has always been, and will always be, necessary for China to develop its own high technology so that it can take its place in this field. If it were not for the atomic bomb, the hydrogen bomb and the satellites we have launched since the 1960s, China would not have its present international standing as a great, influential country. These achievements demonstrate a nation's abilities and are a sign of its level of prosperity and development.[15]

Deng's view has been embraced by the succeeding leaders of China and, indeed, by the whole nation. Development of nuclear weapons has been held as the new, valuable spiritual wealth created by the Chinese people in the 20th century for the Chinese nation. In September 1999, a special conference was held in Beijing to solemnly give commendation to those scientists and technological specialists who had made outstanding contribution to the development of China's projects of "two bombs and one satellite." In the conference, Jiang Zeming, the then Party Secretary General stressed that:

> [T]he progress of 'two bombs and one satellite' has not only resulted in the qualitative leap forward of China's national defense capability, but also contributed to the broad development of science and technology of the nation, promoted its socialist construction, and foster a contingent of science and technology, who are particularly able to be hard-working, to tackle key problems, to bring about innovation, and to carry out collaboration.

> This progress has greatly strengthened the confidence and strength of the whole nation to march forward and to go all out to make the country stronger. The great cause of 'two bombs and one satellite' is the important symbol of the progress of the development of the new China, the glory and pride of the Chinese nation. It is also the magnificent feat of bravely scaling new heights in science and technology in the history of human civilization.[16]

In this spirit, China's national defense science and technology industrial department decided in 2000 to regard the "two-bombs, one-satellite" as its trade spirit to promote the cross-century reform and development of the national defense science and technology industry and set off an upsurge in learning and carrying forward this spirit in the whole industry.[17]

Under the circumstances, developing nuclear weapons seems to have created significance for China beyond the basic defense needs. Whether this national sense of pride will influence China's attitude towards nuclear disarmament in the future may be an open question. But, obviously, much depends on the evolution of the global strategic situation. Furthermore, it would also require some new strategic insights as well as greater political courage of China's leaders to revaluate the role of nuclear weapons in the new strategic situation, and lead the nation to embark on the nuclear disarmament process ahead.

ENDNOTES

[1] Lt. General Li Jijun, Vice President of the PLA's Academy of Military Science, "Traditional Military Thinking and the Defensive Strategy of China," An Address at the US Army War College, Letort Paper No. 1, 29 August 1997, p. 7.

[2] Mao Tse-tung, "On the Ten Major Relationships" (speech given on 25 April 1956), *Selected Works of Mao Tse-tung,* vol. 5 (Beijing, China: People's Publishing House, 1977), 288.

[3] Hans M. Kristensen, "Status of World Nuclear Forces," Federation of American Scientists, http://www.fas.org/programs/ssp/nukes/nukestatus.html, accessed on 18 March 2009.

[4] Second-Phase Actions for the Implementation of the Joint Statement, October 3, 2007. http://www.fmprc.gov.cn/eng/zxxx/t369084.htm.

[5] See Findings of Nuclear Posture Review, US Department of Defense, January 9, 2002. http://www.globalsecurity.org/wmd/library/policy/dod/npr.htm.

[6] Ibid.

[7] George P. Shultz, William J. Perry, Henry A. Kissinger and Sam Nunn, "A World Free of Nuclear Weapons," *The Wall street Journal* (January 4, 2007), page A15, and "Toward a Nuclear-Free World," *The Wall Street Journal* (January 15, 2008), page A13.

[8] Ibid.

[9] "China's National Defense in 2006," issued by the Information Office of the State Council People's Republic of China, 29 December, 2006

[10] For an explanation of Chinese views on National Missile Defense, see David M. Finkelstein, "National Missile Defense and China's Current Security Perceptions," The Henry L. Stimson Center, December 14, 2001.

[11] Statement of the Government of the People's Republic of China, October 16, 1964, People's Daily, October 17, 1964.

[12] "Proposal on Essential Measures for an Immediate Halt to the Arms Race and for Disarmament", Working Paper submitted by the Chinese Delegation at the Second Special Session of the UN General Assembly on Disarmament, June 21, 1982. http://www.nti.org/db/china/engdocs/ch0682.html.

[13] Ibid.

[14] Huang Hua, Speech at the Second Special Session of the US General Assembly Devoted to Disarmament, New York, June 11, 1982. http:www.nti.org/db/china/engdocs/ch0682.html.

[15] "China Must Take Its Place in the Field of High Technology," News report on Deng Xiaoping's remarks when he inspected the electron-positron collider in Beijing, People's Daily, Beijing, October 24, 1988. http://web.peopledaily.com.cn/english/dengxp/vol3/text/c1920.htm.

[16] Speech of Jiang Zeming at the conference to commend the specialists of science and technology who had made outstanding contribution to the research and development of two bombs and one satellite, Beijing, September 18. People's Daily, September 19, 1999, p. 1. The text is in Chinese. The quote is translated by the author.

[17] "Defense Industrial Department Carries Forward Two-Bombs, One-Satellite Spirit," news report of People's Daily, Beijing, April 26, 2000.
http://english.peopledaily.com.cn/english/200004/26_39766.html.

FRENCH PERSPECTIVES ON NUCLEAR WEAPONS AND NUCLEAR DISARMAMENT

Bruno Tertrais

When it comes to nuclear policy, France is the most conservative of the three Western nuclear weapon states, and President Nicolas Sarkozy has confirmed that he will maintain continuity in this domain. Since the end of the Cold War, however, France has also taken major, irreversible unilateral steps toward disarmament—in tune with its policy of "sufficiency" in nuclear deterrence.

Thus, while the issue of nuclear abolition continues to be met with much skepticism in the country, Paris may not want to be isolated if a major global political movement was initiated in this direction. But any decision by France to give up its nuclear weapons entirely would require extraordinary circumstances and profound changes in the strategic and political environment.

FRENCH RATIONALES FOR MAINTAINING NUCLEAR WEAPONS

France maintains nuclear weapons both because of security concerns and to support its regional and global political ambitions.

Security Concerns

While there was undoubtedly a major political dimension in France's original decision to build a nuclear force, security concerns were paramount, and today it is mostly security rationales that explain France's policy to maintain nuclear weapons in the post-Cold War environment.

Among European powers, few countries felt as unsafe as France at the beginning of the second part of the 20th century. French territory had been invaded three times in a few decades, the last one resulting in its humiliating 1940 defeat—an event that traumatized future President Charles de Gaulle to the point of saying in 1943, "We must want the existence of France. Never again will it be self-evident."[*] Thus, in the 1950s, the perception that a major new threat to the country's existence was emerging—the Soviet Western Group of Forces was stationed in East Germany, not far from French territory—caused French leaders to

---

[*] Quoted in Pierre Messmer & Alain Larcan, *Les écrits militaires du général de Gaulle* (Paris: Presses Universitaires de France, 1985), page 201. The 1940 trauma was also a significant motivation for the Fourth Republic's politicians. One of the political fathers of the French atom bomb, Felix Gaillard, said that his first reaction when hearing the news about the first test in 1960 was that France had finally overcome the 1940 defeat (André Bendjebbar, *Histoire secrète de la bombe atomique française* (Paris: Le Cherche-Midi éditeur, 2000), page 290.

perceive a pressing need for a security guarantee. But French leaders did not believe the US nuclear guarantee, then being extended to the West European members of NATO, was enough of an assurance, and sought their own nuclear deterrent.

Today, major threats to Europe have disappeared, but the French still believe there is value in maintaining a nuclear deterrent for security reasons. Two rationales are put forward. The first refers to what the French often call the "life insurance" function. Most French leaders and analysts believe that the world can change rapidly and that the emergence of a new major threat to Europe within fifteen to thirty years is not a far-fetched scenario. Accordingly, it is deemed prudent to maintain a national nuclear deterrent. As then-President Jacques Chirac stated in 2006, "In light of the concerns of the present and the uncertainties of the future, nuclear deterrence remains the fundamental guarantee of our security."[1] He insisted that France is "not shielded from an unforeseen reversal of the international system, nor from a strategic surprise."[2] He emphasized further that the rise of nationalism and the competition between poles of power could give rise to new major threats. In short, the French logic is that even in the absence of a major threat today, it might as well keep its nuclear weapons to protect against the possibility of future threats, so long as the cost of doing so remains bearable.

While mindful that the world has changed drastically and that the notion of a bilateral strategic balance does not make sense anymore, the French consider the unraveling of the arms control process since 2001 to be an additional reason for caution. The US withdrawal from the Anti-Ballistic Missile (ABM) Treaty, Russia's subsequent abandonment of the START-2 Treaty, Moscow's decision to suspend its implementation of the Conventional Forces in Europe (CFE) Treaty and its threat to withdraw from the Intermediate-range Nuclear Forces (INF) Treaty, are all seen as factors that enhance the unpredictability of the strategic environment and thus bolster France's resolve to maintain a nuclear deterrent.

Despite France's traditionally good relations with Moscow and Beijing, the idea that one of these two countries could one day pose a major threat to Europe also is far from being dismissed in French political circles. While Russia is traditionally first on the list of "major" powers that could potentially be a threat to Europe, China now appears to come in second. In 1999, then-Prime Minister Lionel Jospin indicated that the French deterrent should be able to counter any serious threat, "even a distant one."[3] This was interpreted as signifying that the build-up of nuclear arsenals in Asia was deemed a matter of concern for Europe. Arguably, one would be hard pressed to imagine a credible scenario in which China would directly threaten France, but Paris worries about a future scenario in which, for instance, Beijing seeks to deter French involvement in a crisis in Asia by exerting a veiled nuclear threat.

The second security rationale is to guarantee that no regional power could blackmail or pressure France with weapons of mass destruction (WMD). This emerged as a serious concern with the discovery of the scope of Iraq's pre-1991 WMD program, followed by the break-up of the Soviet Union in 1991 and the fear that Belarus, Kazakhstan, or Ukraine would retain the former Soviet nuclear weapons that remained on their soil. Starting in 1992, French official texts and speeches began mentioning the validity of nuclear deterrence to protect against nuclear and other WMD regional threats, provided of course that they were serious enough to threaten the country's vital interests.

Among potential threats to French vital interests, nuclear and ballistic missile proliferation in the greater Middle East is a topic of particular attention. Breaking with a sometimes lenient attitude towards proliferation during the Cold War, France has bolstered its efforts to fight against the spread of nuclear weapons aggressively since the early 1990s. As one of the three European countries which initiated a dialogue with Iran about its nuclear program in the summer of 2003, it has become a key player on the nuclear non-proliferation scene. Specifically, France has made various suggestions to reinforce the existing non-proliferation regime. For instance, French officials have proposed means to ensure that a country leaving the NPT does not go unpunished for the violations it may have committed as a member.

A nuclear-capable Iran with the ability to strike Europe with ballistic missiles would certainly reinforce the general trend in France towards nuclear conservatism and continued modernization of its nuclear forces. Iran has had a tense relationship with France since the 1979 revolution and, in French eyes, the manner in which the current nuclear crisis is resolved is important for the future of non-proliferation and security in the Middle East. In addition, Paris has security agreements with Kuwait, Qatar, and the United Arab Emirates. The contents of these agreements have not been made public, but it could be argued that the opening of a permanent French military base in Abu Dhabi in 2008 is tantamount to extending a security guarantee. In a worse-case scenario of free-for-all nuclear proliferation, the possibility of new nuclear-armed states in North Africa would be a particular source of worry in France. One country of particular concern to the French would be Algeria, for obvious geographical and historical reasons, especially since it had secret nuclear activities in the 1980s.

Asian countries other than China also could be of direct concern to France if they developed Intercontinental Range Ballistic Missiles (ICBMs). This could be the case for North Korea, for example: as Pyongyang's missile ranges increase, geography will ensure that European territory will be technically at risk before US territory is endangered.

With regard to dealing with the consequences of nuclear proliferation, the prevailing opinion in Paris is that nuclear deterrence is a better and safer choice than relying on missile defenses. The kind of scenario that has French officials worried is one, for instance, in which a country tries to block military intervention by threatening to strike French national territory. This concept could be called "counter-deterrence" or "counter-blackmail." No specific countries of concern are identified in French official discourse; Paris has not adopted the US practice of "naming names," in line with a consistent practice of refusing to establish a sharp distinction between "good guys and bad guys" in the international community. However, Iran is now mentioned regularly in official foreign and security policy speeches.

GLOBAL AND REGIONAL AMBITIONS

In its origins, France's nuclear program was partly driven by a quest for global status. It was particularly important for the politicians of the Fourth Republic (1945-1958), as well as for Charles de Gaulle upon his return to power in 1958, to have equal status with the other two major Western powers, the United States and the United Kingdom. In 1954, Pierre Mendès-France, then head-of-government, came back from a meeting at the United Nations stating that "if you do not have the Bomb you are nothing in international negotiations."[4] That same year, a note by the Ministry of Foreign Affairs stated that, "The direction of strategy will from now on, increasingly, belong to the powers possessing the atomic weapon…It is essential that France undertakes an atomic military program. Otherwise, its security will be entirely assured by the Anglo-Saxons."[5] When De Gaulle returned to power in 1958, he considered the bomb "a political means to allow him to sit at the Great [powers'] table."[6]

Today, this concern for global status has largely disappeared. In discussing the need to maintain nuclear forces in 2008, President Sarkozy said clearly, "It is neither a matter of prestige nor a question of rank, it is quite simply the nation's insurance policy."[7] There is no link made today in France between the country's possession of nuclear weapons and its status as a permanent member of the United Nations Security Council. The French consider that they have special responsibilities stemming from this status and that they exert it through voluntary financial contributions to the UN organizations and through significant military contributions to UN-mandated operations. Paris actively supports opening the UNSC to new permanent members, be they nuclear (India) or not (Japan, Brazil, etc.).

However, the possession of nuclear weapons is not without connection to French foreign policy defined broadly. The underlying idea that nuclear weapons make a nation free and independent is still present in the national strategic culture. The country's nuclear status seems to be present in the back of the minds of any French president, prime minister or foreign minister in their daily pursuit of foreign policy. As President Chirac stated in 2006, "[Nuclear weapons] give us, wherever the pressures may come from, the power to be the masters of our actions, of our policy, of the enduring character of our democratic values."[8]

One may even wonder: Would France have taken the stance it did take in early 2003—actively opposing war in Iraq to the point of threatening to veto the passing of a United Nations Security Council resolution—had it not been an independent nuclear power which did not depend on the United States for guaranteeing its security?[†]

Generally speaking, there has never been a direct link between France's political status in Europe and the possession of nuclear weapons. Throughout the Cold War, the European integration process did not see a weakening of France's relative place and role on the continent. Germany, France's foremost partner in this process, was economically strong but politically weak, and the United Kingdom was not a central player in the European game.

However, since the early 1990s, the nuclear issue has been linked with the European integration process in two different ways. One reason, as first raised by President Francois Mitterrand in 1992—at the time the European Union (EU) was created—is the difference in status between, on the one hand, France and the United Kingdom, and, on the other hand, the non-nuclear weapon states of the EU. Mitterrand worried that this difference in status in the EU could make the continuation of political integration more difficult. A second reason is that Paris would like Europe to benefit from the same strategic autonomy that it has enjoyed since acquiring nuclear weapons in the 1960s. French leaders are keen to transpose their concept of strategic autonomy through the possession of nuclear weapons to the EU, suggesting since 1994 that Europe will not be fully autonomous without taking into account the nuclear dimension.[9]

The sensitivity of this issue in Germany, in particular, seems to have precluded any in-depth pan-European debate on the subject, at least publicly. Furthermore, in the absence of a single political authority in the European Union, the French are not willing to share the decision to use nuclear weapons with its partners. A future "European deterrent" would entail consultations before use, some measure of risk- and responsibility-sharing, and perhaps a set of common principles for nuclear

---

[†] Germany became an active opponent of the Iraq war only after the French-German summit of January 2003. It is doubtful that Berlin would have opposed the war actively had it been on its own.

deterrence, but certainly not, for the foreseeable future at least, a common nuclear force with a single finger on the button.

So far, France has fallen short of declaring explicitly that its nuclear deterrent covers its EU partners. But French leaders have suggested increasingly that the country's nuclear deterrent already plays an implicit role in the protection of Europe. In January 2006, President Chirac stated that

> The development of the European Security and Defense Policy, the growing intermeshing of the interests of European Union countries, the solidarity that now exists between them, make the French nuclear deterrent, by its mere existence, an unavoidable element of the security of the European continent.[10]

In March 2008, Sarkozy used almost identical words, but also implied that the "collective solidarity clause" inserted in the new Lisbon Treaty made the existence of French nuclear deterrence even more important for Europe: "By their very existence, French nuclear forces are a key element in Europe's security. Any aggressor who might consider challenging it must be mindful of this (…) Our commitment to the security of our European partners is the natural expression of our ever-closer union."[11]

ROLES, MISSIONS, AND PLANS FOR FRENCH NUCLEAR FORCES

Nuclear forces have a fundamental, but narrow role in French defense policy. Consequently, France deploys relatively small forces but plans to maintain a modern force fully capable of the missions assigned to it.

Roles and missions in French security policy

France takes a fairly traditional approach to the overall concept of deterrence. Few contemporary heads-of-state of nuclear-endowed countries would devote an entire speech to matters related to nuclear deterrence as President Chirac did in January 2006. The White Paper on National Defense and Security that was published in June 2008 has not substantially altered the French stance on nuclear policy.[12] Indeed, President Sarkozy made a speech in March 2008 on strategic issues, which while announcing some reductions in forces and arms control initiatives, essentially reaffirmed President Chirac's statements on the roles and missions of French nuclear forces. President Sarkozy's speech had been informed by the work of the White Paper's commission, which by that time had already examined nuclear questions.

The French nuclear deterrent is intended to cover France's "vital interests." The 1994 White Paper defined them as follows: "The integrity of the national territory, including the mainland as well as the overseas departments and territories, the free exercise of our sovereignty and the protection of the population constitute the core [of these interests] today."[13] This definition has not substantially evolved, although President Chirac stated in his 2006 speech that "the defense of allied countries" could be part of vital interests.[14]

French policy states that an attack on France's vital interests would bring on a nuclear response in the form of "unacceptable damage," regardless of the nature of the threat, the identity of the state concerned, or the means employed. A noted part of President Chirac's 2006 speech was its reference to state-sponsored terrorism: "Leaders of States resorting to terrorist means against us, as those who might consider, one way or the other, weapons of mass destruction, must understand that they risk a firm and adapted response from us. And this response can be of a conventional nature. It can also be of another nature."[15] President Chirac made it clear that it considers that terrorism or weapons of mass destruction would not necessarily represent a threat to the country's vital interests, but that France would not hesitate to use nuclear means should the threshold of vital interests be crossed in the president's view—i.e., if it was clear that this was a state attack. In 2008, President Sarkozy did not reiterate explicitly his predecessor's reference to state-sponsored terrorism, but made it clear that France's deterrent protects the country "from any aggression against our vital interests emanating from a State – wherever it may come from and whatever form it may take."[16]

Current French doctrine is to deter an attack on its vital interests through the threat of destroying the attacker's political, economic and military centers of power. It also includes the option to threaten an adversary who may have misjudged French resolve or miscalculated the limits of French vital interests with a limited strike ("nuclear warning"), aimed at "restoring deterrence."[17] French military authorities let it be known in 2006 that a high altitude electromagnetic pulse (HA-EMP) strike also could be an option.

French policy makes clear that when referring to deterrence, they are referring to nuclear deterrence; the two words are still very much associated in the nation's strategic culture. The 1994 White Paper, for example, expressed considerable reservations about the relevance of "conventional deterrence" as a possible substitute for nuclear weapons.[18]

France has consistently rejected the adoption of a "no first-use" posture. This has been manifested by reservations attached to the Negative Security Assurances (NSAs) conferred in 1995 by France, as by the other declared nuclear powers, to the non-nuclear State Parties to the NPT. Paris sees nuclear retaliation as being consistent with the right to self-defense, as recognized by Article 51 of the UN Charter, and believes this right would prevail in the case of aggression over commitments of nuclear non-use that had been made in peacetime. France also asserts that countries that do not respect their own non-proliferation commitments—including with respect to chemical and biological weapons—should not expect that the NSA would apply to them. These reservations to the NSAs were reaffirmed in 2003.[19] Similar reservations have been made whenever France ratified protocols to treaties establishing nuclear-weapon-free zones.

French authorities, including President Chirac in 2006, regularly reaffirm that their nuclear forces are solely for deterrence and "are in no way war-fighting weapons." [20] In the eyes of French authorities, doctrinal and weapon system adaptations that were made following the end of the Cold War were necessary to ensure the credibility of deterrence in a wider range of scenarios than were necessary in the past, and did not signify a doctrinal change. In 2006, the then-Chief of the Defense Staff let it be known that a minimum yield for new weapons had been fixed, in order to make it clear that France was not adopting a war-fighting strategy: "We have made sure to limit downwards the yield of the weapons we maintain, so that nobody could ever forget that nuclear weapons are, by their very nature, different."[21] In 2008, President Sarkozy referred to the potential use of nuclear weapons as being possible only in "extreme circumstances of self-defense."[22] The use of this expression, taken from the language of the July 1996 International Court of Justice advisory opinion, carried a subtle message. Even though France is reluctant to consider itself legally bound by political commitments made in the context of the NPT review process, such as the idea of a "diminishing role for nuclear weapons in security policies to minimize the risk that these weapons ever be used," Paris was keen to show that it has not broadened the role of its nuclear deterrent.[23]

Finally, there is a traditional defiance in French policy vis-à-vis missile defenses, for both strategic and budgetary reasons. France defended the Anti-Ballistic Missile (ABM) Treaty until 2001, motivated in part by the concern that demise of the Treaty would prompt Russia and other potential adversaries to bolster their defenses, potentially undermining the French deterrent or at least forcing Paris to increase its financial and technical efforts to maintain the credibility of the deterrent. Meanwhile, budgetary limitations have constrained the attractiveness of missile defenses for France itself.

However, since 2001, Paris has shown an increasing pragmatism in this domain. In 2002, it subscribed to the common NATO decision to conduct a feasibility study regarding a missile defense system for the protection of NATO European territory, forces, and population centers.[24] In 2006, President Chirac stated that missile defense could be a complement to nuclear deterrence "by diminishing our vulnerabilities."[25] In 2008, President Sarkozy expressed a similar view: "In order to preserve our freedom of action, missile defense capabilities against a limited strike could be a useful complement to nuclear deterrence, without being a substitute for it."[26] France will thus almost certainly participate in the future NATO missile defense system, be it in a direct way, through its own Sol-Air Moyenne Portée – Terre (SAMP-T) short-range defense systems, or indirectly through technical and industrial inputs by such French companies as EADS and Thales, who are involved in NATO-sponsored studies. In light of France's long-standing reservations about territorial missile defenses, this is a significant evolution.

CURRENT FORCES AND MODERNIZATION PLANS

Nuclear programs make up about 10 percent of the entire French defense budget and about 20 percent of the country's military equipment budget. In the 2003-2008 defense plan, on average, the nuclear budget – as voted by the Parliament in 2002 – would be €2.8 billion per year. The defense nuclear budget voted for 2008 was €2.3 billion in program authorizations and €3.4 billion in payment credits, including €1.3 billion earmarked for transfer to the Commissariat à l'énergie atomique (CEA), which fabricates French nuclear weapons.

Since the 1996 defense review, the number of French strategic submarines carrying nuclear-armed ballistic missiles (SSBNs) has been reduced from five to four. Three SSBNs of the second generation have already entered service; the fourth and final boat of this new series is due to enter service in 2010. Out of four boats in the fleet, three are always in the operational cycle, making it possible to maintain continuous patrols at-sea, with at least one vessel on patrol at all times, and even two for protracted periods of time if the president so decided.[‡]

If the force was fully generated, a total of 48 missiles and perhaps some 250-260 warheads on-board three SSBNs would be available. According to open sources, the M45 submarine-launched ballistic missile (SLBM) has a range of at least 4,000 kilometres and can carry up to six TN75 warheads, each in the 100-150 kiloton range, but some SLBMs carry a reduced payload.[§] The fourth new-generation SSBN will be the first to carry the new M51 SLBM, which initially will be the

---

[‡] The period 2008-2010 is an exception to this rule, as during this period France has only three SSBNs, all in the operational cycle. This is due to the retirement of the last SSBN of the first generation, while the fourth new one will only enter service in 2010.

[§] Theoretically, the French SSBN force could carry a total of 288 warheads (3 boats with 12 missiles per boat, and six TN75 warheads per missile). The number mentioned here is guesswork, taking into account the fact that in 2006, President Chirac stated that the number of warheads on some of the SLBMs had been reduced, allowing for more flexibility in deterrence planning.

M51.1 version, loaded with the same TN75 warhead. A M51.2 will begin entering service in 2015: it will be armed with the new TNO warhead.

The range of the M51 with a full payload of warheads and penetration aids is reported to be 6,000 kilometres. However, many sources suggest that the missile could have a much greater range with a reduced payload (8,000-9,000 kilometres)[27], in particular in its M51.2 version. This would make it able to threaten very distant targets, including in Asia.

France also has two squadrons of land-based Mirage 2000N aircraft and a small naval carrier-based fleet of Super-Etendard aircraft, carrying the 300-kilometre range Air-Sol Moyenne Portée (ASMP) air-breathing missile. The successor to the ASMP is the "improved" ASMP (ASMP Amélioré), which entered service at the end of 2008 and is armed with the new TNA warhead. Rafale aircraft will gradually replace both the Mirage 2000N and Super-Etendard, starting in 2010. The range of the ASMP-A is reported to be 300-400 kilometres, and its accuracy better than that of its predecessor.

In March 2008, President Sarkozy announced a cut of one-third of the air-based leg of the nuclear deterrent – a significant reduction by French standards. This cut includes weapons, missiles, and aircraft: One of three existing nuclear-trained squadrons is to be disbanded. The decision was driven primarily by a reassessment of deterrence needs in the current and projected international environment. It did not necessarily mean that French analysts foresaw a more benign strategic context. The reassessment took into account the ongoing modernization of the French forces, including the greater flexibility given to the strategic submarines by the new missiles and warheads, as well as the coming into service of the ASMP-A, which has a longer-range and is more accurate, and of the Rafale, a more modern aircraft. The decision also relied on political judgment, namely, "how much is enough" to ensure deterrence.

When critics point out that the United Kingdom has retained only a monad since the end of the Cold War (the last British WE-177 bomb was withdrawn in 1998), analysts favoring France's status quo note that the UK's Trident-2 ballistic missile is much more accurate than either the French M45 or the newer M51. They also point out that London's status within NATO's military command—which maintains its own air-launched weapons—makes the need for an independent aircraft-based nuclear component less important. Since the United Kingdom anticipates that dealing with a major threat would probably involve the Alliance as a whole, NATO deterrence would involve both UK missiles and US bombs delivered by European and US aircraft.[**]

As announced by President Sarkozy in March 2008, the current number of nuclear weapons in the French arsenal is less than 300. This is the total number of warheads in the stockpile and not only "operationally available weapons," a measure cited by the United States and the United Kingdom after their own policy reviews of 2001 (for the United States) and 2006 (for the United Kingdom).

The next generation French warheads—the TNA for the ASMP-A, which entered service in 2008, and the TNO for the M51.2, which will enter service in 2015—are called "robust" warheads in France, as they are less sensitive to variations in performance resulting from the ageing of components. This concept was developed during the 1995-1996 final nuclear warhead test series. The concept is not dissimilar to that behind the proposed US Reliable Replacement Warhead program.

The French "simulation" program is aimed at maintaining an enduring, reliable stockpile without "hot" nuclear testing. It includes in particular a high-power laser (Laser Méga-Joule, LMJ), a powerful X-Ray radiography machine (Accélérateur à Induction pour Radiographie pour l'Imagerie X, AIRIX), and a massively parallel computer architecture, aiming at a 100 Teraflop per second capability in 2010.

While specific weapon adaptations have not been made public, it is widely believed that the French have diversified their yield options in recent years. The option of exploding only the first-stage "primary" of a warhead to reduce the yield may have been exploited, since it is known to be an easy adaptation to make from a technical point of view. However, since 1996, all French weapons are lumped together in a single category of "strategic" systems, providing flexibility in nuclear planning and operations. France considers that any use of a nuclear weapon would be such a major decision that the very notion of "non-strategic" or "sub-strategic" weapons or use does not make sense anymore.

In sum, the French nuclear force is just beginning a transition towards a new generation of missiles and warheads, which will stretch from 2008 until 2020.

[**] See Henri Bentegeat in « Rapport d'information fait au nom de la commission des Affaires étrangères, de la défense et des forces armées sur le rôle de la dissuasion nucléaire française aujourd'hui, » page 24. It is anticipated that a reintegration of France in the NATO military structures would not change the status of the French nuclear forces in any way, and that France would not participate in NATO's Nuclear Planning Group.

THE FRENCH APPROACH TO NUCLEAR ARMS CONTROL AND DISARMAMENT

During the Cold War, France put conditions on its possible participation in multilateral nuclear arms control negotiations. As stated by French authorities in 1983, there were three: (1) a reduction in the quantitative and qualitative difference that existed between the French nuclear arsenal and those of the superpowers; (2) a reduction in the conventional imbalance in Europe and the global elimination of chemical and biological weapons; and (3) the end of the offense-defense arms race, with limitations on defensive systems, such as anti-missile and anti-submarine weaponry, capable of neutralizing nuclear deterrence forces. In 1996, President Chirac stated that he still saw no reason to put French nuclear forces on the arms control agenda, mentioning the far greater size of US and Russian arsenals, and the uncertainties about the future of the ABM Treaty and non-proliferation regime.[28]

France considers its nuclear policy to be consistent with its international legal obligations, including Article VI of the Non-Proliferation Treaty. The head of the French delegation to the 2005 NPT Review Conference stated that his country was "intent on reaffirming its commitments under Article VI of the Treaty."[29] France maintains its force at a level of "sufficiency" (a French expression broadly equivalent to "minimum deterrent") and has chosen "not to equip itself with all the nuclear weapons systems it could have given the technological resources at its disposal."[30]

However, the French have also adopted a very strict interpretation of Article VI (which was not even referenced in the aforementioned 2005 brochure). France is keen to emphasize the multidimensional character of Article VI, including the goals of cessation of the arms race and of general and complete disarmament. It considers that its actions in favor of biological, chemical and conventional disarmament (including small arms and landmines) are part of its Article VI record – as is its assistance to nuclear threat reduction in Russia.[31] As far as its own nuclear policy is concerned, the preferred point of reference for French diplomats seems to be the "Decision Number Two" of the 1995 NPT Review Conference, rather than the "Thirteen Steps" of the 2000 Conference.[32] President Sarkozy's disarmament and non-proliferation agenda as laid out in his March 2008 speech is meant to "[take] us forward on the path to both nuclear disarmament and general and complete disarmament," a clear reference to the inseparability, in French eyes, of the two dimensions of Article VI.[33]

France's firmness on the Article VI issue has been made stronger by the unilateral decisions and moves toward reduced armaments it has made since 1990. France has reduced the size of its arsenal by about 50 percent since the height of the Cold War. The nuclear share of the equipment budget has been reduced by half since 1990 (from about 40 percent to about 20 percent). Paris has reduced its number of nuclear delivery vehicles by two-thirds since 1985 and the number of its SSBNs by two-thirds (from six to four). It is the only one of the five NPT declared nuclear weapon-states to have developed, deployed and then abandoned ground-launched ballistic missiles and to have dismantled its nuclear testing site and fissile material production facilities.[††] It was the first of the five NPT nuclear powers to support officially the so-called "zero option" for the CTBT – no test whatever the yield. And it was the first of the five, along with the United Kingdom, to ratify the CTBT in 1998.

Public Opinion

France has never had a significant anti-nuclear movement. The French branches of such transnational organizations arguing in favor of nuclear disarmament as Greenpeace are in no way as strong and influential as they may be in other Western countries. Only a small number of grassroots organizations and interest groups devote their work to disarmament. About forty organizations are affiliated with the international Abolition 2000 network. José Bové, France's most well-known "anti-globalization" activist, is "personally in favor of the unilateral abandonment" of the nuclear deterrent.[34] The Green party, which became a government force in 1997 in an alliance with the Socialist Party, is the only significant force calling for nuclear disarmament. Its platform calls for a commitment to make Europe a nuclear-weapon-free-zone, a freeze on the nuclear deterrence budget, and the cancellation of the M51 program.[35] But the Greens tend to focus their criticism of French nuclear policy on the civilian side – as does the Sortir du nucléaire network, a federation of 765 small local associations. In recent years, due to the evolution of the Holy See's official stance, the Catholic Church has joined anti-nuclear movements in condemning nuclear deterrence and asking for unilateral disarmament. However, bishops remain fairly discreet on this issue – as on most public policy matters due to the strong separation that exists in France between the churches and the state.

A major reason why the anti-nuclear movement in France has never been as strong as in the United Kingdom is that, as suggested above, for the French, nuclear weapons remain the positive symbol of an independent foreign and defense policy, in particular from the United States. French political culture has long identified nuclear technology with independence. Also, the withdrawal from the NATO integrated command in 1967 largely insulated French public opinion from the broader Western strategy debate. During the Cold War, the nuclear debate in Europe was linked with the relationship with the United States and NATO. France was largely spared from this debate and did not have massive anti-nuclear protests.

[††] The Centre d'Expérimentations du Pacifique is now dismantled. The highly-enriched uranium production facility at Pierrelatte will be fully dismantled by 2010. The plutonium production facility at Marcoule has been disabled and dismantlement has begun; however, for technical reasons, it will be fully dismantled only by 2040.

Finally, the French nuclear procurement cycle tends to be spread out over time and rarely lends itself to any critical decision point or moment. The current modernization of nuclear systems, for example, is spread out over more than twenty years. The first new-generation SSBN entered service in 1997; all four of them will be armed with the new-generation warhead only in 2020.

It is therefore not surprising that French public opinion supports the continued possession of nuclear weapons, and that this support has remained fairly high since the end of the Cold War. In June 2007, in response to the question, "Could a country like France ensure its defense without the deterrent force (nuclear force)?" 57 percent answered "No", against 34 percent "Yes." The number of those in favor of "modernizing" (43 percent) and "maintaining in the current state" (35 percent) of the French deterrent has grown steadily since 2000. Conversely, those in favor of "reducing" are now a small minority (17 percent).[36] An Internet poll (4,573 respondents) conducted in October 2006 gave similar results: 71 percent judged that the possession of nuclear weapons by France was "vital" or "useful," against 27 percent who thought it was "useless" or "dangerous." The majority believed that nuclear weapons protected the country against military threats, be they nuclear or non-nuclear.[37]

Prospects for Further Nuclear Reductions

Under what circumstances could France's arsenal be further reduced? It is to be noted that because the future French SLBM warhead, the TNO, will be bigger and heavier than the current one (the TN75), each M51 SLBM will probably carry a smaller number of warheads than the current M45 SLBM. Thus, after 2010, when the M51 comes into service, a French president may be in a position to say that France is reducing the number of operationally available SLBM warheads.

For France to go significantly further, the international framework of strategic stability and non-proliferation would need to be maintained, and other nuclear weapon states would need to be ready to participate as well. As President Chirac stated in 2006, "it is obvious that we will only be able to go forward on the road towards disarmament in the event that the conditions of our overall security are maintained and if the will to make progress is unanimously shared."[38] This position was reaffirmed by French representatives to the 2008 NPT Preparatory Committee.[39] President Sarkozy also insisted in 2008 that collective security and disarmament should be based on "reciprocity."[40] Implementation of the Sarkozy initiatives of March 2008, which include, inter alia, the closing down of all testing sites and fissile material production installations by all states possessing nuclear weapons, might create a favorable atmosphere, but there is no reason why they, in themselves, would lead France to further reduce its arsenal.

What about the impact of further US and Russian reductions? France indicated in 2005 that if "the disproportion [between its forces and those of the US and Russia] changed its nature, it could envision to draw consequences" from such an evolution.[41] If the United States and Russia reduced their arsenals to, say, about 1000 nuclear weapons each, it is doubtful that France would immediately feel compelled to reduce its arsenal. France's weapons are not intended to seek to destroy the nuclear forces and conventional arsenals of other countries. Therefore, French political leaders have stated repeatedly that the level of the country's arsenal is not dependent upon those of others.

On the other hand, if following such significant reductions in US and Russian arsenals, there was then a serious proposal initiated or supported by the United States to seek multilateral and proportional reductions, the French position might change. For political reasons, France would probably not ignore a general trend towards drastic nuclear reductions – especially if British, Chinese and French participation was a precondition for Moscow and Washington to move in this direction. In such a case, France might then perhaps be willing to move to a British-like posture: eliminating its aircraft delivered weapons and maintaining four SSBNs only, with a stockpile of perhaps no more than 150-200 warheads.

The Possibility of Reducing to Zero

Given the importance of nuclear weapons for France, the abandonment of nuclear deterrence by Paris is an extreme hypothesis. What could be the extraordinary circumstances under which France would give up this capability? Three different scenarios need to be envisioned.

Scenario One: Abolition by Example

Abolition by example is hardly a credible scenario. A British decision to give up its own deterrent, for instance, would not be enough: The "exemplary effect" that could be expected would in all likelihood be offset by the realization that France would then be the sole nuclear power in Europe – probably giving it a greater sense of responsibility, as well as a new status on the continent. An American decision to renounce nuclear weapons would be different – but France would still claim that it is the forces of its adversaries that matter for French decisions, not those of its allies.

Scenario Two: A Unilateral Decision to Disarm

A unilateral decision by Paris to disarm is hardly credible either. A consistent feature of the French nuclear stance is the insistence on the need to retain nuclear weapons as long as other states can pose a major military threat to France. This was made clear at several occasions by various French leaders. As early as 1961, President de Gaulle said that "as long as others have the means to destroy her, [France] will need to have the means to defend itself."[42] In 1998, Prime Minister Lionel Jospin said that "as long as general and complete disarmament will not be realized, nuclear weapons will remain necessary [for France.]"[43] Finally, in 2000, President Jacques Chirac said that "as long as risks persist and we have not achieved general and verified disarmament, which does not concern nuclear weapons alone, France will retain the capability to protect itself from any threat to its vital interests."[44]

Nevertheless, the circumstances under which potential major threats to the security of France have disappeared can be imagined. A first prerequisite would be a fully democratic Russia, firmly entrenched in the "Western camp" in terms of fundamental values and policies. As the biggest nuclear power in Europe's neighborhood, Russia's status is the most important feature of France's strategic environment. A second condition would be that proliferation is being "rolled-back" convincingly. The risks of short- to medium-term nuclear proliferation in the Middle East and North Africa would have to disappear. The development of medium- and long-range ballistic missiles in the same region would need to have ceased, as well. This does not mean that all major threats would have disappeared – only that the calculus of costs and benefits of maintaining a nuclear deterrent would then be drastically changed, to the point that it would be difficult for a French government to fund and prepare the "generation after next" of nuclear forces, those which would need to be fielded in the 2030s.

The continued possession by the United States of a nuclear deterrent might help a French decision to go to zero. The US extended deterrent to Europe would remain a "last line of defense" in case of a sudden and dramatic reversal of the strategic environment. In other words, paradoxically, a French decision to forego its nuclear arsenal may be impossible if the United States was to disarm unilaterally.

Scenario Three: A US-led Initiative to Go to Zero

France's participation in a coordinated move toward zero would be another extreme scenario. However, it is possible to imagine the conditions under which Paris would willingly participate in such a move.

The prospect of a major proliferation wave among Europe's regional neighbors would not suffice for Paris to consider abolition. If they confronted a proliferation "cascade," as has been speculated upon as a possible reaction to Iran's acquisition of a nuclear weapon capability, the French reaction would be, "better a bird in a hand than two in the bush;" that is, French officials would believe that the safer bet would be to maintain France's nuclear deterrent rather than participating in a global attempt to abolish nuclear weapons. They would maintain that if there were a serious possibility of a world with 30 nuclear powers, then the political conditions for the global abolition of nuclear weapons would hardly be present.

For France to go along with a US initiative to abolish nuclear weapons, there would need to be a dramatic improvement in the international environment.‡‡ The coming into force of the CTBT and of a Fissile Material Cutoff Treaty would probably be essential components of such an improvement. Also, nuclear proliferation would have had to be stopped demonstrably and verifiably, and France would have to be convinced that all nuclear-capable states were ready to participate in a global move towards zero.

From a French point of view, there also would also need to be significant progress towards non-nuclear stability and disarmament. This would require, at the least, fully implementing and maintaining such existing instruments as the Conventional Forces in Europe Treaty, the Biological and Toxin Weapons Convention, and the Chemical Weapons Convention. A limitation on ballistic missile proliferation would also need to be ensured, and a NATO missile defense architecture which could effectively shield Europe from any significant missile attack (whatever the payload such missiles would carry) might be needed as an insurance policy. A democratic evolution in Russia, better relations between Moscow and its immediate neighbors, as well as the political stabilization of the greater Middle East region—from Morocco to Pakistan—would certainly be needed to help France consider a move toward zero.

Scenario Four: A "Great Powers" Initiative to Go to Zero

A variant of the previous scenario might alter the perspective. While Paris would find it easy to resist a US-only initiative—as it has done in the past on many different occasions—it would be more difficult politically to do so if both Russia and China also took part in it. Beijing's participation would be seen as critical, because it would then imply very strong pressure on New Delhi, and therefore on Islamabad, to give up nuclear weapons, as

---

‡‡ One alternative might be a scenario in which nuclear use had taken place and triggered a general trend towards general nuclear disarmament.

well.[§§] Pressure on Pakistan would also work indirectly through China, which would probably use its full weight to obtain Islamabad's cooperation.

In such a dramatic scenario, there would in all likelihood be strong pressures from within the European Union for France to follow suit. Assuming the United Kingdom was ready to play along, there would then be very strong pressures from such key countries as Germany, Italy, Spain, and Sweden, in which public support for nuclear deterrence has never been very strong. Only some East European countries, such as Poland and the Baltic States, might refrain from such pressures, given their traditional fear of Russia – which may lead them, in the absence of a US nuclear guarantee, to see UK and French forces with increased sympathy. Given France's determination to continue to be one of the key political actors in Europe, such political pressure would be hard to resist. Before giving up its arsenal, however, Paris would certainly attempt to secure its existence for several years, waiting for concrete disarmament steps by the major nuclear players – notably the United States and Russia, given the size of their arsenals – and for proof that verification measures would be effective.

CONCLUSION

In sum, the only credible circumstances where France would be willing to seriously consider the global abolition of nuclear weapons are those in which there is no foreseeable major threat against its vital interests and those of its European partners. However, it would be difficult for Paris to stay away from a coordinated US-Russia-China initiative to begin negotiations for a treaty to eliminate nuclear weapons from all nations.

[§§] France could probably live with the idea that Israel would remain nuclear as long as there is no durable peace in the region. And North Korea would not pose a direct problem for Europe's security as long as it does not have ICBMs.

ENDNOTES

[1] Allocution de M. Jacques Chirac, Président de la République, lors de sa visite aux forces aérienne et océanique stratégiques, (Landivisiau – l'Île Longue (Brest), 19 January 2006).

[2] Allocution de M. Jacques Chirac, op. cit.

[3] Allocution de M. Lionel Jospin, Premier Ministre, devant l'Institut des Hautes Etudes de Défense Nationale (Paris: 22 October 1999).

[4] Quoted in Dominique Mongin, *La bombe atomique française 1945-1958* (Brussels: Bruylant, 1997), page 333.

[5] Quoted in Georges-Henri Soutou, "La politique nucléaire de Mendès-France," *Relations Internationales*, Vol. 59 (Fall 1989), page 320.

[6] General Alfred Buchalet, "Les premières étapes, 1955-1960," in Université de Franche-Comté/Institut Charles de Gaulle, *L'aventure de la bombe*: *De Gaulle et la dissuasion nucléaire 1958-1969* (Paris: Plon, 1985), page 52.

[7] «Discours de M. le Président de la République – Présentation du SNLE Le Terrible » (Cherbourg), 21 March 2008.

[8] Allocution de M. Jacques Chirac, op. cit.

[9] Livre Blanc sur la Défense 1994 (Paris: Editions 10/18, 1994), p. 98.

[10] Allocution de M. Jacques Chirac, op. cit.

[11] Discours de M. le Président de la République, op. cit..

[12] Défense et sécurité nationale: le Livre blanc (Paris: éditions Odile Jacob, 2008).

[13] Livre blanc sur la Défense 1994, op. cit., page 4.

[14] Allocution de M. Jacques Chirac, op. cit.

[15] Allocution de M. Jacques Chirac, op. cit.

[16] Discours de M. le Président de la République, op. cit.

[17] Discours de M. le Président de la République, op. cit.

[18] See Livre Blanc sur la Défense 1994, op. cit., page 99.

[19] See Rapport de la France sur l'application de l'article VI et de l'alinéa C) du paragraphe 4 de la décision de 1995 sur les principes et objectifs de la non-prolifération et du désarmement nucléaires, Deuxième session du comité préparatoire de la conférence d'examen du TNP de 2005 (Geneva), 30 April 2003.

[20] Conférence de presse conjointe de M. Jacques Chirac, Président de la République et de Mme Angela Merkel, Chancelière de la République Fédérale d'Allemagne à l'occasion de la rencontre franco-allemande (Versailles), 23 January 2006.

[21] Henri Bentegeat, in Rapport d'information fait au nom de la commission des Affaires étrangères, de la défense et des forces armées sur le rôle de la dissuasion nucléaire française aujourd'hui, par M. Serge Vinçon, Sénateur, Document n° 36 (24 October 2006), page 25.

[22] Discours de M. le Président de la République, op. cit.

[23] 2000 Review Conference of the Parties to the Treaty on the Non-Proliferation of Nuclear Weapons, Final Document, Volume I, NPT/CONF.2000/28 (New-York, 2000), page 15.

[24] See Prague Summit Declaration, Issued by the Heads of State and Government participating in the meeting of the North Atlantic Council in Prague on 21 November 2002, para. 4.

[25] Allocution de M. Jacques Chirac, op. cit.

[26] Discours de M. le Président de la République, op. cit.

[27] See for instance *Jane's Strategic Weapons Systems*, *M-5/M-51* (23 June 2006), and Jean-Dominique Merchet, « Premier tir d'essai 'réussi' du missile stratégique M51 », *Libération* (10 November 2006).

[28] Discours du Président de la République, M. Jacques Chirac, à l'Institut des Hautes Etudes de Défense Nationale (Paris), 8 June 1996.

[29] 2005 Review Conference of the State Parties to the Treaty on the Non-Proliferation of Nuclear Weapons, General Debate, Statement by H. E. M. François Rivasseau, Ambassador, Permanent Representative of France to the Conference on Disarmament (New-York), 5 May 2005, page 7.

[30] Ministère de la défense, Secrétariat général de la défense nationale, & Ministère des affaires étrangères, Fighting Proliferation, Promoting Arms Control and Disarmament : France's Contribution (2005), page 64.

[31] Conférence des Etats Parties chargée d'examiner en 2005 le Traité sur la Non-Prolifération des Armes Nucléaires, Comité I, Intervention prononcée par S.E.M. François Rivasseau, Ambassadeur, Représentant Permanent de la France auprès de la Conférence du Désarmement (New-York), 19 May 2005.

[32] See 2005 Review Conference of the State Parties to the Treaty on the Non-Proliferation of Nuclear Weapons, General Debate, Statement by H. E. M. François Rivasseau, Ambassador, Permanent Representative of France to the Conference on Disarmament (New-York), 5 May 2005.

[33] Second Session of the Preparatory Committee for the 2010 NPT Review Conference, Statement by H.E. Ambassador Jean-François Dobelle, Permanent Representative of France to the Conference on Disarmament, Head of the Delegation, "Cluster 1" (Geneva), 30 April 2008.

[34] José Bové, interview to I-TV television channel, « Le Franc-Parler », 30 October 2006.

[35] Les Verts, « Le monde change, avec les Verts changeons le monde » (3 August 2006), page 78.

[36] Annual poll by BVA for the French Defense Ministry. The data for 1991-2006 was published in Les Français et la Défense : 15 ans de sondages (1991-2006) (Paris : Ministère de la défense, Délégation à l'Information et à la Communication de la Défense, May 2008). The data for 2007 are not yet publicly available but were communicated privately to the author.

[37] Opinion poll conducted by Expression Publique, October 2006.

[38] Allocution de M. Jacques Chirac, op. cit.

[39] See Second Session of the Preparatory Committee for the 2010 NPT Review Conference, Statement by H.E. Ambassador Jean-François Dobelle, Permanent Representative of France to the Conference on Disarmament, Head of the Delegation, "Cluster 1", Geneva, 30 April 2008.

[40] Discours de M. le Président de la République, op. cit.

[41] Conférence des Etats Parties chargée d'examiner en 2005 le Traité sur la Non-Prolifération des Armes Nucléaires, Comité I, Intervention prononcée par S.E.M. François Rivasseau (2005).

[42] Press conference, 11 April 1961, in Charles de Gaulle, *Discours et Messages*, vol. III (Paris: Plon, 1970), page 72.

[43] Discours du Premier ministre, M. Lionel Jospin, à l'Institut des Hautes Etudes de Défense Nationale, 3 September 1998.

[44] Jacques Chirac, interview to Armées d'Aujourd'hui, January 2000.

INDIAN PERSPECTIVES ON THE GLOBAL ELIMINATION OF NUCLEAR WEAPONS

Rajesh M. Basrur

India's security concerns since its independence in 1947 have revolved around four central themes: protection of the nation's security from external threats, internal consolidation of national identity, achievement of balanced economic growth, and creation of a stable democratic polity. Policymakers have faced serious challenges in all four areas and have had perforce to divide their political and material resources among them. A young nation-state in the making with a weak economy seeking to build democracy in a fragmented society must necessarily restrict its allocations to the military sector. As a part of the overall security landscape, nuclear weapons occupy a relatively small space. Indian thinking about nuclear weapons, moreover, has been shaped by the thinking of M.K. Gandhi, the man who led the country's movement for independence for some three decades. Gandhi's espousal of non-violence as a political strategy and his moral rejection of nuclear weapons laid the foundations of a deep unease with the bomb.[1] Consistent with this perspective, Prime Minister Jawaharlal Nehru, who held the reins of security policy until his death in 1964, was unwilling to seek nuclear weapons because he believed they would engender insecurity rather than security and preferred to focus on universal nuclear disarmament. But Nehru was enough of a realist to leave the door open to the future development of nuclear weapons in case the need arose. As he noted, while India did not need nuclear weapons, "there is always a built-in advantage of defence use if the need should arise."[2] As a result, India abjured nuclear weapons, but developed its civilian nuclear program with an eye to its military potential.

Through a series of cautious responses to external threats, the military potential gradually evolved and India became a declared nuclear-armed state in 1998. Yet the normative aspect has never lost its salience. The balance between a norm-driven rejection of nuclear weapons and a realist-driven awareness of nuclear threats has consistently been tilted in favor of the former.[3] Thus, India is inclined to be well disposed, perhaps more than most other nuclear-armed states, toward the current effort to marginalize and eventually eliminate nuclear weapons.

INDIA'S SECURITY CONCERNS

There has been much debate over India's motivations for nuclearization. Among the factors said to have been influential are national security, the interests of the bureaucracy and the nuclear-scientific community, the political outlook and calculations of the Bharatiya Janata Party (which was in power in 1998), considerations of national prestige, and resistance to international pressure driven by a desire to be autonomous.* All of these arguments have some truth to them, which is hardly surprising, since major historical processes and events are rarely attributable to a single factor. But this debate is skewed and misleading because most of the discussion has occurred in the context of the series of nuclear tests conducted by India in 1998. The reality is more complex.

In assessing India's motivations in becoming a nuclear-armed state, it is important to recognize that the chronology of its nuclearization is distributed over a long period punctuated by three major events. First, India became a *nuclear-capable power* in 1974, when Prime Minister Indira Gandhi ordered a single successful test. But thereafter, she made no effort to build an arsenal. Technical capability was not translated into military capability. The bomb was actually produced circa 1989, when, eschewing further tests, Prime Minister Rajiv Gandhi authorized the construction of the first nuclear weapon, thereby marking India's emergence as a *covert nuclear power*. The bomb lay confined to the basement, its organizational infrastructure largely undeveloped. The series of tests conducted by the coalition government of Prime Minister Atal Behari Vajpayee in 1998 made India a *declared nuclear power*. In each case, security considerations played a significant role, but in different ways. In each case, threat perceptions were different.

Mrs. Gandhi's bomb was motivated by an all-consuming fear of loss of India's political autonomy vis-à-vis the external world. India's colonial past lay heavy in the minds of post-independence leaders, who fashioned a foreign and security policy characterized by resistance to external domination. Its chief tenets were nonalignment, autarky, and opposition to the presence of foreign forces in its neighborhood. India's 1974 test was not a direct response to the Chinese threat. Limited movement toward a nuclear weapons program had been authorized by Mrs. Gandhi's predecessor, Lal Bahadur Shastri, in the wake of China's 1964

---

*For a range of discussions on the Indian decision to go nuclear, see Scott Sagan, "Why Do States Build Nuclear Weapons? Three Models in Search of A Bomb," International Security (Winter 1996/97), pp. 54-86; Stephen P. Cohen, "Why Did India 'Go Nuclear'?" in Raju G. C. Thomas and Amit Gupta, eds., India's Nuclear Security (New Delhi: Vistaar Publications, 2000); Sumit Ganguly, "Explaining the Indian Nuclear Tests of 1998," Ibid.; Devin T. Hagerty, "South Asia's Big Bangs: Causes, Consequences, Prospects," Australian Journal of International Affairs (April 1999), pages 19-29; Prem Shanker Jha, "Why India Went Nuclear," World Affairs (July-September 1998), pages 80-96; Pratap Bhanu Mehta, "India: the Nuclear Politics of Self-Esteem," Current History (December 1998), pages 403-406; Deepa Ollapally, "Mixed Motives in India's Search for Nuclear Status," Asian Survey (November/December 2001), pages 925-942; George Perkovich, India's Nuclear Bomb: The Impact on Global Proliferation (Berkeley, Los Angeles and London: University of California Press, 1999); Kalpana Sharma, "The Hindu Bomb," Bulletin of the Atomic Scientists (July-August 1998), pages 30-33; and K. Subrahmanyam, "Nuclear India in Global Politics," World Affairs (July-September 1998), pages 12-40.

test, which had occurred soon after India's painful rout in the Sino-Indian border war (1962). At the time of the test, little thought was given to the need for nuclear weapons in response to the Chinese military threat, as India was quickly building up its conventional capabilities, more than doubling its forces within the next two years and enhancing its training and logistics as well.[4] Mrs. Gandhi's disinclination for a nuclear build-up in response is therefore understandable, though she was far more inclined toward realpolitik than Nehru or Shastri. The test was a *political* response to the growing perception that India's autonomy was threatened by the ingress of external forces in the region and by the evolving balance of power that was transforming the wider regional strategic landscape at the time. In particular, there was much apprehension among Indian decision makers about what was viewed as an emergent US-Pakistan-China axis, which hemmed India in geopolitically. In responding to the 1971 crisis in East Pakistan (which eventually led to the birth of Bangladesh), India felt compelled to undermine its autonomy by signing a quasi-alliance with the Soviet Union—the August 1971 Treaty of Friendship—which also had been hedging its subcontinental bets by making overtures to Pakistan.[5] Both India's regional security and its global position as a leader of the Non-Aligned Movement quickly deteriorated. Above all, the symbolic warning conveyed to India by the dispatch of a US naval task force into the Bay of Bengal in December 1971 had profound effects on the Indian leadership.[6] The 1974 test was thus a symbolic response to India's perception that it had lost its autonomy and become dependent on the Soviet Union owing to the shifting power balances of the time. In short, it represented a response not so much to a direct military threat as to its perception of a serious deterioration in its overall security environment.

Since the test occurred at a juncture when Mrs. Gandhi was surrounded by increasing domestic political turmoil, it has been claimed that her decision may have been a survival tactic.[7] But this is not a satisfactory explanation. The pivotal decision to go ahead with the test appears to have been made in the period between late 1971 and September 1972, much before Mrs. Gandhi's domestic troubles erupted.[8] The process took time for technical rather than economic or political reasons: though there was some anticipation of an adverse international reaction and negative economic consequences, there was an expectation that India would be able to ride them out.[9]

The militarization of India's nuclear capability occurred in quite different circumstances. By the 1980s, Pakistan was known to be reaching for the bomb, largely through the clandestine efforts of A. Q. Khan. This generated a new and more immediate threat to Indian security since India saw Pakistan as an irredentist state that had twice gone to war with it over Kashmir. In the Indian perception, there were two secondary contributors to the threat. China, pursuing a strategy of containing India by using Pakistan as a surrogate, had supplied technology and possibly nuclear materials and warhead designs for the Pakistani bomb.[10] The United States, meantime, had turned a blind Cold War eye to growing evidence of Pakistan's quest as it needed Islamabad's close cooperation in building up the armed resistance of the mujahideen to the Soviet occupation of Afghanistan. Even so, Rajiv Gandhi, cast in his mother's mold as a realist uneasy with the bomb, sought to propagate universal disarmament and presented a plan toward this end at the United Nations in 1988.[11] But the effort failed, and Rajiv ordered the construction of India's first bomb in 1989.[†] In sum, the making of India's bomb was not an immediate and proactive response to the perception of a major security threat, but rather a case of reluctant nuclearization arising from concerns about the deteriorating security environment.

India's third major nuclear event was the decision to test in 1998. What motivated Vajpayee and the BJP to overtly go nuclear? The BJP as a party had always been a strong advocate of going nuclear. Yet Vajpayee, as Minister for External Affairs in the cabinet of Morarji Desai in the late 1970s, had voted against that path as he felt it would have serious adverse effects on India-Pakistan relations.[12] Analysts who point to domestic political incentives for the tests fail to observe that, first, the BJP was surely aware that Mrs. Gandhi's government had nearly collapsed under the weight of popular opposition within months of the 1974 test; and second, that Prime Minister P.V. Narasimha Rao of the Congress Party had authorized a test in 1995 before retracting it under American pressure.

The evolution of the nonproliferation regime in the 1990s provides a security-related explanation. Though the bomb had been built around 1989, it had remained covert since then and no effort had been made to create a full-fledged infrastructure for it. The Indian position had always been one of building capability and keeping the option to develop an arsenal open. Simultaneously, India had consistently called for disarmament, arguing that it could not close its option so long as others retained their nuclear weapons. Post-Cold War, the US-led drive to tighten nonproliferation made India's position increasingly uncomfortable.[13] While the US retained nuclear weapons as centerpieces of its national security strategy, the odds against India's retention of its open option were lengthened. The indefinite extension of the Nuclear Nonproliferation Treaty (NPT), which India rejected precisely because it would have closed the

---

[†] K. Subrahmanyam, "Indian Nuclear Policy, 1964-98 (A Personal Recollection)," in Jasjit Singh, ed., *Nuclear India* (New Delhi: Knowledge World, 1998), page 44; Raj Chengappa, *Weapons of Peace* (New Delhi: HarperCollins, 2000), pages 332-6. Was Rajiv's disarmament genuine or just a tactical move preceding the bomb decision? There is some evidence for the former, none for the latter. V. S. Arunachalam, his scientific advisor, argues from personal knowledge that he was "genuinely against the bomb," though he "did not want India to be found wanting in a crisis either." See Chengappa, *Weapons of Peace*, page 304. There is also an undeniable continuity in reservations about the bomb over the generations from grandfather to grandson.

door to nuclearization, was a blow, but as an outsider, India could tolerate it. The negotiations over the Comprehensive Test Ban Treaty (CTBT) took a more unpleasant turn from the Indian standpoint. The entry into force (EIF) clause of the treaty envisaged putting pressure on all nuclear-capable states to join. In effect, India was pushed into a corner, its open door on the verge of being slammed shut. It was either sign up or break out, and India chose the latter. The tests, therefore, were a response to the broad, but still substantial, threat to India's security choices.

This brief review brings into relief the security concerns underlying Indian policy, but it also highlights two important points in the current context. First, nuclear weapons have never been central to Indian security thinking in the way that they have been for several other states. Second, India's commitment to disarmament on a universal and non-discriminatory basis has been consistent. Thus, it would be reasonable to say that India's position is one which would be comfortable with a serious drive by the major nuclear powers to eliminate nuclear weapons.

NUCLEAR WEAPONS IN INDIA'S NATIONAL SECURITY STRATEGY

There are two inherent and yet divergent conceptions of the role of nuclear weapons. One is technical: they are seen from this perspective as military instruments that can be utilized for "warfighting." Even those who reject the idea of fighting a nuclear war recognize that unless the weapons were actually functional, and thus could, in principle, be used in a war, they would not deter nuclear use by others. On the other hand, the political concept of nuclear weapons works in the opposite direction, with the bomb viewed as essentially unusable. The balance between the two conceptions is important in shaping the ways in which nations respond to proposals for disarmament. A security strategy that does not give a central place to nuclear weapons and minimizes their role is more in tune with the thrust of disarmament than one that does.

India's concept of the bomb leans heavily toward the political side of the balance. There are several reasons for this. First, as noted above, there is a deep normative discomfort with weapons of mass destruction among Indian leaders. This has not dissipated in the two decades since the first bomb was put together. Second, India's historical experience since independence is one which regards the level of "unacceptable damage" – the basis of its deterrence posture – as low. In the first quarter century after independence in 1947, India fought four wars: three with Pakistan (1947-48, 1965, and 1971) and one with China (1962). None of these wars was highly destructive in terms of its human toll or economic effects.[14] More importantly, civilian populations were not targeted in any of them. This stands in great contrast with the US and the Soviet Union, both of which inflicted large-scale civilian losses during the Second World War. Their historical experience has shaped Indian leaders' belief that deterrence has a relatively low threshold: it does not require the threat to destroy many millions of people in order to deter. A small and low-profile deterrent force is enough.

Third, in contrast with the Second World War and the Cold War, the security threats faced by India have been of limited proportions. The territorial disputes with Pakistan and China do have tremendous symbolic importance, but they are hardly matters of national survival or of an all-or-nothing character. Fourth, as a democratic developing country with limited resources, India simply does not have the luxury of giving in to the temptation of adopting a nuclear doctrine that requires a large deterrent force. Fifth, political leaders in India retain a residual suspicion of the military and hence are reluctant to let the armed forces expand their functions, roles and powers beyond a limited extent.

Accordingly, Indian nuclear strategy is very low-key, reflected in its "recessed" posture.[‡] Unlike the forces of the United States and the Soviet Union/Russia, Indian nuclear weapons have never been deployed in ready-for-use form, let alone kept on alert. Delivery vehicles do not have weapons mated with them. The bombs themselves are kept unassembled. Moreover, there is no evidence that the weapons were assembled even at the height of the Kargil conflict (1999), when Indian and Pakistani troops engaged in several weeks of fighting, or in the 2001-02 crisis, when India threatened "limited war" against Pakistan.

Given this reality, it is not surprising that there is little or no interest in nuclear warfighting and therefore in developing tactical weapons. The author's post-1998 interviews with a large number of individuals from the strategic elite revealed no significant interest in such weapons.[15] Indian nuclear doctrine unequivocally states that retaliation against a nuclear attack will be "overwhelming," indicating a clear preference for a countervalue rather than a counterforce response.[16] The nuclear-capable missiles currently being developed, on which more is said below, are of the middle- and intermediate-range variety. The short-range Prithvi missile has been the mainstay of the missile force hitherto, but, vis-à-vis Pakistan, most of whose major cities are well within their reach, their function is strategic and not tactical.

Could Indian thinking change? Conceivably, the military-technical approach could gain the upper hand in the event there is a concatenation of circumstances:

[‡] The term is attributed to Jasjit Singh, a leading Indian strategic commentator. See his "A Nuclear Strategy for India," in Jasjit Singh, ed., *Nuclear India* (New Delhi: Knowledge World, 1998).

the rapid rise of a serious military threat from Pakistan or China; simultaneous domestic and external crises; and the erosion of civilian leadership. The probability seems remote. External failure in 1962 and 2001-02 had no effect on the domestic power equation. If anything, the political leadership on both occasions showed itself to be adept at retaining its status and position. There is little reason to expect the militarization of Indian thinking about nuclear weapons under the pressure of changed political circumstances.

Nuclear Weapons and India's Regional and Global Aspirations

With the growth of India's economy and the concomitant rise of its military capabilities, it is a valid question whether Indian leaders view nuclear weapons as desirable accoutrements of power. If they were, they could serve two purposes. First, they could be used as instruments for the purpose of specific political gains: as back-ups to conventional forces used for intervention abroad, or as instruments for coercing adversaries directly. Second, as symbols of great power, nuclear weapons could conceivably be used as a platform for acquiring enhanced global status. As is often pointed out, all of the permanent members of the Security Council are also the only "recognized" nuclear weapon states (though this fails to recognize that only the US was a nuclear power in 1945). A brief discussion will show that neither aspect is relevant to India's regional and global aspirations.

At the regional level, India was long viewed as a "hegemon," and not a particularly benign one either, since it incorporated one small neighbor into its territory (Sikkim), signed unequal treaties with two others (Bhutan, Nepal) and intervened militarily in three (Pakistan in 1971, Sri Lanka in 1987, and the Maldives in 1988). But since the 1990s, the situation has been reversed. Relations with all its immediate neighbors are on the upswing.[17] After two major confrontations, India and Pakistan have realized that there is no military solution to the Kashmir issue and have begun fording the gulf between them. India-Sri Lanka relations have reached a stage where Sri Lankan leaders have repeatedly pressed for free trade, a defence pact, and even Indian involvement in their ethnic crisis. India has signed a new and more egalitarian treaty with Bhutan and indicated its willingness to do the same with Nepal. Relations with Bangladesh have improved significantly, reflected in the April 2008 revival of cross-border train service after four decades. India, for its part, has shown no inclination to intervene in any of these states despite its growing power and despite the high level of instability in all except Bhutan.

Nuclear weapons have played no role in any of India's South Asian relationships except with Pakistan, in which a number of confidence-building measures, including nuclear risk reduction measures, have been put in place as part of an ongoing process of dialogue. Moreover, India has continually collaborated with the United States in engaging its neighbors, often letting it take the initiative.[18] This stands in stark contrast with its past tendency to resist the involvement of the US in South Asia. Given its low nuclear profile and the reorientation of its role in its neighborhood, it seems fair to say that India is highly unlikely to conceive of nuclear weapons as having any part to play in shaping its growth as a regional power.

As a rising power, India has begun to spread its strategic wings to its neighboring regions. The "Look East" policy has seen its increasing involvement in Southeast Asia and a growing interest in the politics of Northeast Asia.[19] However, the focus is mainly on economic gains. On the military-strategic side, India has shown an interest in greater involvement through multilateral frameworks such as the Association of Southeast Asian Nations (ASEAN) and the ASEAN Regional Forum. In 2007 there was preliminary movement toward a proposed quadrilateral grouping or "quad" (also called the "coalition of democracies") involving the US, Japan, Australia, and India, but Indian interest was motivated more by a desire not to be left out of a possible bigger role in the east and quickly waned when China reacted negatively.[20] To its northwest, India has long had an interest in Afghanistan and Central Asia and a milestone of sorts was marked by the establishment of a minor "air base" at Ayni in Tajikistan, but only helicopters are deployed there and the base is jointly controlled by Tajikistan, Russia, and India.[21] Interest in the Middle East (which Indians usually call West Asia) is stronger still and expanding because the region is a vital source of oil and natural gas.[22] Nuclear weapons, however, would provide India with little leverage, particularly with two nuclear powers, the US and Israel, already in place. Iran may follow in years to come. Interestingly, while India has taken a legalistic position on Iran's nuclear potential, it does not see that country as a significant threat and has moved to establish closer economic cooperation with it, notably through the long-delayed Iran-Pakistan-India pipeline project.[§] The overall picture is one of a rising South Asian power engaging with neighboring regions in a limited and often multilateral way.

Of the remaining potential threats to India's security, the only significant one is China.[23] It is true that India has lived with Chinese nuclear weapons for a long time. But it has also factored China into its nuclear thinking all along. The first moves to develop India's nuclear weapons capability were made in the wake of the 1962 war and China's subsequent nuclear test. During the 1980s, Chinese

---

[§] K. Alan Kronstadt and Kenneth Katzman, *India-Iran Relations and U.S. Interests*, Congressional Research Service, Washington, DC, August 2, 2006. The Iran-Pakistan-India pipeline, considerably delayed because of US pressure and the political dynamics surrounding the India-US nuclear deal, has come close to fruition at the time of writing (May 2008). See Sajid Chaudhry, "Pakistan, India Agree to Finalise IPI Gasline Project," *Daily Times* (April 26, 2008).

assistance to Pakistan was an important security concern. The 1998 tests were explicitly said to be a response to China as "potential threat number one."[24] India's intermediate-range missile program and research and development on a submarine-based missile can only be attributed to a potential Chinese threat, even if that threat is not currently viewed as a serious one by the political leadership. That said, India-China relations are on a relatively even keel today. Trade has risen sharply from US$1.8 billion in 1999-2000 to $38.6 billion in 2007, making China India's largest trading partner.[25] Despite lingering security concerns, India does not see China as a serious threat. Yet it has hedged its bets: though both countries deny it, it is evident that the India-US nuclear agreement has underneath it a desire to have in hand an insurance policy against a future threat from China.[26] India is also keeping its options wide open by developing capabilities sufficient to deter China, as it has done with the intermediate-range Agni-III missile, which has been successfully tested but is not yet operational.

With respect to India's global aspirations, the symbolic aspect of nuclear weapons is significant, but in a limited way. It is well known that post-independence, India has sought a major role in world politics. Under Nehru, the drive was idealistic, resting on claims about India's size, civilizational uniqueness, nonviolence, and leadership of post-colonial societies. The 1962 debacle with China tempered Indian optimism, but did not wipe it out. The current "awakening of the sleeping giant" syndrome carries with it some of the flavor of the past and is widely expressed in the preoccupation with catching up with China and with acquiring a seat at the table of major world powers. In part, the Indian quest for permanent membership on the Security Council reflects this (though there are more practical benefits to be gained as well). Popular perceptions about India's emergence as a world power are optimistic and even exaggerated.[**] But the leadership is pragmatically aware that India has a long way to go before it can come anywhere close to being able to shape the global agenda.[27] Besides, its worldview is one which regards increasing integration and interdependence as central characteristics of the world economy and world politics.[28] In this context, nuclear weapons cannot have much of a role.

Critics of the India-US nuclear agreement – the so-called 123 Agreement – have argued that the deal will enable India to divert much of its domestic stocks of uranium toward building an increasingly large nuclear arsenal. But that is a misjudgment of the place of nuclear weapons in India's security strategy. The critics are mainly Americans, who tend to think that the expansion of an arsenal is easy to conceive of and implement if one has the means. There is nothing in

---

[**] A 2007 poll by Bertelsmann Stiftung found that 79 percent of Indians believed India would be a "world power" by 2020, whereas only 29 percent of respondents from eight other nations believed the same. Cited in Reshma Patil, "We Will Be Better Than US: Indians," *Hindustan Times* (December 13, 2007).

the thinking of the Indian political leadership that supports this viewpoint. On the contrary, India's extraordinarily restrained nuclear posture points toward the opposite. The crisis of 2001-02 has been particularly instructive. India has learned from the experience that its "advantage"—India would suffer relatively less damage than Pakistan in the event of a nuclear exchange—offers no comfort when a nuclear conflict draws uncomfortably close.[29] If India is deterred by a few dozen non-deployed Pakistani nuclear weapons, how can it possibly think of its own weapons as significant symbols of its rising power? Moreover, Indians place great stress on the concept of No First Use (NFU), which they believe restricts them to a retaliation-only option against weapons of mass destruction. There are no signs of a shift to conceiving of nuclear weapons as instruments for the projection of Indian power.

The India-US nuclear deal is important to Indians in other ways. It represents three things: the removal of the final obstacle to India's right to secure itself as it sees fit; the dismantling of what it regards as discriminatory international arrangements on the control of nuclear arms that it has consistently rejected; and a sign of acceptance into the fold of major powers. Thus, while nuclear weapons are not viewed as instruments for directly extending India's military reach, they do play a role in India's global security concerns in this restricted sense. What this means is that nuclear weapons per se are not objects of high value, but rather that the nature of the international regime for their governance is. In light of India's consistent commitment to disarmament, this is not problematic. Any arrangement that is universal and non-discriminatory and that does not put India at a disadvantage vis-à-vis other nuclear powers is likely to be acceptable to it.

INDIA'S NUCLEAR TRAJECTORIES

The development of the Indian nuclear arsenal is not easy to gauge. Though official data are not available, the following are widely accepted as reliable.[30] India is estimated to have about 50-60 nuclear warheads. Delivery vehicles potentially include the following aircraft: Mirage 2000H, Jaguar IS, Mig-27, and Sukhoi Su-30 MKI. Newer platforms will almost certainly be available with the major expansion envisaged by the Indian Air Force. The Prithvi-I land-based short-range ballistic missile (150 km) has been inducted into the army and is believed to be deployable. The medium-range Agni-I (700 km) and Agni-II (2000 km) missiles are said to have been inducted as well, but their operational status is not certain.[31] The former was tested by the army for only the second time in March 2008.[32] The bomber force and the Prithvi-I are sufficient to strike Pakistan, but not China. Hence, the development of the intermediate-range Agni-III, which has a range of about 3,000 km and has been tested successfully twice (after an earlier failure), in April 2007 and May 2008, is considered crucial for deterring China should the need arise. The missile is expected to be ready for operational use by 2010.

Whether the Agni family of missiles will complete the strategic development of India's deterrent force is a moot point. How much is enough? No one seems to know for sure. While the political trajectory of India's nuclear strategy is flat, the technical trajectory is rising. On one hand, India has adhered to its minimalist approach: its weapons remain in a non-deployed posture; it has declared and stayed committed to a self-imposed moratorium on further testing; and it has expressed a continuing interest in disarmament. On the other hand, research and development work on a range of weapons continues.

The BrahMos short-range cruise missile (290 km) is officially dubbed a conventional weapon, but is reported to have the potential capability to carry a small nuclear weapon.[33] This capability could be enlarged. While it is now assigned to the Army, air and naval versions are under development. A longer range cruise missile is also being developed.[34] It is reported that an extended-range (5,000 km) version of the Agni-III (possibly to be called Agni-IV) is also being developed.[35] Also on the drawing board is the Nirbhay (1,000 km) medium-range missile for land, air and sea platforms. Testing was slated to begin by 2009, though the Defence Research and Development Organization (DRDO) is still looking for engines.[36] A submarine-launched ballistic missile of 700 km range has been tested at least three times and a sea-launched cruise missile is being developed, though readiness is not anticipated for another three to four years.[37] In any case, the launch platform for missiles based undersea, the nuclear submarine envisaged under the Advanced Technology Vessel project, is not expected to be ready until 2010 or 2012.[††] In an indication of still greater ambitions, the DRDO's V. K. Saraswat speculated in August 2007 that the need might arise for a 10,000 km-range missile in the future.[38]

There are two reasons for the divergence of the political trajectories. First, there is lack of clarity in doctrine. This is most clearly visible in the Draft Nuclear Doctrine (DND), which was released in August 1999.[39] The DND represents not so much a clear articulation of strategy as a congeries of diverse views cobbled together for public airing. It gives a minimalist call for non-deployment, NFU and arms control, but simultaneously flags a maximalist approach in advocating the building of multiple redundancies to ensure the survivability of forces. The most elaborate statement of minimum deterrence doctrine made so far, an interview given by then External Affairs Minister Jaswant Singh in 1999,

---

[††] One report (Ibid.) gives the date as 2010. An earlier one says 2012. Rajat Pandit, "N-Submarine May Be Operational by 2012," *Times of India* (March 18, 2007).

reflected the same ambivalence.[40] That Indian civilian officials are unclear about the concept of minimum deterrence is evident from the author's conversations with several. But there is little doubt that nuclear weapons are not viewed in a serious operational way by political decision makers. This is not surprising, for all the National Security Advisers since 1998 have been former bureaucrats with little exposure to the rarefied world of nuclear doctrine.

Second, though civilian control of the armed forces is strong in an organizational sense, the military has considerable leeway in deciding what it needs. As Sunil Dasgupta observes, this represents a grand post-Independence civil-military bargain, "an implicit agreement between the military and political leaderships that allowed the Army freedom of action within the institution in return for submitting to the new nationalist leadership on political-strategic matters."[41] Typically, the Army's requirements are technical-operational and the understanding of nuclear issues is heavily influenced by American deterrence literature – a literature which has produced an incredibly large arsenal. The Army's perspective coincides with those of one small group of weapon producers. The nuclear scientists, though influential (they are closely associated with negotiations on the India-US nuclear deal), are no longer pressing for the expansion of capabilities and have publicly accepted that India needs no more weapon tests.[‡‡] The technocrats spearheading the expansion of India's arsenal are the missile engineers of the DRDO, who have been under pressure from the political leadership because of numerous inefficiencies and delayed projects.[42] There is, of course, the possibility that such pressure groups will be able to offer resistance to a disarmament programme, but given the overall *political* consensus on nuclear policy, such resistance is likely to be manageable.

While this analysis explains the existence of a minimalist posture side-by-side with the development of an ever-widening range of weapons, it does not mean that India would be a hard nut to crack vis-à-vis a serious campaign to eliminate nuclear weapons completely. The civilian leadership is amenable to a sharp turn in nuclear policy precisely because its standpoint is political, unhampered by the arcane verbiage of deterrence doctrine. Moreover, if it cracks the disarmament whip, neither the generals nor the missile makers have the clout to resist. India's political leadership has invariably had behind it the force of public opinion while being constantly sensitive to it.[43]

[‡‡] Some retired scientists have spoken about the need for further testing, apparently with encouragement from political parties opposed to the India-US nuclear agreement, but there is no evidence that they have obtained much purchase. See Sandeep Dikshit, "Top Scientists Caution on Deal," *Hindu* (July 19, 2008).

INDIA'S PROLIFERATION CONCERNS

Notwithstanding India's image as a nonconformist state vis-à-vis the nonproliferation regime, proliferation is certainly a concern. The concern begins at home. From the outset, control over the nuclear apparatus has been tight. Apart from tightening physical security over nuclear materials, the Government of India has strengthened its legal framework, which has been in existence since the passing of the Atomic Energy Act of 1948 and encompasses laws regulating exports.[44] As concerns about proliferation have grown, these laws have been strengthened. In 2005, the Indian Parliament passed the Weapons of Mass Destruction and their Delivery Systems (Prohibition of Unlawful Activities) Act, which aims to contain the risk of proliferation of all weapons of mass destruction. The law, which applies to India's territory, its Exclusive Economic Zone, and to its citizens residing anywhere, prohibits the transfer of weapons of mass destruction and technology to foreign individuals and entities. It provides for heavy fines and imprisonment of persons found guilty of transgressions. India has also engaged in a series of initiatives with the United States to contain the terrorist threat. The Indo-US Joint Working Group on Terrorism and Law Enforcement was established in January 2000. This yielded cooperation in numerous areas, such as legislative and administrative changes, interdiction of terrorist finance networks, counterterrorism training, and aviation security. Indo-US cooperation under the Next Steps in Strategic Partnership (NSSP) initiative, launched in January 2004, has opened up a wide vista of cooperation, including defense collaboration, transfer of military and dual-use technology, and cooperation in the area of energy. A significant concession on the part of the Indian government has been the acceptance of a US export control attaché in New Delhi for end-user verification of technology transfers.

At the multilateral level, India has cooperated with the International Atomic Energy Agency (IAEA) in several ways. In January 2002, India joined the Convention on the Physical Protection of Nuclear Materials. Thereafter, it actively participated in the search for orphaned nuclear materials in Georgia and, in 2003, conducted an international training course on Security for Nuclear Installations in collaboration with the IAEA. In addition, India has actively participated in discussions on evolving the IAEA Code of Conduct on the Safety and Security of Radioactive Sources. In February 2005, representatives from India, the US, and the IAEA met in pursuance of the Regional Radiological Security Partnership program, and India agreed to provide infrastructure and expertise on a regular basis for conducting international training courses in India under the aegis of the IAEA on issues related to the security of radiological sources and materials and also for locating orphaned radioactive sources in countries lacking adequate resources for the purpose.

With respect to other states, Indian officials have expressed a number of security concerns. There is evidence that in the past, as noted above, Pakistan has been the beneficiary of illegal proliferation activities, obtaining assistance from China in its quest for the bomb. Notwithstanding Chinese assurances, such concerns have not disappeared altogether. In November 2006, the US conveyed its apprehensions about Pakistan receiving assistance from Chinese "entities."[45] Given the perception among many in India that China continues to harbor the intent to contain India, this remains a problematic issue, the more so since China has been reluctant to engage fully with India in a nuclear dialogue. Evidence also points to North Korean assistance to Pakistan in the development of the latter's missile capabilities.[46]

A major worry for India has been the proliferation of nuclear technology by the A. Q. Khan network in Pakistan.[47] There is no clear evidence that state officials were directly engaged in the activities of the Khan network but, at the same time, it is evident that both civilian and military leaders could not have been completely ignorant of the goings on and were at least responsible for allowing it to happen.[48] From the Indian standpoint, Pakistani proliferation is worrisome in three respects. First, it is evidence of potential two-way streets that enhance Pakistan's capabilities, such as the acquisition of missile capabilities by Pakistan from North Korea in exchange for nuclear weapon expertise. Second, Indians fear that loose Pakistani controls may result in the acquisition of nuclear capabilities by terrorists bent on wreaking havoc in Indian territory. And, third, the proliferation of illegal nuclear commerce has the potential to unravel the nuclear nonproliferation regime and generate instability.

As regards Iran, Indian policy has been opposed to Iranian actions that have placed doubts over its adherence to NPT commitments. Consequently, over the objections of its domestic political allies, the Government of India twice (September 2005 and February 2006) voted against Iran in the IAEA. In February 2007, it imposed a specific ban on nuclear trade with Iran. But India has favored engagement rather than the imposition of sanctions and has opposed the use of force against Iran. This has been motivated partly by fear of the Middle East going up in flames, thereby destabilizing the energy market, and partly by India's interest in building the Iran-Pakistan-India gas pipeline, a project already delayed by US pressure.

Despite its rejection of the NPT, India's attitude toward nonproliferation is favorable. Minister for External Affairs Pranab Mukherjee made this plain in February 2008: "We do not wish to see the emergence of additional nuclear weapon states, for it will only further endanger international security."[49] Mukherjee went on to add that, "our goal continues to be a world free of nuclear weapons." Such a world would not only eliminate the nuclear threat from states, it would also prevent non-state actors from obtaining nuclear weapons. The chief problem, as mentioned elsewhere, will be to ensure compliance.

MOVING TO ZERO

In the event of a serious initiative to eliminate nuclear weapons, with respect to its immediate security concerns, India would be looking for three things: (1) the participation of Pakistan in the dialogue; (2) likewise, China's participation in the move to disarm; and, (3) the non-discriminatory character of the emerging regime. The first is not likely to be problematic. Following a series of crises, Pakistan, like India, has realized the difficulty of attempting to use coercion in a nuclear weapons environment. India and Pakistan already have in place a series of nuclear confidence building measures and a continuing dialogue on a range of political and security issues.[50] A shift from bilateral nuclear risk reduction to a multilateral framework should not be difficult for either country. In the past, India has rejected limited multilateral frameworks such as nuclear weapons free zones, but these were unacceptable precisely because they were not universal and comprehensive. A non-discriminatory framework would not be problematic. Still, difficulties may arise for two reasons. First, sections of the Pakistani ruling elite may prefer to retain the option of keeping up the pressure on India by supporting terrorist groups active in Kashmir. A serious dialogue will not be possible unless India feels assured on this count. Pakistanis will tend to counter that the resolution of the Kashmir issue is a prerequisite, but such arguments are not convincing. India and China have been able to improve relations significantly despite a long-standing border dispute. Second, Pakistan will be uncomfortable with denuclearization because it views its nuclear forces as deterrents to India's greater conventional capability. India will have to engage with Pakistan with respect to this concern and India may have to provide security assurances on this score as part of a larger bargain. The same applies to India's expectation of assurances from China, but is less vital since India is rapidly strengthening its conventional capability. This also points to a critical issue closely linked with nuclear disarmament more broadly: the effects it would have on the balance of conventional forces would be particularly discomfiting for those who see themselves ending up at a disadvantage.

China has so far been reluctant to engage with India on nuclear issues. During the 1990s, it tried jointly with the US to establish its nonproliferation credentials by putting pressure on India to cap its nuclear program. However, India's position was – and is – that no regional arrangement on arms control/disarmament is acceptable. India will therefore insist that China be included in any nuclear disarmament talks at the same stage as it is involved. A welcome step toward this end would be direct, preliminary talks between China and India to clear the air on any potential disagreements and to exchange views on the nature, scope and timing of multilateral negotiations for disarmament. The participation of China (and Pakistan) would meet the most direct Indian security concerns, since its main adversaries would be committed to a common process of restraint and transparency. Ultimately, a "zero treaty" would effectively mitigate the two biggest (currently, the only) threats to India's security.

India's expectation of a non-discriminatory elimination regime could create some complications with respect to the process. Were the initial moves to emerge from the NPT process, say, by way of "authorizing" certain states to negotiate an elimination treaty, how would India, an outsider, be accommodated? Careful language would have to be used that simultaneously satisfies treaty states that no special concession or indirect "recognition" of India's nuclear weapons status is recognized; and does not rub Indian legal and political sensitivities the wrong way. Ideally, the language should eschew reference to the legal status of the participants in the newly launched process.

India's position on disarmament has often been viewed as pontifical and rhetorical. Yet it has been based on a set of three consistent principles: (1) that nuclear weapons are morally objectionable because they are indiscriminate and inhumane; (2) that in a practical sense they are dangerous weapons because their potential for damage far exceeds their contribution to security; and, (3) that nuclear disarmament must be universal and complete. Though long regarded as idealistic and unrealizable, these principles are in fact realistic, as they combine a desired moral objective with an emphasis on the practical effects of the weapons and on recognition that the unique possession of a class of weapons by any one state is a potential threat to all others. Thus, India has rejected any arms control/disarmament arrangements that it views as discriminatory and hence at least potentially violative of its security in an anarchic world.[51] At the same time, it has over the decades initiated and supported universal and non-discriminatory measures to reduce the nuclear threat generally. It thus joined the Limited Test Ban Treaty, which applied equally to all countries, but not the Non-Proliferation Treaty, which established two classes of nations – nuclear weapon states and non-nuclear weapons states. India also advocated a comprehensive test ban, but, as noted earlier, backed away when its open door policy toward nuclear weapons came under pressure. Consistent with this position, it has rejected regional agreements to eschew nuclear weapons, such as nuclear weapon free zones, but has accepted the idea of bilateral nuclear risk reduction measures. With regard to specific quantitative disarmament measures, it will only accept obligations under a universal, multilateral framework.

Despite its long-proclaimed commitment to disarmament, India in practice has no experience with it. On the contrary, its entire experience with respect to nuclear stabilization has been limited to confidence building measures (CBMs), where the focus is on political assurance rather than verifiable limits. The advantage of CBMs is that they can be–like iterated games–a learning process for the players, who learn over time the benefits of cooperation. So far, India has agreed on nuclear CBMs only with Pakistan. These include an agreement not to attack each other's nuclear facilities (1988); a quasi-formal understanding on retaining their moratoria on nuclear testing (1999); an agreement to notify each other of impending ballistic missile tests, and another to establish a secure hotline between their foreign secretaries (2005).[52] These agreements have worked well so far, notably the oldest of them, which has survived the twin tests of time and recurrent crises. But disarmament is a different cup of tea as it requires high degrees of assurance regarding compliance – an issue that India will have to tackle if negotiations commence.

India's last major effort to push for disarmament came in the closing years of the Cold War. At the United Nations General Assembly's Third Special Session on Disarmament in 1988, Rajiv Gandhi personally presented a step-by-step plan for universal and complete nuclear disarmament. But the time was not ripe and the proposal evoked barely a ripple of global interest. Still, interest in disarmament has remained strong regardless of the party in power. Even the Bharatiya Janata Party (BJP), commonly labeled a right-wing "Hindu nationalist" party, explicitly announced through its government's doctrine (January 2003) its commitment to "global, verifiable and non-discriminatory nuclear disarmament."[53] In short, disarmament has remained on the agenda regardless of the time frame and the party in power. A serious proposal to eliminate nuclear weapons will therefore evoke a positive response from the Indian government. It may be noted, too, that Rajiv Gandhi's proposal called for a time-bound framework and that this has been reiterated by later leaders. In the Indian perception, unless there is a clear schedule, efforts to disarm will be hampered by procrastination, as has been the case with the disarmament provisions of the NPT.

India's current policy on disarmament reflects a continuing commitment to its old goals. In February 2008, the Indian Ambassador to the Conference on Disarmament (CD), Hamid Ali Rao, presented a seven-point agenda for nuclear disarmament, which called for

- Unequivocal commitment to the goal of total elimination of nuclear weapons;
- Reduction in the salience of nuclear weapons in security doctrines;
- A no first use agreement among all nuclear-armed states;

- An agreement not to use nuclear weapons against non-nuclear-armed states;
- A convention prohibiting the use or threat of use of nuclear weapons;
- A convention proscribing the development, production and stockpiling of nuclear weapons; and
- Verifiable and non-discriminatory elimination of all nuclear weapons.[54]

Given this background, a serious initiative for elimination by leading nuclear weapons states, with the US taking the lead, would be welcomed by India. The Indian reaction to the initiatives set in motion by a group of four American senior statesmen have been positive. Yet there have been some concerns that the US-led move might be too conservative in its reach or shaped by the interests of the big powers. The Indian Prime Minister's Special Envoy, Shyam Saran, asserted in February 2008 that the US leaders' characterization of the goal of elimination as "the top of a very tall mountain" did not go far enough and that "the need of the hour is to bring it down into plain sight."[55] Saran warned that current moves toward disarmament may even mask a discriminatory objective: further tightening of current arrangements that focus on technology denial and efforts to control specific targets – terrorists, clandestine traders, so-called "rogue states," and developing countries generally – rather than on an undiluted quest for complete elimination.[56] A universalist approach is a *sine qua non* for India's participation in a drive to eliminate nuclear weapons. This necessarily includes strong guarantees against cheating. But so far, not much attention has been paid to the nitty gritty issues; the focus is on obtaining agreement on the basic principle of universal disarmament, which has been repeatedly asserted.[57]

What specific initiatives would arouse Indian enthusiasm? The suggestions that follow are indicative. The key, it is worth reiterating, lies in ensuring that the process is non-discriminatory and universal. But the process itself could be set in motion by American initiatives that demonstrate a clear intent to shift away from a stance that has tended in the post-Cold War era to hold nuclear weapons dear, to take for granted an untenable notion of nuclear superiority, and to focus single-mindedly on retaining superiority by countering all threats to it.

Once the US got the ball rolling, its momentum would facilitate bilateral negotiations between the US and the other nuclear superpower, Russia. At the review meeting of the NPT states in April 2008, representatives of both countries claimed that they had reduced their weapon stocks significantly. But the smaller nuclear powers and the non-nuclear weapons states will not be satisfied unless there is concrete and substantial movement toward force reductions in keeping with the promise of the treaty. The Russian leadership will require some persuasion to get on board since, to all appearances, it views nuclear capability as inseparable from its standing as a power. In December 2007, First Deputy Prime Minister Sergei Ivanov asserted, "Military potential, to say nothing of nuclear potential, must be at the proper level if we want . . . to just stay independent" and that "the weak are not loved and not heard, they are insulted, and when we have parity they will talk to us in a different way."[58] To demonstrate commitment to global disarmament, the US and Russia would have to take very specific and tangible steps. These could include a joint declaration on moving toward zero, the launching of talks on de-alerting, confining naval and air forces to their bases, and/or deep cuts in strategic and tactical nuclear forces, including forces in reserve/storage.

The bilateral process could be kept short and quickly expanded to incorporate all the major nuclear-armed states and subsequently all states. An immediate outcome would be a declaration committing the nuclear-armed states to the elimination of nuclear weapons within a specified time frame. Negotiations on a comprehensive test ban could be resumed. During the 1990s, India walked out of the CTBT talks and tested its weapons. But following the 1998 tests, Indian political leaders and scientists publicly declared there was no need for further tests. Currently, Indian officials are wary of the CTBT because of its recent history, but in fact there is no substantial reason for India not to sign on since they have crossed the nuclear Rubicon and do not feel fresh testing is essential. In the context of an initiative to eliminate all nuclear weapons, negotiations on the Fissile Material Cutoff Treaty would also likely be received positively by India. Such resistance as there is with regard to the resultant capping of Indian capabilities will dissipate if the treaty is parleyed within the framework of elimination.[§§]

The Government of India also would expect to see at an early stage discussions leading to a convention on NFU and non-use against non-nuclear states. These are not substantive measures and may not appear to be very useful since adherence to them could only be verified ex post facto. Nonetheless, the Indian approach favors cumulative engagement, commitment and political understanding for building confidence. Only with progress of this kind would it be possible to move toward more advanced and difficult negotiations on a universal treaty to outlaw the development, production and stockpiling of all nuclear weapons. At an early stage, India can be expected to demonstrate its commitment to the process by joining other nuclear powers in increasing transparency, notably by declaring its facilities, delivery vehicles and fissile

---

[§§] India does insist, however, that the treaty include provision for verification – an issue on which it has had differences with the US. "U.S. Braces for Face-off over Weapons Treaties," *Washington Times* (February 11, 2008).

material stocks. On the organizational aspect, India would favor a process that builds a multilateral institution, perhaps on the lines of the World Trade Organization, which would eventually regulate the full spectrum of activities and processes related to nuclear weapons and associated materials and technologies. Thus, a greatly strengthened IAEA or a newly launched organization could have under its purview: oversight of the process of dismantling nuclear weapons in the later stages; monitoring, auditing and inspection of all military and civilian nuclear facilities; centralization of the supply of nuclear fuel for civilian reactors to countries in need; regulation of nuclear waste disposal; and maintenance of a database on all sources of fissile material.

END-STATES

Though Indians have tended to be optimistic about the prospects for disarmament, they are sufficiently realistic to recognize that the process will be a complex one and will face numerous hurdles in trying to harmonize divergent state interests. The prospect of further expansion of the nuclear club is not viewed with equanimity. Because of its geographic distance, North Korea's nuclearization has not been received with alarm, and doubtless the nuclearization of Japan would be viewed in the same way. Though it is much closer, the same approach has been taken with respect to Iran. But India has made it clear that it is opposed to proliferation because it causes general destabilization which could affect its security either through state-to-state proliferation (e.g. the Pakistan-North Korea connection mentioned above) or through state proliferation to non-state actors.[59]

The alternative to elimination, it is understood, would be the emergence of new nuclear-armed states, which is not a prospect contemplated with sanguinity. Over the past decade, India has been on the defensive on nuclear matters, partly because of nonproliferation pressures and partly because of the severity of its crises with Pakistan. But it has been quick to sense the current mood and appears ready to grasp the moment and help develop a global consensus on elimination. The possibility of rapid proliferation is not currently seen as high, but if evidence indicating this were to appear, Indian leaders would worry much more than they do now and would press harder for a global effort to disarm.

A well-known objection to nuclear disarmament is that if nuclear weapons are eliminated, conventional war will become more likely. This is by no means a trivial argument, but its salience depends on each state's specific security environment. The potential problem is unlikely to trouble India directly. As shown above, India was not disposed to go nuclear despite facing a security threat from a nuclear power, China. It did conduct a symbolic test in 1974 in response to a perceived sense of isolation in an insecure strategic environment, but thereafter eschewed weapons production. For India, in short, nuclear weapons were never a requirement for deterring a conventional threat. That remains true today. In the past, the United States was something of a worry, not as a potential aggressor but as a state that threatened to make inroads into what India conceived of as its regional sphere of influence, i.e. South Asia and the Northern Indian Ocean. That is no longer the case. India not only does not view American military power with distrust but is engaged in unprecedented military cooperation with the US. Nor do the conventional forces of China and Russia seriously worry it. On the contrary, with its rising economic strength, India has embarked on a program of military modernization that is the source of greater confidence in its conventional capabilities.

Nevertheless, the wider issue of the nuclear-conventional linkage is one that has been recognized. India's Ambassador to the United Nations, Nirupam Sen, drew attention to this in April 2008 while speaking on nuclear disarmament and called for reductions in conventional weapons as well.[60] This is neither an immediate nor an overriding concern, but one that is acknowledged as an inevitable obstacle in the path of nuclear elimination. As mentioned earlier, Pakistan's concerns in this respect will also bring home the problem, unless India's relations with that country are dramatically transformed, which seems unlikely.

CONCLUSION

This review of India's security concerns and its position on nuclear disarmament shows that a serious proposal to eliminate nuclear weapons within a certain time frame would receive strong support from an Indian government. The idea of disarmament is deeply embedded in India's strategic culture and retains its salience two decades after India built its first nuclear weapon. Indian security concerns, effectively met by Chinese and Pakistani inclusion in the process and more generally by its universal nature, will not be an obstacle to its participation in the negotiations. As a rising power of the future, India's outlook on the world is one which emphasizes not only distaste for the risks posed by nuclear weapons, but also the centrality of global interdependence, which makes the resort to such weapons counterproductive. Given its self-image as a major power in the making, India will see a movement for nuclear elimination as an opportunity to take a leadership role. With its history of extraordinary restraint, its minimalist posture, and its reputation as a large democracy, it is particularly well placed to play such a role. The inconsistency between its minimalism and some of its more ambitious nuclear plans is unlikely to be problematic. The political leadership has a firm grip on the policy process and will not have much difficulty in overcoming resistance from both the armed forces and the technical bureaucracy which produces the weapons. Its hand will be particularly strong because nuclear disarmament enjoys support across the board from all political parties. So long as the process is characterized by undiluted equity, India will almost certainly be a principal player in the global drive to eliminate nuclear weapons.

ENDNOTES

[1] For a compendium of Gandhi's views on nuclear weapons, see Y. P. Anand, *What Mahatma Gandhi Said about the Bomb* (New Delhi: National Gandhi Museum, 1998).

[2] Ashok Kapur, *India's Nuclear Option: Atomic Diplomacy and Decision Making* (New York: Praeger, 1976), page 194.

[3] Rajesh M. Basrur, *Minimum Deterrence and India's Nuclear Security* (Stanford, CA: Stanford University Press, 2006), chapter 3.

[4] James Barnard Calvin, *The China-India Border War* (Quantico, Virginia: Marine Corps Command and Staff College, April 1984), accessed at Global Security.org <http://www.globalsecurity.org/military/library/report/1984/CJB.htm>.

[5] Rajesh M. Basrur, "1971 in Retrospect: A Reappraisal of Soviet Policy in South Asia," *International Studies* (July- September 1988), pages 241-257.

[6] Andrew Latham, "Constructing National Security: Culture and Identity in Indian Arms Control and Disarmament Practice," *Contemporary Security Policy* (April 1998), page 139.

[7] Scott D. Sagan, "Why Do States Build Nuclear Weapons? Three Models in Search of A Bomb," *International Security* (Winter 1996-97), pages 65-69.

[8] George Perkovich, *India's Nuclear Bomb: The Impact on Global Proliferation* (New Delhi: Oxford University Press), page 172.

[9] Ibid., page 174.

[10] "China's Nuclear Exports and Assistance to Pakistan," Center for Nonproliferation Studies, Monterey Institute of International Studies, Monterey, CA, August 1999 <http://cns.miis.edu/research/india/china/npakpos.htm> (accessed April 30, 2008). See also T. V. Paul, "Chinese-Pakistani Missile Ties and the Balance of Power," *Nonproliferation Review* (Summer 2003), pages 1-9.

[11] See "A World Free of Nuclear Weapons: Prime Minister Rajiv Gandhi at the United Nations," available at <http://www.indianembassy.org/policy/Disarmament/disarm15.htm> (accessed February 4, 2008).

[12] K. Subrahmanyam, "Politics of Security: When Vajpayee Said 'No' to Going Nuclear," *Times of India* (April 10, 2004). <http://timesofindia.indiatimes.com/articleshow/608713.cms>.

[13] Jyoti Saksena, "Regime Design Matters: The CTBT and India's Nuclear Dilemma," *Comparative Strategy* (July 2006), pages 209-229.

[14] The point has been made with reference to India-Pakistan wars in Kotera M. Bhimaya, "Nuclear Deterrence in South Asia: Civil-Military Relations in Decision-Making," *Asian Survey* (July, 1994), pages 644-645.

[15] Rajesh M. Basrur, "Nuclear Weapons and Indian Strategic Culture," *Journal of Peace Research* (March 2001), pages 181-198.

[16] Government of India, Ministry of External Affairs, *Draft Report of National Security Advisory Board on Indian Nuclear Doctrine* (August 17, 1990).

[17] Rajesh M. Basrur, "Global Quest and Regional Reversal: India's Policy toward Its Neighbours," *Ethnic Studies Report* (forthcoming).

[18] Ibid.

[19] G. V. C. Naidu, "Looking East: India and the Asia-Pacific," in N. S. Sisodia and C. Uday Bhaskar, eds., *Emerging India: Security and Foreign Policy Perspectives* (New Delhi: Institute for Defence Studies and Analyses and Promilla & Co., in association with Bibliophile South Asia, 2005); and Christophe Jaffrelot, "India's Look East Policy: An Asianist Strategy in Perspective," *India Review* (April 2003), pages 35-68.

[20] Rahul Singh, "China Miffed as India Cements Ties with 3 Nations," *Hindustan Times* (August 21, 2007).

[21] Stephen Blank, "India's Rising Profile in Central Asia," *Comparative Strategy* (April-June 2003), pages 139-157; Shishir Gupta, "Tajik Air Base Is Ready, Gives India Its First Footprint in Strategic Central Asia," *Indian Express* (February 25, 2007).

[22] M. Hamid Ansari, "Imperatives of Indian Policy in West Asia," in Sisodia and Bhaskar, eds., *Emerging India*; S. D. Muni and Girijesh Pant, *India's Energy Security: Prospects for Cooperation with Extended Neighbourhood* (New Delhi: Rupa, in association with Observer Research Foundation, 2005).

[23] Jing-dong Yuan, "The Dragon and the Elephant: Chinese-Indian Relations in the 21st Century," *Washington Quarterly*, 30, 3 (Summer 2007), pp. 131-144; George Perkovich, "The Nuclear and Security Balance," in Francine R. Frankel and Harry Harding, eds., *The India-China Relationship: Rivalry and Engagement* (New Delhi: Oxford University Press, 2004).

[24] The assessment came from India's Minister for Defence, George Fernandes, in May 1998. See "China Is Enemy No. 1: George," *Indian Express* (May 4, 1998).

[25] The 1999-2000 figure is from "India-China Bilateral Trade Statistics, IndiaChina.org < http://www.indiachina.org/trade_statistics.htm> n.d.. The 2007 figure is from "China Emerges India's Largest Trade Partner," *India Post* (March 24, 20080 http://indiapost.com/article/perspective/2359/

[26] Stephen Blank, "The geo-Strategic Implications of the Indo-American Strategic Partnership," *India Review* (January-March 2007), pages 1-24.

[27] Amelia Gentleman, "India Can't Wait to Put the 'Super' before 'Power,' " *International Herald Tribune* (November 23, 2006).

[28] "India as a Rising Great Power: Challenges and Opportunities," Speech by M. K. Narayanan, India's National Security Advisor, at the IISS-Citi India Global Forum, April 18-20, 2008 <http://www.iiss.org/conferences/iiss-citi-india-global-forum/igf-plenary-sessions-2008/fourth-plenary-session-india-and-the-great-powers/fourth-plenary-session-m-k-narayanan/> (accessed April 25, 2008).

[29] Basrur, *Minimum Deterrence and India's Nuclear Security*, Chapter 4.

[30] The data are drawn from "India's Nuclear Forces, 2007" *Bulletin of the Atomic Scientists* (July/August 2007), pages 74-77.

[31] Robert S. Norris and Hans M. Kristensen, "India's Nuclear Forces, 2007," *Bulletin of the Atomic Scientists* (July/August 2007), page 76.

[32] T.S. Subramanian and Y. Mallikarjun, "Agni-I Test-Fired Successfully," *Hindu* (March 24, 2008).

[33] "India Developing Submarine Launched Ballistic Missiles," *International Herald Tribune* (September 11, 2007).

[34] Y. Mallikarjun, "DRDO Begins Work on Agni-IV," *Hindu* (August 9, 2007).

[35] Ibid.

[36] Neelam Mathews, "India Plans to Test New Medium-Range Missile in 2009," NewKerala.com, July 24, 2007 <http://www.newkerala.com/july.php?action=fullnews&id=48537> (accessed July 25, 2007).

[37] Rajat Pandit, "N-Submarines Will Make India's Deterrence Credible," *Times of India* (September 24, 2007); Wade Boese, "India Test-Launches Submarine Missile," *Arms Control Today*, April 2008 <http://www.armscontrol.org/act/2008_04/IndiaTest.asp> (accessed April 30, 2008).

[38] Mallikarjun, "DRDO Begins Work on Agni-IV," op.cit.

[39] *Draft Report of National Security Advisory Board on Indian Nuclear Doctrine*, op.cit.

[40] "India Not to Engage in A Nuclear Arms Race: Jaswant," (Interview), *Hindu* (November 29, 1999), page 14.

[41] Sunil Dasgupta, "The Indian Army and the Problem of Military Change," in Swarna Rajagopalan, editor, *Security and South Asia: Ideas, Institutions, and Initiatives* (London and New Delhi: Routledge, 2006), page 88.

[42] Manu Pubby, "Need to Revamp, Give Us Roadmap in a Fortnight: Govt Tells DRDO," *Indian Express* (April 27, 2008).

[43] David Cortright and Amitabh Mattoo, eds., *India and the Bomb* (Notre Dame, IN: University of Notre Dame Press, 1996), pages 117-118.

[44] S. Gahlaut, "Nonproliferation Export Controls in India," in M. D. Beck, R. T. Cupitt, S. Gahlaut, and S. A. Jones, eds., *To Supply or to Deny: Comparing Nonproliferation Export Controls in Five Key Countries* (New York: Kluwer Law International, 2003).

[45] "US Concerned about China-Pak 'Proliferation' Ties," *Daily Times* (November 15, 2006).

[46] Gaurav Kampani, "Second Tier Proliferation: The Case of Pakistan and North Korea," *Nonproliferation Review* (Fall-Winter 2002), pages 107-116.

[47] *Nuclear Black Markets: Pakistan, A.Q. Khan and the Rise of Proliferation Networks: A Net Assessment* (London: International Institute for Strategic Studies, 2007).

[48] Bruno Tertrais, "Kahn's [sic] Nuclear Exports: Was There a State Strategy?" in Henry D. Sokolski, ed., *Pakistan's Nuclear Future: Worries beyond War* (Carlisle, PA: Strategic Studies Institute, U.S. Army War College, January 2008).

[49] "Pranab: We Don't Wish to See More Nuclear States," *Indian Express* (February 6, 2008).

[50] Rajesh M. Basrur, *India's Minimum Deterrence Posture and the India-Pakistan Composite Dialogue* (Landau Network Centro-Volta, Como, Italy), March 2006.

[51] Arundhati Ghose, "Negotiating the CTBT: India's Security Concerns and Nuclear Disarmament," *Journal of International Affairs* (Summer 1997), pages 239-261.

[52] Rajesh M. Basrur, *Minimum Deterrence and India-Pakistan Nuclear Dialogue: Case Study on India* (Landau Network Centro-Volta, Como, Italy), March 2006.

[53] Government of India, Press Release, "The Cabinet Committee on Security Reviews operationalization of India's Nuclear Doctrine," January 4, 2003.

[54] Pranab Dhal Samanta, "India For No-nuke World Order, Ready to Make No-first Use [sic] a Multilateral Pact," *Indian Express* (March 3, 2008).

[55] Shyam Saran, "Cold Warriors Do A Flip," *Times of India* (February 26, 2008).

[56] Ibid. For a similar criticism of the US-centric approach, see R. Rajaraman, "Get Rid of Nuclear Weapons," *Times of India* (March 5, 2008).

[57] See, e.g. "Indian Prime Minister Pitches Global Disarmament," *Voice of America*, June 9, 2008 < http://voanews.com/english/2008-06-09-voa13.cfm>; "Total Nuclear Disarmament Is the Aim: Pranab," *Hindu* (June 25, 2008)< http://www.thehindu.com/2008/06/25/stories/2008062560801200.htm >.

[58] Cited in Robert S. Norris and Hans M. Kristensen, "Russian Nuclear Forces, 2008," *Bulletin of the Atomic Scientists* (May/June 2008), page 54.

[59] Government of India, Press Release, "NPT Skewed, New Nuclear Nations Threat to World Peace: Pranab Mukherjee," February 5, 2008.

[60] "India Calls for Global Disarmament," *Financial Express* (April 9, 2008).

IRANIAN PERSPECTIVES ON THE GLOBAL ELIMINATION OF NUCLEAR WEAPONS

Anoush Ehteshami[*]

Iran's nuclear program has emerged as one of the major security concerns of the early 21st century. Since early revelations about the extent of Iran's public and clandestine nuclear-related activities were revealed in late 2002, it has rarely moved off the international agenda. For the West, it has become a signature battle for the containment of hostile, or potentially hostile, regional powers. The harsh rhetoric of Iran's combative, neo-conservative president, Dr. Mahmoud Ahmadinejad, has not helped matters, of course, but in reality the die for this tense situation were cast at the height of the Khatami Presidency (1997-2005), toward the end of which Tehran announced to the International Atomic Energy Agency (IAEA) the termination of its self-imposed moratorium on uranium enrichment. This action, taken in July 2005 just weeks before Ahmadinejad's formal inauguration as president, has done more than any of the new president's subsequent pronouncements to widen the gap between the international community and Iran. In essence, Tehran's decision to proceed with uranium enrichment reignited a cycle of IAEA engagements which, in September 2005, led the IAEA board to pronounce Iran "non-compliant" with the Non-Proliferation Treaty (NPT), of which it is a signatory, and to refer the matter to the UN Security Council.

The situation became so difficult that between late 2006 and early 2008 Iran was the subject of three UN Security Council resolutions, each imposing sanctions on Iran and each designed to increase the economic costs of Iran's violation of previous Security Council demands.[1] By early 2008 it was clear that Tehran had made the decision to simply ignore the UNSC resolutions. Indeed, according to the IAEA report in February 2008, Tehran claimed, the Agency was now satisfied that Iran's program did not violate its NPT obligations. The actual words of IAEA Director General Mohamed El Baradei were, "We have managed to clarify all the remaining outstanding issues, including the most important issue, which is the scope and nature of Iran's enrichment programme." However, he did go on to express concern that Iran still had much explaining to do:

> As a result of Iran running an undeclared nuclear programme for almost two decades, there has been confidence deficit on the part of the

---

[*] Professor Anoush Ehteshami is Professor of International Relations at the School of Government and International Affairs at Durham University. The views expressed in this paper are his alone, and not necessarily those of any institution.

international community about the intentions, future intentions of Iran's nuclear programme. Therefore the Security Council asked Iran to suspend its enrichment-related activities. I hope that Iran will continue to work closely with the Security Council, to create the conditions for Iran and the international community to engage in comprehensive negotiation that would lead to a durable solution. A durable solution requires confidence about Iran's nuclear programme, it requires a regional security arrangement, it requires normal trade relationship between Iran and the international community. As the Security Council stated, the ultimate aim should be normalization of relationships between Iran and the international community.[2]

The sense of concern and urgency was repeated in El Baradei's follow-up report to the IAEA Board and also the UN Security Council. According to press reports, this report contends that, "Iran may be withholding information needed to establish whether it tried to make nuclear arms…The tone of the language suggesting Tehran continues to stonewall the U.N. nuclear monitor revealed a glimpse of the frustration felt by agency investigators stymied in their attempts to gain full answers to suspicious aspects of Iran's past nuclear activities."[3]

Initially obtained by the Associated Press, the restricted report forwarded to the Security Council and to the IAEA Board said that Iran remained defiant of the Council's demands that it suspend uranium enrichment. Iran apparently expanded its operational centrifuges machines generating enriched uranium by about 500 since the last IAEA report in February, according to the follow-up report. The report states that,

> Iran has not provided the Agency with all the information, access to documents and access to individuals necessary to support Iran's statements [that its activities are purely peaceful in intent]. The Agency is of the view that Iran may have additional information, in particular on high explosives testing and missile related activities which…Iran should share with the Agency.[4]

It goes on to say that the allegations of nuclear military programs "remain a matter of serious concern."[5]

For the Ahmadinejad Administration, however, the February IAEA report effectively closed the book on the controversy, giving Iran a clean bill of health and, in the process, also condoning Iran's enrichment activities as part of any NPT member's inalienable right to all aspects of nuclear technology for peaceful purposes. Much of the diplomatic activity to contain Iran's nuclear program had already taken place, of course, culminating during President Khatami's term in office in the EU3 countries' (Britain, France and Germany) November 2004 "Paris Agreement" with Iran, which stated that in return for security guarantees and substantial economic support Iran would agree to suspend uranium enrichment. The spirit of the Paris Agreement endured and led to further diplomatic negotiations with Tehran by the "5+1" group (the five permanent members of the UN Security Council and Germany). The result was a comprehensive package of incentives put to Tehran by the 5+1 group in June 2008. So, while the Security Council was imposing sanctions on the country for non-compliance, its core members were also extending the hand of compromise to Tehran.

Indeed the momentum for dialogue had gained so much speed by 2008 that even the sceptical Bush Administration had directly bought into the process, and as a sign of its seriousness, dispatched William Burns, a senior State Department official, to the July 2008 round of meetings with Iranian officials in Geneva. However, within two months of the Geneva meeting, the IAEA reported that not only was Iran stonewalling the Agency about several aspects of its nuclear program, but that between 2005 and 2008 Iran had substantially improved the efficiency of its centrifuges that produce enriched uranium.[6] Then came the news from the IAEA's latest report to the Security Council in March 2009 that the country had already accumulated more than 1,000 kilograms of low enriched uranium (LEU), apparently under-reporting its stock of LEU by some 200 kilograms. For the United States, this revelation meant that if the LEU were enriched further, by early 2009 Iran would have enough fissile material to make one nuclear bomb.[7]

The sense of crisis, which had been prevalent since rumors of an imminent Israeli strike on Iran appeared in the summer of 2008, intensified with this news. Indeed, the *New York Times* reported in June 2008 that the Israeli Air Force was already practicing for an aerial bombardment of Iranian nuclear targets.[†]

President Barack Obama's election later that year and his apparently new agenda and outlook on Iran may shift this situation in a positive direction. President Obama entered the White House professing a new policy of engagement with the Middle East. He expressed interest in reaching out to Iran and Syria, working towards peace in Palestine, reducing America's military presence in Iraq, and generally mending bridges with the Muslim world. While yet to be matched by concrete proposals, this message of hope and diplomatic engagement is important as it

---

[†] "More than 100 Israeli F-16 and F-15 fighters participated in the manoeuvres, which were carried out over the eastern Mediterranean and over Greece during the first week of June [2008], American officials said." The article further reported that, "Mike McConnell, the director of national intelligence, said in February that Iran was close to acquiring Russian-produced SA-20 surface-to-air missiles. American military officials said that the deployment of such systems would hamper Israel's attack planning, putting pressure on Israel to act before the missiles are fielded." *New York Times* (June 20, 2008).

provides the new administration with breathing space as it sets about to implement America's new policies and priorities. But it is important to point out that there are also some clear continuities with the previous administration's positions. Indeed, a skeptic might be forgiven for concluding that the US outlook has remained very similar to the mindset as the Bush era. One key driver of US policy remains the absolute security of Israel, which the new Secretary of State, Hillary Clinton, spelled out in tones that echoed those of President Bush during her visit to Israel in early March 2009. While it is likely that this policy priority will remain paramount for any US administration for the foreseeable future, it is instructive that under President Obama the absolute security of Israel is also being linked to the containment of Iran, and is evidently directly affecting the Obama Administration's agendas with such global actors as China and Russia. Clearly, containment remains the policy goal, even in the efforts to establish direct contact with Tehran. These started in the last year of the Bush Administration and led to a high-level face-to-face encounter between Under Secretary of State William Burns and the Secretary of Iran's National Security Council, Saeed Jalali, in July 2008.

Iran's isolation also is being pursued through a new bridge-building exercise with Syria and an attempt to reshape the Levant's politics. Ironically, even the new Administration's efforts to reignite the Israel-Palestine peace process are seen by cynics as an effort to curtail Iran's influence in the region. Thus, while President Obama is seen as a breath of fresh air, friends and foes alike in the region remain suspicious and wary, uncertain of the direction in which his professed priorities will take the region.

Despite these diplomatic initiatives and the December 2007 US National Intelligence Estimate's conclusion that Tehran had suspended its weapons-design and related programs in 2003, Iran's nuclear program continues to be viewed with great suspicion by the United States and by the United States' key European allies (notably Britain, France, Germany, and also Italy). In the Middle East region, too, Iran's nuclear-related activities have caused real concern, with Israel and some of Iran's smaller Arab neighbors harboring security anxieties. The stated fear is that Iran is pursuing a two-track nuclear program, with the military program disguised by Iran's massive civilian program. The broad assumption is that Iran's extensive industrial and intellectual nuclear know-how will serve its military and security needs sooner or later. The strategic concern is that no later than 2015, and perhaps as soon as 2010/11, Iran will have likely mastered the techniques necessary to utilize nuclear materials in a weapon, could be able to assemble a nuclear bomb, and also could be in a position to deliver nuclear payloads with a wide range of surface-to-surface ballistic missile systems to distant targets. There is also an equal concern that once Iran has a nuclear weapon, it will then be able to dictate its agenda to its neighbors—to become dominant in the Gulf sub-region in more ways than one.

This paper provides a brief assessment of Iran's nuclear program within the context of the country's overall security planning and analysis of Iran's security calculations, its perception of its security environment and the strategic setting in which Tehran operates. On the basis of this analysis, the paper develops a wider ranging discussion of the possible drivers of proliferation in the Middle East region and the ways and means of mitigating nuclear proliferation.

WHAT FACTORS COULD MOTIVATE IRAN TO ACQUIRE NUCLEAR WEAPONS?

Iran's motives in pursuing nuclear capabilities cannot be much different from those of the countries that preceded it down the nuclear path, but naturally the context is different in every case. In examining the context for Iran's calculations, they can usefully be divided into security concerns, regional ambitions, and global ambitions.

Iran's Security Concerns

There are some generally accepted explanations as to why states acquire nuclear weapon capabilities. It generally comes down to two perceptions on the part of the states' leaders and decision-makers: (1) an acute sense of insecurity and vulnerability, and (2) a strong desire to secure the freedom to project power unhindered. Though these twin objectives are linked in the majority of cases, to date it has been the former which has swayed most decision-makers. In the Middle East and the Indian sub-continent, particularly, insecurity has been the real driver for those parties which have acquired a nuclear-weapons capability, including India, Israel and Pakistan. At various points in their histories, the leaders of these countries became convinced that the possession of nuclear weapons would deter attacks on them, even attacks with conventional forces. Of course, this belief has not always proven to be true, as demonstrated by the Egyptian/Syrian attack on Israel in 1973; still, this perception of insecurity has been the determining factor in these nations' decisions to acquire nuclear capabilities.

Analysts have justified Iran's pursuit of nuclear capabilities on the basis of the security dilemmas facing Tehran and, indeed, other regional actors. The ruling Iranian establishment is said to be vulnerable to the US' repeated calls for 'regime change' in Iran. The US did change the Iranian regime through a covert operation once – in 1953 – and the period between 2002 and 2008 is replete with direct and indirect threats by the Bush Administration to repeat history or to conduct military strikes against Iranian nuclear and military facilities. Of course, it should also be acknowledged that the bellicose language from the US is sometimes a response to provocations from Tehran. To be sure, Iran has provoked the US on more than one occasion, beginning with the embassy seizure in 1979, continuing with the Hezbollah bombings of the US Marine barracks and US embassy in Beirut in 1982, the bombing of the US Air Force barracks in Saudi Arabia in the 1990s, and current activities in Iraq. So, what ought to be acknowledged is that there is a long and tangled history of perceived injustices, provocations, and resulting hostility on both sides.

Without strategic allies and lacking an effective conventional military machine, Iran may feel a need to be able to deter this persistent enemy, as well as other threats, by every means possible. For Ray Takeyh, for example, the primary motivation for Iran's nuclear drive is to be found in its desire "to negate the American and Iraqi threats."[8] Israel and its nuclear weapons capability, for Takeyh, are not seen by Iran to be a sufficient factor to justify the program or to constitute an existential threat to Tehran.

This view is not held universally. The rationale for acquisition of nuclear weapons by Tehran, Shahram Chubin argues, is not found in Iran's strategic environment, because it "does not create the insecurity driving Iran's nuclear program."[9] The program, he states, "is driven more by frustration over status and the ambition to be taken more seriously and to play a larger, more global role."[10] He also asserts that the one source of insecurity, namely the United States, "does not account for the start of the nuclear program or its persistence." The US, thus, for Chubin, is a secondary factor and not the primary cause of Iran's proliferation.

For most analysts, Iran faces a real security dilemma in its tense relations with the United States which, at the very least, provides additional incentives for Iran's nuclear drive. Kasra Naji, for example, notes that President Bush's 2002 "axis of evil" comment during his State of Union address led to an acceleration of Iran's nuclear drive.[11]

Iran's bitter experience in the war with Iraq (1980-88) is another factor driving its nuclear program. The country suffered very high casualties during this conflict and was the victim of attacks with lethal chemical weapons. Many Iranians believe that if they had possessed nuclear weapons, Iraq would not have dared used chemical weapons against them, or that they could have retaliated effectively. The Iraq war experience is one side of the strategic coin that defines Iran's perception of its need for nuclear capabilities, with the other being its single-minded effort to be independent and self-sufficient in as many realms as possible.

The strong US military presence on Iran's doorstep is clearly a concern. The US Navy is a resident navy in the Persian Gulf and is also its largest and most powerful. Unlike any other naval force in the region, it has extensive support and logistics facilities in several Gulf Arab states. In Qatar, Bahrain (since the Second World War), the UAE, and Oman, it has substantial military assets and a strong military presence in Kuwait as well – if for no other reason than to support the US forces in Iraq. In short, the US has a very substantial military presence in the Persian Gulf through its navy alone, added to which is its major air base in Qatar.

Close to Iran's borders, the US military is also omnipresent on land, as far as Tehran is concerned. In Iraq and Afghanistan, there are over 150,000 well-armed and well-supported US military forces in place. The United States also has established a minor military foothold in Azerbaijan and Turkmenistan. Add to these the close partnership between the US and Pakistan and the picture is complete as far as Tehran's perception of encirclement is concerned. Further still are the strategic partnerships Israel, as the closest Middle East ally of the United States, is developing, including Israel's growing relations with Turkey (a NATO member) and India. All three countries are of great importance to Iran's strategic planners and Israel's links to both is a worrying development as far as Tehran is concerned.

In short, the strong US military (and political) presence in southwest Asia, which of course is there to deal with a diverse set of American concerns in the absence of any substantial and meaningful dialogue between the two countries, has encouraged the sense of insecurity in Iran, coming as it has in the cascade of security-related developments since 9/11.

Furthermore, Iran's awareness of Israel's nuclear capability means that if it expects a confrontation with Israel in the medium-term, it would make sense from Tehran's perspective to have a nuclear deterrent in place to counter Israel's considerable military advantages. Israel's possession of nuclear weapons for decades has played a large role in Iran's motivations, particularly given that Israel was also able to remove Iraq's nuclear program in 1981 without retaliation from Baghdad. Iran wants to be able to deter Israel from threatening nuclear use in the event of a new war with Syria or further conflict in Lebanon that would involve Iran. Others fear that Tehran could use its nuclear capabilities, once developed, in a coercive way vis-à-vis Israel in the Palestinian context. Iran, indeed, acknowledged at the height of the Gaza conflict in January 2009 that it could not mobilize in support of Hamas and that its hands were tied "in this arena," according to Ayatollah Khamenei.[12]

The strategic shifts in the region have further shaped Iran's security perceptions. The wars in Iraq and Afghanistan since 2001, for example, have removed two of Iran's worst enemies. Tehran's security has increased since the removal of the Taliban in Afghanistan and Saddam Hussein in Iraq. Tehran has been able to extend its reach well into Iraq as a consequence of regime change in Baghdad in 2003, and as a further consequence has been accused of developing a 'Shia crescent' extending through Iraq into the Levant area. In terms of strategic developments, Iran, it could be argued, is the only two-legged runner in a race of one-legged competitors in a dysfunctional regional system. Iran's nuclear program, thus, could mark a new watershed in the region's strategic relations. On the one hand, fear of Iran could provide the glue finally to bring the Arab countries and Israel together—to confront a common security foe that might require joint action. On the other hand, the view that Iran's nuclear ambitions will not go unchecked, and that the international community is impotent in dealing with this threat, could fuel a new nuclear arms race in the region. A third possibility would be one of rapid engagement: a so-called grand bargain between Iran and the United States could be a major priority of the new Obama Administration, in an effort to end Tehran's revisionist position.[13] Success would have strategic consequences for the region and, particularly, for US relations with its traditional Arab allies and Israel.

At the same time, however, lack of security in both Iraq and Afghanistan is not good for Iran; nor indeed is the resultant extension of the US military presence in both countries beneficial to Tehran. The view that Iran is able to 'bleed' the US to distraction in Iraq, and therefore use its proxies to ensure that Washington cannot engage it militarily, has only limited validity if one considers Iran's potential gains in a stable and peaceful Iraq and Afghanistan. The thesis that US involvement in Iraq and Afghanistan is a trap for the US also overlooks the many options available to the US were it to choose to use force as a means of dealing with Iran. The US is not as handicapped militarily as many pundits purport, and it retains considerable residual power to check the projection of Iran's power. Nor, during the Bush Administration, did the US reject the option of taking limited military action if it so chose, which pushed Iran to either escalate or accept a stand-off. Neither of these two options would suit Iran's long-term interests and there are voices in Tehran who would rather find ways of sustaining the *status quo* than being forced to expose the country's hand. A weak Iranian response to the US challenge, after so much baiting, can only result in the denting of Iran's international image and self-declared superiority. Iran's propaganda after all is anticipating its armed forces to deliver 'deadly blows' to the US.‡

In sum then, Iran's apparent strategic gains from the wars in Afghanistan and Iraq should not be viewed from a static position. For every gain there is a potential price to be paid and a whole range of other pressures to accommodate and problems to manage. Iran's neighborhood is dynamic and that dynamism is a two-edged sword in strategic terms. While oil prices were over $100/barrel, the US bogged down in

---

‡ As much was claimed by the Revolutionary Guards' Commander in Chief Mohammed Ali Jafari in an interview to the Jam-e Jam satellite television station in late June 2008. See Y. Mansharof and A. Savyon, "Iranian Threats in Anticipation of Western Attack," *Inquiry and Analysis - No. 455*, Middle East Media Research Institute, (July 15, 2008).

Iraq, and its neighbors apparently too weak and divided to challenge Iran, it seemed assured of its supreme position. But the dramatic drop in oil prices over a short period of time – from $147/barrel in July to under $40/barrel by December 2008 – coupled with the apparently greatly improved US position in Iraq and the resurgence of an 'Arab core' led by Saudi Arabia, have dented Tehran's self-confidence, showing the country's vulnerabilities to international forces.[14] Iran's strategic rise exposes it to classic counter-balancing in a region such as the Middle East, in which power politics continue to dominate the region's inter-state relations. Those fearful of Iran's rise and its nuclear plans have shown the tendency to at least consider 'band-wagoning' against it as a way of curtailing its influence.

For Tehran, the utility of a nuclear-weapon capability would be its deployment in circumstances in which the country was directly threatened or in which its wider strategic interests were indirectly threatened. The possible scenarios in which Iran might see utility for its nuclear weapons could be: (1) conflicts between Israel and Iran's allies, Syria or Hezbollah/Lebanon, in which Israel might otherwise be tempted to make nuclear threats; (2) situations in which France threatened to act on its threat to utilize its nuclear forces against any state that made weapons of mass destruction available to terrorist organizations and thereby threatened France's national security interests; or (3) serious conflicts between Iran and the Gulf Arab states in which Iran's nuclear weapons might be used to deter US intervention.

Iran's Regional Ambitions

Iran is said to have regional ambitions, and from the dominant Arab perspective, is seen also to be entertaining unreasonable claims to the region's politico-security agendas hitherto regarded as Arab concerns. Claims that Iran entertains the ambition to dominate the region originate from two sources. The first is Iran's own bellicose statements and pronouncements that leave observers with little doubt that many Iranian leaders regard the present epoch to be their historic opportunity. Iran's so-called "neo-cons," the Rightist factions who have supported President Ahmadinejad's neo-populist and neo-revolutionary policies, supported by the Leader (Ayatollah Ali Khamenei), are convinced that Iran should be bold and determined enough to fulfill its historic mission to lead the region and the wider set of Muslim countries to a just world.[15] Some amongst the elite interpret this as a messianic role, while for others it is just a matter of policy.

Leading Muslims, though, is not the same as striving for domination of them or hegemony of Tehran's immediate neighborhood. Furthermore, domination and hegemony are two very different things. For hegemony to work, Iran would need the consent of the neighboring countries, which is unlikely to be forthcoming for the foreseeable future. None of Iran's neighbors, including the new Shia-dominated

Iraq, are prepared to accept Iranian control of the Persian Gulf or its right to dictate the politics of the Levant.

But nor is domination a simple proposition when Iran's neighbors clearly have opportunities to counter Iran's efforts. Note in this regard both the large and smaller Gulf Cooperation Council (GCC) states' rush to begin their own nuclear programs since 2007, and their emerging military partnerships with not only the United States, but other Western countries (e.g., France) as well. These countries are neither helpless nor hapless. They have effective means of responding to perceived threats and challenges. Iran's gains in the Levant, for example, are matched by Saudi Arabia's flexing of its own considerable muscles when it comes to the security and political agendas of Palestine, Lebanon, and even Syria (Iran's only ally).[16]

There is real concern amongst Iran's close neighbors, in particular, and of course in Israel that Iran's ambitions run potentially counter to their interests. Though Arab public opinion has generally been supportive of Iran's efforts to "stand up to the US and Israel," as is often the perceived context of this issue, at elite levels, the leaders of GCC countries, in particular, have since 2005 been willing to make public comments about the dangers of Iran's program—seeing the program very much in geo-political balance of power terms.[17] Fears of Iran's actions remain despite repeated high level contacts between Tehran and GCC capitals since 2005.

Yet, despite these expressed fears, not a single Arab leader foresees military confrontation in the Persian Gulf. The nightmare of a nuclear Iran is haunting enough, but worse still is the vision of a wounded Iran hitting out at its neighbors. The consequences of a violent reaction (terrorism or a military attack) by Iran against the populations of neighboring countries is playing into Tehran's hands, ensuring that Iran's neighbors remain paralyzed in policy terms. This position leaves the door open for Iran's further penetration of the Arab heartland and core Arab issues (such as Palestine). Even in indirect ways, Iran's nuclear posture is feeding its regional ambitions.

In addition, the perception of Iranian domination is also being fed by strategic developments in the region since 2001. As has been said already, Iran stood to gain from the regime changes in Iraq and Afghanistan. Indeed, between late 2001 and late 2004, Iran had to do very little to benefit from sea-changes in its neighborhood.

In more recent years, however, Iran has had to be much more nuanced in its behavior, as even before the opportunities afforded Iran in the aftermath of the fall of the Taliban and Saddam Hussein had been realized, President Bush had included Iran in the 'Axis of Evil' statement in his State of the Union speech in January 2002. Thus, for every apparent gain in Iraq or Afghanistan, Iran has had to contend with more pressure from the US and its allies. The fact that, according to US intelligence, Iran apparently halted its active military nuclear program in the spring of 2003 can be said to be largely due to the United States' willingness to replace the Iraqi regime, in principle, because of its belief that Saddam Hussein was pursuing weapons of mass destruction. The US problems in Iraq since then, and perceptions of Iran's net gains in Iraq since 2004, tend to overshadow the fact that Tehran was extremely concerned during the military assault on Iraq in 2003 that US forces could easily target Iran and energize internal opposition to the regime there. The fear that Iran could be next existed for much of 2003, even inviting a conciliatory letter of compromise from Ayatollah Khamenei to President Bush. At that point, Iran was on its back foot, trying to reach an accommodation with the United States.

Nevertheless, Tehran does have regional ambitions and it sees the present situation as ideal for the advancement of its interests and objectives in the Middle East. In this context, the Islamic Republic has always been happy to combine soft and hard power for its purposes. If religion and culture form the heart of its soft power, then military prowess must represent its hard shell. In the latter case, non-conventional weapons could well play a part, particularly if the deterrence of threats by the US and Israel is the object of Iran's exercise. In short, the key question is whether Iran is developing nuclear capabilities primarily in support of its desire to project power in the region, or is it simply trying to protect itself by balancing the power of others? Though it is difficult to separate the two in practice, where one chooses to place the emphasis will inevitably have operational implications for other actors.

Iran's Global Ambitions

In global terms, Iran's ambitions can be understood in the context of developments across Asia, in which Iran views itself as a key actor and stakeholder. In Asia, there are already a number of actors with nuclear weapons and, of course, one of Iran's key neighbors (Pakistan) is already a nuclear-weapon state. The dynamics of Asian geo-politics are a major factor as one looks at the range of factors behind Iran's conception of its nuclear role. By some Asian standards – namely by looking at the economic power bases of China, India, Indonesia, and Japan – Iran is less of a significant actor than its ambitions indicate. But, if one takes into account Iran's geo-political, cultural, demographic, and energy resources, then the country is an Asian power of considerable importance. In the Asian mix of powers, Iran has the potential to be a 'swing' state of significant weight, able to affect Asia's emerging new power lines as Eurasia begins to adjust to the rapid rise of China and India and the relative decline of Russia. Its partnerships with all of Asia's diverse major actors, including North Korea, mean that it has to be able to carry its own weight in this unstructured and unregulated regional setting, which encompasses and accommodates well over half of humanity. No other Middle East state has the same vulnerabilities and opportunities in Asia as Iran, so its "look east" policy has significance both strategically and operationally.

With India and Pakistan recently declared to be nuclear-weapon states, there is a sense that Iran is next in a hierarchical framework of proliferation. But Iran does not need nuclear weapons to deter Asian adversaries, far from it. Iran is actually increasingly reliant on a number of Asian countries for counteracting the pressures from the trans-Atlantic western alliance. Increased economic pressure from the US and the EU, for example, are driving Iran to loosen its financial presence in Europe and to shift its considerable deposits to the Far East.

But to be able to preserve its own position, and for these powers to take Tehran seriously as a big player, even an ambiguous nuclear posture can be beneficial. This is a trick that Iran clearly learned from North Korea as it was developing its nuclear program in the 1990s, and from the regional states' reactions to North Korea's nuclear diplomacy. There is much to be gained from pursuing nuclear capabilities, if its consequences can be controlled and do not lead to military confrontation, as happened in the case of Iraq in 2003. Let us not forget that it was Baghdad's deliberately ambiguous posture in the 1990s and early 2000s, ironically intended to deter Iran, which US leaders used to justify military action.

It may be premature to see Iran's nuclear program as leading to a 'grand bargain' with the United States but, nevertheless, it is possible to see the nuclear program's depth and diversity as providing Iran with a wide range of negotiable pawns in any deal with the international community. Unlike Libya and more like North Korea, the more complex the program the greater the opportunities for negotiations.

The danger is that such implicit and ambiguous threats can also lend support to those who advocate preventive military action against Iran: "Because the ultimate goal of prevention is to influence Tehran to change course, effective strikes against Iran's nuclear infrastructure may play an important role in affecting Iran's decision calculus," according to advocates of military action, Clawson and Eisenstadt.[18] The depth and complexity of Iran's program, according to these analysts, implies Iran's retention of a 'breakout option' that must be stopped even by force.

A nuclear posture therefore strengthens Iran's profile in an Asian neighborhood full of heavy-weights and nuclear weapon states, and also strengthens its negotiating hand with its adversaries. There is obviously an awareness of this among Iranian leaders for it has been noted that, in the words of the former chief nuclear negotiator Ali Larijani, "If Iran becomes atomic Iran, no longer will anyone dare challenge it, because they would have to pay too high a price."[19] This analysis does not sit easily with some clerics, who have commented that Iran should regard the possession of nuclear weapons as *haram* and therefore against the republic's principles. The reality is that the key policy makers are fully aware of advantages of implicit nuclear capabilities for Iran's global power games.

IRAN'S NUCLEAR PLANS

Much speculation surrounds Iran's actual nuclear plans. Takeyh, for example, has boldly argued that under the cover of civilian nuclear research program, "Iran is gradually accumulating the technology and the expertise necessary for the construction of nuclear weapons."[20] Fitzpatrick claims that "at the very least, it seems, Iran is seeking to have a nuclear-weapons capability that can be quickly put into place when it makes the final decision"—the 'bomb in the closet' option.[21] Kam is of the view that for the Iranian leadership, "the acquisition of nuclear weapons is a strategic priority of paramount importance," and that "Iran sees nuclear weapons as a requirement for building its position as a regional power."[22] Perkovich believes that "political leaders [such as Khamenei and Rafsanjani] see nuclear weapons as an almost magical source of national power and autonomy."[23] From the outside at least, there seems to be a logic to the program that will lead to nuclear weapons.

Indeed, since 2003 we have learnt much about the extent of Iran's nuclear program and its technical enhancement plans, which include an impressive and diverse set of initiatives. As noted earlier, Iran's nuclear program appears to be comprehensive and also supported by a concerted drive toward the mastery of the entire fuel cycle and its applications. As the UK Parliament's Select Committee on Foreign Affairs put it in its most recent report, Iran is engaged in "the mining and milling of uranium, the conversion of uranium, the enrichment of uranium, fuel fabrication, reactor construction, and reprocessing R&D."[24] The same report also notes that the potential for an Iranian nuclear 'break-out' remains strong given the diversity and richness of its nuclear program.

Iran's nuclear program may be designed to make the country less reliant on the outside world, but in practice its current success is due largely to a wide range of international links which have included Russia, Pakistan, North Korea, and China. Each has provided unique insights for the Iranians. Russia, of course, remains Iran's main nuclear partner, engaged in completing the engineering and construction of the 1,000 megawatt Bushehr nuclear power plant since the mid-1990s and also committed to providing its fuel. Russia is also Iran's main military supplier, exporting a wide range of equipment to its southern neighbor. Compared with Russia, China plays a more circumspect, but nevertheless significant, role in Iran's nuclear program. It is reported by US intelligence, for instance, that since the 1980s China has been responsible for helping the Islamic Republic build fuel fabrication, uranium purification, and zirconium tube production facilities, and even provided it with the equipment used in electromagnetic isotope separation enrichments of weapons grade uranium.[25] China has also been a major military partner of Iran, helping it to develop its naval, as well as complex land-based and sea-launched missile forces.[26] Another residual partner has been North Korea, whose engagement with Iran dates back to the Iran-Iraq war. Indeed, much of Iran's sophisticated and advanced domestic surface-to-surface missile (SSM) program is nurtured by North Korean modifications of Soviet-type hardware. Through the 1990s, the post-Cold War period, North Korea went further and played an important role in facilitating Iran's nuclear research and development. Verified intelligence reports also speak of North Korean willingness to transfer plutonium to Iran and also its help to Iran to build large, hardened, underground bunkers for its most sensitive facilities.

The final key outside player in facilitating Iran's nuclear achievements to date has been the AQ Khan network. Dr. Khan, of course, is the godfather of Pakistan's successful nuclear weapons program and leader of the world's most successful nuclear smuggling group. According to the US, the Khan network is responsible for supplying Iran with its first P-2 centrifuges and designs, in a sense being responsible for getting the entire uranium enrichment program on the road.

But what is Iran's nuclear program? Essentially, there are four known elements in Iran's nuclear-related activities: uranium enrichment, reprocessing activities and hot cells construction, heavy water reactor projects, and uranium conversion. Of these, enrichment, reprocessing activities, and reactor projects are on-going concerns of the UN Security Council, and it should be noted that repeated Security Council resolutions have pointedly asked for Iran's suspension of its enrichment program—as indeed have the European Union and the G-8.

Enrichment activities have grown steadily since 2002 and Iran is not only intent on intensifying the output of its fuel enrichment plant by adding new centrifuges and cascades, but notified the IAEA in April 2008 that it was planning to introduce a new generation of locally designed sub-critical gas centrifuges (IR-3). In total, Iran has converted 320 tonnes of uranium into UF6 between March 2004 and 2008. The total amount of UF6 fed into the operating cascades between February 2007 and May 2008 was 3970 kilograms, producing low enriched enrichment (up to 4.7 percent U-235 according to the Iran's own Atomic Energy Agency). Iran is likely to accumulate 600kg-700kg of low enriched uranium during the course of 2008. The possession of such a stockpile has been described by scientists as a 'breakout capacity'—the brink of nuclear weapons status—since if 600-700kg of low enriched uranium were run though Iran's enrichment facilities again, it would provide enough fissile material for one bomb.[27]

It should be noted further that as of early 2008 Iran had completed the installation of eighteen 164-machine cascades at the Natanz enrichment plant, which were operating at full capacity, though obviously with the expected technical problems that such a sophisticated facility would face in the beginning of its operations. These data mean that there are nearly 3,000 (2,952 to be precise) operational centrifuges at this facility. But Iran's intention is to grow the centrifuges to a massive total of 50,000, which could be an aspirational figure given the complexities and intensities of such an undertaking, though still highly significant.

In terms of reactor projects, Iran is hoping to generate some 20,000 megawatts of nuclear electricity by 2030 through its light-water reactors. How safe and how well safeguarded these will be remains an international concern. Safety concerns include operational issues, as well as the big problem of nuclear waste disposal, which is a major concern for even established nuclear energy states, such as the United Kingdom, France, and Japan. Issues to do with the location of such reactors also have to be settled: concerns about pollution—radioactive materials seeping into the Persian Gulf and therefore the main water supply of the Gulf Arab states—are matched by those regarding the potential problems of power plants located in an earthquake prone country such as Iran.

Experts remain concerned that Iran's program continues to contain a military dimension, despite the fact that "no evidence has surfaced pointing to a parallel, covert facility," according to Mark Fitzpatrick.[§] However, Fitzpatrick himself has stated that there are ten reasons to suspect that Iran's nuclear or nuclear-related activities have a military dimension.

1. The role of the military in the administration of Iran's Gchine uranium mine and mill;
2. Polonium-210 experiments, which could be deployed as long-life batteries for deep-space satellites, but also as nuclear bomb neutron initiators;
3. Defense-based centrifuge workshops involved in production of parts for the P-2s;
4. Traces of highly-enriched uranium found by IAEA inspectors at the Lavisan military base Physics Research Center;
5. Iran's possession of a 15-page document from the AQ Khan network, "describing procedures for the re-conversion and casting of uranium metal hemispheres," which the IAEA has characterized as related to the manufacture of nuclear bombs components;

[§] Quoted in House of Commons Foreign Affairs Committee, Global Security: Iran (London: Her Majesty's Stationary Office, March 2008), page 11.

6. The military-controlled "Project 111," which is said to be an effort to reshape nose cones of Shehab-3 SSMs as nuclear implosion weapons;
7. Documents from a laptop computer provided by a defector showing blasts data consistent with the critical mass of an atomic explosion;
8. Documents from the same laptop source concerning conversion of uranium dioxide into uranium tetraflouride undertaken by the IRGC;
9. Drawings of subterranean shafts with remote-control censors to measure data relating to an underground atomic test; and
10. The military's deep involvement in many aspects of the nuclear program, including high explosives, nuclear ore processing, and parts fabrication, among others. [28]

Together, these ten factors can be made into a case that Iran is pursuing a clandestine nuclear weapons operation, but Fitzpatrick also notes that Iran has willingly accommodated a highly intensive and intrusive IAEA inspections regime since 2003 in its efforts to dispel the suggestion that it is pursuing a weapons capability. These inspections continue to show that Iran does not seem to be developing a weapons program. But of course inspectors can only visit the sites they know about and also do not have access to Iran's off-limits military sites.

Iran's multi-faceted program reflects Tehran's real drive and desire to become self-sufficient in the nuclear realm. It is interesting that Iran has refused to curtail any part of its program, partly for the fear that this might adversely affect the rest of it, or that indeed such delays could set the program back. The drive for self-sufficiency may have been the starting point, but the self-generated momentum of such a comprehensive program cannot be underrated. Experience shows that, once unleashed, it takes the convergence of a set of international factors and domestic actors to contain a nuclear program. Examples are many: South Africa, Libya, Argentina, and Brazil.

In sum, it is therefore not very surprising to find some analysts that see Iran's nuclear program, along with North Korea's, as the "greatest proliferation dangers to world security."[29] In strategic and operational terms, as Cordesman and Al-Rodhan note, an Iranian nuclear capability will inevitably change the military map of the region.[30] Iran's development of its SSM forces and its drive to acquire a satellite system, the first of which was launched in February 2009, are seen as part of its concerted effort to get to the point of being able to deliver a nuclear weapon at considerable distances.

IRAN'S PROLIFERATION CONCERNS

Iranian leaders, to a man (literally), have spoken about the dangers of proliferation in the Middle East, even welcoming the news that Libya had surrendered its clandestine nuclear program to the IAEA. The long shadow cast by Iraq's use of chemical weapons and ballistic missiles against civilian and military targets in the 1980s remains vivid in the Iranian mindset and Iranian leaders rarely miss an opportunity to remind visiting guests that their country remains one of the few victims of deadly non-conventional weapons attacks since the First World War. That experience, it is reiterated, had made Iran a strong advocate of disarmament. Proliferation, according to this logic, is bad for Iran and for its future. Yet, Tehran was one of the first to congratulate Pakistan on its nuclear achievement when it announced its nuclear weapons status in the second half of the 1990s. Also, under the Ahmadinejad presidency, Iran has been offering a range of Muslim countries (Kuwait, Sudan, Syria, Turkey, to name but a few), as well as other nations of compatible political persuasion, the gift of its nuclear know-how and technologies, apparently by-passing the IAEA's strict guidelines about nuclear states' obligations toward non-proliferation. In short, Iran's record with regard to counter-proliferation is inconsistent.

But the main direction of Iran's proliferation concerns has invariably veered toward Israel, which it, and virtually every other regional state, see as the only nuclear weapon state, and therefore chief proliferator, in the Middle East. Largely for this reason, Iran has embraced the Arabs' concept of a Middle East nuclear-weapons-free-zone. But given the largely rhetorical orientation of this position, it is unlikely to cause Iran to develop a well-thought out policy for preventing the proliferation of non-conventional weapons in the Middle East.

MOVING TO ZERO

If one assumes, as do Cordesman and Al-Rodhan, that were Iran, "to acquire nuclear weapons…it will use them largely as a passive deterrent and means of defense," then we must also make the working assumption that there is not a military solution to the current situation. Rather, Iran's position should encourage the opportunity for a negotiated settlement of the nuclear dispute. But, if we accept the contrary argument that Iran will deploy its nuclear weapons arsenal, "to put direct or indirect pressure on its neighbours, threatening them to achieve goals it could not achieve without the explicit or tacit threat of weapons of mass destruction," then clearly getting to a negotiated settlement will require the exercise of some tough choices.[31]

There is also the larger global picture to consider. Since the end of the Cold War, every established nuclear-weapon state has gone out of its way to reaffirm its deterrent capability and several have introduced programs to modernize their nuclear forces, as well. In the cases of UK and France, the explicit rationale for this has been the threat from emerging nuclear weapon countries, such as Iran. Fear of proliferation will only entrench these nuclear-weapon powers.[32] "Deterrence," former President Chirac of France said in 2001, "must also enable us to deal with the threats to our vital interests that regional powers armed with weapons of mass destruction could pose."[33] Britain's promised multi-billion dollar investment in the modernization of its Trident force is also seen as providing a credible independent deterrence against emerging powers. Indeed, Prime Minister Brown has made this very case on numerous occasions in the House of Parliament. To clarify, however, France and Britain have decided to replace their submarines, but have not yet committed the cash to doing so. But both have reaffirmed their deterrent doctrines while reducing the size of their nuclear stockpiles. The picture is mixed elsewhere too.

The United States and Russia, of course, have also been engaged in the modernization of their nuclear forces, and Moscow announced in March 2009 a program of military modernization starting with its nuclear forces. The US has made substantial cuts in its nuclear forces, to be sure, and is modernizing very slowly. Moreover, there is a new atmosphere in Washington, as reflected by the initiatives of former secretaries of state George Schultz and Henry Kissinger, former secretary of defense William Perry, and former senator Sam Nunn, and also by the fact that both presidential candidates, Senators John McCain and Barack Obama, made speeches devoted to nuclear problems in which they expressed support for goal of disarmament and outlined specific measures toward that end. With Obama now in the White House, there is hope and expectation that his administration will commit seriously to fulfilling this campaign pledge. China, India, and Pakistan, finally, are modernizing their nuclear forces more rapidly than the others, but their programs seem to have a more focused regional dimension to them. All three nations continue to express rhetorical support for disarmament, but maintain that given the much larger size of their nuclear arsenals, it is up to the US and Russia to take the first steps.

In short, there are slowly emerging global initiatives that arguably could eventually tie Iran into a serious disarmament effort. However, there does not appear to be in place at present an internationally-driven disarmament movement sufficient to cajole Iran into joining, and for this Tehran rightly assumes that the efforts to get it to halt its civilian nuclear program suggest that it is being picked on. Though, of course, its own incendiary statements and behaviour do not quite help it get away with this cultivated innocent image.

Moving to zero requires flexibility from Iran and also an offer that Tehran could simply not refuse. As will be shown below, some progress on the latter has certainly already been made, but we need to make a final assessment of Iran's end-game. Is it to acquire a nuclear-weapons capability, and is this for deterrence or for power projection?

Bahgat notes that "it is apparent that convincing Iran to give up its nuclear program would require prolonged and complicated negotiations. The crux of these negotiations is to persuade Iran's policy makers that the risks of pursuing a nuclear program exceed the rewards."[34] Before this stage can be reached, however, governments must understand Iran's maximalist position regarding its nuclear rights under the NPT and weigh it against the possibility of offering credible security guarantees as part of a set of incentives to Iran to give up its nuclear program. On the first issue, Iran will need to be persuaded that being asked to end (or curtail) its fuel-processing capabilities may be asking it to compromise its NPT rights, but, at the same time, the IAEA can demonstrate that this proposal is not politically driven. The issue, as Huntley has usefully shown, is the fact that as many as 40 countries may now possess the industrial and scientific infrastructure for nuclear weapons manufacture: "This concern has generated new proposals to restrict fuel-cycle capabilities of non-nuclear countries more widely."[35] By all estimates, Iran is one such country and its offer of sharing this know-how with others—though probably made with the best of intensions—is actually to encourage unregulated proliferation.

The trick is preventing a global initiative to restrict fuel-cycle capabilities internationally from becoming hostage to those groups in Iran who might successfully foment pro-nuclear nationalism through their manipulation of Iran's complex political identity. The answer to this dilemma lies in the mix and nature of the rewards being offered and the price that non-compliance would otherwise cost. First, a serious initiative by the nuclear weapon states to negotiate a disarmament treaty that includes global agreement that fuel cycles must all come under multinational control need to be put in place. Second, while these negotiations are proceeding (or getting started), near-term resolution of the current crisis must be considered on the basis of the November 2004 Paris Agreement, with the amendment that the 5+1 agree to make available aid and wider support *at the same time* as Iran is ceasing enrichment activities. The problem so far has been that Iran has been asked to end enrichment before the incentives would kick-in.

A general regional proliferation, following Iran's apparent intransigence, is not in Iran's security interests and the strategic fall-out from Iran's efforts in this field could be strongly demonstrated to Iran by the IAEA, particularly if it is true that "Tehran might fear the prospects of American and Israeli nuclear retaliation less than Western strategists would hope."[36] In other words, once the threat of the use of force had receded, then the door would have been opened for deeper discussions about the security consequences for Iran and other regional states of proliferation of nuclear know-how, and the falling into wrong hands of a 'dirty bomb' or equivalent that could directly damage Iran's own security.

In this broader context, revisiting of the November 2004 Paris agreement between the EU3 and Tehran may provide some useful insights regarding the appropriate next steps.[37] First, the agreement was reached on the back of Iran's consent to the EU3's request that it should suspend its enrichment activities, which it said it would do on a temporary basis and as a gesture of goodwill. "In the context of this suspension," the agreement notes,

> The E3/EU and Iran have agreed to begin negotiations, with a view to reaching a mutually acceptable agreement on long-term arrangements. The agreement will provide objective guarantees that Iran's nuclear program is exclusively for peaceful purposes, it will equally provide firm guarantees on nuclear, technological and economic cooperation and firm commitments on security issues…A steering committee will set up working groups on political and security issues, technology and cooperation, and nuclear issues.[38]

As part of the same agreement, the EU3 also committed the Union to "actively support the opening of Iranian accession negotiations at the World Trade Organization (WTO)," and the parties confirmed their determination to combat terrorism (a code word for EU's acceptance of the anti-Tehran, Iraq-based Mujahedin-e Khalq (MEK) Organization as a terrorist movement).

The Paris agreement is a remarkable document for its tone and foresight and also for what it commits the West to supporting—CBMs, nuclear cooperation, WTO accession, lifting of sanctions and restrictions, and removal of the MEK as a deep and poisonous thorn in Tehran's side. This agreement was indeed on the verge of being revolutionary, given the tensions that had largely characterized Iran's relations with the West to this point. But the Paris agreement was followed a few months later by a further remarkable document: The EU3's detailed proposal, billed as a "framework for a long-term agreement" between Iran and the EU. Issued on the 5th of August 2005 by the EU3, just a few days into President Ahmadinejad's presidency, the framework document provides a comprehensive blueprint for a new start between Iran and the international community. Under the general headings of "political and security co-operation," "long-term support for Iran's civil nuclear programme," and "economic and technological co-operation," the document details mechanisms for addressing many of Iran's concerns as fully as possible. By this juncture, of course, the US administration had dropped its opposition to Iran's WTO membership and had also agreed to the suggestion that Iran's civilian aircraft fleet be allowed to purchase parts directly from the manufacturers—the Bush Administration was prepared to board the train.

It is worth noting some of the most salient aspects of the framework proposal: Help in building a safe and economically viable civil nuclear power generation and research program; access for Iran to the international nuclear technologies market; assurances for external supplies of nuclear fuel; establishment of a buffer store of fuel; Iran being declared as a long-term source of fossil fuels for the EU; providing assistance in the fields of environmental, communications and information technologies; cooperation in the fields of air, maritime and railway transport, and agriculture and food industries. In other words, for the EU to provide help, cooperation, and assistance in every conceivable area that would help make Iran develop as a strong and robust state and economy.

Indeed, many of the incentives raised in the framework document can be found in the much more talked about the 5+1 6th of June 2006 package of incentives offered to Tehran (which now included the US, as well as China and Russia). In return for stiff assurances on Iran's nuclear program, the 5+1 package makes a series of eye-catching commitments on nuclear cooperation, help in the application of nuclear science and R&D, economic assistance, high technology cooperation, civil aviation support, etc. This was seen by most outside observers as a significant incentive package, but it too failed to move matters forward. In the summer of 2008, the world was still waiting Iran's formal response to an even better package offered in June of that year.

The Paris agreement and its successors, though remarkable in many ways, had failed to end the crisis and by 2008 there were three UNSC sanctions resolutions on the books against Iran and a host of other unilateral sanctions imposed by the US and the EU. Yet, there is evidence to suggest that Tehran was interested in furthering the debate beyond sanctions resolutions. It is useful to note, for the record, that European diplomats had reported that Mr Mottaki and Mr Jaleli had expressed strong interest in the 5+1 2006/08 packages, under which the international community would help Iran to develop a state-of-the art civil nuclear energy program if it suspended uranium enrichment. Under the proposal, Iran would continue enrichment but, as a first step, declare that it had frozen installation of more centrifuges at its nuclear facilities. In return, the permanent members of the United Nations Security Council plus Germany would freeze steps to apply more sanctions.

By the time this package was prepared and delivered, of course, Tehran had moved well away from a compromise. It should be recalled that on the 8th of August 2005

Iran broke the seals on its conversion plant in Isfahan, and after being reported by the IAEA Board as 'non-compliant' with its NPT obligations in September 2005, resumed enrichment in January 2006. By the autumn of 2006, by which time Iran's president had repeatedly questioned the right of Israel to exist as a sovereign country and had also engaged in Holocaust denial at public national and international gatherings, the EU3 had had enough. It was, ironically, the party championing the introduction of the first set of UNSC sanctions against Iran.

This position is a world removed from the relationship that the Paris agreement had heralded just two years earlier. It is little wonder then that both sides are now even more wary. The June 2006 package (which also evolved into a similar 2008 package) is probably the defining edge of the abyss if we are to believe the reports that Israeli forces were poised to attack Iran's nuclear facilities during the autumn of 2008, apparently convinced that Iran was weaponizing without delay.[**]

Having seen what might have been achieved, in terms of the Paris agreement and the 5+1 offers, and the scale of breakdown in the negotiations since, it is easy to be pessimistic. Yet glimmers of hope still exist and one can find silver linings not only in the new US administration's expressions of commitment to find a negotiated solution to the crisis, but also in Iran's nuanced responses to international pressures and offers of negotiations. It is also worth noting that in a poll of 35,000 Iranians in June 2008, 50 percent of the respondents said that Iran should accept the 5+1 package with some modifications and a further 21 percent said that Iran should accept the package in its entirety. Thus, the vast majority, over 72 percent of those polled, want a negotiated compromise on the basis of the package of incentives. Only 24 percent of the Iranians polled said the package should be rejected.[39]

Readers must also be conscious of the fact that alongside any package of rewards, the Western nations should pursue strategies that will "relieve Iran's regional tensions and avoid provoking nationalistic reactions [which] could not only deflate Iranians' perceived strategic need for nuclear weapons but also help promote more moderate domestic forces less dependent on threat-based nationalism for support."[40] The international community still finds it very difficult to strike the right balance between these imperatives.

Thus, despite the upbeat assessment of Iran's response to the 5+1 group's package of incentives, it was apparent to observers that the dynamics of the relationship were far from accommodating a speedy settlement. Iran's fears of Western motives had not gone away, nor indeed were the Western countries any closer to understanding what Iran's perception of its own role in the region was going to look like in the

---

[**] This is the view expressed by John Bolton, former US ambassador to the UN. See *The Daily Telegraph* (June 24, 2008).

future, any future—whether nuclear-free or with a weapons capability. Thus, on the 15th of June 2008, it was reported that a senior US official in Washington had told journalists that if Tehran refused the generous offer, the US would push the EU to step up sanctions—particularly on Bank Melli, Iran's largest commercial bank with an international network of branches and links.[41] Sure enough, within a few days of this report, it was announced on the 23rd of June that the EU had approved without debate the imposition of new sanctions against Iran, including freezing the assets of Bank Melli. This happened despite the fact that Iran's promised 'considered response' to the package had not yet been delivered.

As we begin to look at end-states, it is worthwhile reflecting on Iran's so-called 'strategic' offer of negotiating with the 5+1 group of countries in search of a solution to the on-going dispute between it and the Security Council, even though Tehran continues to regard the involvement of the Security Council as unlawful. Iran's Foreign Minister Mottaki, in his letter of 13th of May 2008 to the UN Secretary General Ban Ki-moon, expressed a desire to try and settle the dispute on the basis of "real and serious cooperation among the concerned parties [i.e., 5+1]."[42] The material sent to the UN Secretary General is billed by Mottaki as a package of comprehensive solutions to "the regional and global problems and challenges." Though divided into three distinct baskets, at its heart the section entitled "The Nuclear Issue" is clearly the driver of the other two—"Political and Security Issues," and "Economic Issues." But even under the latter two baskets one can find evidence for compromise, albeit a hesitant one. Take the political and security issues basket, for example. Mottaki offers to cooperate, "to assist the Palestinian people to find a comprehensive plan…to resolve the 60-year old Palestinian issue," as "a symbol" of Iran's commitment to its offer of dialogue. No mention of the end of Israel here, although cynics could interpret this statement as saying the end of Israel in more polite words. But the choice of words is very interesting, in that it tries to appear constructive and also willing to engage with the 'Palestinian people' as a whole (i.e., not only Hamas) to find a comprehensive plan for ending the conflict. What the statement does not say is that Iran and the Palestinians should join forces and follow Iran's lead in forming an anti-Israel coalition. What is said and also what is not said are both significant.

The nuclear basket, itself divided into seven sub-sections, offers three very interesting propositions: "establishing enrichment and nuclear fuel production consortiums in different parts of the world—including Iran," "nuclear disarmament and establishment of a follow up committee," and "improved supervision by the IAEA over the nuclear activities of different states." This represents Tehran's efforts to find a constructive response to the '5+1' package. Its horizons are limited, for sure, but it is not a blanket rejection of the operational aspects of the package either. It concedes some ground while wanting to see the IAEA more actively engaged.

This document appears to be Tehran reaching out to the 5+1 group as best it can, given its self-imposed ideological and political constraints, offering to partner with the West in dealing with the region's crises collectively and collaboratively. Despite the many short-comings of the proposal, it is clear that its whole tenor, and the demeanour of the submission, is designed to be conciliatory—the kind of style that we have not seen since August 2005. But is it enough? The answer is clearly not. Riccardo Redaelli argues that one of the key ingredients of progress must be in efforts to de-securitize Iran's foreign policy agenda, alongside a "step-by-step roadmap for defusing the crisis."[43] But before such a roadmap can be implemented, the ground rules for engagement must be established and the international community must show a general willingness to consider nuclear disarmament as a priority.

Also, the essence of Iran's security doctrine needs to be taken into account. For the Islamic Republic, defense (and therefore deterrence) has been a policy imperative. So long as this is the case, the West's conventional and non-conventional capabilities will be regarded as potentially threatening. Tehran regards US conventional forces more dangerous in practical terms than its nuclear arsenal, for example. So, changing the Iranian mindset, so that the West is no longer seen as an existential enemy, will take time and much effort on both sides. A glimpse of what is possible was found in the Paris Agreement and its successors; but at the same time we have also seen how easily matters can spin out of control and even nosedive. For the moment, the best that we can hope for is for the dogs of war to be kept at bay until the new administrations in Tehran and Washington have been able to take stock and decide to show the courage that would enable them to retrace their steps back from the edge. Once this happens, anything is then possible!

ENDNOTES

[1] UN Security Council Resolutions 1737 (2206), 1747 (2007), and 1803 (2008).

[2] IAEA Staff Report, "Latest Iran Safeguards Report Circulated to IAEA Board," 22 February 2008.

[3] George Jahn, "IAEA: Iran may be withholding info in nuke probe," *International Herald Tribune* (May 26, 2008).

[4] IAEA, Report by the Director General, "Implementation of the NPT Safeguards Agreement and Relevant Provisions of Security Council Resolutions 1737 (2006), 1747 (2007) and 1803 (2008) in the Islamic Republic of Iran," 26 May 2008, page 4.

[5] See International Herald Tribune (May 26, 2008).

[6] Elaine Sciolino, "Nuclear Agency says Iran has Improved Enrichment," *International Herald Tribune* (September 16, 2008), http://www.nytimes.com/2008/09/16/world/africa/16iht-16iran.16181716.html?_r=1.

[7] Jay Solomon, "U.S. says Iran has Matter for Bomb," *Wall Street Journal* (March 3, 2009).

[8] Ray Takeyh, "Iran Builds the Bomb," *Survival*, vol. 46, no. 4 (Winter 2004-05), page 53.

[9] Shahram Chubin, Iran's Nuclear Ambitions (Washington, DC: Carnegie Endowment for International Peace, 2006), page 16.

[10] Ibid.

[11] Kasra Naji, Ahmadinejad: The Secret History of Iran's Radical Leader (London: IB Tauris, 2008).

[12] Michael Slackman, "Iran Tones Down its Support for Hamas," *International Herald Tribune* (January 13, 2009).

[13] See Flynt Leverett and Hillary Mann Leverett, "The Grand Bargain: Five Presidents Have Treated Iran as a Threat. The Next Needs to Think of it as an Opportunity," *Washington Monthly* (Aug./Sep./Oct. 2008), pages 31-36.

[14] "Iran: The Party's Over," *The Economist* (November 20, 2008), http://www.economist.com/world/mideast-africa/displaystory.cfm?story_id=12650281.

[15] See Anoushiravan Ehteshami and Mahjoob Zweiri, Iran and the Rise of its Neoconservatives: The Politics of Tehran's Silent Revolution (London: IB Tauris, 2007).

[16] For examples, see Anoushiravan Ehteshami, Competing Powerbrokers of the Middle East: Iran and Saudi Arabia (Abu Dhabi: Emirates Center for Strategic Studies and Research, 2008).

[17] Emile El-Hokayem and Matteo Legrenzi, The Arab States in the Shadow of the Iranian Nuclear Challenge (Washington, DC: Henry L. Stimson Center, May 2006).

[18] Patrick Clawson and Michael Eisenstadt, <u>The Last Resort: Consequences of Preventive Military Action against Iran</u> (Washington, DC: Washington Institute for Near East Policy, 2008), page 7.

[19] Ali Larijani, quoted in Chubin, *op. cit.*, page 33.

[20] Ray Takeyh, "Iran Builds the Bomb," *Survival*, vol. 46, no. 4 (Winter 2004-05), page 51.

[21] Mark Fitzpatrick, "Assessing Iran's Nuclear Programme," *Survival*, vol. 48, no. 3 (Autumn 2006), page 13.

[22] Ephraim Kam, <u>A Nuclear Iran: What Does it Mean, and What Can be Done</u> (Tel Aviv: Institute for National Security Studies, 2007), page 26.

[23] George Perkovich, <u>Dealing with Iran's Nuclear Challenge</u> (Washington, DC: Carnegie Endowment for International Peace Working Paper, 28 April 2003), page 4.

[24] House of Commons Foreign Affairs Committee, <u>Global Security: Iran</u> (London: Her Majesty's Stationary Office, March 2008), page 38.

[25] Anthony H. Cordesman and Khalid R. Al-Rodhan, <u>Iranian Nuclear Weapons? Options for Sanctions and Military Strikes</u> (Washington, DC: Center for Strategic and International Studies, August 2006).

[26] Kori N. Schake and Judith S. Yaphe, <u>The Strategic Implications of a Nuclear-Armed Iran</u> (Washington, DC: National Defense University, 2001).

[27] *Financial Times* (June 29, 2008).

[28] Mark Fitzpatrick, "Assessing Iran's Nuclear Programme," *Survival*, vol. 48, no. 3 (Autumn 2006), page 9.

[29] Mark Fitzpatrick, *op.cit.,* pages 61-80.

[30] Anthony H. Cordesman and Khalid R. Al-Rodhan, *op.cit.*

[31] Both quotations are from Cordesman and Al-Rodhan, *op.cit.*, page 3.

[32] Barry Blechman, ed., Unblocking the Road to Zero: Perspectives of Advanced Nuclear Nations – France and the United Kingdom (Washington, DC: Henry L. Stimson Center, February 2009).

[33] Quoted in David S. Yost, "France's Evolving Nuclear Strategy," *Survival*, vol. 47, no. 3 (Autumn 2005), page 118.

[34] Gawdat Bahgat, <u>Proliferation of Nuclear Weapons in the Middle East</u> (Tampa, FL: University Press of Florida, 2007), page 41.

[35] Wade L. Huntley, "Rebels Without a Cause: North Korea and Iran and the NPT," *International Affairs*, vol. 82, no. 4 (July 2006), page 733.

[36] Richard L. Russell, Weapons Proliferation and War in the Greater Middle East: Strategic Contest (London: Routledge, 2005), page 87.

[37] Yaphe and Lutes note that the non-nuclear benefits of this offer were indeed substantial. See Judith S. Yaphe and Charles D. Lutes, Reassessing the Implications of a Nuclear-Armed Iran (Washington, DC: National Defense University, 2005).

[38] Signed in Paris on November 15, 2004.

[39] The poll was conducted by Tabnak organization news site, www.tabnak.ir.

[40] *Ibid*, page 736.

[41] *Financial Times* (June 15, 2008).

[42] The unofficial translation and release of this package was undertaken by the US-based American Iranian Council. See *American Iranian Council Update*, no. 77 (22 May 2008).

[43] Riccardo Redaelli, "Why Selective Engagement? Iranian and Western Interests Are Closer Than You Think," *Policy Analysis Brief* (June 2008), page 1.

ISRAELI PERSPECTIVES ON THE GLOBAL ELIMINATION OF NUCLEAR WEAPONS

Shlomo Brom

Israel is in a unique position among the perceived nuclear powers—a state recognized as a nuclear power outside the five nuclear states accepted by the Nuclear Proliferation Treaty (NPT), but not admitting to be one. The three other states that were in a similar position, India, Pakistan and North Korea, performed tests, declared their nuclear capabilities, and are striving to become accepted nuclear powers. Israel sticks to a policy of nuclear ambiguity or opacity; it is very comfortable with the perception that it is a nuclear power but does not admit it. That makes Israel a unique country and an interesting case when trying to understand perspectives on the global elimination of nuclear weapons.

THE ISRAELI NUCLEAR OPTION – MOTIVATIONS AND PURPOSES

Israel's nuclear ambitions are almost as old as the state itself. When the state of Israel exited the 1948-1949 War of Independence victorious but bruised, David Ben-Gurion, Israel's first prime minister, was acutely aware of the existential security predicament Israel faced because of the asymmetry between it and its Arab neighbors. He viewed the Arab-Israeli conflict as deep and lasting and believed that it could be resolved only after the Arabs had accepted the existence of Israel as an established and irreversible fact. The combination of asymmetrical capabilities and lasting conflict caused Israel to assume a deterrent posture that prevents its Arab neighbors from posing an existential threat to Israel. Moreover, Ben-Gurion believed that a deterrent based only on conventional military capabilities would not be credible because the Arabs would assume that they would eventually be capable of changing the conventional balance of forces due to their greater resources. In this sense, the Israeli nuclear option was supposed to be the great equalizer that corrects the asymmetry in the balance of resources.[1]

Thus, from its inception, the role of the nuclear option was to prevent the realization of existential threats to the young state. During the first 30 years of Israel's existence, the existential threat was conceptualized by a scenario in which a coalition of Arab states launched a massive land invasion against the state of Israel. This doomsday scenario was realized twice, in the 1948-49 war and in the 1973 war, but there was a substantial difference between the two wars. While the first was a total war in which the declared objective of the invading Arab armies was to destroy the infant state, the second was a limited war aimed at regaining the territories occupied in 1967 by achieving limited territorial gains and exerting a significant cost on the Israeli Defense Force (IDF). The accepted assessment in Israel is that one of the main reasons for Egypt and Syria's limited objectives in the 1973 war was their recognition of Israel's nuclear option. This is cited frequently as proof of the validity of Israel's nuclear strategy.[2]

During the first years of development of Israel's nuclear option, two schools of thought ruled the debate. The first supported the idea that the nuclear option should be the principal mainstay of Israel's deterrent posture, even at the expense of Israel's conventional forces, thus avoiding possible bankruptcy because of huge defense expenditures. This paradigm also had supporters in Israeli academia[3]. The second school of thought considered the nuclear option an instrument of last resort, an insurance policy that hopefully would never be used. Supporters of the second school argued that Israel should build up its conventional military power and manage its wars as if the nuclear option did not exist. Eventually, the second school of thought gained dominance in the Israeli strategic community. What Israel's prime minister, Levy Eshkol, referred to as "The Samson Option" became the basic Israeli strategic concept—the nuclear option as a national insurance policy.[4]

According to one source, when the Israeli nuclear doctrine was first formulated in 1965-66, four concrete scenarios were presented as existential threats and thought to justify the use of nuclear weapons: (1) a successful Arab military penetration into populated areas within Israel's (pre-1967) borders; (2) the destruction of the Israeli Air Force; (3) the exposure of Israeli cities to massive and devastating air attacks or to possible chemical or biological attacks; and (4) the use of nuclear weapons against Israeli territory.[5]

Much has changed in the Middle East and in the Arab-Israeli relationship in the more then 40 years since the doctrine's development. Israel has succeeded in retaining a qualitative edge and conventional military superiority over any probable anti-Israel Arab military alliance. That is due, to a great extent, to US support and its pledge to maintain Israel's qualitative advantage. Israel's continuous military superiority is one of the reasons for a change in the Arab approach towards Israel. Two Arab states, Egypt and Jordan, have concluded peace treaties with Israel, while others have been involved in peace negotiations with Israel at various times. Currently, no Arab government declares that Israel should not exist and/or states that its objective is to destroy the state of Israel. The only government that holds these positions is Iran, a Muslim non-Arab country. The culmination of this change in the positions of the Arab governments was the so-called "Arab peace initiative," which was adopted as an Arab League resolution in Beirut on March 28, 2002. It offered Israel normalization of relations and comprehensive peace agreements with all Arab states, with the condition that Israel reach peace agreements with Syria and the Palestinians.*

Nevertheless, Israel's strategic thinking is still affected by a sense of vulnerability and fragility. Israelis think that the peace agreements are fragile because they were concluded by governments whose citizens' attitudes are very hostile to Israel. Most regimes in the Arab Middle East are non-democratic and have to deal internally with strong Islamic oppositions. From the Israeli perspective, the current regimes may crumble and be replaced by Islamic governments not committed to upholding the agreements made by the former leaders The events in Iran 30 years ago have had a lasting effect on Israeli perceptions. Until 1979, Israel and the Shah's government of Iran were allies with a joint strategy aimed at defending their mutual interests vis-à-vis the Arab states of the Middle East. The Islamic revolution in Iran reversed everything and turned Iran into Israel's most vitriolic enemy. Israelis are concerned that similar developments in Arab states that concluded peace treaties with Israel are possible.[6]

The nature of security threats to Israel has changed as well. Most of the classic last resort scenarios that dominated the 1965-66 debate have lost much of their relevancy. The states that are still hostile to Israel are not capable of launching seriously threatening land invasions or devastating air attacks against Israel. Most of the relevant threats today are not existential threats. Instead they threaten to prevent Israeli citizens from living normal, routine, and secure lives through the use of terrorism or extended harassment by rockets launched from a distance. There is only one existential threat that is looming in the future, that of a hostile state committed to the idea of destroying Israel obtaining nuclear weapons and acting on calls for Israel to be "wiped off the map."[7]

There is also debate in Israel today about whether chemical and biological weapons pose an existential threat. It is acknowledged that the military utility of these weapons against armed forces equipped with suitable protective gear is limited. The concern is their use against Israel's civilian population, which would be more vulnerable. The Israeli response to this threat is a combination of passive defense, such as the distribution of personal protection gear and building codes that require a room that can be easily sealed in each apartment or house, and active defense with a national missile defense system. The assumption is that the effectiveness of a chemical or biological attack will depend to a great extent on the number of missiles that hit their targets. The missile defense system probably could not intercept all incoming missiles, but it could diminish substantially the number of missiles that

---

*See the text of the Arab Peace Initiative at http://www.albab.com/arab/docs/league/peace02.htm.

reach their destinations. Nevertheless, there is still concern that all these protective means would reduce casualties, but not to a point that would prevent these attacks from having a devastating effect on public morale.

Thus, Israel apparently also considers its nuclear option as means to deter its enemies from use of chemical and biological weapons.[8] Prior to the first Gulf War, Israel's military and political leaders threatened a devastating response if Iraq used chemical and biological weapons in an effort to deter Saddam Hussein.[9] These threats were supported by Israel's ballistic missile test in the Mediterranean on December 22' 1990.[10] The assumption that such a test would deter Hussein was probably based on the common understanding that Israeli ballistic missiles are intended to be delivery vehicles for nuclear weapons.

Israel is anxious to link the nuclear option only to last resort scenarios. Use of nuclear weapons in war-fighting roles would contradict this doctrine. At the same time there is uncertainty as to the true extent of Israel's nuclear capabilities. In 1991, for example, Seymour Hersh, in his book, *The Samson Option*, proposed that Israel might possess hundreds of nuclear weapons of all types, from low-yield enhanced radiation designs, including those in the form of mines and artillery shells, to large thermonuclear weapons.[11] There is no evidence to support this speculation, however, and it seems to the writer that Israel has adhered to its basic doctrine of the nuclear option as a "last resort."

WHO IS THE THREAT?

In Israeli thinking, a threat is created when there is a combination of intentions and capabilities. Thus, Israel does not look at Turkey's military capabilities as a threat, although Turkey has in its possession the largest military force in the Middle East. Turkey is not considered a threat because it is not hostile to Israel; the two countries have a friendly relationship. The same was true for Iran before the 1979 revolution. Israel cooperated strategically with the Shah's Iran and was not concerned by the accelerated military build up that took place under the Shah's regime. There were also indications at the time that the Shah had nuclear ambitions, which were not cause for concern in Israel. After the 1979 revolution, however, Israel's perception of Iran changed completely. Iran's Islamic regime is extremely hostile to Israel, does not recognize its right to exist, and declares that it should be wiped out.[†] As a

---

[†] Ahmadinejad (President of Iran): "Our dear Imam (referring to Ayatolla Khomeini) said that the regime occupying Palestine should be wiped off the map and this was a very wise statement." Islamic Republic of Iran Broadcasting (October 26, 2005). Ahmadinejad: "Although the main solution is for the elimination of the Zionist regime, at this stage an immediate cease-fire must be implemented.," in Sean Young, "Ahmadinejad: Destroy Israel, End Crisis," *The Associated Press* (August 3, 2006).

result, Israel perceives that Iran poses the most severe threat to its security and even existence.

At present none of the existing nuclear powers are perceived as threats to Israel. At the time of the inception of Pakistani military nuclear capabilities, the term "Islamic bomb" was frequently used when referring to the Pakistani program, and there were some rumors that Israel was cooperating with India in preparing plans for an attack on the Pakistani nuclear facilities. These rumors were never verified and it now seems they were false. Throughout the years, the relationship between Israel and Pakistan has not been contentious and Israel has not felt threatened by Pakistan. This may change if the nature of the Pakistani regime changes and it becomes an Islamic regime adhering to anti-Israeli ideology.

Israel's perception of the threat posed by Iran has intensified over the past 20 years. Iran has made its intentions clear. Iranian leaders have repeatedly declared that Israel has no right to exist and should be wiped off the earth. The Israeli perception is that Iran has continuously shown that it is serious by assisting any party willing to act violently against Israel and putting pressure on those groups to bolster their activities against Israel. This has been a comprehensive policy executed without exceptions. Assistance has been given to Shiite groups, such as Hizballah, in Lebanon and to some Sunni groups, including some Palestinian terror groups associated with Fatah that were operating in the West Bank. In fact, Iran was using these groups as proxies in its war against Israel.[12]

Currently, Iran does not possess capabilities that enable it to pose a direct threat to Israel. Its vast army does not pose a threat because of its distance from Israel. Its air force capabilities are very limited, especially from distant ranges. It has a small inventory of long range ballistic missiles that can reach Israel, but they would probably have difficulties penetrating the Israeli missile defense shield in meaningful numbers.[13] Iran is intensifying Israeli threat perceptions, however, by the anticipation that Iran may acquire nuclear weapon capabilities that will be combined with its proven hostile intentions towards Israel.

Following the Israeli attack and destruction of Osiraq, the Iraqi reactor, in 1981, many researchers proposed that Israel had adopted a comprehensive preventive counter-proliferation doctrine sometimes referred to as the "Begin Doctrine." This may be the Israeli doctrine, but its application is dependent upon the feasibility of carrying out such a course of action and its costs.[14]

The execution of this policy is especially tough in the case of Iran for a number of reasons: Iran's distance from Israel and the lack of closer bases from which Israel can operate; the potential global repercussions of such an Israeli operation, such as its potential effect on the global energy market leading to a dramatic increase in the price of oil; and potential Iranian reprisals against Israel.[15]

These restraints have two main implications. The first is a clear preference of the Israeli government for a political solution that would arrest the Iranian nuclear program short of a weapons capability. This solution should be based on a combination of sticks and carrots. A system of severe international sanctions—economic and political—would be applied against Iran as long as it does not stop its attempts to produce fissile material and other activities that have potential military use, combined with a threat of military attack.[16] On the other hand, the great powers need to show a willingness to assist Iran in nuclear enterprises that have no military implications. If such a political effort fails, Israel will very seriously consider the military option. The second major implication is that Israel might decide that the "Begin Doctrine" cannot be applied in the case of Iran because the military option is not viable, and Israel will have to face an extremely hostile state armed with nuclear weapons. That possibility is a source of deep concern in Israel.[17]

Part of the discourse surrounding this subject in Israel dwells on the question of whether the current Iranian regime can be considered a rational actor. Some argue that as an extreme Islamic government committed to its fatalistic ideology, it might make decisions that would not be considered rational according to Western norms. Others argue that the current regime is more pragmatic and rational than its rhetoric suggests, in the sense that it makes calculations of costs and benefits and decides accordingly. In either case it is acknowledged that the value system of this Iranian regime is different than that of Western societies; for example, it is thought that the value ascribed to human life is lower. There is a greater tendency to be willing to make sacrifices in human life for the greater good. That implies that this kind of regime might take greater risks than others. On the other hand, analysis of the Iranian modus operandi does not substantiate the assumption that Iran is willing to pay very high costs whether in human life or other resources unless it perceives no other choice. It is true that Iran suffered a very large number of casualties in the Iran-Iraq war, but that was in a war that it did not initiate and was considered an existential war from the point of view of the regime. The fact of the matter is that the regime took the painful decision to stop the war far absent of victory when the number of casualties started to mount and ballistic missile attacks on Iranian cities were causing a relatively large number of casualties among Iranian civilians. Since then, Iranian conduct has been characterized by caution. They are not averse to using violence against perceived adversaries, but they prefer not to be directly involved and to use proxies, thus minimizing the costs involved and possible retaliation. That is also the way Iran operates against Israel.[18]

Israel believes that the nuclearization of Iran may bring about a chain reaction of proliferation. Other actors in the Middle East, such as Egypt, Saudi Arabia, and Algeria, who were willing to accept Israel's nuclear option because it was undeclared and because Israel is perceived as a responsible actor in the region, may find it impossible to live with a nuclear-capable Iran without having a similar capability to deter it.[19]

All these developments and assumptions are leading to a situation in which, gradually, the deterrence of other regional nuclear powers is becoming the main purpose of the Israeli nuclear option. The other purpose of the nuclear option, as the ultimate insurance policy, is becoming less significant, but only in relative terms.

DOES ISRAEL HAVE REGIONAL AMBITIONS?

Nuclear programs are sometimes motivated by regional ambitions. There is a perception in Israel that one of Iran's main motivations in pursuing its nuclear program is a desire to gain the status of a regional power and have a hegemonic position in the Gulf area. That may also motivate a state like Egypt to follow Iran, because Egypt considers itself the leader of the Arab World and a leading player in the Islamic world. States tend to apply their way of thinking to other states and so there is a suspicion in the Arab World that Israel strives for hegemonic posture in the Middle East. This perception, for example, was one of the main determinants of Egypt's policies towards Israel during the Arms Control and Regional Security (ACRS) talks in the 1990s.‡ Egypt wished to curb what it considered Israel's growing connections with, and influence on, states in the Middle East.[20]

That is certainly not the Israeli perception. Israel looks upon itself as an inherently isolated state in the region because of its very character. It is a Jewish state in a region which is mostly Arab and predominantly Islamic. It is considered by many to be a foreign implant on the region's soil. Its presence is accepted as fact but that does not mean that it is liked. How can a state that is in such a situation have ambitions for regional leadership or hegemony? Actually, Israel is somewhat schizophrenic about its own identity as a Middle Eastern state because it considers itself a part of the West, linked more strongly to Europe than to the Middle East. That was the reason Shimon Peres' ideas of the "New Middle East" were received with scorn by many Israelis. Some activities initiated by Mr. Peres to make progress toward this "New Middle East" were among the reasons that created a perception

---

‡The Arms Control and Regional Security Group was one of the multilateral negotiations groups that were established following the Madrid Conference in 1991.

among some Arab observers of an Israeli drive towards leadership, while in reality they reflected only an Israeli desire to be accepted as a normal state.[§]

This lack of regional ambitions was one of the reasons behind Israel's motivation to retain a low nuclear profile and to remain faithful for so many years to the policy of nuclear opacity.

DOES ISRAEL HAVE GLOBAL NUCLEAR AMBITIONS?

Israel does not pretend to be a power on the world stage. Through all its history, it has always been anxious to have a world power as its ally, being aware of its inherent weakness as a small isolated nation that does not belong to any block. Ironically, only in 2008, sixty years after it was admitted to the organization, did one of the groups of states that exist in the UN (the European group) agree to accept Israel as a member state. Therefore, the Israelis believe it is ridiculous to expect that the nuclear option would grant Israel with prestige and power in the global arena.

However, that does not mean that the Israeli nuclear option has no role in the global arena. It serves also as a deterrent vis-à-vis global powers and the international community. The aim of the deterrent on this level is not to deter global powers from attacking Israel. Israel is not concerned about the possibility of attacks by non-regional powers. Israel perceives that many of the world's powers are concerned about scenarios that might push Israel to realize its nuclear option. These concerns provide strong motivation for world powers to prevent the occurrence of such scenarios. In fact, Israel presents two alternatives to the world community: help us to remove threats to our existence or we will be pushed to do things that you will regret. Realizing the first alternative, of course, serves the Israeli objective of preventing the realization of existential threats, while not forcing its nuclear option.

One example that shows the effect of the Israeli nuclear option on the global stage is the US commitment to maintain the qualitative edge of Israel's armed forces. For many years, the US was reluctant to become Israel's weapon supplier. It changed its policy during the Kennedy Administration, and it seems that information about the Israeli nuclear program exposed during this period played an important role in the president's decision, because he was aware of the linkage between the Israeli nuclear program and Israel's levels of threat perception. In the meetings between President Kennedy and Prime Minister Eshkol and in the exchange of letters among

---

[§] Mr. Peres' "New Middle East" idea was his program to create a regional community that would live in peace and openness and have strong mutual economic ties in the Middle East. During the 1990s, he initiated a number of regional conferences to discuss economic cooperation. In the Arab world, prone to conspiracy theories, it led to a suspicion that after failing to achieve regional hegemony with its military superiority, Israel was trying to achieve the same goal with its economic power.

them that followed, Eshkol's main goal was the creation of a link between the Israeli nuclear program and US attentiveness to Israeli security demands, which he felt he achieved.[21] Another example is the 1973 war, considered the only case in which there was real debate by Israeli leaders about exercising the nuclear option. It is assumed that this was a major US consideration in deciding, after some delay, to provide replenishment to Israel through air lifts and in giving massive military assistance to Israel after the war.[22]

ISRAEL'S NUCLEAR PLANS

As previously stated, there is a great deal of uncertainty about the true extent of Israel's nuclear capabilities. It is generally assumed that Israel is the sixth nuclear nation in terms of the size of its arsenal. It is widely believed that Israel's status as a nuclear weapon state resembles that of the old members of the nuclear club (such as France and the UK) in terms of the quality of its arsenal, delivery means, and command and control more closely than that of the new members (such as India and Pakistan),[23] but there is no authoritative information on the composition and quality of Israel's arsenal. Speculation on the number of warheads range from 60 to 200, and cover the full range from mines and shells to large thermonuclear weapons, once again with no authoritative information.**

The assumption that Iran may succeed in obtaining nuclear weapon capabilities leads to speculation that Israel may consider modifications to its current nuclear posture. Those considerations probably would focus on three subjects: (1) what should be done to strengthen Israel's deterrence? (2) how much and in what way would the relationship with the US contribute to the deterrence of Iran? and (3) How will it influence Israel's public policy; namely, how will it affect the nuclear opacity policy?

Concerning Israeli indigenous capabilities, the main question will probably be whether Israel can achieve sufficient deterrence by presenting a credible second strike capability. Answers to that question may have implications for the nuclear arsenal itself, but, more importantly, may affect the delivery means. It is assumed that Israel has a variety of delivery options that include Jericho II ballistic missiles and its fleet of F-16 and F-15 aircraft. It may be that media reports about Israel's acquisition of German manufactured submarines that are equipped with Israeli manufactured cruise missiles are an indication of first steps being taken to enhance Israel's second strike capability.[24] There is no real public discourse on these subjects and no authoritative information, although there have been some beginnings of academic discussion.[25]

**According to a US Defense Intelligence Agency report issued in 1999, Israel had 60-80 nuclear weapons. According to the 2007 SIPRI report, Israel has 100-200 nuclear weapons.

Israel will have to strike a balance between its dependence on its own deterrent and dependence on US extended deterrence. Decision makers are obviously aware of the inherent problems of extended deterrence and its credibility. Would the US be willing to threaten Iran with the use of nuclear weapons and face the possible scenario of a nuclear clash with another nuclear power, albeit a small one, for Israel? How much can Israel trust such assurances?

Israel must also consider how it could build a US-Israel relationship that would make extended deterrence more credible. Could the conclusion of a defense treaty be an effective way of doing it? The discussion of the feasibility and desirability of such a defense treaty is public and open, although not always related directly to the question of nuclear deterrence.[26]

The need to project a credible deterrent posture may finally lead Israel to re-evaluate the efficacy of the "nuclear opacity policy."[27] There is no previous experience with a stable balance of deterrence between two nuclear powers in a situation in which one of the powers declares and exposes its capabilities to cause unbearable pain to the other side. It is possible that Israel would decide that "opacity" makes deterrence too fragile, and that Israel has no alternative but to radically change its exposure policy, with the possible political pressure put on Israel to disarm. The decision will, of course, be dependent on Iran's conduct. Will it move itself to an overt nuclear posture or emulate the Israeli policy of nuclear opacity?

PROLIFERATION CONCERNS

According to the Israeli mindset, the proliferation effects of a successful Iranian program in military nuclear development should be a major source of concern. Although it may be possible to achieve a stable balance of mutual deterrence between Israel and Iran, the nuclearization of Iran could accelerate nuclear proliferation in the Middle East. It is not a coincidence that in the 11 months between February 2006 and January 2007, at least 13 countries in the Middle East announced new or revived plans to pursue civilian nuclear energy.[28] The reasons are not the rising costs of fossil energy, which are often cited, but political considerations stemming from the concerns raised by Iran's nuclear program. The purpose of some of these announcements may be to deliver a message to the international community that Iran should be stopped, otherwise further proliferation is unavoidable. However, Israel has to take into account that some of these announcements may reflect real intentions. Thus, it seems reasonable that a state such as Egypt, which perceives itself as a major Middle Eastern power and the leader of the Arab world, would find it very difficult to withstand a situation in which the only two perceived nuclear powers in the Middle East are non-Arab states.

ISRAEL'S PAST APPROACH TOWARDS NUCLEAR ARMS CONTROL IN THE MIDDLE EAST

Israel's traditional approach to nuclear arms control in the Middle East is schizophrenic. On the one hand, Israel acknowledges the importance of the NPT as a global regime that for a long time was quite successful in limiting the proliferation of nuclear weapons and creating a norm of non-proliferation. On the other hand, Israel is not willing to join the NPT and give up its own nuclear option. This contradictory, and some would say "hypocritical" approach, is manifested clearly by the Israeli policy on establishing a Nuclear Weapons Free Zone (NWFZ) in the Middle East. On the one hand, the Israeli government adopted this idea rhetorically as part of the broader concept of establishing a zone free of surface-to-surface missiles and of chemical, biological and nuclear weapons in the Middle East, with adherence to the agreement verifiable by each of the parties.[29] On the other hand, Israel was not willing to actually enter talks to establish the zone and treated the idea more as a visionary goal that might be implemented in the context of a comprehensive peace in the Middle East. The debate between Egypt and Israel on that subject was one of the main reasons that, in 1995, led to the end of talks in the framework of the Arms Control and Regional Security group (ACRS) that was part of the Multilateral Middle East peace talks begun at the Madrid conference in 1992.[30]

The place of nuclear arms control on the official Israeli agenda and in unofficial discourse depends on two main parameters: the level of external pressure and the level of optimism about possible developments in the peace process. Global initiatives, especially when they come from the US, force the Israeli government to consider nuclear arms control ideas and decide on a position. Moreover, at a time of optimism, when the general perception is that there has been progress in the peace process, threat perceptions change and there is a greater willingness to take risks and consider arms control ideas that may limit Israel's military capabilities along with those of its adversaries.

For both those reasons, arms control was relatively higher on the Israeli agenda during the first half of the 1990s, at the height of the peace process. It gradually faded away when the peace process stumbled into serious difficulties, and it completely disappeared from Israel's agenda at the beginning of the present decade when the Bush Administration adopted a negative policy towards arms control initiatives in general.

If one wishes to understand Israel's policy toward nuclear arms control, it is necessary to revisit Israeli policy statements during the 1990s and analyze what effect the last decade's developments may have had on Israeli positions. Probably the most authoritative presentation of Israel's arms control policies was made by a former director general of the Israeli Ministry of Foreign Affairs, Ambassador Eytan Bentsur, in a statement before the UN Conference on Disarmament on September 4, 1997.[31] In this statement, Bentsur listed the guiding principles of Israel's approach to regional security, arms control, and disarmament.

- Peace must come with security—meaning that even in times of comprehensive peace, Israel cannot give up the security capabilities that offset its strategic vulnerabilities and disadvantageous disparities vis-à-vis neighboring states.
- The peace process should be free of terrorism and violence—states using these instruments cannot be partners in any regional security process and arms control negotiations.
- Regional cooperation is an essential part of security and stability.
- Peace and normalization are one and indivisible.

One important implication of these principles is that the Israeli approach to arms control is regional. Global conventions and regimes are important, but they do not respond effectively to the specific problems and characteristics of the Middle East. Based on the four general principles, Ambassador Bentsur proceeded to list several basic premises:

- Arms control and the regional security process should enhance the security of every state participating in it. This premise reflects the perception in Israel that, from the point of view of the Arab states, the purpose of the arms control process is to weaken Israel by denying it the capabilities that offset its vulnerabilities.
- All steps taken in such a process should increase the overall stability of the region.
- Each state is entitled to equally high levels of overall security, defined as the freedom from threats to its existence and well-being.
- Every state has the right to define the threats it considers relevant to its own security – arms control and regional security process should provide adequate responses to these defined threats.
- The process should take into account not only individual states, but also possible coalitions – any agreement that is based on the conception of a balance of forces should take into account that Israel may face different potential Arab/Muslim anti-Israel coalitions in the Middle East.

In the next phase of the presentation, Bentsur provided the main guidelines for the Israeli positions on arms control and regional security processes:

- The peace process is paramount and the eventual peace must be durable and comprehensive.
- The peace process must be regional and embrace every state in the region. Confidence building and security measures have to be developed within this framework.
- A step-by-step approach is required—any attempt to rush the process will make it collapse.
- The progress achieved in the transformation of the region into a more peaceful, stable, and secure environment will govern the pace and scope of the negotiation and implementation of arms control measures.

Ambassador Bentsur concluded his statement by elaborating Israel's positions on specific arms control initiatives, among them several relating to nuclear arms control:

- The Non-Proliferation Treaty – Israel supports the NPT but <u>does not</u> find it an adequate response to its own security problems and regional concerns, so Israel does not intend to become a signatory-state.
- The Comprehensive Nuclear-Test-Ban Treaty (CTBT) – Israel signed the CTBT and is cooperating in making its monitoring mechanism reliable.

That was the approach when there was still some hope that the peace process would positively change Israel's strategic environment and would eliminate some of the threats that it faces. The collapse of the Oslo Process after the failure of the Camp David summit in 2000 and the long years of bloody conflict with the Palestinians that followed, coupled with the war in Lebanon in the summer of 2006, have certainly hardened Israeli positions on arms control. First, there is a general feeling that threats to Israel have become more severe and therefore Israel cannot do anything that may hurt its strategic insurance policy. Second, there is a general lack of confidence in Israel's ability to deal with security threats in the traditional ways it dealt with them in the past. The less than satisfying performance of the Israeli Defense Force in the war in Lebanon contributed much to this feeling of insecurity. Third, there is great suspicion of the intentions of Israel's Arab neighbors. This results in suspicion that any agreement concluded with them, including arms control agreements, would probably be violated. The perception in Israel is that a number of Arab and Muslim Middle Eastern states (Iran, Libya, and Syria) that are signatories of the NPT violated the treaty and were engaged in covert nuclear weapon programs. Given these past violations, why would Israel sign a treaty that would deny it an essential security asset while giving its adversaries opportunities to cheat and gain a clear advantage?

More generally, there is no discourse on regional cooperation. A deep sense of disappointment in the peace process dominates the Israeli landscape and the public does not want any more illusions. Past statements by former Prime Minister and current President Shimon Peres about a "New Middle East" that would create cooperation among a variety of issues are being ridiculed. It is very difficult to sell ideas on cooperative security in this atmosphere; instead there is a growing tendency to take unilateral steps. Former Prime Minister Sharon's plan of unilateral disengagement from some of the Palestinian territories was one indication of this trend. Another indication was the Israeli decision following the receipt of reliable intelligence on the building of a secret plutonium production reactor in Syria to destroy it instead of filing a complaint with the IAEA. In Israel, unilateral counter-proliferation reigns and cooperative non-proliferation is not trusted.

The end result is that although there are no declaratory changes in Israel's arms control policies and the sets of principles and premises listed by Ambassador Bentsur are still valid, they are considered to be a set of conditions that will not be fulfilled at any future date. Shelving the idea of becoming more engaged in arms control became easier because of the corresponding change in the US arms control stance. It is always easier for Israel to follow US policies. Under these circumstances, Israel expects no real pressure to change its arms control policies.

MOVING TO ZERO

Following the early general elections that took place in Israel in February 2009, a new coalition government was formed by Prime Minister Benjamin Netanyahu. This coalition is composed mostly of right wing parties, and as such will probably adopt a tougher and more hawkish policy on security matters then the previous government. The change of government will make it less probable that Israel will be forthcoming towards a Global Zero initiative than it would be under a center-left government, which would inherently be more attentive to international initiatives.

In any event, a necessary condition for any Israeli government to respond positively to a zero nuclear weapons initiative is the adoption of such an initiative by the US administration. Israeli leaders would not pay attention to such an initiative if it were to come from other actors. Israeli leaders believe that the US would shoot down the initiative and Israel would not really have to deal with it. Israeli attention to the initiative would also be dependent on Israel's assessment of the seriousness of the US in pursuing the initiative: how determined it is and its willingness to put real pressure on Israel to implement the initiative. Israel faced down earlier US arms control initiatives that it did not like because the US was not serious enough. One example was President George H.W. Bush's Middle East arms control initiative that was announced in May 1991 after the first Gulf War in a speech made by Mr. Bush at the Air Force Academy. The initiative suggested a cut-off of fissile material production and elimination of ballistic missiles in the Middle East.[32] The proposal was opposed by Israel and others in the Middle East and faded away very quickly. At that time, the Bush Administration was not determined enough to make it happen and decided to withdraw the idea after it was met with negative responses in the Middle East. In the future, depending on US actions, Israeli leaders may assume that, although the US has adopted the vision of the global elimination of nuclear weapons, it does not really intend to implement the idea in the hope that other actors will shoot it down.

Even if this pre-condition was fulfilled and the Israeli leadership became convinced that the US administration was serious, Israel would probably try to postpone its engagement in negotiations for a treaty to eliminate nuclear weapons by a specific date for as long as possible. Israelis are great believers in "slippery slope" theories, which is natural for a small state such as Israel. They believe that once Israel joins negotiations of this kind, it will face great difficulties in weathering pressure to make incremental concessions to its basic positions that will build up to a fundamental change in positions. Former Prime Minister Sharon used the metaphor of cattle in a slaughterhouse for such situations. The cattle are pushed towards fences that make the space around them gradually narrower and narrower until they face the knife of the meat packer.[33]

The main obstacles, which would have to be overcome before Israel could consider nuclear disarmament seriously, are Israel's deep sense of insecurity (strengthened by recent events such as the war in Lebanon) and its mistrust of the effectiveness of global regimes in the specific Middle East regional environment. Assuming that the US and other nuclear powers adopted the idea of eliminating nuclear weapons globally and wished to convince Israel to cooperate with this idea, they will have to deal with these two important issues. The two issues are connected to the Middle East itself, and no out-of-region developments, including developments in Europe, could influence Israeli actions.

Israel would feel more secure if there was serious progress in the peace process and if significant steps were taken against the main challengers of the peace process— Iran and Syria—that also pose central threats to Israel's security. If steps were taken to neutralize the Iranian threat, if Syria were taken out of the group of states that are in conflict with Israel, and if real progress towards a settlement with the Palestinians were achieved, the Israeli leadership would be much more open to arms control ideas, as it was during the first half of the 1990s. The US, as well as other world powers, would have to deal with these problems before approaching Israel with an initiative that Israel would perceive as a demand to give up its insurance policy against existential threats.

Assuming that it is unlikely for the Iranian, Syrian, and Palestinian conflicts all to be resolved in the next few years, other options for strengthening Israel's self-confidence may be considered as a way of making Israel more open to nuclear disarmament ideas. One such idea that is already part of the discourse in Israel, albeit in limited circles, would be a proposal to offer Israel a formal defense treaty with the US and/or membership in NATO. The purpose of such a proposal would be to offer Israel compensation for what it may deem a weakening of its ability to defend itself. These ideas are very controversial in Israel, and strong voices argue that the price Israel would have to pay for a defense treaty with the US or membership in NATO, in terms of loss of freedom of action and the damage to its indigenous defense capabilities, far surpass the advantages of these two ideas.[34] Given the strength of these concerns, it is doubtful that an offer of this kind would convince Israel to join a global zero initiative. It is more probable that if the government of Israel agreed to the idea of global zero because the previously mentioned conditions had been met, it would ask as a pre-condition for a package of steps that would shore up its security; and a defense treaty with the US or membership in NATO may be part of such a package. Israelis appreciate the contribution of the US and other allies to their security, but as an addition, not as a replacement for their own capabilities. The ethos of being able to defend itself plays a major role in the Israeli psyche.

In short, the US and its partners in a disarmament initiative will have to deal with the question of how to adapt the initiative to Middle Eastern realities. They may have to take steps to devise a regional monitoring and enforcement system that would be more strict and reliable then what may be needed in other regions. The Israelis maintain that international norms are not accepted as widely in the Middle East. For example, even when non-use of chemical weapons was an entrenched international norm, various actors in the Middle East made use of them anyway.[††] Additionally, more then one Middle Eastern nation has assumed that signing on to international treaties does not imply that they necessarily have to comply with them, as has been the case with several signatories of the NPT. From the point of view of Israel, arms control will have no real value without very strong regional mechanisms for verification and compliance. But even the inclusion of such mechanisms in a treaty would not be sufficient if there were no real determination to implement them. For example, there is disappointment in Israel about the way the Chemical Weapons Convention (CWC) is implemented. The Convention includes very strong monitoring mechanisms, such as challenge inspections, but they are not being utilized. There are strong suspicions in Israel that Iran, a signatory of the CWC, has not complied with its commitments and the Organization for the Prohibition of Chemical Weapons (OPCW), the agency established for this purpose,

---

[††] Egypt in Yemen (1963-1966), Iraq and Iran (1982-1988), Libya in Chad (1981).

is not using the strong enforcement instruments available in the CWC because of political reasons.[35]

Finally, Israel will make a strong connection between its approach toward a nuclear disarmament initiative and the positions of the other Middle Eastern states. That means that such an initiative would not be considered as long as other Middle Eastern states refused to accept it. Moreover, Israel would have a problem with a nuclear disarmament initiative if it were not also connected to the disarmament of chemical weapons, biological weapons, and ballistic missiles. Any progress towards nuclear disarmament would be conditional upon full acceptance by all Middle Eastern states.

END-STATES

When push comes to shove and it becomes clear to Israel's leadership that Iran is not going to be prevented from acquiring nuclear weapons by international sanctions, dialogue, or preventive military attacks, either because there is no way of stopping the Iranian program or because the costs are too high, Israel will consider two possible ways of dealing with the new situation. The first is to live with a mutual balance of terror based on the threat of mutually assured destruction. That would compel Israel to make large investments to acquire credible second strike capabilities. Moreover, Israel would still be left with strong doubts about how reliable its nuclear deterrence could be in a multi-nuclear environment characterized by high levels of hostility to Israel. The second alternative is to look for a way to turn the Middle East into a nuclear-free zone, acknowledging that there are severe doubts concerning the implementation of such an agreement and concerns that giving up the nuclear insurance policy would create a situation in which it would be easier for Israel's adversaries to pose other threats to Israel. Currently, given the heightened security concerns of Israelis and high level of mistrust of the other parties in the Middle East, it seems that the choice would be to continue to depend on nuclear deterrence.

Israel is pre-occupied with its own security concerns, and its attitude is influenced more by the regional situation than by developments in the global arena. The damage to the global nuclear regime caused by a nuclear arms race in the Middle East would be of minor concern to Israel, and would not play an important role in the decisions of the Israeli leadership. Global norms are important to Israel as long as they inhibit nuclearization of the Middle East. If the Middle East proves to be a region in which global norms do not play a real role, then they are of no real concern to Israel. Israel is not really concerned about the possibility that a nuclear conflict in some other area would overflow to its region. The question of whether there would be 20 or 30 nuclear weapon states on the globe by 2025 is of little concern to Israel, as long as they are not Middle Eastern states hostile to Israel.

An interesting question arises about the relationship between conventional balances of forces and a nation's willingness to eliminate all nuclear weapons. In the Israeli case, the original motivation for the decision to build a nuclear option was the concern that a combined land invasion of Israel by its Arab adversaries would pose an existential threat to the state of Israel. In recent decades, this threat has subsided. On one hand, the relationship between Israel and many Arab states has changed, and the political situation in the Middle East has made the formation of an anti-Israeli Arab military coalition unlikely. On the other hand, Israel succeeded in building conventional military capabilities that surpass the capabilities of its potential adversaries. These developments may lead Israel to become more agreeable to ideas of nuclear disarmament. One may also argue that similar developments have occurred in the global arena; the largest powers will probably maintain their conventional weapons superiority in a world without nuclear weapons, and therefore be able to maintain some measure of world order. Israel, in contrast to India and some others, is not concerned by such a prospect. The largest powers are not threatening Israel and their ability to maintain some world order is a stabilizing factor that may contribute to the removal of existential threats to Israel.

Nevertheless, it is doubtful whether this kind of argument in favor of nuclear disarmament would make inroads in Israel. Israel's understanding is that the collapse of the Soviet Union did not lead to a new world order, but to a new world disorder. The international environment is now more anarchic then it used to be, and military superiority of the largest power is not sufficient to instill order in this chaos. The best example of this failure is the repercussions of the US attempt to reform the Middle East by use of force in Iraq.

Israelis also think that political environments can change, especially in the volatile Middle East, and there is no guarantee that Israeli conventional military superiority can be retained indefinitely. The Israelis had a sobering experience in the 2006 war in Lebanon, in which a ruthless adversary succeeded in bypassing Israel's military superiority by engaging in a war of terror against its citizens.

CONCLUSIONS

In the current regional context, it will be extremely difficult to convince the government of Israel or the Israeli public that moving to zero nuclear weapons is good for Israel.

This may change if real steps are taken to change the regional environment and if this nuclear initiative is connected to complete chemical weapons, biological weapons, and ballistic missiles disarmament in the region. Israel would also have to be convinced that an agreement on the global elimination of nuclear weapons would have effective regional monitoring and compliance mechanisms that would be utilized if violations take place. That will be something very difficult to sell to a suspicious Israeli audience.

The Israeli government would be in a difficult position if all the nuclear powers joined a disarmament initiative. In such a case there will be no nation Israel could hide behind to wait for the initiative to be shot down. In such a situation, it is difficult to make a credible forecast of Israel's capability to withstand the pressure of the great powers. What is quite certain is the fact that Israel would fight hard.

ENDNOTES

[1] Avner Cohen, Israel and the Bomb (New York: Columbia University Press, 1998), pages 9-14.

[2] See, for example, Ariel Levite and Emily Landau, Israel's Nuclear Image – Arab Perceptions of Israel's Nuclear Posture (Tel Aviv: Tel Aviv University – Papyrus Press, 1994), page 43; in Hebrew.

[3] See Shai Feldman, Israeli Nuclear Deterrence: A Strategy for the 1980s (New York: Columbia University Press, 1982).

[4] Avner Cohen, op. cit., pages 235-9.

[5] Ibid., page 238.

[6] See, for example, MK Yuval Steinitz, Chairman of the Knesset Committee for Foreign Policy and Security Policy, warning against US weapon deals with Egypt and Saudi Arabia and asserting that they may turn into enemies of Israel, in Yuval Steinitz, "Egypt, Israel and the Harpoon Missile," Jerusalem Post (March 29, 2002); Moshe Arens, former minister of defense, writing about the Islamic threat to the Arab regimes, in Moshe Arens, "Those that Use Democracy to Hurt Democracy," Haaretz (November 13, 2001).

[7] Nuclear Programmes in the Middle East – In the Shadow of Iran, an IISS Strategic Dossier (London: The International Institute for Strategic Studies, 2008), page 128.

[8] Amir Oren, "What Did Deter Saddam?" Haaretz (March 27, 2008).

[9] "Prime Minister Yitzhak Shamir and Defense Minister Moshe Arens have both repeatedly pledged to respond massively in the advent of any Iraqi attack," according to David Makovsky, "Scenarios: will Israel hit Iraq?," Jerusalem Post (January 4, 1991). "The Jewish state has repeatedly vowed to make Iraq pay a 'horrible and terrible' price for any chemical attack, a clear hint that it would retaliate with chemical or even nuclear arms. Frightened Jews are a very dangerous people, said Gen. Peled." Anton La Guardia, "The Middle East: Israelis Face Bloody Price of First War on Civilians," The Daily Telegraph (November 10, 1990). Former Prime Minister Rabin said: "Israel has a response that will inflict multiple pains," On Levy, Daniel Ben-Simon, and Dan Avidan, "Rabin's Reaction to Saddam Hussein's Threats, Israel Has a Response that Will Inflict Multiple Pains on Iraq," Davar (April 3, 1990). In another article, Gerald M. Steinberg, "Can Saddam Hussein Be Deterred?" Jerusalem Post (August 10, 1990), the author analyzes the Israeli strategic thinking about the best way to deter Saddam Hussein.

[10] Allison Kaplan and Bradley Burston, "Israel Missile Test Alarms Gulf Force," Jerusalem Post (December 23, 1990).

[11] Seymour M. Hersh, The Samson Option: Israel's Nuclear Arsenal and American Foreign Policy (New York: Random House, 1991), pages 291, 312, 319.

[12] Ephraim Kam, From Terror to Nuclear Bombs: The Significance of the Iranian Threat, (Tel Aviv: Ministry of Defense Press, 2004), pages 248-256, 263-280 (in Hebrew).

[13] Anthony Cordesman, Iran: "Hegemon" or "Weakling," (Washington, DC: Center for Strategic and International Studies, March 2, 2007).

[14] Shlomo Brom, "Is the Begin Doctrine Still a Viable Option for Israel?" In Henry Sokolsky and Patrick Clawson, eds., Getting Ready for a Nuclear-Ready Iran, (Carlisle, PA: Strategic Studies Institute, 2005), pages 137-138.

[15] See the analysis of possible repercussions in Ephraim Kam, A Nuclear Iran: What Does it Mean, and What Can be Done, (Tel Aviv: INSS, Memorandum 88, February 2008), pages 32-45.

[16] Interview of Ms. Zippi Livni, Israel's Foreign Minister, on Israeli radio station on Dec. 24, 2006: http://www.mfa.gov.il/MFAHeb/Foreign+Minister/FM+Livni+speeches+and+interview/Fm+Livni+interview+-+sanctions+against+Iran+241206.htm (in Hebrew).

[17] Avner Cohen, "Israel: A Sui Generis Proliferator," in Muthiah Alagappa, ed., The Long Shadow – Nuclear Weapons and Security in 21st Century Asia, (Stanford, CA: Stanford University Press, 2008), pages 259-261.

[18] Kam, op.cit., pages 248-83; Shimon Shapira. Hizballah, Between Iran and Lebanon (Tel Aviv: Hakibutz Hameuhad, 2000).

[19] See, for example, the analysis in "Nuclear Programmes in the Middle East - In the Shadow of Iran, An IISS Strategic Dossier (London: IISS, 2008).

[20] Emily Landau, Egypt and Israel in ACRS: Bilateral Concerns in a Regional Arms Control Process, (Tel Aviv: JCSS, Memorandum No. 59, June 2001).

[21] Zaki Shalom, Between Dimona and Washington – The Struggle for the Development of Israel's Nuclear Option, 1960-1968 (Beer Sheva: Ben Gurion University Press, 2004), pages 118-128 (in Hebrew).

[22] Nuclear Programmes in the Middle East, op. cit., page 28.

[23] Ibid., page 131.

[24] Nuclear Programmes in the Middle East, op. cit., pages 133-134.

[25] Ephraim Kam, op. cit.

[26] See, for example, Ministry of Foreign Relations, Report of the Second Forum on Israel-USA Relations (June 29, 2006), http://www.mfa.gov.il/MFAHeb/Department+activities/north+america/Israel-Usa+Forum+280606.htm;

Zvi Gil, "A Defense Treaty with the USA," Bama Magazine (June 11, 2006), http://stagemag.co.il/Articles/682;

Ami Dor-On, "A Balance of Terror Against the Terror Plague" (July 3, 2008), http://www.nfc.co.il/ArticlePrintVersion.aspx?docId=27171&subjectID=3.

[27] Kam, *op. cit.,* pages 79-80.

[28] Nuclear Programmes in the Middle East, *op. cit.,* pages 7-8.

[29] "A Farewell to Chemical Arms," Address by the Foreign Minister of Israel, Mr. Shimon Peres, at the Signing Ceremony of the Chemical Weapons Convention Treaty, Paris (13 January 1993), http://www.fas.org/news/israel/93011-peres.htm.

[30] Emily B. Landau, Arms Control in the Middle East – Cooperative Security Dialogue and Regional Constraints (Brighton: Sussex Academic Press, 2006), pages 46-48.

[31] "Israel's Approach to Regional Security, Arms Control and Disarmament," Statement by H.E. Mr. Eytan Bentsur, Director General of the Ministry of Foreign Affaires, before the Conference on Disarmament, Geneva (4 September 1997), http://www.mfa.gov.il/MFA/MFAArchive/1990_1999/1997/9/Israel-s%20Approach%20to%20Regional%20Security-%20Arms%20Contr.

[32] Andrew Rosenthal, "Bush unveils plans for arms control in the Middle East," New York Times (May 30, 1991).

[33] Aluf Ben, "A Successor, not a Follower," Haaretz (August 12, 2005).

[34] See, for example, a report on a discussion on this subject carried out under the auspices of the Israeli Ministry of Foreign Affairs in June 2006, http://www.mfa.gov.il/MFAHeb/Department+activities/north+america/Israel-Usa+Forum+280606.htm?DisplayMode=print (in Hebrew)

[35] Shmuel Limone, "The Chemical and Biological Weapons Conventions," Strategic Assesment, Vol. 7, No. 1 (May 2004); Interview with Col. (ret) Shmuel Limone, member of the Israeli observer delegation to the Conference of the States Parties of the OPCW (December 20070.

REALISTIC PROACTIVISM:
JAPANESE ATTITUDES TOWARD GLOBAL ZERO

*Matake Kamiya**

US President Barack Obama's speech in Prague on April 5, 2009 declared "America's commitment to seek the peace and security of a world without nuclear weapons," and was warmly received by Japan. The very next day, Prime Minister Taro Aso expressed his support for Obama's speech to reporters by saying, "[i]t was a wonderful speech. It is a very positive trend that the United States, who possesses nuclear weapons, addresses [the issue of nuclear elimination] seriously."[1] Obama's recognition that "[a]s the only nuclear power to have used a nuclear weapon, the United States has a moral responsibility to act" was particularly esteemed in Japan as a courageous remark.[2] Moved by the speech, Mayor Tadatoshi Akiba of the city of Hiroshima, where the first atomic bomb used in war was detonated on August 6, 1945, launched the "'Obamajority' campaign" to expand international support for the goal of a "world free of nuclear weapons."[3]

In Japan, it has been generally understood that President Obama's declaration about the desirability of eliminating nuclear weapons is closely related to the Global Zero movement. For instance, an article in the May 29 issue of the Japan Atomic Energy Commission magazine discussed the launch of Global Zero at a conference in December 2008 and its announcement of a plan for the next 25 to 40 years leading to the phased elimination of nuclear weapon. The magazine said that, "President Obama's speech in Prague was indeed the declaration that the United States will assume leadership to take the first step to that direction."[4] One of Japan's largest national daily newspapers, *Asahi Shimbun,* reported that President Obama, despite North Korea's nuclear test only several hours before his historic speech, delivered his planned speech on nuclear disarmament[5] Taken together, Global Zero and Obama's speech have been received in Japan as indications that issues of nuclear disarmament and nuclear abolition, which had historically been dominated by idealists, are now led by realistic security thinkers, as well as political leaders, all over the world.[6]

Despite an initial warm reception, however, the overall Japanese reaction to Global Zero and Obama's speech in Prague has been cautious and modest. Many mainstream security thinkers in Japan have pointed out the importance of observing

*Matake Kamiya is a professor of international relations at the National Defense Academy of Japan. The views expressed in this paper are the author's own and do not represent those of the National Defense Academy or of Japan's Ministry of Defense.

the backdrop of such developments carefully. They have pointed out that the motivations behind such movements include fear of accelerating nuclear proliferation and increasing fear of nuclear use.[7] Given the realities of the early 21st century, it will be necessary to construct a totally new mechanism of world order and international security to realize a world free of nuclear weapons. Such a total transformation of the world will surely take time, which may explain why President Obama said that a world free of nuclear weapons would perhaps be unattainable during his lifetime.[8] Obama's speech on April 5 demonstrated his determination to achieve the goal of nuclear abolition. In reality, however, a world with nuclear weapons will, as Obama himself admits, last for many more years. In this situation, the president's seriousness about nuclear disarmament has to be buttressed by sober consideration of the world order during the period when the world is moving to a world free of nuclear weapons but will still have (a decreasing number of) such weapons. A particularly vital question with regard to Japan's security during this period is: Is there any realistic security mechanism that can substitute for extended US nuclear deterrence and, if there is, how can it be achieved?[9] Former Foreign Minister Yoriko Kawaguchi also emphasized the necessity to demonstrate a "realistic alternative" to the US nuclear umbrella in order to change the minds of those who believe it to be a necessary part of Japan's security.[10] In short, although welcoming the growing momentum behind nuclear disarmament in the international community, Japan finds itself in a difficult gap between the ideal and reality.

Observing Japanese cautiousness toward Global Zero and Obama's speech, some foreign observers have started to express concerns about the possibility that Japan might develop its own nuclear weapons, particularly after North Korea conducted its second nuclear test on May 25, 2009.

For Japan, however, facing a dilemma between the non-nuclear ideal and the nuclear reality is not new at all. Throughout the post-World War II period, Japan has consistently been the earnest advocate of nuclear disarmament as the only country ever to have experienced nuclear devastation. At the same time, however, Japan has faced the nuclear arsenals of two giant neighbors, Russia and China, for many decades. Firmly maintaining its non-nuclear policy in a troubled security environment, Japan has relied upon the US extended nuclear deterrence within the framework of the US-Japan alliance.

Simultaneously facing the first opportunity to bring the world closer to its long-cherished ideal of nuclear elimination and the increasing danger of nuclear proliferation and even nuclear use, particularly in the area surrounding Japan, what changes have (or have not) taken place in Japan's threat perceptions? Have these changes brought about any alterations in Japan's nuclear plans and/or Japan's non-nuclear policy? What is Japan's perception of Global Zero? This paper attempts to answer these questions.

FACTORS THAT CONCEIVABLY COULD LEAD TO A NUCLEAR JAPAN

Foreign observers have often pointed out that both the continuing development of military, and especially nuclear, capabilities by Japan's neighbors and growing doubts about the US security commitment and nuclear umbrella might lead Japan at some future point to reconsider its non-nuclear weapon status.

Security Concerns

Three states in Japan's immediate vicinity – North Korea, China, and Russia – are modernizing and extending their military and nuclear capabilities, causing growing concern among Japanese officials and ordinary citizens. Of the three, North Korea is perceived as an immediate threat, China as a longer term danger, and Russian nuclear forces are barely mentioned.

North Korea's Nuclear and Missile Development

A series of provocative actions by North Korea could be considered nuclear brinksmanship, including underground nuclear detonations in October 2006 and May 2009. These have escalated tensions in Northeast Asia, but did not create panic among the Japanese, already inclined to think the worst of Pyongyang.

The Japanese, of course, were outraged by North Korea's behavior. On May 25, 2009, the day when North Korea conducted its second nuclear test, Japanese TV and radio news programs were filled with on-the-street interviews with Japanese people, each of them expressing anger, anxiety, and words of condemnation against the despicable action taken by Pyongyang. Japanese government and political leaders wasted no time to condemn the test. Immediately afterwards, the Japanese government protested to North Korea through the "embassy route" in Beijing.[11] On the same day, Prime Minister Taro Aso issued an official statement to condemn North Korea and said:

> A nuclear test by North Korea is totally unacceptable, as it constitutes a grave threat to Japan's security as well as seriously undermines the peace and security of Northeast Asia and the international community when taken together with North Korea's enhancement of its ballistic missile capability, which could serve as the means to deliver weapons of mass destruction.[12]

On May 26 and 27, both Lower and Upper Houses of Japan's Diet passed unanimously respective resolutions that condemned the test and called on the

Japanese government to, "take resolute measures, such as a strengthening of sanctions," against North Korea.[13]

On the international scene, the Japanese government moved quickly to formulate a wide international coalition against the nuclearization of North Korea. The test took place on the very day that the Asia-Europe Meeting (ASEM) was about to start in Hanoi. The Japanese government pressed for and received a joint statement condemning the test; separate from the conference's normal closing statement. The joint statement described the test as "a clear violation of the Six-Party agreements and the relevant UNSC [United Nations Security Council] resolutions and decisions."[14] Prime Minister Aso convened Japan's Security Council within nine hours of the test and requested a new UN Security Council sanctions resolution against Pyongyang.[15] On June 12, the UNSC unanimously adopted Resolution 1874, which "condemned [the test] in the strongest terms" and tightened sanctions against Pyongyang.[16]

In addition, the Japanese government unilaterally approved additional sanctions which go beyond those listed in UNSC Resolution 1874, including a total export ban to North Korea.[17] Japan had already imposed unilateral sanctions after North Korea's missile-launch in July 2006 and its first nuclear test in October of the same year, including a total ban on imports from North Korea and port calls by North Korean ships. Moreover, reacting to Pyongyang's Taepodong-II missile test in April 2009, Japan had just tightened its sanctions. The additional measures taken by Tokyo, therefore, are largely symbolic and can be expected to do only marginal economic damage to Pyongyang.

Japanese leaders have long seen North Korea as a serious threat to Japan's security, well before the country conducted nuclear tests. Such a threat perception was explicitly stated in the current "National Defense Program Guideline (NDPG)" of Japan, which was adopted in December 2004. In contrast to previous NDPGs, dating back to 1976 and which referenced an unstable situation on the Korean Peninsula but refrained from candidly indicating that North Korea posed a security threat to Japan, the 2004 NDPG called North Korea a "major destabilizing factor to regional and international security."*

---

* The Japanese government has formulated three "Boei Keikaku no Taiko (National Defense Program Outlines)", beginning in 1976. In 1995, the entirely new "National Defense Program Outline in and after 1996" was formulated in response to the drastic changes in the international security environment after the end of the Cold War. In 2004, the third of such documents, "National Defense Program Guideline in and after FY2005," was adopted so that Japan's security policy could meet the challenges of the post-9/11 era. (Although the English translation of the title of the document was changed from "outline" to "guideline," the title in Japanese remained the same as before: "Boei Keikaku no Taiko.") In this paper, the abbreviation "NDPG" is used for simplification. Currently, preparations to update the 2004 Guideline are underway. (The English translations of each of the three documents can be found at: "National Defense Program Outline" [http://www.ioc.u-tokyo.ac.jp/~worldjpn/documents/texts/docs/19761029.O1E.html]; "National Defense Program Outline in and after

North Korea is engaged in the development, deployment and proliferation of weapons of mass destruction and ballistic missiles, and it maintains a large number of special operations forces. Such military activities by North Korea constitute a major destabilizing factor to regional and international security, and are a serious challenge to international non-proliferation efforts.[18]

The government's threat perception is shared almost identically by its successor, the long-time opposition Democratic Party of Japan (DPJ), which handily won the August 31st election this year. On February 26, 2003, the Project Team on North Korea of the DPJ issued a document which explained the party's North Korea policy, and called North Korea's nuclear program "a grave problem that has influence on our nation," and insisted that ballistic missile tests by Pyongyang "may invite a serious threat to the security of our nation" and "a firm response will have to be taken."[19] The two nuclear tests by North Korea have certainly strengthened such threat perceptions among Japanese leaders. For instance, in a press conference held the day after the May 2009 test, Defense Minister Yasukazu Hamada was asked if he believed the test had heightened the military threat posed to Japan and replied:

> Of course, I do. If they improve the accuracy [of their nukes] by conducting nuclear tests, since they have recently shown a certain level of things with regard to delivery vehicle [by the Taepodong-II test in the previous month], certainly it is natural to think of them as threat.[20]

Japanese leaders' anger against, and sense of threat from, North Korea are real, and are widely shared by the general public. Public opinion polls have clearly shown that the sentiment of the Japanese people has become stronger following each of the two nuclear tests conducted by Pyongyang. In a public opinion survey conducted by the Japan Association for Public Opinion Research only four weeks before North Korea's first nuclear test, 38 percent of the respondents felt the threat of North Korea "very much," and 46 percent felt it "to some extent."[21] In a poll conducted by *Yomiuri Shimbun* immediately after the test, 81 percent of the respondents said that his/her threat perception of the North had become stronger. (Fifty-three percent chose the answer "has become stronger very much," and 28 percent chose "has become stronger to some extent.") In the same poll, 74 percent "support[ed]" tough UNSC sanctions resolution against North Korea, and 17 percent were "generally favorable" with regard to such a resolution. Nearly 70 percent also "support[ed]" the Japanese government's unilateral sanctions against Pyongyang, and 18 percent were "generally favorable" for such measures.[22] Another poll conducted by the *Asahi Shimbun* also revealed that the test raised the level of concern among the

FY 1996" [http://www.mofa.go.jp/region/n-america/us/q&a/ref/6a.html]; and "National Defense Program Outline, FY2005-" [http://www.kantei.go.jp/foreign/policy/2004/1210taikou_e.html].)

Japanese about Pyongyang. In the poll, 44 percent of the respondents felt a "strong threat" from North Korea, and 38 percent felt "some level of threat." In comparison, an earlier poll in July that year conducted by the same newspaper company found that 38 percent felt a "strong threat" and 39 percent felt "some level of threat." In the *Asahi* October poll, 62 percent of the respondents said that the international community should put more emphasis on sanctions than on talks with North Korea.[23]

The nuclear test in May 2009 has further hardened public sentiment against North Korea. In a poll taken by the semi-national Japan Broadcasting Corporation, known as NHK, from June 5-7, 65 percent of the respondents said that Japan should strengthen its unilateral sanctions against North Korea, while only eight percent said it did not need to do so.[24] In another poll taken by *Yomiuri Shimbun* during the same period, 88 percent of the respondents said the international community should strengthen sanctions against Pyongyang, while only six percent said it did not need to do so. Only 46 percent of the respondents, however, believed that international sanctions would actually lead to termination of North Korea's nuclear and missile development program. Forty-five percent believed that sanctions were unlikely to have such an effect.[25]

Despite their heightened anger and threat perception, it is noteworthy that the Japanese public has by and large reacted calmly to North Korea's brinkmanship. For example, on May 25, stock prices in Japan rebounded after three consecutive business days' of decline, "shrugging off jitters over North Korea's claimed nuclear test which unnerved some other key Asian markets."[†]

In the previous month, North Korea's demonstration of its delivery vehicle capacity by the launch of the Taepodon-II missile (which Pyongyang claimed to be an Unha-II rocket carrying a Kwangmyŏngsŏng-II satellite) also triggered a sharp but calm response from Japan. Prime Minister Aso, with a stern face, said to reporters that, "The launch by North Korea is an extremely provocative act and Japan absolutely cannot ignore it."[26] Japanese TV and radio stations immediately broadcast special reports about the launch. However, NHK TV's "News at Noon," which was broadcast only a half an hour after the launch, was extended by only 15 minutes.

The calm response by the Japanese public to the May 2009 test has been clearly reflected in the rapid decline of media coverage of the topic. For instance, Japan's largest national daily *Yomiuri Shimbun* carried 218 articles including the keywords "Kita-Chosen (North Korea)" and "kaku-jikken (nuclear test)" during the first week

---

[†] "Tokyo Stocks Rise Despite N. Korea Nuclear Test," *Kyodo News on the Web*, May 25, 2009, http://home.kyodo.co.jp/?%253Fid=1564 (accessed on May 25, 2009).

after the test. The number of articles, however, dropped to 47 for the second week, and continued to decline to 33, 29, and 18 for the third, fourth, and fifth weeks, respectively. In contrast, during the same five weeks, *Yomiuri* consistently maintained high coverage of the 2009 swine flu pandemic. The number of articles including the keyword "shingata-infuruenza (new type influenza)" that appeared in the *Yomiuri Shimbun* for the same five weeks, respectively, were: 338, 225, 238, 251, and 220.[27]

Japanese security experts Hajime Izumi and Katsuhisa Furukawa observed that the reaction in Japan to North Korea's first nuclear test in October 2006 was similarly "much more restrained than predicted by some foreign experts, particularly in the United States." The Japanese public was concerned about the development, as shown in the public opinion polls. However, "in general [the Japanese public] did not demonstrate active interest in taking any specific measures, such as establishing underground shelters," and "the Japanese media focused primarily on the radioactive contamination risks the test might pose to Japan." "Having recognized that such risk was almost nonexistent, the public interest on this issue faded away promptly,"[28]

In a public opinion survey on "public consciousness about risks" conducted by the Mitsubishi Research Institute, Inc. from Jun 9-10, 2009 which asked each respondent to name three developments between January and May 2009 which he or she found "most frightening," 32 percent chose "the new type influenza" as the most frightening, while 22 percent chose "the missile shooting and the nuclear test by North Korea."[29]

The relatively calm Japanese reaction to North Korea's nuclear brinkmanship reflects the perception that North Korea's nuclear weapons development is not an isolated issue, but part of a broader "North Korea problem" centered around nuclear weapons development, ballistic missiles development, and abductions.

Deep suspicions and misgivings about North Korea had already been growing in Japan since the early 1990s. During the Cold War, strong leftist orientation among Japanese media encouraged reporting that was sympathetic to Pyongyang.‡ Influenced by such reports, the Japanese people held a relatively benign image of North Korea through the late 1980s. But since the end of the Cold War, Japanese

---

‡ Fuji Kamiya, Japan's leading Korea expert since the 1960s, recalled: "[T]he Japanese media eagerly praised North Korea, while treating South Korea as a bad guy. As was typically observed in the case of the Chollima movement, they consistently overestimated and admired them [what North Korea did]. In contrast, with regard to South Korea, their reports exaggerated the negative aspects [of what South Korea did] due to their preoccupation with biases and prejudices [toward South Korea]." Fuji Kamiya *Kokusai Seiji no Han-seiki: Kaiko to Tenbo* [The Half Century of the International Politics: Retrospect and Prospect] (Tokyo: Sansei-do, 2001), page.179.

media reports about North Korea have become more objective. Consequently, the Japanese have become much more familiar with the strange belief system shared among North Korean leaders, the extremely oppressive nature of the regime in Pyongyang, and the history of North Korea's anti-Japan activities, including the abduction of Japanese citizens to advance its espionage efforts in the 1970s and 1980s.

From 1993 to 1994, when Pyongyang's nuclear and missile development programs were first disclosed, the Japanese began to recognize North Korea as a potential threat to their security. In 1997, an ex-North Korean agent who had defected to Japan confirmed the kidnapping of a 13-years-old girl, Megumi Yokota, two decades earlier.[§] That was followed by the launch of the first Taepodong missile on August 31, 1998. The shock of the launch to the Japanese was arguably comparable to the one received by the Americans at the Soviet launch of Sputnik in October 1957. For most Japanese, the launch was the first occasion in the postwar period in which they felt their country was immediately threatened by a hostile external power. Although Japan had confronted Russian (Soviet) and Chinese military power, including their nuclear and ballistic missile arsenals, most Japanese had actually never perceived these threats as immediate, given their protection by the US military umbrella.

In the case of the Taepodong launch, however, the fact that North Korea launched a missile that actually flew over the main island of Japan and splashed down into the Pacific Ocean was enough to send shivers up just about every Japanese spine. The possibility that North Korea, viewed by most Japanese as the most enigmatic and the most unpredictable country in the region, had the capability to attack Japan with ballistic missiles was horrifying. The North Korean spy ships incidents that took place in March 1999 and in December 2001 further intensified the perceived threat from Pyongyang.[**]

Kim Jong-Il's handling of the abduction issue at and after the first Japan-North Korea summit meeting badly damaged the perception of North Korea among the Japanese. When Kim admitted that his country had abducted thirteen Japanese nationals in the 1970s and 1980s and made a verbal apology for doing so, the majority of the Japanese public actually accepted Kim's words and supported Prime

---

[§] At the first summit meeting between Japan and North Korea in September 2002, at which it was revealed that North Korea actually had abducted thirteen Japanese nationals in the 1970s and 1980s, Megumi Yokota was included among the eight abductees who were claimed by North Korea to have already died.

[**] Even before these incidents, it is believed that North Korean ships frequently intruded into Japan's territorial waters and extended economic zone (EEZ) in order to gather information, replace spies stationed in Japan, smuggle drugs into Japan, and even to abduct Japanese citizens. At the first Japan-North Korea summit meeting, Kim Jong-Il admitted that spy ship activities had actually been carried out by "certain military officers" in waters near Japan and pledged that such incidents would not take place again.

Minister Junichiro Koizumi's decision to resume normalization talks with North Korea.[††] Kim's deeds that followed, however, outraged the Japanese. The Japanese were particularly upset at Pyongyang's negative response to Tokyo's demand for detailed information about the eight abductees whom North Korea claimed to have had died, including information on the causes of their deaths. Most Japanese believed that North Korea tried to deceive Japan by providing obviously fake information. According to North Korea, many of the eight people died due to unnatural causes, such as car accidents, drowning, carbon monoxide poisoning, and suicide.[30] The family members of Shuichi Ichikawa, for example, who North Korea claimed to have drowned while swimming in the ocean, argued that he was actually unable to swim and rarely went swimming while he was in Japan.[31] Moreover, many errors with regard to birth dates and home addresses in Japan were found on the death certificates that were given to Tokyo, and coincided with misinformation that the Japanese side had mistakenly given to North Korea several years earlier.[32] In a public opinion survey conducted by the *Asahi Shimbun* in October 2003, 88 percent of the respondents said that they did not trust North Korea's explanations with regard to the abduction issue, while only three percent answered affirmatively.[33]

Pyongyang's attitude toward the five surviving abductees added fuel to the fire. North Korea's decision in October to allow them to return to their homeland almost a quarter century after being kidnapped by North Korean agents was welcomed by the Japanese. When they expressed their desire not to return to North Korea again and to live in Japan with their family members permanently, Pyongyang demanded that Tokyo send them back to North Korea. Japanese anger toward North Korea grew even stronger when Pyongyang declared at the normalization talks, which were resumed in late October after two years of suspension, that the abduction issue had already been solved; it was and still is widely believed in Japan that at least tens of more Japanese had actually been kidnapped by the North in the past.

The resurgence of the North Korean nuclear crisis in October 2002, triggered by the North Korean acknowledgement to the US envoy that it was conducting a uranium-enrichment program, took place at a time when the reputation and credibility of North Korea among the Japanese public had already hit rock bottom.

For almost a decade before the current nuclear crisis started, the Japanese had lived with "North Korea problems." Having faced a series of provocative moves by

---

[††] In a public opinion survey conducted by the *Asahi Shimbun* on September 18, the day after Koizumi's visit to Pyongyang, 81 percent of the respondents said that they evaluated the outcome of the summit meeting positively, while only 16 percent said that they evaluated the outcome negatively. Fifty-eight percent of the respondents said they endorsed Koizumi's decision to resume normalization talk with North Korea in October. *Asahi Shinbun* (September 19 and 20, 2002).

Pyongyang, the Japanese were surely irritated, but such experiences ironically and unintentionally had given them confidence that Pyongyang, despite its harsh rhetoric and confrontational postures, was effectively deterred by the US-Japan alliance. The Japanese had grown accustomed to the harsh way Pyongyang spoke and behaved. In other words, they had acquired immunity from North Korean provocations. Consequently, even the explicit warning issued by Pyongyang in April 2003 that Japan should recognize that it is "within the striking range of the DPRK" and should behave well was almost ignored by the Japanese media and barely induced any reactions from the Japanese public.[34]

The relatively calm reactions of Japan and its people to the renewed North Korean nuclear crisis do not mean that Tokyo has taken a soft policy stance toward Pyongyang. Since the crisis resumed in the fall of 2002, Tokyo has consistently taken "a hard-line approach toward North Korea similar to that of the Bush administration" and "[t]he Japanese public has come to support" it.[‡‡] Such a tendency has been clearly observed in Tokyo's immediate responses to the Taepodong-II test and the nuclear test in the spring of 2009. For the Japanese, the renewed nuclear brinkmanship by Pyongyang represents only an additional episode in the long list of "North Korea problems" they have been forced to face since the early 1990s. Being deeply concerned and angered by North Korea's repeated missile and nuclear tests, and being totally disillusioned about the trustworthiness of that country as a negotiating partner, the Japanese tend to see wicked North Korea as being up to its old tricks.[35]

Growing Anxiety about China's Nuclear Arsenal

Not many in Japan perceive an immediate threat to its security from China. However, China's rapidly growing military strength, particularly its nuclear and missile capabilities, has gradually aroused anxiety among the Japanese. The results of the annual "Japan-US Joint Public Opinion Polls," conducted by the *Yomiuri Shimbun* and Gallup Inc., have demonstrated this trend eloquently: In November 1997, in answer to the question, "Please choose as many countries or regions from the following that you think will possibly become a military threat to Japan," only 25 percent of the Japanese respondents chose "China/Taiwan." In November 2008, 59 percent chose "China" and six percent "Taiwan."[36] At the governmental level, the 2000 edition of Japan's annual defense White Paper explicitly stated, for the first time, that China's intermediate-range ballistic missiles would cover Japan. Until that year, the White Paper, entitled, *Defense of Japan* traditionally refrained from using terms which could imply that Japan perceived China as a threat.[37] The 2000 edition, however, maintained that "with regard to intermediate-range ballistic

---

[‡‡] Katsu Furukawa, "Japan's View of the Korea Crisis," http://cns.miis.edu/research/korea/jpndprk.htm (accessed on September 15, 2003).

missile, China possesses a total of approximately 70 missiles whose ranges cover the Asian region *including Japan* [emphasis added by the author]."[38]

Since then, similar expressions of concern have repeatedly appeared in *Defense of Japan*. The 2008 edition states that China's intermediate- and medium-range ballistic missiles (IRBMs/MRBMs) are "covering the Asia-Pacific region including Japan" and "[t]hese missiles are capable of carrying nuclear warheads."[39] It also says that, "there is concern about how China's military strength will impact the regional situation and Japanese security," particularly because, "China does not show a clear, specific future vision."[40] Besides IRBMs and MRBMs, China's short-range ballistic missiles (SRBMs) in the vicinity of Taiwan constitute a source of security concern for Japan, because such missiles are within range of the Okinawa (Ryukyu) Islands.

The increasing sense of unease among the Japanese about China's military buildup is also reflected in Japan's current NDPG. The 2004 NDPG,, for the first time since 1976, explicitly named China as a major security concern for Japan, with particular attention to its nuclear and missile capabilities. It maintains:

> China, which has a major impact on regional security, continues to modernize its nuclear forces and missile capabilities as well as its naval and air forces. China is also expanding its area of operation at sea. We will have to remain attentive to its future actions.[41]

China's military buildup has loomed particularly large because of the long-time stagnation of Japan's own defense spending. While China's defense budget has seen two-digit growth for 21 consecutive years, Japan's defense budget decreased for the seventh consecutive year in fiscal 2009 to a 14-year low.[42] Hisayoshi Ina, a political columnist and the vice chair of the editorial board of *Nihon Keizai Shimbun (Nikkei)*, has pointed out that while China's defense budget has increased nearly five-fold from 1997 to 2007, Japan's defense budget has increased less than two percent during the same decade. Ina named this stagnation of Japan's defense spending the "Koizumi Disarmament" and said that it irritated the US government while pleasing China.[43] In fact, on May 20, 2008, in an address to the Foreign Correspondents Club of Japan, the US Ambassador to Japan, J. Thomas Schieffer said:

> ...it is *troubling* to note that the ratio of defense spending [of Japan] to gross domestic product has been steadily shrinking. This year that number will be less than 1%, 0.89% to be precise, a ratio lower than any NATO or developed country in the OECD [emphasis added].[44]

The relationship between China and Taiwan, which the current NDPG says "remains unpredictable," adds another source of anxiety for Japan. Shortly after the issuance of the NDPG, on February 19, 2005, the US-Japan Security Consultative Committee (2+2) issued a joint statement which included, as a "common strategic objective of Japan and the US, the need to "encourage the peaceful resolution of issues concerning the Taiwan Strait through dialogue."[45] Since it was the first time that Tokyo and Washington have ever issued a joint statement concerning the Taiwan Strait in the more than fifty year history of the US-Japanese alliance, it was widely perceived as a signal that the two allies view the Taiwan Strait issue as a mutual security concern.[46] Many also called the move "a demonstration of Japan's willingness to confront the rapidly growing might of China."[47] On April 29, in an address given in New York, Japan's Foreign Minister Nobutaka Machimura, talked about making the peaceful resolution of the Taiwan Strait issue a common strategic objective for Japan and the United States, and said that Taiwan has been included in the Treaty of Mutual Cooperation and Security between Japan and the United States of America.[48]

In recent years, an increasing number of Japanese politicians, both in the ruling and opposition parties, have become more candid about expressing their anxiety over China's military buildup, particularly of its nuclear arsenal.[49] For example, on December 9, 2005, in an address at the Center for Strategic and International Studies in Washington, DC, the former head of the DPJ, Seiji Maehara, who is widely recognized as a promising candidate to be a future prime minister, said:

> As an undeniable reality, a situation has come into being in which China has become increasingly powerful both economically and militarily. China, against the background of its economic development, has maintained double digit growth of its military expenditures for nearly twenty years, and has advanced the expansion and modernization of its military force. Some have pointed out that the real military spending of China is twice or three times larger than the officially announced figure by the Chinese government. *This represents a realistic threat* [for Japan] [emphasis added].[50]

Thirteen days later, in a regular press conference, Foreign Minister (an later) Prime Minister) Taro Aso commented on Maehara's remark and was summarized in the government minutes:

> Double-digit growth of defense expense, for 17 consecutive years. And if its content is unclear, in terms of transparency, it may breed distrust. They would not need to say it isn't a threat, if it were visible from outside, like Japanese one is. They might not have to say what was better left unsaid,

only if it were clearly visible. Since this is my impression, it can be said the remark of Mr. Maehara, that it is breeding a threat or anxiety, is a fair one.[51]

In response to a question if he also felt China a threat, Aso replied:

A neighbor with one billion people, *possessed of nuclear bombs* and its military budget growing by double digits for 17 consecutive years. And if its content is unclear, as a consequence *my feeling is that it is on the course to constitute a considerable threat* [emphasis added].[52]

Most recently, during his visit to the Czech Republic and Germany in early May 2009 to attend the 18th Japan-EU Summit Meeting, Prime Minister Aso said that the security environment in Northeast Asia is increasingly hostile due to North Korea's missile launch in April *and* China's modernization of its nuclear arsenal [emphasis added].[53] On June 25, 2009, at the working dinner of the G8 Foreign Ministers' Meeting held in Trieste, Italy, Foreign Minister Hirofumi Nakasone also expressed concern about China's expanding nuclear arsenal. According to a Japanese official, Nakasone said that China "is the only country in the P-5 that has not worked on nuclear disarmament and is instead beefing up its strategic arms." After the session, the foreign minister told reporters that, "[i]n particular, I pointed out the need to work toward nuclear disarmament by all nuclear states, including China and others who remain outside the framework of the NPT, and other (G-8) countries expressed similar understanding (about the need)."[54]

Despite this growing displeasure at China's military buildup and, particularly, its expanding nuclear arsenal, Japan's response has been modest at best. There is a widespread view in the Japanese security and foreign policy community that China represents a more serious and longer-term threat to Japan's security than North Korea. Some officials and commentators go so far as to argue that North Korea's provocations provide Japan with legitimate reason to build up defense capabilities to meet the threats and uncertainties related to China.[55] However, not much has been done by the Japanese government so far. In fact, as mentioned above, Japan's defense budget decreased for the seventh consecutive year in fiscal 2009 to a 14-year low. Japan's most conservative national daily, *Sankei Shimbun,* complained in September 2008 that "Japan's build-up of the defense capabilities [against China's military expansion] has remained too restrained to be sufficient for a response to the realistic threat [of China]," despite the fact that the 2008 edition of the defense White Paper emphasized concern about the impact of China's military strength on regional and Japanese security.[56] A well-known political commentator and president of Japan's Institute for National Fundamentals, Yoshiko Sakurai, who has staunchly advocated for Japan's reconstruction as a normal country, also raised a question:

"Do Japanese politicians recognize how severe the current state [of China's threat is for Japan]?"[57]

The limited nature of Japan's reaction to China's military expansion can be mainly attributed to the following three factors: First is the socio-psychological influence of Japan's modern history with China. Since the end of the World War II, Japan's posture toward China has been "reactive rather than active," and "remarkably less confrontational than that of the United States." Many Japanese believe that maintenance of reasonably good relations with their giant neighbor is essential both for Japan's security and its economic interests. In addition, the pacifist orientation among the post-war Japanese generations has led to a desire to avoid involvement in political and military confrontations with their neighbor. Moreover, a sense of guilt resulting from the pre-war history has restrained Japanese attitudes toward China even more.[58]

Second, sober analyses of China's military strength have been widely shared among mainstream thinkers of Japanese security and foreign policy community. They have worried increasingly about China's rapidly expanding military power. At the same time, the majority believe that China does not pose an immediate military threat to Japan. For instance, in a paper published in February 2004, commissioned by the Ministry of Finance to review Japan's provision of official development assistance to China despite China's military expansion, a leading China expert in Japan, Junichi Abe, maintained:

> …If we place China's military strength in the international security mechanism in East Asia, which is structured around the Japan-US alliance at the core and [other bilateral] defense networks between the United States and South Korea, Thailand, Singapore, and Australia, the level of its "threat" is relatively low. At least in Japan, there are few who seriously consider China's "military threat" as a realistic problem (apart from [the possibility in] the distant future)…It is highly unlikely that China will challenge the security mechanism in East Asia, which is supported by the military power of the United States…It must be concluded that use of force [by China] against our country, who represents the key to the US military presence in Asia, is not a rational option [for China].[59]

Finally, the security threat posed by North Korea looms much larger and more immediate than that posed by China. For instance, in an address given at the Brookings Institution in Washington, DC on April 17, 2009, Japan's former Prime Minister Shinzo Abe said, "[a]t any rate, for its neighbors, China poses great uncertainties." Immediately after that, however, Abe maintained that "North Korea remains the biggest threat to security in our part of the world."[60]

Russia

In the latest 2008 edition of the defense White Paper, a short section entitled "Russian Forces in the Far East Region" says that Japan needs to continue to pay attention to Russian nuclear forces in the region:

> The current presence of the Russian military forces in the Far East region is comparatively much smaller than its peak. However, a considerable scale of military forces including nuclear forces still remains in the region…It is necessary to continue to monitor the positioning and trends of Russian forces in the Far East region in the future while taking into consideration that the overall forces tend to focus on maintaining combat readiness of the strategic nuclear unit as well as dealing with conflicts by inter-theater mobility of its permanent combat-ready troops.[61]

The "Overview" section of the "Security Environment Surrounding Japan," however, does not mention Russian nuclear forces at all.[62]

Similarly, the 2009 edition of *East Asian Strategic Review*, written by the researchers at the National Institute for Defense Studies, says no more than the following about the impact of Russian nuclear forces on Japan:

> …[i]n terms of strategic nuclear weapons, its arsenal remains the second largest after the United States' and it has begun to modernize its outdated conventional forces. Thus, Japan and other neighboring nations are obliged to keep an eye on trends in the Russian Armed Forces.[63]

US Secretary of Defense Robert Gates, in a speech at the Sophia University in Tokyo on November 9, 2007, said that "the Northeast corner of the Pacific remains one of the last places on earth with the potential for a nuclear confrontation."[64] Quoting his remark, *Yomiuri Shimbun* insisted that "we cannot escape from the reality [which Secretary Gates mentioned], because we have to face to nuclear weapons of not only North Korea but also of China *and of Russia*. The 'Nuclear threat' confronting Japan has grown bigger than we realize [emphasis added]."[65]

Still, Japan's current NDPG pays only modest attention to nuclear weapons in the Russian Far East:

> …although Russia has drastically reduced its armed forces in the Far East since the end of the Cold War, massive military might, including nuclear arsenals, continue to exist in the region, and a number of countries are pouring in efforts to modernize their military forces.[66]

In fact, since the end of the Cold War, discussions in Japan about the impact of Russian nuclear force on its security have been lukewarm at best. Most of the concerns expressed in Japan with regard to Russian nuclear arsenal have been about insufficient controls on nuclear weapons and materials.

The Role and Credibility of the US Nuclear Umbrella

Surrounded by nuclear neighbors, Japan has maintained its non-nuclear weapons policy despite its latent technological capabilities. It is widely agreed among mainstream security thinkers in Japan that the alliance with the United States and the US commitment to defend Japan in case of enemy attack, including the provision of extended nuclear deterrence, has reassured the Japanese people.

The current NDPG puts it simply: "To protect its territory and people against the threat of nuclear weapons, Japan will continue to rely on the US nuclear deterrent."[67] A comprehensive national security policy proposal published by the National Security Research Project of the Tokyo Foundation on October 8, 2008, which is widely considered among the security and foreign policy community in Japan as one of the most important non-governmental inputs to the ongoing preparation of the next NDPG by the Japanese government, emphasizes the indispensability of the US extended nuclear deterrent for Japan's security:

> ...the BMD system alone is not sufficient to suppress the threat of ballistic missiles [against Japan]. A system of deterrence by punitive measures is also necessary. Given the current situation of North Korea possessing nuclear weapons, Japan-U.S. joint efforts to effectively maintain *the deterrence system including conventional and nuclear weapons* are crucially important. *Such a system requires American commitment to resolutely responding to armed attacks against Japan. In addition to the nuclear extended deterrence*, Japan and the U.S. should make joint efforts to establish a system of operational cooperation so that a thorough counteroffensive using conventional weapons alone can be carried out [emphasis added].[68]

In the most recent "Public Opinion Survey on the Self-Defense Forces and Defense Issues," conducted by Japan's Cabinet Office in January 2009, to the question "[W]hat way do you think Japan should adopt to defend it security?", 77 percent of the respondents said that "Japan should, as it currently does, defend its security by the US-Japan Security System [i.e., alliance] and the Self-Defense Forces." Sixty-five percent of the respondents believed that the strength of the Self-Defense Forces (SDFs) "should be as it is at the present," and only 14 percent said it "should be strengthened." Seventy six percent of the respondents believed that the alliance with the United States is "contributing" to peace and security of Japan, while only

16 percent answered "not contributing."[69]   Although this poll did not specifically ask respondents about the credibility of the US nuclear umbrella, taking into consideration the fact that there is a widely shared, if vague, understanding among Japanese citizens that their country is protected by American nuclear weapons against the nuclear weapons of other countries, these results strongly indicate that the vast majority of the Japanese people still trusted the US nuclear umbrella at the beginning of 2009, and desired that the umbrella should be maintained.

It is true, however, that there is a growing uneasiness among Japanese political elites about the credibility of the US extended nuclear deterrence vis-à-vis China and North Korea.   For instance, an article carried in *Yomiuri Shimbun* on June 16 maintained, "In the face of North Korea, who repeats missile shootings and nuclear tests despite dissuasions from the international society, credibility of the strategy [of US extended deterrence] has been considerably shaken."[70]   On June 23, 2009, *Mainichi Shimbun* carried an editorial titled, "Viewpoint: Nuclear Umbrella."   It starts with the sentence, "An English word 'vulnerable' may best describe the current state of Japan."   Taking a clear position that Japan's nuclearization would be "irreparably harmful" for Japan, the editorial maintains that "the role of the United States is indispensable, in order to give the Japanese citizens a sense of being protected," and raises a question for the readers: "[W]ill the US forces retaliate with nuclear weapons in case North Korea shoot a nuclear missile against Japan?"[71]   On July 3, *Sankei Shimbun* carried an article which insisted:

> What is important for Japan now is a multi-partisan discussion in a calm manner about how the U.S.-Japan Security System and the [US] extended deterrence (nuclear umbrella) should be to deal with new threats such as North Korea's nuclear development…In the recent US-ROK summit meeting, South Korea demanded the United States to reconfirm the guarantee of the US extended deterrence for it, and the two leaders documented the guarantee. As is clear from this development, we are in the era in which credibility of US "nuclear umbrella" over its allies are questioned again. For Japan, too, there is an increasing necessity of thorough discussion about Japan's own deterrence posture including the pros and cons of acquiring a capability to attack enemy's bases and of possession of nuclear weapons, as well as about the extent to which nuclear deterrence through the US-Japan Alliance are actually functioning.[72]

Such anxiety about the credibility of the US nuclear umbrella was quite common among West Europeans during the Cold War period, as well, due to the inherent difficulties of "extending" deterrence.   Extended nuclear deterrence is a threat of nuclear retaliation by one state on behalf of its allies, and such a threat "implies that the US is willing to risk its own destruction in the interest of deterring an attack on an ally which does not possess a basic deterrent of its own."[73] In order to make extended deterrence credible, and therefore effective, the United States must convince the targeted states that there is a real likelihood of US nuclear retaliation in case of attacks on US allies. At the same time, the United States must reassure its allies of the continuing trustworthiness of US promises to retaliate. A difficulty for extended deterrence is that the reassurance of allies often requires "a greater degree of certainty that nuclear retaliation will be forthcoming [in case of enemy attacks] than the degree of certainty that is sufficient to deter an adversary in a crisis."[74]

The credibility of US nuclear deterrence was one of the central themes of the security debate among Europeans throughout the Cold War. Many doubted whether the United States would dare to risk destruction of its own cities if the Soviet Union attacked only Europe. And the US worked hard to clear these doubts through repeated declarations, by deploying tactical nuclear weapons in Europe, some of which would be delivered by the forces of the allies, and by developing war plans that would have made nuclear use virtually automatic in the event of war. In Japan, however, the credibility of the US nuclear umbrella was rarely discussed until recent years. Japan's defense posture during the Cold War was based on the assumption that any nuclear attack on Japan would be part of a total nuclear exchange between the Soviet Union and the United States. It was so unlikely that the Soviet Union would attack Japan alone that the Japanese had little reason to worry about the possibility of "decoupling." Today, however, there is growing concern among Japanese about the future possibility that North Korea, armed with nuclear weapons and ballistic missiles, may find an incentive to attack Japan alone, or that Japan might become the sole target of a Chinese nuclear attack in a Sino-Japanese conflict. At the beginning of the twenty-first century, an increasing number of Japanese have come to realize that they now have to face up to the famous question raised by French President Charles de Gaulle in the 1960s: Would a US president actually trade New York for Paris?[75]

Of course, it should be remembered that the "supposedly dangerous situation" in Europe depicted by de Gaulle actually continued for three decades until the end of the Cold War and the collapse of the Soviet Union. The US extended nuclear guarantee to Europe "worked" even during a time of strategic parity between the two superpowers. Obviously, "[m]ost American and European leaders realized that in practice the issue was not what the American President could be assumed to do but how the Soviet Union assessed its risk, if it would want to take initiative."[76] This difference is widely appreciated among mainstream security thinkers in Japan. It is therefore groundless to argue that increasing concern among the Japanese about the credibility of the US nuclear umbrella automatically will lead to it being dysfunctional. Besides, Japan has a long history of being protected under the US extended nuclear deterrence. As a leading Japanese expert of nuclear strategy Shinichi Ogawa argues,

> The US-Japan alliance is intact today, and no significant event has occurred that might lead a third party to conclude that the alliance is on the verge of collapse. It is improbable that the Japanese public has suddenly lost confidence in the U.S. nuclear commitment.[77]

One more point should be added, however: If Japanese confidence in the US commitment was shaken in the foreseeable future, distrust would more likely be caused by political, rather than military, reasons. In recent years, despite the widespread perception among the Japanese that the United States is "contributing" to peace and security of Japan (as was shown above), a sense of distrust of the United States has also been growing. According to the annual "Japan-US Joint Public Opinion Polls," conducted by the *Yomiuri Shimbun* and Gallup Inc., in November 2002, 49 percent of the respondents trusted the United States (eight percent chose the answer "trust very much" and 40 percent chose "trust to some extent"), while 39 percent did not (9 percent chose the answer "do not trust at all," and 30 percent chose "have some distrust").[78] Six years later, in November 2008, these figures had changed greatly: only 32 percent trusted the United States (six percent chose "trust very much," and 26 percent chose "trust to some extent"), while nearly 60 percent did not (21 percent chose "do not trust at all," and 39 percent chose "have some distrust").[79] One major reason for this change in Japanese perceptions was, of course, US unilateralism during the Bush Administration and the Iraq War. In the 2008 poll, the vast majority of the respondents (83 percent) believed that credibility of the United States decreased during the eight years of the Bush Administration.[80]

There is, however, another important reason for declining trust in the United States. There is a widespread sentiment among the Japanese that the United States has failed to give them satisfactory reciprocation for their efforts to help the US after the 9/11 terrorist attack and during the Iraq War, with the latter being particularly important. Although many countries, even close allies, condemned the United States for starting an illegitimate war against Iraq, the Japanese government not only refrained from criticizing its ally, but tried to screen it from international blame. Although the majority of the Japanese public was critical of the Iraq War, Tokyo dispatched SDF troops to Iraq to help US reconstruction efforts. It was not an easy decision for the Japanese government, since this deployment of troops was the very first time Japan had sent its armed forces to the territory of a country in which military conflicts were still in progress since WWII. It marked a "historic watershed in Japan's policies on international contributions, which had centered mostly around cooperation for UN peacekeeping operations" and the "opening of a new era for the role of the SDF."[81] The reaction of the Japanese public to this deployment was very noteworthy. Despite a deep pacifist orientation embedded in post-war Japanese society, and notwithstanding the fact that a majority in Japan did not support the US-led war against Iraq and exhibited a strong sense of dissatisfaction with the US handling of the post-war situation there, the SDF deployment to Iraq won acceptance among the Japanese people. In a poll conducted by the *Yomiuri Shimbun* on April 17 and 18, 2004, about three months after the SDF troops were sent to Iraq, a full 60 percent of the respondents were supportive of the deployment, as opposed to 37 percent who were not.[82]

The Japanese government, as well as its people, expected that such a show of goodwill, friendship, and partnership would ensure the US reciprocated by supporting Japan against North Korea. Immediately after Pyongyang conducted its first nuclear test in October 2006, however, the Bush Administration replaced its original policy of not rewarding North Korea's bad behavior with a new, conciliatory policy line, including direct bilateral talks with Pyongyang and reopening of the Six-Party Talks. Although this policy change was received favorably by the majority of the international community as a sign of a shift from unilateralism to multilateralism, it was a profound shock to Japan. The Japanese were particularly deeply disappointed to see the United States make such a fundamental policy shift on the most vital issue for Japan's security *unilaterally*, without sufficient consultations with Japan. When the Bush Administration rescinded the designation of North Korea as a State Sponsor of Terrorism in October 2008, going against Japan's insistence that the delisting should not be implemented until Pyongyang took concrete actions to resolve the issue of the abduction of Japanese citizens, the Japanese were disappointed even further.

Such unilateral policy changes by the United States have created a sense that the US is not willing to pay sufficient respect even to Japan's most vital security interests. If it continues to remain so neglected, such sentiments could raise voices in Japan questioning Washington's sense of solidarity with Tokyo, and undermine the security alliance itself. If, on the other hand, this political nightmare is avoided by closer consultations between the two allies, there will not be much reason, at least for the time being, to worry about Japan's loss of faith in the US nuclear umbrella.

JAPAN'S NUCLEAR PLANS AND NON-NUCLEAR WEAPONS POLICY

Since Japan launched a nuclear energy development program in the mid-1950s, the government—as well as political leaders—has repeatedly declared that the country will never possess nuclear weapons. In 1955, the Diet adopted the Atomic Energy Basic Law that strictly limits the use of nuclear energy to peaceful purposes. During deliberations on the bill, Liberal Democratic Party (LDP) Lower House member

Yasuhiro Nakasone, one of the sponsors of the bill, maintained that "weapons which utilize atomic energy to kill and wound people," would be excluded from Japan's atomic energy research and utilization program.[83]

In April 1958, Prime Minister Nobusuke Kishi declared at an Upper House session that Japan would choose not to possess any nuclear weapons, though its postwar "Peace Constitution" did not prohibit the possession of strictly defensive nuclear weapons.[§§] In April 1960, he maintained at a Lower House session that "Japan will not arm itself with nuclear weapons, nor will it allow the introduction of nuclear weapons [into its territory]."[84] It should be noted that Nakasone and Kishi were generally considered to be among the most hawkish nationalists within Japan's political circles at that time. In May 1967, the Director General of the Defense Agency (currently the Ministry of Defense), Kanehichi Masuda, told the Upper House that "the government has maintained the principles of not manufacturing, possessing, or allowing the introduction of nuclear weapons into Japan since the Kishi cabinet."[85] Formulated as the "Three Non-Nuclear Principles (*Hikaku San-Gensoku*)" by Prime Minister Eisaku Sato at Lower House sessions in December 1967 and January 1968 and formalized in a resolution by the Diet in November 1971, these principles were subsequently upgraded to the status of "national principles" (*kokuze*), and each subsequent administration, LDP or non-LDP, has repeatedly reaffirmed its unwavering support for these principle as national policy.[***] The Japanese government signed the Treaty on the Non-Proliferation of Nuclear Weapons (NPT) in 1970 and the Diet ratified it in 1976.

The current "Framework for Nuclear Energy Policy," which was adopted by the Japan Energy Commission in 2005 to define the basic principles of Japan's nuclear energy policy, maintains:

> The goals of research, development and utilization of nuclear energy in Japan, according to the Atomic Energy Basic Law, are to secure energy resources for the future, to promote academic progress and industrial advancement and thereby, to contribute to the welfare of society and the improvement of people's living standard, based on the premise of safety assurance, while strictly limiting the activities involved to peaceful purpose.[86]

[§§] "Dai-23-kai Kokkai, Sangi-in, Shoukou-Iinkai-Kaigi-roku, Dai-5-gou (The 23th Session of the Diet, the House of Councilors, Commerce and Industry Committee, Proceedings, No.5)" (December 15, 1955), page 8. See also, Akira Sakuragawa, "Nihon no Gunshuku Gaiko (Japan's Disarmament Diplomacy)" *Kokusai Seiji* 80 (October 1985), page 64. During the 1950s, when Kishi made this remark, it was expected that very small nuclear warheads which could be used for strictly defensive purpose might come into being as a consequence of advance of science and technology. Since "strictly defensive nuclear weapons" have never been invented, possession of any existing nuclear weapons by Japan would be unconstitutional.

[***] Sato was Kishi's younger brother.

As the only country to have suffered nuclear attack, Japan takes these commitments seriously. It promotes research, development, and utilization of nuclear energy strictly for peaceful purposes, while setting the goal of eliminating all nuclear weapons and adhering to the "Three Non-nuclear Principles" of not possessing, not producing, and not permitting the introduction of nuclear weapons into Japan. In addition to ratifying the Non-Proliferation Treaty (NPT), it has concluded a Comprehensive Safeguards Agreement and signed the "Additional Protocol" with the International Atomic Energy Agency (IAEA). In addition, it has developed and improved corresponding domestic safeguards systems.[87]

As of March 31, 2009, Japan had 53 nuclear reactors in operation, 4 reactors under construction, and 12 additional reactors planned.[88] The total number of Japan's reactors (69) is the second largest in the world, next to the United States (113 reactors, as of January 1, 2009). According the 2007 edition of Japan's *White Paper on Nuclear Energy*, published in March 2008:

> Japan's basic policy of back-end of nuclear fuel cycle has been to reprocess spent fuel, to dispose of only non-recyclable fission products and transuranic elements as high-level radioactive waste, and to effectively utilize collected plutonium and uranium, etc.[89]

An important part of Japan's nuclear energy policy is the "Pluthermal Program," the program to utilize MOX fuel (fuel consisting of a mixture of uranium and plutonium oxides) in light water reactors. Although Japanese electric utilities announced in 1997 that they would start using MOX fuels in 16 to 18 light water reactors by 2010, the Federation of Electric Power Companies of Japan announced on June 12, 2009, that many of the electric power companies will have to postpone the program by up to five years, mainly because discussions are still under way with the local governments and citizens.[90] However, Japan has maintained a basic policy of promoting nuclear fuel cycle activities for "the reprocessing of spent fuel and effective utilization of recovered plutonium and uranium improve such characteristic of nuclear power generation as excellent supply stability," and enhance the energy security of Japan, which is poorly endowed with energy resources.[†††]

Being the only non-nuclear weapons state that implements a full, closed nuclear fuel cycle, Japan has achieved a high level of nuclear technology. Technologically,

---

[†††] *White Paper on Nuclear Energy 2007 (Summary)*, p.15. According the 2008 edition of Japan's *White Paper on Energy*, as of 2006, Japan imported 99.6 percent of its oil consumption, 96.4 percent of natural gas consumption, 74 percent of LP gas consumption, and "almost all (more than 99%) of coal consumption. *Energy Hakusho 2008* (White Paper on Energy 2008) (Tokyo: Agency for Natural Resources and Energy, 2008), pages 137, 138, 140, and 141. Japan also imports all of the uranium necessary for its nuclear power plants.

Japan would be capable of developing nuclear weapons if it invested considerable money, resources, and time. The Japanese government, however, has carefully limited Japan's nuclear activities within the realm of peaceful uses, while setting the goal of eventually eliminating all nuclear weapons. On November 30, 2006, at a session of the Committee on Security of the House of Representatives, Foreign Minister Taro Aso described this situation by saying. "…it is certain that we [i.e., Japan] have technologies to produce them [i.e., nuclear weapons]. However, we have never said that we would use them to possess nuclear weapons immediately."[‡‡‡]

Japan has taken various specific measures to guarantee that its nuclear program would not be diverted from peaceful purposes. As noted, Japan has concluded the Comprehensive Safeguards Agreement and the Additional Protocol with the International Atomic Energy Agency (IAEA). In addition, it has developed domestic safeguards systems. Since 1994, Japan disclosed specific figures for the quantities of plutonium in its stocks to further promote the transparency of its nuclear fuel recycling program. In recent years, Japan has established the means for the implementation of large-scale safeguards activities at the new Rokkasho Reprocessing Plant in cooperation with the IAEA. Japan has also introduced various proliferation resistant technologies in its nuclear activities. For instance, for reprocessing spent fuel from light water reactors, Japan developed a technology called "PU-U co-conversion," which eliminates the need to handle pure plutonium oxide powder. This technology has also been used in the Rokkasho Reprocessing Plant.[91]

Japan has intentionally avoided possessing weapons-grade plutonium. Nearly all the plutonium stockpile in Japan consists of reactor-grade plutonium. It may be possible to produce small-scale nuclear "bombs" with reactor-grade plutonium. However, as Professor Tetsuo Sawada, an expert on nuclear engineering and nuclear nonproliferation at the Tokyo Institute of Technology, points out, producing bombs with reactor-grade plutonium involves an extremely dangerous process technologically, and such bombs should be too unstable and too unreliable militarily to be deployed as actual warheads.[92] In fact, no country has ever tried to produce nuclear weapons with reactor-grade plutonium.

Were Japan to decide to develop its own nuclear weapons, it would surely choose to do so with weapons-grade plutonium, because it would be much easier, safer, and cheaper. However, the amount of weapons-grade plutonium that Japan could obtain by running existing nuclear power plants would be limited. For a major power like

---

[‡‡‡] "Dai-165-kai Kokkai, Shuugi-in, Anzenhoshou-Iinkaigi-roku, Dai-11-gou (The 165th Session of the Diet, the House of Representatives, Security Committee, Proceedings, No.11)" (November 30, 2006), page 16.

Japan, possessing only a small number of nuclear warheads would be militarily meaningless.[93] In order to obtain a militarily-meaningful nuclear arsenal, Japan must produce hundreds of warheads. In order to do so, however, Japan would have to spend many years to construct new facilities to extract a large amount of weapons-grade plutonium from its existing stocks.[94]

As for uranium, despite having the technological capability to produce weapon-grade, highly-enriched uranium, Japan has refrained from generating such materials. In the past, Japan purchased a limited amounted of highly-enriched uranium from the United States and retained it for use in peaceful research reactors. Since 1996, however, Japan has agreed to return that highly-enriched uranium to the US in order to remove the risks of proliferation to third countries and terrorists, and by the summer of 2008, 579.7 kilograms of highly-enriched uranium, which represented "almost all of highly enriched material in Japan's principle research reactors," was actually transferred to nuclear research facilities in the United States.[95] According to Andrew Beineawski, an official of the US Department of Energy, the repatriation operation was initiated by the US as part of a counter-proliferation project called the Global Threat Reduction Initiative. Beiniawski said, "Japanese research reactors have been very successful in shipping their spent HEU fuel to the United States. These shipments contribute to HEU minimization efforts worldwide." The remaining ten-odds kilograms of highly-enriched uranium still in Japan is scheduled to be returned to the United States by 2012.[96]

As Ambassador Yukiya Amano, newly-elected Director General of the IAEA, maintained, the Japanese government judged by the end of 1970s that "using highly enriched uranium is a matter of concern from the security point of view, is not a necessity, and is not helpful to ensure the confidence of the international community, as far as Japan is concerned," and "decided and has been reducing the enrichment level" since then.[97] Japan's attitude toward highly-enriched uranium demonstrates that Japan has not entertained any idea of diverting such materials for weapon purposes.

In their detailed study published in 2003 on Japan's nuclear energy program and its implications for Japan's potential nuclearization, Jeffrey W. Thompson and Benjamin L. Self concluded that "Japan's nuclear energy program would not support the development of a nuclear arsenal."[98] In fact, on June 14, 2004, Director-General of the IEAE Mohamed El Baradei officially announced at the organization's board of governors meeting that a four-year investigation of nuclear power use had revealed that Japan's nuclear program was limited to peaceful purposes, and there was no reason to suspect that it would be diverted to nuclear weaponry. This was the very first time that the IAEA had reached such a conclusion for a non-nuclear state that has promoted the use of nuclear energy on a significant scale. As a result, Japan has joined the group of countries to which "Integral Safeguards" are applied, requiring only half the previous number of inspections. Before they were granted to Japan, "Integral Safeguards" had been applied only to Australia, Norway, and Indonesia. These three countries, however, possessed only research reactors, so this was the very first time that they had been granted to a state which possesses numerous nuclear reactors for commercial purposes.

The IAEA's decision to give such exceptional treatment to Japan represents the Agency's conviction that Japan has no intention of producing nuclear warheads. It is also noteworthy that Japan has intentionally refrained from developing key technologies that would permit it to obtain delivery vehicles for nuclear warheads. For Japan, tactical nuclear weapons would be nearly useless, because, as an island country, it would find few meaningful targets for such weapons. In order to obtain a militarily-meaningful nuclear arsenal, Japan would have to possess ballistic missiles. Although the country has advanced rocket production and space-launch capabilities, it would take many years before the country would actually be able to deploy ballistic missiles for military purposes. Japan has developed the solid-fuel M-V rocket, which is capable of launching probes for interplanetary missions. However, the rocket which the Japanese government has positioned as its "primary large-scale launch vehicle" has been the H-II, not the M-V.[99] In fact, production of the M-V series was discontinued after the launch of M-V-7 in September 2006 for cost and other reasons.[100] As the Federation of American Scientists simply put it, the H-II is "_ENTIRELY_ unsuited for conversion to ballistic missile applications [emphasis in the original]" because it is powered by liquid oxygen and liquid hydrogen.[101]

According to Thompson and Self, "Japan has invested heavily in rockets that would _not_ make effective ballistic missiles." They also note:

> To the extent that technical consideration of military applicability entered into the engineering context . . . it seems that the civilian rocket programs at ISAS [the Institute for Space and Aeronautical Sciences] and NASDA [the National Space Development Agency] steered _away_ from rather than toward, such capabilities. Military rocketry research at the Technology Research and Development Institute (TRDI), inside the Defense Agency, has been restricted to small rockets for tactical use, such as surface-to-air missiles.[102]

In addition, Japan has not developed an accurate inertial guidance system and reentry mechanisms that would be essential for ballistic missiles. Even if Japan acquired all the technologies to produce ballistic missiles, it would still face another technological obstacle to obtain a reliable nuclear deterrent. Due to its geographical narrowness, if Japan introduced long-range, land-based ballistic missiles, they would inevitably be vulnerable to a first strike. Japan would have to deploy submarine-launched ballistic missiles (SLBMs) to have a credible second-strike capability, but that would require a considerable fleet of nuclear submarines to carry them. For that purpose, Japan would have to build naval nuclear reactors, as well as an extensive terrestrial or satellite communications grid to support their activities. Japan currently does not possess any nuclear-powered ships, due mainly to the accidental radiation leaks that accompanied its first nuclear-powered ship, "Mutsu," off the coast of Aomori Prefecture during its experimental voyage in 1974, and the consequent deep public distrust of nuclear vessels. Japan also would have to conduct research on launching ballistic missiles from submarines. The time required for Japan to be able to acquire all these technologies would probably be measured in decades, not years. None of the necessary development programs have been ever started by Japan.

In conclusion, Japan's nuclear infrastructure has been oriented exclusively to peaceful uses of nuclear energy. In order to guarantee that its nuclear program would not be diverted from peaceful purposes, Japan has taken various specific measures. Consequently, despite all its latent nuclear know-how and potential, Japan is not capable of acquiring a militarily significant nuclear arsenal in a short period of time. Because Japan is an open society and all of its nuclear power activities are subject to IAEA safeguards, it would be impossible for the country to start a project in secret to obtain all the necessary technologies described above and to build covertly a militarily-meaningful nuclear arsenal of its own.

Moreover, there is very little support for nuclearization in Japan. Indeed, until the late 1990s, it was a near taboo in Japanese society and particularly for Japanese politicians to discuss even the hypothetical possibility of Japan obtaining nuclear weapons. Since the turn of the century, the prohibition against such discussions have gradually declined, due mainly to the development of North Korea's nuclear weapons and missiles. On the one hand, there is an emerging, but still limited, group of people who believe that Japan should acquire its own nuclear deterrent to deal with North Korea. On the other hand, there is a growing number of the mainstream security thinkers who argue that the Japanese need to discuss the pros and cons of Japan's acquisition of a weapons' capability in order to gain a clearer understanding among themselves as to why their country chooses to maintain a non-nuclear policy, and to show such an understanding to the international community, as well.[103]

When North Korea conducted its first nuclear test on October 9, 2006, Prime Minister Shinzo Abe promptly declared that Japan would maintain its non-nuclear policy:

> ...yesterday, in a telephone conversation with the US President Bush, President and I agreed that the alliance relationship between Japan and the United States will remain firm to the future, and that we will securely maintain deterrent power, and that such a relationship will keep standing firm. On the basis of these facts, with regard to an option for our nation to possess nuclear weapons, I, of course, do not have any intention to change our position that we do not have such an option at all to the future. I would like to state clearly that the Three Non-Nuclear Principles will not be changed at all.[104]

Some Japanese lawmakers, however, openly advocated discussing the rights and wrongs of nuclearization, and surprised outside observers. For example, on October 15, 2006, Chairman of the LDP's Policy Research Council Shoichi Nakagawa appeared on the "Sunday Project," a nationally broadcast news and discussion program, and said that "discussion [about Japan's nuclear acquisition] should be allowed," because "it could be logical to argue that the existence of nuclear weapons would lower the probability of being attacked."[105] Two days later, at a session of the Committee on Security, the House of Representatives, Foreign Minister Taro Aso said that, "Rather than remaining ignorant [on the matter of Japan's nuclear acquisition], one viable option is to choose not to possess such weapons after sufficient studies [about the matter]."[106] On the next day, at a session of the Committee on Foreign Affairs, the House of Representatives, Aso made another remark on the issue. While repeatedly maintaining that there was no change in the policy of the Japanese government to maintain the Three Non-Nuclear Principles, the foreign minister said that various discussions about Japan's nuclear possession was important for Japan's security:

> ...at the moment when the country next to us comes to possess [nuclear weapons], it is not good that we are not allowed to even discuss about it, that we are not allowed to even talk about it, and we are not allowed to do anything about it. As a way of thinking, it might be possible to say that even exchanges of various ideas should not be allowed. But as another way of thinking, doing various discussions [about Japan's nuclear possession] is important. I belong to the latter way of thinking.[107]

On October 22, former Director General of the Defense Agency Shigeru Ishiba, a well-know opponent to Japan's nuclearization, also insisted that "discussion about nuclear possession should be done publicly."[108]

These politicians did not advocate that Japan should go nuclear. In fact, results of surveys of Diet members' opinions on this issue demonstrated overwhelming objection to Japan's acquisition of nuclear weapons. In a survey conducted by the *Yomiuri Shimbun* with the cooperation of Professor Ikuo Kabashima of the University of Tokyo from November to December 1998, Japanese legislators were "in almost total agreement across party lines" on the issue of Japan's possession of nuclear weapons. Among 431 respondents (59 percent of all the Diet members), only 17 were "in favor" or "somewhat favor" of the idea.[109] In another survey conducted jointly by the *Asahi Shimbun* and Professor Kabashima in 2003, which covered the House of Representatives, the more powerful chamber of the Diet, among 394 respondents (83 percent of the Lower House members), only one said that he or she was "somewhat receptive" to nuclear armament of Japan, while 36 said "neither yes nor no" and the remaining 357 said "no." In their analysis of these results, the *Asahi Shimubn* and Professor Kabashima concluded that "although talking about Japan's nuclearization has become topical in and out of Japan these days against the background of the nuclear development of North Korea, it is proper to say that the consensus 'against nuclear possession [by Japan]' has been formed across party lines in the House of Representatives."[110]

Shoichi Nakagawa and some other politicians insisted that Japan should study and discuss the costs and benefits of going nuclear. A large segment of the Japanese lawmakers, however, seemed to be intolerant of such a discussion. According to the *Asahi Shimbun*, severe criticism immediately erupted from the ruling coalition over the remark by Shoichi Nakagawa. LDP leaders such as Director General of the Defense Agency Fumio Kyuma and former Secretary General of the LDP Koichi Kato said that such a statement might "send a wrong message" to the world. LDP's Secretary General Hidenao Nakagawa expressed openly his displeasure with Shoichi Nakagawa's remark. Chairman of Policy Research Council of another member of the ruling coalition, the New Komei Party, Tetsuo Saito, also insisted that "even a discussion [on this topic] is not acceptable because it will invite international suspicion [against Japan]."[111] Consequently, on October 16, the day after his appearance on the "Sunday Project," Shoichi Nakagawa had to make a follow-up remark: "Of course, I am also against the argument that Japan should go nuclear."[112] On October 27, Prime Minister Abe declared that he would not let the government or the LDP discuss the issue, although personal discussion by politicians could not be suppressed.[113]

After the test of the Taepodong-II by Pyongyang on April 5, 2009, nuclear debate resurfaced among Japanese lawmakers. On the day of the launch, Shoichi Nakagawa said, "How to give damages to [North Korea's] missile base, [and] how to counter nuclear delivery system [of North Korea] if it is completed. Our discussions may include a talk about nuclear weapons."[114]

On April 7, Lower house member and Chairman of the Party Organization Headquarters of the ruling Liberal Democratic Party, Goji Sakamoto, also said that it should be OK for Japan to discuss nuclear possession, although he later explained that he "does not advocate Japan's nuclear possession," and "made a hypothetical remark to show the firm stance [of Japan] to North Korea."[115] On April 19, Nakagawa insisted again that the Japanese should discuss the nuclearization of their country, adding that "actual possession of nuclear weapons and discussion about nuclear weapons are totally separate issues."[116]

Again, however, not many Japanese political leaders reacted favorably to such arguments. In a regular press conference on April 7, 2009, Chief Cabinet Secretary Takeo Kawamura reacted to the earlier remark by Nakagawa and simply stated that "such an option is out of the question for Japan, who has maintained the Three Non-Nuclear Principles." LDP's Secretary General Hiroyuki Hosoda said on the same day that "no one believes that Japan can go nuclear."[117] In that evening, former Director General of the Defense Agency and former Vice President of the LDP Taku Yamasaki criticized Nakagawa by saying, "such is an argument that could, if you use an extreme expression, lead to the destruction of the human species."[118]

Such attitudes of Japanese politicians reflect the state of public opinion in Japan with regard to nuclear options. Ambassador Tetsuo Kawato, a highly respected strategist and Visiting Professor at Waseda University, reported:

> In the recent ado about North Korea's missile and nuclear tests, in Japan, discussion about acquisition of nuclear weapons has not gained momentum, to an inexplicable degree. My students say: "Such weapons are unnecessary. We think that the U.S. nuclear umbrella has not been torn yet, and Japan is in the NPT and has promised to the world not to go nuclear." I basically agree with them. In the world, the idea that nuclear weapons are unusable and obsolete has been gradually spreading (except for terrorists)...[119]

At the time this paper was written, no public opinion survey with regard to Japan's nuclear option had been conducted after North Korea's 2009 missile and nuclear tests. In the *Mainichi Shimbun* survey conducted from November 25 to 26, 2006, shortly after Pyongyang's first nuclear test, 78 percent of the respondents were against Japan's acquisition of nuclear weapons, while 14 percent supported the idea. In the same poll, 69 percent of the respondents said that discussion of the issue was OK (61 percent of the respondents said that Japan should not go nuclear but discussion should be allowed).[120] In a survey conducted by the Fuji TV's news program "Shin-Houdou 2001" on April 2, 2009, 73 percent of the respondents were against Japan's nuclearization, while 19 percent were for the idea.[121]

These results were identical to the results of earlier polls. In polls conducted in June 1969, April 1978, and April 1981, the *Yomiuri Shinbun* posed the same question: "Do you want Japan to possess nuclear weapons?" In the 1969 poll, 72 percent of respondents answered "no," while 16 percent answered "yes." In 1978, the percentage of those who answered "no" rose to 74 percent, whereas the percentage of those who answered "yes" dropped to 10 percent. In 1981, the percentage of those who answered "yes" remained at 10 percent, but the percentage of those who replied "no" leapt to 82 percent.[122]

Another poll conducted by the National Institute for Research Advancement (NIRA) in October 1999, which targeted 2,000 members of the Japanese public, as well as 400 "informed Japanese people," produced an even more striking outcome. Asked what policy option Japan should adopt to protect itself from other nations' nuclear weapons if the US-Japanese Security Treaty were dissolved or rendered meaningless for some reason, only seven percent of the general public and less than fifteen percent of "informed people" responded that they believed that Japan should possess its own nuclear weapons.[123]

Taken together, these results show the consistency and persistency of public attitudes in Japan against nuclearization, a result which rests on two major factors: strong anti-nuclear sentiment and sober cost-benefit calculations. To put it in other words, Japan is *not willing, nor interested* in becoming a nuclear power.[124]

Shared Aversion to Nuclear Weapons

The Japanese share a deep-seated aversion to nuclear arms, a feeling that transcends differences in political ideology and beliefs. An almost instinctive dread of, and hatred for, nuclear weapons widely held across the spectrum of Japanese society is both one of the most fundamental roots of Japan's non-nuclear stance and an extremely powerful deterrent against Japanese nuclear proliferation. The origin of such strong anti-nuclear attitudes lies in Japan's tragic experience as the only nation ever to suffer a nuclear attack. The two bombs dropped on Japan in August 1945 killed about 140,000 in Hiroshima and about 70,000 in Nagasaki. In the years that followed, tens of thousands more died from so-called atomic bomb disease—various illnesses caused by exposure to radiation. Even today, many Japanese suffer the after-effects of this exposure. Naturally, Hiroshima and Nagasaki have greatly influenced post-war Japanese culture. Over the past half-century, countless books, nursery tales, television and radio programs, movies, comic books, animated features and other forms of communication about the bombs have exposed later generations to the horrors of nuclear war.§§§

---

§§§ Many Japanese often feel that people in other countries, particularly those in nuclear weapon states, do not have sufficient understanding of nuclear devastation. For instance, in his recent address on Japan's approach to global nuclear disarmament, Japan's Foreign Minister Hirofumi Nakasone said: "In one scene of a blockbuster movie

Another factor often overlooked by outsiders, but no less important in shaping Japanese anti-nuclear sentiment than Hiroshima and Nagasaki, was the harm done to Japanese fishermen by US nuclear testing in the South Pacific in March 1954. The radioactive fallout from the first US hydrogen bomb test on Bikini Atoll severely contaminated the *Fukuryu-maru No. 5*, a Japanese tuna-fishing boat known as the *Lucky Dragon* outside Japan, and its crew of 23, even though the boat was located 35 kilometers from the danger zone declared by the United States at the time of the explosion. The entire crew suffered from atomic bomb disease; one crew member died, and the rest were hospitalized for more than a year. The Japanese were both horrified and outraged to see that their compatriots were victims of nuclear weapons yet again, particularly because the tragedy occurred in peacetime.[125]

The *Fukuryu-maru* incident left a deep and lasting impression among the Japanese population that one could become a victim of nuclear weapons anywhere or anytime. Shortly afterward, the first nation-wide grassroots movement against nuclear weapons sprang up in Japan and, by the end of 1954, more than 20 million Japanese had signed the Suginami Appeal for the Prohibition of Atomic and Hydrogen Bombs.[126] In April 1954, both houses of Japan's Diet unanimously passed resolutions that called for the prohibition of nuclear weapons and international control of nuclear energy. Japan's non-nuclear policy has consistently reflected this profound hatred for nuclear weapons, which has been deeply embedded in post-war Japanese culture and society.

Costs and Benefits of Nuclearization

As vigorous and ingrained as anti-nuclear sentiment may be, it is not the sole factor behind Japan's non-nuclear stance. Japan's decision to remain non-nuclear is also based on its national interests. In Japan, sober perceptions of the costs and benefits of going nuclear have been widely shared.

First, it is generally understood that Japan's decision to go nuclear would surely undermine the stability of the international environment in which the country lives. As a resource-poor country, friendly international relations are Japan's only hope to maintain its security and prosperity. According the 2008 edition of Japan's *White*

---

released last year [i.e., *Indiana Jones and the Kingdom of the Crystal Skull*], the hero survived a nuclear blast by hiding inside a refrigerator. I was surprised at the soft image about nuclear blasts that was indicated by this scene. A nuclear blast would destroy everything in an instant. I was worried that such a naive perception could spread worldwide." "Conditions towards Zero—'11 Benchmarks for Global Nuclear Disarmament,'" Statement by Mr. Hirofumi Nakasone, Minister for Foreign Affairs of Japan, http://www.mofa.go.jp/policy/un/disarmament/arms/state0904.html (accessed on June 1, 2009). See also "Japan FM says Indiana Jones Trivializes Nuke," *FOX 40 News* (by AFP) (April 28, 2009), http://www.fox40now.com/news/entertainment/43850047.html (accessed on May 3, 2009).

Paper on Energy, as of 2005, Japan's energy self-sufficiency rate was only 4 percent (18 percent when nuclear power is included).[127] In fiscal year 2006, Japan was self-sufficient for only 39 percent of its calories, which was the lowest among major industrialized countries. In fact, Japan is the world's largest food importing country.[128] As an island nation, Japan depends on sea-lanes for imports and exports. Thus, the Japanese are not merely speaking rhetorically when they say that peace and stability of the international community is indispensable to achieve peace and prosperity for Japan, that world and regional peace are inseparable from the country's security and prosperity, or that Japan cannot promote its national interests without peace and stability of the international community, as the government's *Diplomatic Bluebooks* recently emphasized.[129]

Since the end of World War II, Japan has used every opportunity to show the international community and especially its East Asian neighbors that it has been reborn as a "*heiwa kokka* (nation of peace)." Japan's post-war, exclusively defense-oriented policy has played a particularly large role in restoring the trust of other East Asian countries by providing clear evidence of Japan's resolve not to become militaristic again. In abiding by this policy, Japan has voluntarily limited the resources and missions of its SDFs to the minimum necessary to maintain national self-defense. It has refrained from acquiring offensive weapons, such as intercontinental ballistic missiles, long-range strategic bombers, and offensive aircraft carriers, and has imposed strict conditions on when and how the SDFs can mobilize lawfully. Were Japan to go nuclear, almost sixty years of abiding by such conditions would immediately go up in smoke.

Japan's defense authorities soberly recognize this reality. The final report of an unofficial study conducted from 1994 to 1995 by Defense Agency officials and SDFs officers at the behest of Administrative Vice-Minister Shigeru Hatakeyama maintained that even under the worst case scenarios, i.e. a breakdown of the US-Japan alliance, a collapse of the nuclear non-proliferation regime, and/or the drift of other countries toward nuclearization, possession of its own nuclear arsenal would not be beneficial for Japan:

> Even in these cases, it must be questioned to what degree it could be meaningful for the trading country [i.e., Japan] which depends on the stability of the international society to possess its own nuclear weapons in order to secure its survival and to protect its interests.[130]

The report also insisted that "the Japanese military side" should express their position not to support any nuclear option because "from the perspective of security policy of our country, suspicions about [Japan's] nuclear possession will be detrimental to trust building with the neighboring countries."[131]

According to the author's conversations with anonymous high-ranking officials of the SDFs, the Ministry of Defense, and the Ministry of Foreign Affairs, such views are still widely shared among Japan's military leaders as well as its foreign and defense policy elites.

Second, contrary to what most foreign observers as well as those who advocate Japan's nuclearization believe, going nuclear would actually threaten Japan's military security. A decision to build a nuclear arsenal might trigger an arms race in Northeast Asia, possibly prompting the two Koreas and Taiwan to accelerate their nuclear development or go nuclear as well, ultimately reducing regional and global security.

Japan's defense authorities soberly recognize this reality, too. The above-mentioned report prepared by Defense Agency officials and SDFs officers in 1995 concluded that Japan's possession of its own nuclear arsenal had little if any strategic merit.[132] In a 1996 presentation, Lt. Gen. Noboru Yamaguchi of the Japanese Ground SDF (reportedly a participant in the 1994-95 study group) asserted that even without the protection of the US nuclear umbrella, Japan would be worse off with its own nuclear arsenal.[133] He emphasized that, as an island country with a large part of its population living in a small number of densely populated cities, nuclear armament would not suit Japan because of its inherent vulnerability to nuclear attack. As a result, Japan is better off in a world in which just a few states possess nuclear weapons capability. Consequently, going nuclear would only endanger Japan because such a move would motivate numerous other currently non-nuclear states to pursue proliferation, while bringing only minimal military benefits to Japan. In 2003, Shinichi Ogawa, Senior Research Fellow at the National Institute for Defense Studies and also reportedly another participant in the 1994-95 study group, argued in *The National Institute for Defense Studies News* that, "the political and security repercussions of Japanese nuclear weapon development would be very negative." According to Ogawa,

> [M]ost worrisome would the reaction of Japan's neighboring countries…Japanese nuclear weapon development, even if its intention were totally defensive, would be likely to invite caution and countermeasures from China, Russia, and South Korea even in its early stages. As a result, Japan might face a serious security problem before it succeeded in attaining the necessary SSBN/SLBM force…Japan's nuclearization may invite a serious security threat well before a strategically meaningful nuclear force can be built and deployed.[134]

Third, Japan's decision to develop nuclear weapons would inevitably have a detrimental effect on the country's relationship with the United States—Japan's most important bilateral relationship. It is clearly understood among the security and foreign policy community in Japan that most US political leaders, as well as its security and foreign policy elites, do not want to see Japan become a major military power, much less a nuclear power. The Japanese have observed that every major advance of North Korea's nuclear and/or ballistic missile programs—in 1994, 1998, 2002, 2006 and 2009—triggered, with disturbing regularity to their eyes, suspicion among American elites of Japan's intention to go nuclear. The most recent statement to that effect came from Joseph S. Nye at a hearing by the US House Committee on Foreign Affairs Subcommittee on Asia, the Pacific and the Global Environment.[135] Nye, who is well-known in Japan, not only as an advocate of the concept of soft power but also as a key decision-maker on the US side when the US-Japan Alliance was "redefined" in the mid-1990s, testified that "North Korea's detonation of a second nuclear device and launching of rockets over Japan has created anxieties that lead some observers to wonder whether Japan will reverse its long standing decision not to seek a national nuclear deterrent capability."[136]

Fourth, contrary to the views of many foreign observers, the decision to go nuclear would only weaken Japan's political power internationally. In fact, Japan has won the respect of other nations with its decision to forego nuclear weapons, despite its advanced nuclear technological capability. The phrase a "world free of nuclear weapons," did not originate with President Obama. As the only country to have experienced the devastation caused by the use of atomic bombs, Japan has consistently made efforts "to take a leading role to bring about *a peaceful and safe world free of nuclear weapons* as soon as possible [emphasis added]."[137]

Since 1994, Japan has submitted a resolution to advocate the abolition of nuclear weapons to the UN General Assembly every year, resolutions which have won the overwhelming support of the international community, despite objections from the United States since 2001.****

In July 2009, when Japanese Ambassador Yukiya Amano was elected to be the new Director-General of the IAEA, the Japanese media, almost in unison, stressed the significance that the leader of the "nuclear watchdog" would be from Japan, the only nation ever to suffer nuclear devastations.[138] After his election, Amano himself said that "Japan can be called a model country that carries out both peaceful use of nuclear energy and nonproliferation. I'd like to put Japan's experience in this area into good use for the world.[139]

**** From 1994 to 1999, the resolution was called, "Nuclear Disarmament with a View to the Ultimate Elimination of Nuclear Weapons"; from 2000 to 2004, the resolution was titled, "A Path to the Total Elimination of Nuclear Weapons"; and from 2005 to 2008, the resolution was termed "Renewed Determination towards the Total Elimination of Nuclear Weapons."

In short, Japan has built considerable soft power as a promoter of nuclear disarmament and non-proliferation. Nuclearization would only undermine Japan's international position and the reputation it has built for itself thus far. As the second largest economic power in the world, Japan, unlike India, does not need to acquire nuclear weapons to assert its prestige in the world.

JAPAN'S POSSIBLE RESPONSES TO NUCLEAR PROLIFERATION

American researchers, who conducted an extensive review of articles on Japan's security policy published in Japan in recent years, as well as a series of interviews with Japanese political leaders, government and military officials, and security experts, reported that "prominent Japanese opinion-makers and experts revealed a near-consensus of opposition to the development of nuclear weapons."[140] The central reason for such attitudes among Japanese elites is the widely-shared understanding that going nuclear would bring more harm than good to the country. In fact, Japanese security experts who examined the pros and cons of Japan's going nuclear in the past came to that conclusion almost unanimously.

Consequently, most political leaders, as well as almost all of mainstream security thinkers in Japan, share the understanding that even in the face of growing nuclear threats in the region, acquiring nuclear weapons does not represent a sound strategy for Japan. It is widely believed that Japan, which has imposed various constraints on its own defense capabilities under article 9 of the constitution, as well as through the policy of an exclusively non-offensive defense (*senshu bouei*), can do a great deal in the realm of improving its conventional forces before thinking about nuclear weapons. In recent years, the importance of developing and deploying an effective missile defense system in cooperation with the United States has been emphasized in order to enhance deterrence by denial, and to mitigate the consequences of an attack if deterrence failed. For example, in his address given only two days after North Korea's first nuclear detonation, the LDP's Secretary General Hidenao Nakagawa said, "For us, rather than to acquire nuclear weapons, it will be more beneficial realistically to concentrate Japan's strategy and resources on building a missile defense system to neutralize nuclear missiles."[141] It is also believed that strengthening the alliance with the United States including the US extended nuclear deterrent over Japan should be sufficient to deter North Korea. Shinichi Ogawa represents the majority view among Japanese security experts on the latter point:

> If there were any scenario in which US nuclear forces could not deter a North Korean nuclear strike against Japan, it would be North Korea's "final blow"… Such a "final blow of a loser about to die" could not be deterred by any means, including American or Japanese nuclear weapons. Likewise, if it is held that US nuclear forces cannot deter North Korea

because its leadership has a peculiar and irrational way of thinking, then Japanese nuclear forces cannot either.[142]

Based on such perceptions, the author predicted in 2002 that "[e]ven an acceleration of North Korea's nuclear program would not likely cause Japan to follow suit."[143] The prediction stands today, even after the two nuclear tests by North Korea.

As demonstrated above, Japan has many reasons to remain non-nuclear. The strategic implication of the nuclearization of North Korea in the narrow military sense is limited. North Korea is a weak country in almost all indicators of national power. The economy of North Korea has been in a miserable condition for years. Its people have suffered from food and energy shortages during that period, and their average life expectancy has declined significantly. Even militarily, North Korea is weak. American military and security experts have been quite confident that, if the North attacked the South, the US-ROK alliance would easily defeat the North in several weeks or shorter. Pyongyang's nuclear detonations have not given North Korea any real military strength. Given the credible US nuclear deterrent, Pyongyang's nuclear bombs will remain weapons that cannot be used unless the North Korean government is willing to commit suicide.

Here, however, one caution is in order. It is incorrect and dangerous for the international community to take Japan's non-nuclear stance for granted. Despite the extremely strong desire of Japan to remain non-nuclear, Japan would have to make new cost-benefit calculations when international developments force it to reevaluate important foreign and security policy decisions, as every nation does, and the decision with regard to nuclear weaponry is no exception. In other words, Japan's current decision to remain non-nuclear would not be continued automatically, but would be affected by the international environment.

From this point of view, two areas deserve special attention. First, the political implications of Japan going nuclear (and remaining non-nuclear) should be seriously reconsidered by the international community. Non-nuclear major powers, like Japan, should not be regarded as politically inferior to nuclear-armed major powers, and, for example, excluded indefinitely from having a permanent seat on the UN Security Council. There has been frustration among the Japanese that countries like China and Russia do not treat Japan as an equal politically because Japan has refrained from possessing a full-fledged military and developing a nuclear arsenal. Such frustration, if left neglected, could lead to an overestimation by Japanese leaders of the benefits of going nuclear.

Second, if the international community does not respond strongly to the acquisition of nuclear weapons by countries other than Japan, it could also have an undesirable effect on Japanese perceptions of the cost-benefit equation of becoming a nuclear weapons state. Up to the present, such a calculation by Japan has been based on the assumption that any country which develops nuclear weapons against the non-nuclear norm shared by the international community would face tough reactions by the international community. In 1998, the Japanese were shocked and disappointed to see that only a very few countries, including Japan, undertook tough and substantial sanctions against India and Pakistan after their nuclear tests. In 2006, international reaction to North Korea's first nuclear test served to deepen the frustration of the Japanese. In their eyes, the reaction from China and the United States was particularly indecisive. Although the Japanese welcomed China's vote for the UN Security Council Resolution 1718 to impose sanctions against North Korea, they were irritated by China's repeated urge "to the countries concerned to adopt a prudent and responsible attitude in this regard and refrain from taking any provocative steps that may intensify the tension."[144] The typical Japanese reaction was, "If you want to preach that way, don't do it to 'the countries concerned' (obviously including Japan), but to North Korea, with whom you have had special relationship for a long time."

The US reaction was even more disappointing than China's from a Japanese viewpoint. Observing that Washington abandoned its opposition to bilateral talks with Pyongyang shortly after the nuclear detonation by North Korea, many in Japan wondered whether nuclearization would invite international punishment or international reward. After the United States and North Korea held talks on the normalization of their diplomatic relations in New York in March 2007, former Director General of the Defense Agency Kazuo Aichi expressed his regret at the US policy flip-flop by saying:

> In short, North Korea, without doubt, has benefited from expressing clearly its possession of, or its willingness to possess, nuclear weapons. This means that the result completely opposite to what the United States desired has been brought about. That is to say, although the United States has accepted direct talks with North Korea due to fears of nuclear proliferation, it [i.e., the US acceptance of such talks] has actually made the world recognize how beneficial the acquisition of nuclear weapons could be. The consequence [of North Korea's nuclearization] could lead to emergence of other countries who would attempt to acquire nuclear weapons. It is a truly ironic consequence. The United States should have demonstrated that anyone who tried to acquire nuclear weapons would be taught a lesson.[145]

The conclusion of the US-Indian Nuclear Cooperation Agreement was disturbing to the Japanese, too. Although the Japanese government accepted the deal, the Japanese people were generally upset because they perceived it as another case of the United States rewarding behavior that went against the international non-nuclear norm. While the United States tried to treat India as an exception to its nuclear non-proliferation policy, many in Japan saw that as unrealistic and worried that the conclusion of the agreement would set a precedent that going nuclear could pay. To convince the public that developing nuclear weapons will do more harm than good, mainstream security experts in Japan point to the expected harsh reaction from the international community as a central premise of their calculation. These experts, including this writer, have felt since North Korea's first nuclear test that an increasing number of people have started to express at least some skepticism about such explanations.

Although the vast majority of people in Japan remain anti-nuclear today, the results of the nuclear cost-benefit calculation are less obvious than it had been. Repeated failures by the international community to demonstrate firm resolve to stand united against nuclear proliferators could undermine Japan's incentives to remain non-nuclear. For example, suppose Japan found itself in a situation in which all of its neighbors—North Korea, South Korea and Taiwan, in addition to China and Russia—had acquired significant nuclear arsenals, or in a situation in which there were twenty or thirty or even more nuclear weapon states. In either situation, no one could predict confidently that the Japanese would still find convincing reasons for their country to maintain a non-nuclear-weapons policy. From this standpoint, the passage of UN Security Council Resolution 1874, placing tighter sanctions on North Korea following its second nuclear test, was an encouraging sign. Many in Japan, however, felt that it took too much time for China and Russia to reach agreement with Japan, the United States, South Korea, and other countries with regard to the contents of the sanctions, and that the sanctions themselves were not quite sufficient to teach Pyongyang a lesson.

PROACTIVE BUT CONDITIONAL: JAPAN'S APPROACH TO MOVING TO ZERO

On April 27, 2009, Japan's Foreign Minister Hirofumi Nakasone delivered a major address entitled "Conditions towards Zero—11 Benchmarks for Global Nuclear Disarmament" at the Japan Institute of International Affairs (JIIA) Forum in Tokyo.[146] As he mentioned in the address, the Japanese have recently sensed "a momentum building toward nuclear disarmament for the first time in many years," beginning with the article, "A World Free of Nuclear Weapons," published in *The Wall Street Journal* on January 4, 2007 by the so-called "Gang of Four"—George P. Shultz, William J. Perry, Henry A. Kissinger and Sam Nunn.[147] Japan, which has seen itself as the champion of nuclear disarmament and has proposed a resolution for the total elimination of nuclear weapons to the UN General Assembly every year since 1994, naturally welcomed this momentum, which was strengthened by the launching of the "Global Zero" movement in December 2008 and US President

Obama's speech in Prague on April 5, 2009. In fact, even before these latest developments, together with Australia, Japan had established the International Commission on Nuclear Non-Proliferation and Disarmament co-chaired by Japan's former Foreign Minister Yoriko Kawaguchi and Australia's former Foreign Minister Gareth Evans in September 2008 with the aim of "reinvigorat[ing] international efforts on nuclear non-proliferation and disarmament."[148] When the commission held its first meeting in Sydney in October 2008, the Japanese government issued a statement which expressed its hope that "the International Commission will be able to present a path toward a peaceful world free of nuclear weapons."[149]

The address by Nakasone eloquently demonstrated the proactive attitude of the Japanese government to "take advantage of the growing momentum" toward global nuclear disarmament. Expressing his strong support of US President Obama's commitment to taking realistic and concrete steps toward the realization of a peaceful, safe, nuclear-free world, Foreign Minister Nakasone proposed "eleven benchmarks" for promoting global nuclear disarmament, categorized under "three major pillars."

> **Pillar I:** nuclear disarmament by all states holding nuclear weapons;
>
> **Pillar II:** disarmament and non-proliferation measure to be taken by the entire international community;
>
> **Pillar III:** measures to support countries seeking to promote peaceful uses of nuclear energy.

As part of the first pillar, all nuclear weapon states, including those countries that are not signatories of the NPT but actually possess nuclear weapons, would take "concrete measures to significantly reduce" their nuclear arsenals. Nakasone proposed five benchmarks as part of this pillar:

i) "Leadership of and cooperation between the United States and Russia," including promotion of a comprehensive bilateral strategic dialogue to conclude a successor treaty to the START I Treaty;

ii) "Nuclear disarmament by China and the other states holding nuclear weapons," with particular emphasis on the vital importance of reducing all nuclear arsenals;

iii) "Transparency over nuclear arsenal," including "regular and sufficient information disclosure concerning their own nuclear arsenals," by all nuclear weapons states;

iv) "Irreversible nuclear disarmament," including dismantlement of nuclear warheads, nuclear testing sites, and facilities to produce fissile material for weapon purposes by all nuclear weapon states;

v) "Study on future verification," to which Japan is ready to contribute by utilizing its own advanced science and technology.

As part of the second pillar, the entire international community would adopt and comply with "universal norms for disarmament and non-proliferation." Nakasone proposed three benchmarks for this pillar:

I. "Ban on nuclear tests," for which "Japan will work with China, India, Pakistan and other countries" whose ratifications are necessary for the CTBT to enter into force, to help gain their early ratification of the treaty, and would draw up, "a program to promote the early entry-into-force of the CTBT," which is to "make demarches on early ratification" and to "contribute to the establishment of a global verification system."

II. "Ban on production of fissile material for nuclear weapon purposes," including the conclusion of a Fissile Material Cut-off Treaty and the declaration by all countries of a moratorium to freeze the production of fissile material for weapon purposes pending the conclusion of the treaty.

III. "Restrictions on ballistic missiles" for which "Japan supports the globalization of the Intermediate-Range Nuclear Forces Treaty between the United States and Russia, and the EU's move to propose a treaty to ban short- and intermediate-range-ground-to-ground missiles."

Finally, as part of the third pillar, peaceful uses of nuclear energy by non-nuclear weapons states would be promoted, while ensuring nuclear non-proliferation, the prevention of nuclear terrorism, and nuclear safety. Under this pillar, three more benchmarks were proposed by the Japanese Foreign Minister:

I. "International cooperation for civil nuclear energy," for which Japan has taken "an approach, called '3S,' referring to safeguards, nuclear safety, and nuclear security." Japan "intends to help countries in newly introducing nuclear power plants to do so in a way that ensures the 3S," and "has been supporting human resource development and capacity building," particularly in Asia.

II. "IAEA safeguards," with regard to which Japan has been actively working towards universal acceptance of the NPT Comprehensive Safeguards Agreements and the Model Additional Protocol.

III. "Prevention of nuclear terrorism," for which Japan welcomes President Obama's proposal to make a new international efforts to strengthen the control of nuclear material and host a "Global Summit on Nuclear

Security," and will cooperate with the United States for this summit meeting to be held successfully.

Foreign Minister Nakasone also declared that Japan would "do its utmost" to accomplish the eleven benchmarks, and would host an international conference, tentatively entitled "The 2010 Nuclear Disarmament Conference" in early 2010 "to encourage concerted actions by the international community to promote global nuclear disarmament." Nakasone concluded his address by saying:

> As the Foreign Minister of the only country to experience the devastation of nuclear bombings, I would be most delighted if the outcome of this conference, together with the 11 benchmarks that I proposed, led to a successful conclusion of the 2010 NPT Review Conference and helped us take a great step toward nuclear disarmament.[150]

The Japanese government officially proposed the eleven benchmarks to the Third Session of the Preparatory Committee of the 2010 Review Conference of the Parties to the Treaty on the Non-Proliferation of Nuclear Weapons, held in New York in May 2009.[151]

The central purpose of Nakasone's address was to educate and encourage the Japanese people to support him and his government in playing a leading role in promoting global nuclear disarmament and seeking a world free of nuclear weapons, as well as to demonstrate to the world Japan's proactive stance on these issues. In the same address, however, the Foreign Minister also emphasized the importance of facing up to the reality of the international security environment when tackling nuclear disarmament and nuclear non-proliferation. In this portion of his speech, Nakasone particularly stressed the significance of US extended nuclear deterrence for the security of Japan:

> When we advance nuclear disarmament and non-proliferation, it is of course necessary to take into consideration the security environment that we face in reality. In light of the situation in East Asia that I mentioned earlier, it goes without saying that the extended deterrent including nuclear deterrence under the Japan-US security arrangements is of critical importance for Japan.[152]

In fact, the logic of this argument by Nakasone is identical to the logic expressed by President Obama in Prague.

Make no mistake: *As long as these weapons exist*, the United States will maintain a safe, secure and effective arsenal to deter any adversary, and guarantee that defense to our allies [emphasis added].[153]

In his JIIA address, Japan's foreign minister responded to this well-known phrase by declaring that Japan would maintain a stance that considered the US extended deterrent significant for its security, *as long as nuclear weapons exist.* "I believe that the world has now arrived at a stage where it should consider more specifically a realistic approach to nuclear disarmament whereby international stability will be preserved both in establishing the goal of the world free of nuclear weapons as well as in the process of attaining it," said Nakasone.[154]

In the article explaining the eleven benchmarks, Nakasone expressed his belief that "there is no contradiction whatsoever between fulfilling the most important obligation [of the state] of national security and advocating nuclear disarmament and nuclear non-proliferation to all the countries in the world."[155]

Many Japanese mainstream security thinkers seem to agree with Nakasone. For instance, in his keynote paper to a round-table discussion among security experts, entitled "Path to 'Global Zero," which appeared in the *Asahi Shimbun*, Associate Professor Toshihiro Nakayama of Tsuda College stated:

> ..."A world free of nuclear weapons" is "the world it ought to be." However, the distance between "the world it ought to be" and the reality is so grave...The Japanese share a special sentiment toward nuclear issues. However, if we take the Obama initiative seriously, we have to talk not only about "the world it ought to be," but also about a path to "the world it ought to be." That is to say, we will have to talk and think about the global nuclear order which will stay around for some time yet."[156]

Based on such thinking, Nakayama argued at the round table that if the Japanese are willing to take Global Zero as a realistic, not merely idealistic, issue, "it is indeed necessary to start our thinking from the 'nuclear umbrella.'"[157]

Associate Professor of Keio University Ken Jimbo agreed with Nakayama by saying, "The understanding should be shared in Japan that [US] nuclear forces are ready today to respond to various developments, though the United States is reducing the roles of nuclear weapons. Such is the healthy situation, I think."[158]

In another round-table discussion arranged by the monthly foreign policy journal *Gaiko Forum,* entitled "Between Disarmament and Security," a political columnist of the *Asahi Shimbun,* Fumihiko Yoshida, emphasized the necessity to reassure

Japan by a "redefinition" of extended nuclear deterrence into a new form that could be consistent with President Obama's scenario of nuclear disarmament. The president of Japan Association of Disarmament Studies, Mitsuru Kurosawa, while welcoming the growing momentum toward nuclear disarmament, expressed his belief that extended nuclear deterrence will remain necessary as long as nuclear weapons exist. Director of the Disarmament, Non-proliferation and Science Department of the Foreign Policy Bureau of the Ministry of Foreign Affairs Toshio Sano emphasized that Japan's quest for nuclear disarmament will have to be compatible with Japan's efforts for national security.[159]

Since the early Cold War period, Japan has long coexisted "peacefully" with its nuclear neighbors, Russia (Soviet Union) and China, without arming itself with nuclear weapons. This peaceful coexistence, however, has never meant that Japan had abandoned its efforts to protect itself from the nuclear weapons of these neighboring countries. Firmly maintaining its non-nuclear policy, Japan has maintained its security by the combination of a limited build-up of its own conventional forces (with various self-imposed restraints) and the security alliance with the United States, including the US nuclear umbrella. In light of North Korea's acquisition of nuclear weapons, China's growing nuclear and missile arsenals, and Russia's remaining nuclear forces, non-nuclear Japan will have to promote its security by improving its conventional weapon capabilities, including missile defense capabilities, *and* strengthening the alliance with the United States, including reassurance from US that it continues to extend its nuclear umbrella over Japan.

That is why a Japanese signatory to Global Zero, former President of the Japan Institute of International Affairs Ambassador Yukio Satoh, who believes that "[e]liminating the threat of nuclear weapons is critically important for the future of all humanity,"[160] said that:

The argument made by the aforementioned four eminent strategists in the tone-setting joint article published in The Wall Street Journal ... was received with mixed reactions in Japan: welcome for the sake of nuclear disarmament and caution from the perspectives of security and defense. As depending upon the US' extended nuclear deterrence will continue to be Japan's only strategic option to neutralize potential or conceivable nuclear and other strategic threats, the Japanese are sensitive to any sign of increased uncertainties with regard to extended deterrence."[161]

Thus, Japan's attitude toward Global Zero is identical to that of President Obama's. First, both are highly proactive in promoting global nuclear disarmament, and are willing to take concrete measures for that purpose. Second, although both believe in the desirability of a world free of nuclear weapons, both acknowledge the difficulty of realizing such a world. "I'm not naive. This goal will not be reached quickly—perhaps not in my lifetime. It will take patience and persistence," said President Obama in his address in Prague.[162] The Japanese government has often used the phrase "ultimate elimination of nuclear weapons," recognizing that it will take a long time to achieve elimination. Third, despite their proactive stance to promote the ideal of a nuclear-free world, both President Obama and Japan have made it clear that both have no intention of jeopardizing the security of their respective nations for the sake of global nuclear disarmament. President Obama's initiative has been recognized by the world as "realistic" because he made it clear that the United States will maintain a credible basic and extended deterrent until all other nuclear weapon states follow his initiative to reduce and eventually eliminate the role of nuclear weapons. Japan has also followed a realistic policy with regard to nuclear disarmament. Strongly committed to the ultimate elimination of nuclear weapons, and to the maintenance of its own non-nuclear policy, Japan works hard to maintain the US guarantee to defend Japan, including its nuclear umbrella.

The Japanese have learned the degree of patience and persistence required to inch toward the goal of global nuclear disarmament through their own experiences. A Japanese diplomat, who prefers to remain anonymous, said:

> Japan has tried hard to promote nuclear disarmament. But how often Japan has had to be chagrined at not being listened to by nuclear weapons states, including the United States. Due to its non-nuclear status, and due to the reality of its reliance on the US nuclear umbrella, Japan has lacked an effective leverage to move nuclear weapons states. Now, because of the 'Gang of Four,' the Global Zero movement, and President Obama's speech in Prague, nuclear weapons states have finally became somewhat serious about nuclear disarmament. I believe Japan can utilize this opportunity to get closer to the Japan's long-cherished dream of nuclear abolition.[163]

Both houses of the Japanese Diet, which on May 26 and 27, 2009, respectively, adopted resolutions condemning North Korea's second nuclear test and calling on the Japanese government to "take resolute measures, such as a strengthening of sanctions," against Pyongyang, also adopted unanimously, on June 16 and 17, respectively, for the first time in the history of the Japanese Diet, another set of resolutions requesting the Japanese government strengthen its efforts toward the abolition of nuclear weapons.[164] The contrast between these resolutions represents a clear manifestation of the nature of Japan's realistic approach toward Global Zero.

ENDNOTES

[1] "Obama Daitouryou: Kaku-Haizetsu Enzetsu, Yuiitsu no Kaku-Shiyou-koku, 'Dougi-teki Sekinin' ni Genkyuu (President Obama: Address on Nuclear Abolition, Referred to 'Moral Responsibility' of the Only Nuclear Power to Have Used Nuclear Weapons)," *Mainichi Shimbun* (April 7, 2009).

[2] *Ibid*.

[3] "2009-nen 6-gatsu 10-ka Kisha Kaiken: Obamajority Campaign ni Tsuite (Press Conference [of Mayor], June 10, 2009: On Obamajority)," website of the City of Hiroshima, http://www.city.hiroshima.jp/www/contents/0000000000000/1244613195105/index.html (accessed on July 19, 2009).

[4] *Genshiryoku Iinkai Mail Magazine*, No.31 (May 29, 2009).

[5] "Kaku-Naki Sekai he (Toward a World Free of Nuclear Weapons)," *Asahi Shimbun* (May 20, 2009).

[6] "'Kaku-Naki Sekai' ha Genjitsu-ron, Obama Bei-Seiken Tanjou ga Hakusha ('A World Free of Nuclear Weapons' Is Discussed Realistically, Spurred by the Inauguration of the Obama Administration in the US)," *Kyodo-tsushin* (Kyodo News) (January 19, 2009); https://contents.nifty.com/member/service/g-way/mmdb/aps/RXCN/main.jsp?ssid=20090626152809649acropolis02 (accessed on January 22, 2009).

[7] Yukio Satoh, "Kaku-Gunshuku Jidai no Nippon no Anzen-hoshou: Kakudai-Yokushi no Shinnraisei Koujou ga Kagi (Japan's Security in the Era of Nuclear Disarmament: Enhancement of Credibility of Extended Deterrence Is the Key)," *Gaiko Forum*, Vol.22, No.8 (August 2009), p.47; Toshihiro Nakayama, "'Arubeki Sekai' made Tsuzuku 'Kaku no Chitsujo' Kangaeyo (Think about the 'Nuclear Order' That Will Last Unitil 'the World It Ought to Be' Is Realized)," submitted to the round-table discussion: "Path to 'Global Zero," *Asahi Shimbun*, (July 17, 2009).

[8] Satoh, "Kaku-Gunshuku Jidai no Nippon no Anzen-hoshou," page 47.

[9] For typical examples of this line of argument, see Fumihiko Yoshida, "Obama Daitouryou ga Tou Wareware no 'Honki' (President Obama Has Raised Questions about Our 'Seriousness')," concluding remark to the round-table discussion: "Path to 'Global Zero,'" *Asahi Shimbun* (July 17, 2009); and Toshihiro Nakayama's remark in this round-table discussion.

[10] "'Kaku-Naki Sekai' ha Genjitsu-ron."

[11] Ministry of Foreign Affairs, "Japan Protests against North Korea's Nuclear Test Announcement," May 25, 2009, http://www.mofa.go.jp/announce/announce/2009/5/1192257_1134.html (accessed on May 26, 2009).

[12] "Statement by the Prime Minister of Japan," (May 25, 2009), http://www.kantei.go.jp/foreign/asospeech/2009/05/25seimei_e.html (accessed on May 26, 2009).

[13] "Lower House Condemns North's Nuke Test," *Asahi Shimbun* (May 27, 2009), http://www.asahi.com/english/Herald-asahi/TKY200905270006.html (accessed on May 30, 2009); "Upper House Adopts Resolution Condemning North Korean Nuclear Test," *Kyodo News*

on the Web (May 27, 2009), http://home.kyodo.co.jp/modules/fstStory/index.php?storyid=441025 (accessed on May 30, 2009); "Kita-Chosen Kaku-Jikken Jisshi ni Taisuru Kougi Ketsugi (A Resolution to Protest against the Conduct of the Nuclear Test by North Korea)" House of Representatives website, http://www.shugiin.go.jp/itdb_annai.nsf/html/statics/ketugi090526.html (accessed on June 15, 2009); "Kita-Chosen Kaku-Jikken Jisshi ni Taisuru Kougi Ketsugi (A Resolution to Protest against the Conduct of the Nuclear Test by North Korea)" House of Councilors website, http://www.sangiin.go.jp/japanese/ugoki/h21/090527-3.html (accessed on June 15, 2009).

[14] "Statement of the ASEM 9th Foreign Ministers Meeting on the Nuclear Test Conducted by the DPRK on May 25, 2009," http://www.mofa.go.jp/policy/economy/asem/asem9/state0905.html (accessed on June 19, 2009).

[15] "Aso Shushou no Ichinichi: 5-gatu 25-nichi (How Prime Minister Aso Spent the Day: May 25)," *Yomiuri Shimbun* (May 26, 2009); "Kita-Chosen Kaku-Jikken: Seifu ga Kougi, Kokuren Anpori ni Seisai-Ketsugi wo Motomeru (North Korea's Nuclear Test: The Government Made a Protest, Requested UNSC a Sanctions Resolution)," *Mainichi Jp* (May 25, 2009), http://mainichi.jp/select/today/news/20090526k0000m010122000c.html (accessed on May 26, 2009).

[16] "Security Council, Acting Unanimously, Condemns in Strongest Terms Democratic People's Republic of Korea Nuclear Test, Toughens Sanctions," SC/9679, June 12, 2009; "Resolution 1874 (2009)," S/RES/1874 (2009), June 12, 2009.

[17] "Waga-Kuni no Tai-Kita-Chosen Sochi ni tsuite (Kanbo-Chokan Danwa) (On Measures Taken against North Korea by Our Country [Statement by Chief Cabinet Secretary])" (June 16, 2009), http://www.kantei.go.jp/jp/tyokan/aso/2009/0616happyou.html (accessed on June 22, 2009).

[18] "National Defense Program Outline, FY2005-" [http://www.kantei.go.jp/foreign/policy/2004/1210taikou_e.html].

[19] The Project Team on North Korea of the DPJ, "Kita-Chosen Mondai ni Kan-suru Genjou no Kangae-kata (How the DPJ Currently Views the North Korea Problems)" (February 26, 2003).

[20] "Daijin Kaiken Gaiyou (The Outline of the Minister's Interview)" (May 26, 2009, 8:48 to 8:53AM), Ministry of Defense Website, http://www.mod.go.jp/j/kisha/2009/05/26.html (accessed on June 6, 2009).

[21] *Kyodo-tsushin* (Kyodo News), September 17, 2006, https://contents.nifty.com/member/service/g-way/mmdb/aps/RXCN/main.jsp?ssid=20090701071740717acropolis04 (accessed on June 7, 2009).

[22] "Kita no Kyoui "Tsuyomaru" 81%, Seisai "Shiji" 90%, Kaku-Jikken uke: Yomiuri Shimbun-sha Yoron-Chousa (81% Say Threat of the North "Has Become Stronger, 90% "Support" Sanction, in Response to Nuclear Test: Yomiuri Shimbun Co. Public Opinion Survey)," *Yomiuri Shimbun*,(October 17, 2006).

[23] "Kita-Chosen Kaku-Jikken, 'Taiwa' yori "Seisai"62%: Asahi Shimbun-sha Yoron Chousa ("On North Korea's Nuclear Test, 62% Says 'Sanctions' rather than 'Dialogue': Asahi Shimbun Co. Public Opinion Survey)," *Asahi Shimbun* (October 11, 2006).

[24] "Kita-Chosen heno Dokuji-Seisai, 'Kyouka-subeki' ga 65%: NHK Yoron-Chousa (65% Say Unilateral Sanctions against North Korea Should be Strengthened: Public Opinion Survey by NHK)," *NHK News*, https://contents.nifty.com/member/service/g-way/mmdb/aps/RXCN/main.jsp?ssid=20090701070313040acropolis04 (accessed on June 16, 2009).

[25] "Tai-Kita-Chosen Seisai "Tsuyomeru bekida" 88%: Yomiruri Shimbun-sha Yoron Chousa" (88% Say Sanctions against North Korea "Should Be Strengthened: Yomiuri Shimbun Co. Public Opinion Survey), *Yomiuri Shimbun*, June 8, 2009.

[26] "North Korean Launch Draws Japan's Anger," *Asahi Shimbun* (April 6, 2009), http://www.asahi.com/english/Herald-asahi/TKY200904060008.html (accessed on April 6, 2009).

[27] The numbers are based on the data preserved at the "Shinbun Zasshi Kiji Oudan Kensaku (Cross-Searchable Database of Newspaper and Magazine Articles)," a database service powered by the G-Search Limited and provided by the Nifty Corporation at http://www.nifty.com/RXCN/ (accessed on June 30, 2009).

[28] Hajime Izumi and Katsuhisa Furukawa, "Not Going Nuclear: Japan's Response to North Korea's Nuclear Test," Arms Control Today (June 2007), http://www.armscontrol.org/act/2007_06/CoverStory (accessed on February 18, 2009).

[29] "Mitsubishi Sougou Kenkyu-jo, Dai-3-kai Shimin no Risk Chousa wo Jisshi (The Mitsubishi Research Institute Conducted the 3rd Survey on Public Consciousness on Risks), on the website of the Mitsubishi Research Institute, Inc., http://www.mri.co.jp/NEWS/press/2009/2010059_1435.html (accessed on July 12, 2009); The Mitsubishi Research Institute, Inc., "The 3rd Survey on Public Consciousness on Risks: Data" (July 10, 2009), http://www.mri.co.jp/NEWS/press/2009/__icsFiles/afieldfile/2009/07/08/pr090710_ssu00.pdf (accessed on July 12, 2009); "Ichiban Kowai News, Shingata-infuru: Kotoshi Zenhan (The Most Frightening News Was the New Type Influenza: In the First Half of This Year)," *Yomiuri Shimbun, evening edition*, (July 11, 2009). Sixteen percent and nearly ten percent of the respondents, respectively, chose "the new type influenza" as the second and the third most frightening developments, while 20 percent and nearly 12 percent chose "the missile shooting and the nuclear tests by North Korea" as the second and the third. In total, 57 percent of the respondents chose the new type influenza, while 54 percent chose North Korea.

[30] *Yomiuri Shinbun*, evening edition (October 2, 2002).

[31] *Yomiuri Shinbun*, Western edition (October 3, 2002); *Yomiuri Shinbun*, evening edition (October 7, 2002).

[32] *Yomiuri Shinbun*, evening edition (October 10, 2002).

[33] *Asahi Shinbun* (October 7, 2003).

[34] "KCNA Urges Japan to Behave with Discretion," *Korean News: News from Korean Central News Agency of the DPRK*, http://www.kcna.co.jp/index-e.htm (accessed on April 15, 2003).

[35] Matake Kamiya, "A Disillusioned Japan Confronts North Korea," *Arms Control Today*, (May 2003).

[36] The results of these polls were printed in *Yomiuri Shimbun* (December 19, 1999 and December 18, 2008).

[37] Yasuhiro Matsuda, "Japanese Assessments of China's Military Development," *Asian Perspective*, Vol.31, No.3 (2007), page 188.

[38] *Defense of Japan 2000*, (Tokyo: Japan Ministry of Defense, 2000), Ch.1, available online at http://www.clearing.mod.go.jp/hakusho_data/2000/honmon/frame/at1201030402.htm (accessed on April 9, 2009); "'Nihon ha Chugoku no Misairu Shatei-nai' Bouei Hakusho, Hatsu no Shiteki ('Japan Is within the Range of China's Missiles': Defense White Paper Points out for the First Time)," *Asahi Shimbun* (July 2, 2000); "The Defense Agency Warns That North Korea Continues to Pose a Threat," *Asahi Evening News* (July 28, 2000).

[39] *Defense of Japan 2008*, (Tokyo: Japan Ministry of Defense, 2008), page 51, available online at http://www.mod.go.jp/e/publ/w_paper/2008.html (accessed on April 9, 2009).

[40] *Ibid.*, page 49.

[41] National Defense Program Outline, FY2005-. Op.cit.

[42] "Japan's Defense Budget to Fall for 7th Straight Year," *Kyodo World News Service* (December 20, 2008).

[43] Hisayoshi Ina, "Bei Iradataseru 'Koizumi Gunshuku' ('Koizumi Disarmament' Has Irritated the United States)," *Nihon Keizai Shimbun (Nikkei)* (August 31, 2008).

[44] Ambassador J. Thomas Schieffer, "Address to The Foreign Correspondents Club of Japan: 'The Price of Security in a Changing World" (May 20, 2008), Tokyo, Japan, http://tokyo.usembassy.gov/e/p/tp-20080520-72.html (accessed on June 19, 2009).

[45] "Joint Statement: U.S.-Japan Security Consultative Committee," Washington, DC (February 19, 2005), http://www.mofa.go.jp/region/n-america/us/security/scc/joint0502.html (accessed on June 19, 2009).

[46] Anthony Faiola, "Japan to Join U.S. Policy on Taiwan: Growth of China Seen Behind Shift," *Washington Post* (February 18, 2005), page A5; J. Sean Curtin, "The Dragon Roars over US-Japan Accord," *Asia Times Online* (February 23, 2005), http://www.atimes.com/atimes/Japan/GB23Dh01.html (accessed on June 20, 2009); and "US-Japan Statement on Taiwan Opposed," *China Daily* (online), (February 20, 2005), http://www.chinadaily.com.cn/english/doc/2005-02/20/content_417717.htm (accessed on June 20, 2009).

[47] Faiola, *op.cit.*

[48] "Taiwan ha Nichibei-Anpo no Taishou (Taiwan Is Included in the Japan-U.S. Security Treaty)," *Asahi Shimbun* (April 30, 2005).

[49] Matsuda, "Japanese Assessments of China's Military Development," *op.cit.,* page 186.

[50] Seiji Maehara, "Minshu-tou no Mezasu Kokka-zou to Gaikou Bijon (DPJ's Vison of Japan and Japanese Diplomacy)," the transcript of an address at the Center for Strategic and International Studies, December 9, 2005, http://www.maehara21.com/kiji/kiji051209.html (accessed on December 15, 2009).

[51] "Press Conference by Foreign Minister Taro Aso" (December 22, 2005), http://www.mofa.go.jp/announce/fm_press/2005/12/1222.html (accessed on December 15, 2009).

[52] *Ibid.*

[53] "Beijing Hits Aso for Threat Rhetoric," *The Japan Times* (online), (May 8, 2009), http://search.japantimes.co.jp/cgi-bin/nn20090508a5.html (accessed on May 12, 2009).

[54] Daisuke Yamamoto, "G-8 Urges N. Korea to Abandon Nukes, Expresses Concern about Iran," *Kyodo News on the Web* (June 26, 2009), http://home.kyodo.co.jp/modules/fstStory/index.php?storyid=446388 (accessed on June 26, 2009); "Nakasone-shi, Chugoku no Kaku-gunbi ni Kenen - G8 Gaishou Kaigou ga Kaimaku (Mr. Nakasone Expressed Concern with Chin's Nuclear Arsenal: G8 Foreign Ministers' Meeting Has Begun," *Jiji.com* (June 26, 2009), http://headlines.yahoo.co.jp/hl?a=20090626-00000043-jij-int (accessed on June 26, 2009); "Nakasone-Gaishou, Chugoku wo Nazashi-Hihan (Foreign Minister Nakasone Criticized China by Name)," *Kyodo-tsushin* (Kyodo News), http://news.nifty.com/cs/domestic/governmentdetail/kyodo-2009062601000352/1.htm (accessed on June 26, 2009).

[55] Izumi and Furukawa, *op.cit.*

[56] "Shuchou: Bouei Hakusho, Takamaru Chugoku no Kyoui Chokushi wo (Opinion: Defense White Paper - Face up to the Growing Threat of China), *Sankei Shimbun* (September 6, 2008).

[57] Yoshiko Sakurai, "Chugoku no Kyoui wo Mitsumeyo, Jieitai (Self-Defense Force, You Must Face up to China's Threat)," *Shukan-Shincho* (October 9, 2008), reproduced in Sakurai's blog, http://yoshiko-sakurai.jp/index.php/2008/10/09 (accessed on January 6, 2009). See also the website of Japan Institute for National Fundamentals, http://en.jinf.jp/ (accessed on August 15, 2009).

[58] Matake Kamiya, "Japanese Foreign Policy toward Northeast Asia," Takashi Inoguchi and Purnendra Jain, eds., *Japanese Foreign Policy Today* (New York: Palgrave, 2000), pages 246-248.

[59] Junichi Abe, "Chugoku no Gunji-ryoku to Nippon no ODA (China's Military Power and Japan's ODA,)" Japan Center for International Finance, ed., *Chugoku Shintaiseika ni Okeru Shomondai: Tai-Chu-Shien no Arikata ni tuite* (Various Problems under the New Leadership of China: On Japan's Assistance to China) (Tokyo: Japan Center for International Finance, 2004), page 67.

[60] "A New Era Requires New Political Will: An Address by the Honorable Shinzo Abe, Former Prime Minister of Japan," proceedings prepared from a tape recording, (Washington, DC: The Brookings Institution, April 17, 2009), page 7.

[61] *Defense of Japan 2008, op.cit.,* page 65.

[62] *Ibid.*, pages 1-4.

[63] The National Institute for Defense Studies, *East Asian Strategic Review 2009* (Tokyo: The Japan Times, 2009), page 204.

[64] "Secretary of Defense Robert Gates - Speech and Q&A Session with Students, Sophia University, Tokyo, Japan (November 9,2007)," http://tokyo.usembassy.gov/e/p/tp-20071109-73.html (accessed on December 15, 2008).

[65] Kakusan Fusegeruka, "6 (Can the Proliferation Be Prevented?: Part 6)," *Yomiuri Shimbun* (online) (November 16, 2007).

[66] "National Defense Program Outline, FY2005-" *op. cit.*

[67] *Ibid.*

[68] The National Security Research Project of the Tokyo Foundation, "New Security Strategy of Japan: Multilayered and Cooperative Security Strategy," The Tokyo Foundation Policy Recommendations, The Tokyo Foundation (October 8, 2008), http://www.tokyofoundation.org/en/additional_info/New%20Security%20Strategy%20of%20Japan.pdf (accessed on February 4, 2009).

[69] Public Relations Office, Cabinet Office, "Jieitai, Bouei-Mondai ni Kansuru Yoron-Chousa (Public Opinion Survey on the Self-Defense Forces and Defense Issues)" (January, 2009), http://www8.cao.go.jp/survey/h20/h20-bouei/index.html (accessed on March 19, 2009).

[70] "Kita no Kaku, Takamaru Kyoui (North Korea's Nuclear Weapons: Increasing Threat,)" *Yomiuri Shimbun* (June 16, 2009).

[71] Hiroshi Fuse, "Viewpoint: Nuclear Umbrella" (editorial), *Mainichi Shimbun* (June 23, 2009).

[72] "Kaku 'Mitsuyaku' Rongi, Tou-bekiha Kaku-no-Kasa no Shinrai (Debate over the 'Secret Agreement' on Nuclear Introduction: What Should Be Discussed Is the Credibility of Nuclear Umbrella)," *Sankei Shimbun* (July 3, 2009). In Japan, there has been a debate whether Japan and the United States reached a secret agreement with regard to port calls by US naval vessels carrying nuclear weapons to Japanese ports in negotiations in the late 1960s over the reversion of Okinawa to Japan.

[73] Schuyler Foerster, "Theoretical Foundations: Deterrence in the Nuclear Age," Schuyler Foerster and Edward N. Wright, eds., *American Defense Policy*, sixth edition (Baltimore: The Johns Hopkins University Press, 1990), page 46.

[74] *Ibid.*

[75] The author's argument along this line is quoted in the article written by Michael J. Green and Katsuhisa Furukawa, "Japan: New Nuclear Realism," in Muthiah Alagappa, ed., *The Long Shadow: Nuclear Weapons and Security in 21st Century Asia* (Stanford: Stanford University Press, 2008), page 356.

[76] Godfried van Benthem van den Bergh, *The Nuclear Revolution and the End of the Cold War: Forced Restraint* (Basingstoke and London: Macmillan in association with the Institute of Social Studies, 1992), page 193.

[77] Shinichi Ogawa, "A Nuclear Japan Revisited," *The National Institute for Defense Studies News*, No.64 (April 2003), page .3.

[78] The results of the poll were printed in *Yomiuri Shimbun* (December 5, 2002).

[79] The results of the poll were printed in *Yomiuri Shimbun* (December 18, 2008).

[80] *Ibid.*

[81] *Sankei Shimbun* (January 10, 2004); *Yomiuri Shimbun*, editorial (January 10, 2004).

[82] *Yomiuri Shimbun*, April 20, 2004.

[83] "Dai-23-kai Kokkai, Sangi-in, Shoukou-Iinkai-Kaigi-roku, Dai-5-gou (The 23th Session of the Diet, the House of Councilors, Commerce and Industry Committee, Proceedings, No.5)" (December 15, 1955), page 8. See also, Akira Sakuragawa, "Nihon no Gunshuku Gaiko (Japan's Disarmament Diplomacy)" *Kokusai Seiji* 80 (October 1985), page 64.

[84] *Ibid.*

[85] *Ibid.*, page 65.

[86] Japan Atomic Energy Commission, "Framework for Nuclear Energy Policy (Tentative Translation)" (October 11, 2005), page 4.

[87] *Ibid.*, page 7.

[88] The Japan Atomic Industrial Forum (JAIF), Inc., "World's Nuclear Generating Capacity Down about 1,800MW, Waits to Grow": JAIF Annual Report, World Nuclear Power Plants 2009, *Atoms in Japan Focus* (April 22, 2009), page 5.

[89] Japan Atomic Energy Commission, *White Paper on Nuclear Energy 2007 (Summary)* (March 2008), page.9.

[90] "Power Firms Delay Start of MOX Fuel up to 5 yrs," *The Daily Yomiur*, (June 13, 2009).

[91] "Framework for Nuclear Energy Policy (Tentative Translation)," *op.cit..* page 7. In this method, the plutonium extracted in the form of nitric acid solution [PuNH] is mixed with solution of uranyl nitrate hexahydrate [UNH, UO2(NO3)2_6H2O] before denitration into powder form.

[92] Tetsuo Sawada, "Plutonium Heiwa Riyou to Gunji Tenyou Mondai (Peaceful Use of Plutonium and the Issue of Military Diversion)," Kaku-Fukakusan Taiou Kenkyu-kai (Study Group on Nuclear Non-Proliferation), ed., *Plutonium Heiwa Riyou to Kaku-Kakusan Mondai* (Peaceful Use of Plutonium and the Nuclear Non-Proliferation) (Tokai-mura: Japan Nuclear Cycle Development Institute, 2003), page 80.

[93] This line of argument was first made by the author in Matake Kamiya, "Nuclear Japan: Oxymoron or Coming Soon," *The Washington Quarterly*, Vol.26, No.1 (Winter 2002-2003), page 70.

[94] Interview with Ryukichi Imai, April 25, 1995.

[95] "Bei, Kaku-Heiki 20-patsu-bun Hanshutu, Kou-noushuku Uran 580-kilo (The United States Has Carried out 580 Kilograms of Highly-Enriched Uranium, Sufficient to Make 20 Nuclear Weapons)," *Kyodo-tsushin* (Kyodo News) (December 27, 2008); "Kou-noushuku Uran: Nippon no Kenkyu-you Genshiro kara Bei he 580-kilo (Highly Enriched Uranium: 580 Kilograms from Japanese Research Reactors to the United States)," *Mainichi Shimbun* (December 28, 2008); "Bei, Nippon kara Kou-noushuku Uran 580-kilo Hanshutsu (The United States Has Carried out 580 Kilograms of Highly-Enriched Uranium from Japan)," *Sankei Shimbun* (December 28, 2008); "Japan Sent Uranium to the United States," *The Japan Times* (December 28, 2008). The quotation is from the articles in *Mainichi Shimbun* and *Sankei Shimbun*.

[96] "Bei, Kaku-Heiki 20-patsu-bun Hanshutu. " *Kyodo-tsuhin.*

[97] Yukiya Amano, "Reducing the Enrichment Level of Uranium Fuel (Japan's Experience)," paper presented at the international symposium on "Minimization of Highly Enriched Uranium (HEU) in the Civilian Nuclear Sector," Nobel Peace Center, Oslo (June 19, 2006), page 3.

[98] Jeffrey W. Thompson and Benjamin L. Self, "Nuclear Energy, Space Launch Vehicles, and Advanced Technology: Japan's Prospects for Nuclear Breakout," Benjamin L. Self and Jeffrey W. Thompson, eds., *Japan's Nuclear Option: Security, Politics, and Policy in the 21st Century* (Washington, D.C.: The Henry L. Stimson Center, 2003), page 148.

[99] "H-IIA Launch Vehicle," in the website of the Japan Aerospace Exploration Agency (JAXA), http://www.jaxa.jp/projects/rockets/h2a/index_e.html (accessed on January 6, 2009).

[100] "M-V Satellite Launch Vehicles," in the website of the JAXA, http://www.isas.jaxa.jp/e/enterp/rockets/vehicles/m-v/index.shtml (accessed on January 6, 2009).

[101] "Missile Program," in the website of the Federation of American Scientists, http://www.fas.org/nuke/guide/japan/missile/index.html (accessed on January 6, 2009).

[102] Thompson and Self, *op.cit., p*age 173.

[103] As a typical example, see Takashi Kawakami, "'Fuuin' Sareta Nihon-Kakubuso-ron wo Tokihanate (Liberate "Sealed" Discussions on Japan's Nuclearization)", *Sekai Shuho* (January 16, 2007).

[104] "Dai-165-kai Kokkai, Shuugi-in, Anzenhosho-Iinkaigi-roku, Dai-4-gou (The 165th Session of the Diet, the House of Representatives, Budget Committee, Proceedings, No.4)" (October 9, 2006), page 5.

[105] "Jimin Seichou-Kaichou 'Kaku-Hoyuu no Giron Hitsuyou,' Shushou ha San-Gensoku Kyouchou (Chairman of LDP'S Policy Research Council Says 'Discussion on Nuclear Posession Necessary,' Prime Minister Emphasizes the Three Principles)," *Asahi.com* (October 15, 2006), http://www.asahi.com/politics/update/1015/002.html (accessed on October 19, 2006).

[106] "Dai-165-kai Kokkai, Shuugi-in, Anzenhosho-Iinkagi-roku, Dai-1-gou (The 165th Session of the Diet, the House of Representatives, Security Committee, Proceedings, No.1)" (October 17, 2006), page 24.

[107] "Dai-165-kai Kokkai, Shuugi-in, Gaimu-Iinkaigi-roku, Dai-1-gou (The 165th Session of the Diet, the House of Representatives, Foreign Affairs Committee, Proceedings, No.1)" (October 18, 2006), page 21.

[108] Shigeru Ishiba, "Discussion about Nuclear Possession Should Be Done Publicly," *Nihonkai Shimbun* (October 22, 2006).

[109] Ikuo Kabashima, "A Nuclear Japan?" *Japan Echo*, Vol.30, No.4 (August 2003), http://www.japanecho.co.jp/sum/2003/300411.html (accessed on December 21, 2008); *Yomiuri Shimbun* (December 25, 1998).

[110] *Asahi Shimbun* (August 27, 2003).

[111] "Nakagawa Seichou-Kaichou 'Kaku-Hoyuu no Giron Atteii' Hatsugen, Hikeshi ni (Soothing the Impact of Chairman of Policy Research Council Nakagawa's Remark that 'Discussion about Nuclear Possession Should Be Allowed')," *Asahi.com* (October 16, 2006), http://www.asahi.com/politics/update/1016/019.html (accessed on October 19, 2006).

[112] "Kaku-Hoyuu Meguru Hatsugen, Nakagawa Seichou-Kaichou ga Shakumei (Chairman of Policy Research Council Offered Clarification on His Remark on Nuclear Posession)," *Asahi.com* (October 16, 2006), http://www.asahi.com/politics/update/1016/006.html (accessed on October 19, 2006).

[113] "Kaku Giron, Kojin Hyoumei ha Younin, Mondai no Shinkoku-ka Sakeru: Seifu, Jimin (Discussion on Nuclear Issue, Personal Expressions [of opinions] Would Be OK, to Avoid the Problem from Becoming More Serious: Government and LDP)," *Yomiuri Shimbun* (October 29, 2006).

[114] "'Kaku no Giron Attemo-ii': Nakagawa Zen-Zaimu-shou ('Nuclear Discussion May Be Included,' Said Ex-Finance Minister Nakagawa)," *Jiji.com* (April 5, 2009), http://www.jiji.com/jc/zc?k=200904/2009040500112, accessed on April 9, 2009.

[115] "Jimin, Sakamoto-shi, 'Nihon mo Kaku wo,' Tou Yakuin Renraku-kai de Hatsugen (Sakamoto of the LDP Said at Extraordinary Meeting of the Board or the Party: 'Japan Should Also [Discuss] Nuclear [Possession],'" *Asahi.com* (April 8, 2009), http://www.asahi.com/politics/update/0408/TKY200904080166.html (accessed on June 19, 2009); "Jimin, Sakamoto Soshiki Honbucho, 'Nihon mo Kakuhoyuu, Kokuren Dattai' (LDP Chairman of the Party Organization Headquarters Sakamoto: 'Japan's Nuclear Possession, Withdrawal from the UN')," *Yomiuri Shimbun* (online) (April 7, 2009), www.yomiuri.co.jp/politics/news/20090407-OYT1T01011.htm (accessed on July 4, 2009).

[116] "'Kaku ni Taikou Dekirunoha Kaku,' Kita-chosen Jousei de Nakagawa Zen-Zaimu-shou ('What Can Counter Nuclear Are Nuclear,' Said Ex-Finance Minister Nakagawa on the North Korea Issues), *Kyodo-tsushin* (Kyodo News) (April 19, 2009); "Nakagawa Floats Sobering Option: Going Nuclear," *Japan Times* (April 20, 2009).

[117] Jimin, Sakamoto-shi, "Nihon mo Kaku wo. " *op. cit.*

[118] "Nippon no Kaku-busou Jinrui Hametsu ni, Tai-Kita Reisei Taiou wo, Jimin, Yamasaki-shi (Japan's Nuclearization [Could Lead to] Destruction of Human Species, Cool-Headed Reaction to North Korea Is Needed, Said LDP's Yamasaki, " *Jiji.com* (April 7, 2009),

http://www.jiji.com/jc/zc?k=200904/2009040700776 (accessed on April 11, 2009); "Jimin, Sakamoto Soshiki Honbucho, 'Nihon mo Kakuhoyuu, Kokuren Dattai", *op. cit.*

[119] Tetsuo Kawato, "Kaku-Busou ni Oikomareru Maeni Mada Yareru Koto (What Can Be Done Before Being Forced to Go Nuclear)," at Tetsuo Kawato's blog (June 8, 2009), http://www.tkfd.or.jp/blog/kawato/2009/06/post_117.html (accessed on June 12, 2009).

[120] *Mainichi Shimbun* (November 27, 2006).

[121] http://www.fujitv.co.jp/b_hp/shin2001/chousa/2008/090405.html (accessed on May 26, 2009).

[122] NHK Broadcasting Poll Research Institute, ed., *Zusetsu Sengo Yoron-shi* (Postwar opinion polls illustrated), second edition (Tokyo: Nihon Hoso Shuppan Kyokai, 1982), pages 170-71.

[123] *Japan's Proactive Peace and Security Strategie*s, NIRA Research Report No. 20000005 (Tokyo: National Institute for Research Advancement, 2001), page 270.

[124] Kamiya, "Nuclear Japan," *op.cit.,* page 63.

[125] For details of the *Fukuryu-maru* incident, see Kazuya Sakamoto, "Kaku-Heiki to Nichi-Bei Kankei: Bikini Jiken no Gaiko Shori" (Nuclear weapons and the Japanese-U.S. relationship: The Diplomatic Settlement of the Bikini Incident), *Nenpo Kindai Nihon Kenkyu* 16 (November 1994), pages 243–271; Shigemichi Hirota, *Dai-go Fukuryu-maru* (The *Fukuryu-maru No. 5*) (Tokyo: Shiraishi Shoten, 1989).

[126] Sakamoto, "Kaku-Heiki to Nichi-Bei Kankei," p. 251; Hiroshi Iwadare, *Kaku-Heiki Haizetsu no Uneri* (The surge of movement to abolish nuclear weapons) (Tokyo: Rengo Shuppan, 1982), pages 11-13; Susumu Wada, *Sengo Nihon no Heiwa Ishiki* (Public opinion on peace issues in postwar Japan) (Tokyo: Aoki Shoten, 1997), page 93.

[127] *Energy Hakusho 2008* (White Paper on Energy 2008), page 127; see also footnote 100.

[128] Statistical Research and Training Institute, Ministry of Internal Affairs and Communications, *Statistical Handbook of Japan 2008* (Tokyo: Statistics Bureau, Ministry of Internal Affairs and Communication, 2008), page 62 and 64.

[129] Ministry of Foreign Affairs, *Gaiko Seisho, 2005* (Diplomatic bluebook, 2005), http://www.mofa.go.jp/Mofaj/gaiko/bluebook/2005/index1.html (accessed on January 6, 2009); Ministry of Foreign Affairs, *Gaiko Seisho, 2002* (Diplomatic bluebook, 2002) (Tokyo: Ministry of Finance Printing Bureau, 2002) page 88.; Ministry of Foreign Affairs, *Gaiko Seisho, 2009* (Diplomatic bluebook, 2009) (Tokyo: Jiji Gahou-sha, 2009) page 11.

[130] "Tairyou Hakai Heiki no Kakusan Mondai ni Tuite (On the Issue of Proliferation of Weapons of Mass Destruction)" (May 29, 1995), page 27. Because of the unofficial nature of the study, this final report was not intended for publication and has not been available to the public. A portion of the contents of the report were leaked in, "Anpo Minaoshi: Nichibei Sessho no Uchimaku (Reviewing Japanese-U.S. Security Relations: The Inside Facts About the Bilateral Negotiations)," *Shukan Toyo Keiza*i (December 2, 1995).

[131] "Tairyou Hakai Heiki no Kakusan Mondai ni Tuite," *op.cit.,* page 30.

[132] *Ibid.*, pages 24-29.

[133] Noboru Yamaguchi, "Japan's Nonnuclear Policy in a Post–Cold War Era: A Military Perspective," paper presented at the International Studies Association–Japan Association of International Relations Joint Convention, Makuhari, Japan (September 20–22, 1996).

[134] Ogawa, "A Nuclear Japan Revisited," *op. cit.,* pages 4-5.

[135] "Kita no Kyoui ha Shinkoku, Bei Gikai Kouchoukai deno Nihon Kaku-busou Rongi (Threat of North Korea Is Serious: Discussion on Japan's Nuclear Acquisition at the Hearing of the U.S. Congress)," *Sankei Shimbun* (online), http://headlines.yahoo.co.jp/hl?a=20090703-00000635-san-int, July3, 2009.

[136] Testimony by Joseph S. Nye, Jr., "Hearing on Japan's Changing Role," House Foreign Affairs Committee Subcommittee on Asia, the Pacific and the Global Environment (June 25, 2009),page 1; http://foreignaffairs.house.gov/111/nye062509.pdf (accessed on June 28, 2009).

[137] This phrase appeared in the preface by Foreign Minister Yoriko Kawaguchi to the first edition of Japan's *White Paper on Disarmament* in March 2003. Yoriko Kawaguchi, "Preface to the Publication of 'Japan's Disarmament Policy,'" Directorate General, Arms Control and Scientific Affairs, Ministry of Foreign Affairs, *Japan's Disarmament Policy* (Tokyo: The Center for the Promotion of Disarmament and Non-Proliferation, Japan Institute of International Affairs, 2003). Similar expressions repeatedly appeared in subsequent editions of the *White Paper on Disarmament*, published every two years since fiscal year 2002. The first edition was officially titled *Japan's Disarmament Policy*, and from the second edition, the title was changed to *Japan's Disarmament and Non-Proliferation Policy*.

[138] "Japan Brief, July 9, 2009" on the website of the Embassy of Japan in Austria gives a concise summary of editorials in Japan's five major newspapers on Amano's election. http://www.at.emb-japan.go.jp/English/japaninfo.htm (accessed on July 12, 2009).

[139] Toru Tamakawa, "Amano Elected IAEA Chief," *Asahi.com* (July 4, 2009), http://www.asahi.com/english/Herald-asahi/TKY200907040077.html (accessed on July 12, 2009).

[140] Emma Chanlett-Avery and Mary Beth Nikitin, "Japan's Nuclear Future: Policy Debate, Prospects, and U.S. Interests," CRS Report for Congress, RL34487 (Washington, DC: Congressional Research Service, February 19, 2009), page 7.

[141] "Nakagawa Seichou-Kaichou 'Kaku-Hoyuu no Giron Atteii' Hatsugen, Hikeshi ni." *Op.cit.*

[142] Ogawa, "A Nuclear Japan Revisited," page 2.

[143] Kamiya, "Nuclear Japan," *op. cit.,* page 73.

[144] For example, see "UN Imposes Sanctions on N.Korea for Nuclear Test," *China Daily.com.cn,* (October 15, 20060, http://www.chinadaily.net/world/2006-10/15/content_708287.htm (accessed on January 20, 2009).

[145] "Kaku-Hoyuu Koku ni Natta houga Toku nanoka ('Is It More Beneficial to Become a Nuclear Weapons State?')," *Opinion Letter*, No. 277 (March 22, 2007), in the Website of Kazuo Aichi, http://www.aichi-kazuo.net/004/ (accessed on June 27, 2009).

[146] "Conditions towards Zero—'11 Benchmarks for Global Nuclear Disarmament,'" Statement by Mr. Hirofumi Nakasone, Minister for Foreign Affairs of Japan, http://www.mofa.go.jp/policy/un/disarmament/arms/state0904.html (accessed on June 1, 2009); "Zero heno Jouken—Sekai-teki Kaku-Gunshuku no tameno 11-no Shihyou (Conditions towards Zero—11 Benchmarks for Global Nuclear Disarmament, Japanese version), http://www.mofa.go.jp/mofaj/press/enzetsu/21/enks_0427.html (accessed on June 1, 2009); and http://www2.jiia.or.jp/report/kouenkai/090427-nakasone.html (the summary in Japanese) (accessed on June 1, 2009). See also Hirofumi Nakasone, "'Zero heno Jouken' wo Totonoeru tame (In Order to Fulfill the 'Conditions toward Zero')," *Gaiko Forum*, Vol.22, No.8 (August 2009).

[147] George P. Shultz, William J. Perry, Henry A. Kissinger and Sam Nunn, "A World Free of Nuclear Weapons," *The Wall Street Journal* (January 4, 2007).

[148] http://www.icnnd.org/ (accessed on April 8, 2009). Besides Kawaguchi and Evans, thirteen other Commissioners from thirteen countries, including William Perry from the United States, are serving on the commission. In addition, the Commission's Advisory Board includes Henry Kissinger, Sam Nunn, and George Shultz.

[149] "The First Meeting of the International Commission on Nuclear Non-Proliferation and Disarmament" (October 17, 2008), on the Website of the Ministry of Foreign Affairs, http://www.mofa.go.jp/announce/event/2008/10/1183965_944.html (accessed on April 8, 2009).

[150] "Conditions towards Zero—'11 Benchmarks for Global Nuclear Disarmament," *op.cit.*

[151] http://www.mofa.go.jp/mofaj/gaiko/kaku/npt/jyunbi/03_gh.html (accessed on July 13, 2009); Nakasone, "Zero heno Jouken' wo Totonoeru tame," *op. cit.*, page 13.

[152] "Conditions towards Zero—'11 Benchmarks for Global Nuclear Disarmament.'" Op. cit.

[153] "Remarks by President Barack Obama, Hradcany Square, Prague, Czech Republic" (April 5, 2009), Office of the Press Secretary, The White House, http://www.whitehouse.gov/the_press_office/Remarks-By-President-Barack-Obama-In-Prague-As-Delivered/ (accessed on April 10, 2009).

[154] "Conditions towards Zero—'11 Benchmarks for Global Nuclear Disarmament,'" *op. cit.*

[155] Nakasone, ""Zero heno Jouken' wo Totonoeru tame," *op. cit.*, page 12.

[156] Toshihiro Nakayama, "'Arubeki Sekai' made Tsuzuku 'Kaku no Chitsujo' Kangaeyo (Think about the 'Nuclear Order' That Will Last Unitil the World It Ought to Be Is Realized)," submitted to the round-table discussion: "Path to 'Global Zero,'"*Asahi Shimbun* (July 17, 2009).

[157] The round-table discussion: "Path to 'Global Zero,'" *Asahi Shimbun* (July 17, 2009).

[158] *Ibid.*

159 "Between Disarmament and Security, A Round-table Discussion," *Gaiko Forum*, Vol.22, No.8 (August 2009), pages 20-29.

160 http://www.globalzero.org/en/who/yukio-satoh (accessed on July 5, 2009).

161 Yukio Satoh, "Reinforcing American Extended Deterrence for Japan: An Essential Step for Nuclear Disarmament," *AJISS-Commentary*, No.57 (February 3, 2009), http://www.jiia.or.jp/en_commentary/200902/03-1.html (accessed on February 8, 2009).

162 "Remarks by President Barack Obama, Hradcany Square, Prague, Czech Republic," *op. cit.*

163 This statement was made by a Japanese diplomat, who prefers to remain anonymous, to the author.

164 "Kaku-Haizetsu, Shuuin, Hatsu no Ketsugi, Seifu ni Issou no Doryoku Youkyuu (On Nuclear Abolition, Lower House Passed Its First Resolution, Requested the Government to Strengthen Its Efforts)," *Mainichi Shimbun* (online), June 16, 2009, http://mainichi.jp/select/today/news/20090616k0000e010080000c.html (accessed on June 18, 2009); "Kaku-Haizetsu Ketugi, Sanin mo Zenkai-icchi de Saitaku (Resolution on Nuclear Abolition, Adopted Also Unanimously by Upper House)," *Asahi.com*, http://www.asahi.com/politics/update/0617/TKY200906170094.html (accessed on June 18, 2009); http://www.shugiin.go.jp/index.nsf/html/index_gian.htm (accessed on July 17, 2009); and http://www.sangiin.go.jp/japanese/gianjoho/ketsugi/171/090617.pdf (accessed on July 17, 2009).

NORTH KOREA'S PERSPECTIVES ON THE GLOBAL ELIMINATION OF NUCLEAR WEAPON

Leon V. Sigal and Joel Wit

North Korea's position on the global elimination of nuclear weapons has only been addressed in passing. The government has had little to say about global elimination in negotiations with the United States, in informal discussions with Americans, or in public comments and propaganda beamed at audiences overseas or at home.

What North Korea says about nuclear weapons, its own decision to arm, US nuclear weapons policy, and the nuclear weapons policy of its neighbors does have some bearing on global elimination, but a review of North Korea's positions suggests that global elimination is not central to its concerns. Rather, Pyongyang is focused on eliminating the political, economic, and security threats it perceives to be posed by the United States and its allies. Whether a successful nuclear test will change its stance is not known.

NORTH KOREA'S NUCLEAR MOTIVATIONS

North Korea's nuclear program has been stimulated primarily by security concerns, but there are also domestic, regional and international political motivations behind the program.

Security Concerns

No country's motivation for building nuclear weapons can be known with certainty, but North Korea has been unusually explicit in its public statements about why it acquired nuclear weapons: insecurity. The prime reason for that insecurity is the United States and what Pyongyang calls America's "hostile policy." For North Korea, the concept of Washington's hostile policy is much broader than the threat posed by Washington's nuclear arsenal, and particularly the US threat of first use of nuclear weapons against it. It includes political, economic, and other military factors, such as the danger of invasion by conventional forces, economic sanctions, and attempts to suborn its government. Ending this hostile policy, rather than requiring the elimination of American nuclear weapons, has been the main condition for Pyongyang to eliminate its arsenal.

The North's view is the product of decades of confrontation with the United States starting with the Korean War. Aside from a continuing policy of political and economic hostility, which only began to thaw in the mid-1980s, US threats, both nuclear and conventional, were unusually explicit. Thousands of US tactical nuclear weapons were deployed on the Korean Peninsula as part of a strategy designed to deter a North Korean attack, as well as for possible use in a war. The location of these weapons, along with the positioning of US strategic forces, served to compel North Korean actions in certain circumstances, for instance, to coerce the North into ending the Korean War. North Korea has been the object of nuclear threats by the United States more often than any other country in the world—at least seven times since 1945.[1] On top of clear nuclear threats, the US conventional war plan has long called for American and allied forces to both repel an attack on the South and move into the North in event of a conflict.

The North's reaction to these threats has manifested itself in a number of ways. Aside from periodic propaganda offensives intended to undermine US ties with Japan and South Korea, Pyongyang's construction of an extensive system of underground military installations and tunnels dates back to just after 1963 when the Cuban Missile Crisis cast doubt on the Soviet Union's security guarantee. In addition, North Korea's forward conventional military posture, which clearly threatens Seoul, is probably designed to help deter such an attack. Beyond its bristling rhetoric and steps taken to defend against a possible nuclear attack, the North's interest in acquiring its own nuclear weapons to deter attack seems to date back to the immediate aftermath of the 1963 crisis when Kim Il Sung sent Mao Tse-tung a letter proposing that the two countries cooperate in building the bomb.[2]

By the early 1990s, Pyongyang's strategy seemed to have developed more emphasis on ending hostile relations with Washington, even to the point of constraining its nuclear weapon programs. The collapse of the Soviet bloc, China's establishment of diplomatic relations with the United States and Japan and its tentative movement towards normalizing relations with South Korea, and the deterioration of its own economic and military position vis-à-vis the South required a dramatic rethinking of North Korean security policy. Since Kim Il Sung could no longer count on his erstwhile allies, militarily or economically, he began reaching out to North Korea's lifelong enemies — the United States, South Korea and Japan — in an effort to turn foe into friend. Such realignment would improve North Korea's security and provide a hedge against an increasingly powerful China.

As a result, Pyongyang's strategy included a new component — not only seeking to deal with the threat of a nuclear attack by acquiring its own weapons, but also using that program as a possible bargaining chip to end US hostility. This strategy has formed the basis of North Korean policy towards the US for the past two decades.

The first significant sign of a shift came in 1991 when US withdrawal of its tactical nuclear weapons prompted North Korea to sign a safeguards agreement with the International Atomic Energy Agency and the Joint North-South Declaration on the Denuclearization of the Korean Peninsula. The 1994 US -North Korean Agreed Framework, which laid out a roadmap to denuclearization, seems to have been based on the assumption that Pyongyang would trade its nuclear program for better relations with the United States.

A fundamental turning point in that direction was reached with the visit of Marshal Jo Myong Rok to Washington DC in October 2000 and the trip by Secretary of State Madeleine Albright to Pyongyang a few weeks later. Pyongyang welcomed the US-drafted joint statement made public during Marshal Jo's visit in which the two sides affirmed that "they are prepared to undertake a new direction in their relations." As a crucial first step, the two sides stated that "neither government would have hostile intent toward the other and confirmed the commitment of both governments to make every effort in the future to build a new relationship free from past enmity."[3] That progress was discarded by the Bush Administration, which was more interested in confronting than engaging North Korea and other so-called rogue states.

While diplomatic efforts since the 2002 collapse of the 1994 Agreed Framework have made limited progress in restraining North Korea's revived nuclear program, success in addressing the fundamental political issue of strategic relations between Washington and Pyongyang has been even more elusive. As a result, the North has returned to an emphasis on the US's "hostile policy," which it says is designed to "isolate and stifle" North Korea.[4] The improvement of political relations is absolutely essential to achieve denuclearization. In that context, authoritative North Korean interlocutors have characterized US nuclear strategy as threatening and emphasized the need to remove that threat, but have seldom talked about the need to reduce or eliminate all US nuclear weapons.

North Korea's stance that as long as the United States remains hostile, it will seek nuclear weapons and missiles to deter that threat has permeated all of Pyongyang's major policy moves and statements. For example, the North's resumption of its plutonium production program in 2003 following the collapse of the Agreed Framework was, according to Pyongyang, a response to renewed hostility from the Bush Administration and US refusal to negotiate after confronting the North over its suspected uranium enrichment program.

Drawing lessons from the start of the Iraq war earlier that year, North Korea noted that the United States had first demanded that Iraq submit to inspections, and it did. The United States next demanded that Iraq disarm, and it began to. The United

States attacked it anyway. "This suggests that even the signing of a non-aggression treaty with the US would not help avert war," a DPRK Foreign Ministry spokesman said on April 6, 2003. "Only military deterrent force, supported by ultra-modern weapons, can avert a war and protect the security of the nation. This is the lesson drawn from the Iraqi war."[5] In short, Pyongyang's price for eliminating its nuclear arsenal is that Washington must demonstrate an end to enmity in deeds, not just words. Pyongyang requires a combination of written statements reaffirming respect for the North's sovereignty and non-interference in its internal affairs. This could be accomplished through significant agreements like a peace treaty ending the Korean War and a non-aggression pact or negative security assurance. North Korea also requires concrete demonstrations of non-hostility, such as normalizing political and economic relations and the provision of energy and other assistance.

A February 10, 2005 statement by the Foreign Ministry that declared North Korea to be a nuclear weapons state also put emphasis on US enmity:

> As we have clarified more than once, we justly urged the US to renounce its hostile policy toward the DPRK whose aim was to seek the latter's 'regime change' and switch its policy to that of peaceful co-existence between the two countries…However, the administration turned down our just request and adopted it as its policy not to co-exist with the DPRK.

The statement cited a US nuclear threat, but in the context of more generalized hostility from Washington: "The US disclosed its attempt to topple the political system in the DPRK at any cost, threatening it with a nuclear stick. This compels us to take a measure to bolster [our] nuclear weapons arsenal."[6]

In other public statements, as well as in discussions with US officials, the North Koreans drew attention to the 2001 Nuclear Posture Review, which designated North Korea as a possible target for nuclear attack; and the Bush doctrine of preventive war, promulgated in the president's West Point speech of June 2002.[7] Yet North Korea usually framed the US nuclear threat in the context of broader conventional military, economic, and political threats, as well as by its neighbors, Japan and South Korea. As the February 2005 statement noted,

> We had already taken the resolute action of pulling out of the N.P.T. and have manufactured nukes for self-defense to cope with the Bush administration's evermore undisguised policy to isolate and stifle the DPRK. [Our] nuclear weapons will remain [a] nuclear deterrent for self-defense under any circumstances.[8]

In announcing the October 6, 2006 nuclear test three days before conducting it, the DPRK Foreign Ministry cited the nuclear threat as just one reason among many for the test. Pyongyang denounced the UN Security Council resolution imposing sanctions on the North for its July 4 missile tests, "a de facto 'declaration of war' against the DPRK," and added,

> The US extreme threat of a nuclear war and sanctions and pressure compel the DPRK to conduct a nuclear test, an essential process for bolstering nuclear deterrent, as a corresponding measure for defense.[9]

Nevertheless, the North stated that its aim of negotiated denuclearization of the Korean peninsula remained unchanged and focused on ending its contentious relationship with the United States:

> The ultimate goal of the DPRK is not 'denuclearization' to be followed by its unilateral disarmament but one aimed at settling the hostile relations between the DPRK and the US and removing the very source of all nuclear threats from the Korean Peninsula and its vicinity.[10]

That source of the nuclear threats is not the weapons themselves, but the political context in which they are deployed.

Whether North Korea will change its approach as a result of a successful nuclear test remains unclear. For example, Pyongyang, like China, could seek to link it own nuclear reductions to those of the United States and other nuclear powers. In a recent formulation, a January 13, 2009 statement by the Foreign Ministry spokesman hints at a potential change of approach: "If the nuclear issue is to be settled, *leaving the hostile relations as they are,* all nuclear weapons states should meet and realize the simultaneous nuclear disarmament. This is the only option"[11] (emphasis added by author). While the statement retains a key qualifier, "leaving the hostile relations as they are," it can be argued that the North Koreans have now at least raised an alternative path into the future that has evolved from their previous position. North Korean interlocutors have never broached mutual disarmament in US talks, but hinted at the possibility in informal conversations.

Aside from the threat posed by the United States, the North has mentioned, on occasion, the possible dangers of nuclear weapons acquisition by Japan and South Korea. Whether those statements reflect real concern or are purely opportunistic is unclear, although Pyongyang probably does view Japan as a long-term danger. A case in point came on May 31, 2002, after Pyongyang restarted its plutonium program and Washington refused to hold talks. Chief Cabinet Secretary Yasuo Fukuda contended that Japan's peace constitution did not preclude nuclear weapons and suggested that "depending upon the world situation, circumstances and public opinion could require Japan to possess nuclear weapons."[12]

The North's response again framed the nuclear issue in the context of broader threats. A KCNA report noted Fukuda's comments:

> As evidenced by Japan's arms buildup and the tremendous strength of the 'self-defense forces,' such terms as disarmament, peace and three non-nuclear principles are nothing but a fig-leaf to cover up the revived Japanese militarists' moves to turn Japan into a military power and their policy of overseas expansion.[13]

The statement added that, "It is an open secret that one of the important targets of Japan's avowed policy of becoming a military power is to go nuclear to emerge a nuclear power." The article ended with a warning,

> Japan should discard its nuclear ambition, not oblivious of the lesson of history drawn from the nuclear disaster suffered by it in the past. If Japan persistently opts for nuclear armament, it will only invite an unimaginable nuclear disaster.[14]

More recently, in an authoritative April 2007 article appearing in the communist party's newspaper, the North criticized Tokyo's less than cooperative stance in the Beijing Six Party Talks and observed that "Japan's objective in intensifying its maneuvers against us is to make the settlement of the nuclear issue on the Korean Peninsula out of reach and use it as an excuse to arm itself with nuclear weapons." The article noted that,

> Japan dreams of attaining superpower status after getting out from the United States' "nuclear umbrella" of shamelessly taking an active hand in major international issues on equal footing with other major powers, and of realizing its ambitions for overseas expansion by coming into possession of nuclear weapons.[15]

As for Seoul, when revelations of South Korean enrichment experiments surfaced in October 2004, North Korea's reaction was low-key, exploiting the disclosure to call for six-party discussions of the issue and later for reciprocal inspections in the South. A Foreign Ministry spokesman put it this way,

> The gravity of the situation lies in that South Korea has pursued in secrecy the nuclear weapons program at the tacit connivance of the US and with its cooperation and has now full access to the nuclear weapons development

technology. This cannot but be a serious challenge to the efforts to denuclearize the Korean peninsula...The reality proves that the nuclear issue of South Korea should be discussed and clarified at multilateral negotiations in the future if any discussion is to be made on the issue of denuclearization of the peninsula.[16]

Two months later, a Foreign Ministry spokesman linked the North's denuclearization to the South's more explicitly:

Double standards as regards the nuclear issues of the north and the south of Korea can never be allowed under any circumstances and it does not stand to reason that the DPRK alone should work for denuclearization. It is illogical for the DPRK to unilaterally dismantle its nuclear deterrent force unless the secret nuclear-related experiments of South Korea are thoroughly probed. Under this situation the DPRK is left with no option but to increase its nuclear deterrent force.[17]

Domestic, Regional and International Political Motivations

While Pyongyang's primary motivation for building nuclear weapons seems to be concern about the threat posed by the United States, a number of domestic, regional, and international political factors may also be driving its program.

Some analysts argue that nuclear weapons have become an important domestic prop for the current regime and could give the North greater confidence in pursuing much needed economic modernization. According to this view, Pyongyang's nuclear program has proven to be an important asset in building support among the general population, as well as in strengthening Kim Jong Il's control over the powerful North Korean military. That increased control, along with the greater security against outside threats which these weapons provide, might also enable the North to justify reallocating military resources to civilian use, thereby allowing it to pursue more actively the economic reform program begun in the early 2000s.

The annual 2007 New Year's Day editorial published in the leading newspapers, observed that while the acquisition of a nuclear deterrent "was an auspicious event in our national history," the civilian economy was also critically important to North Korea, arguing that,

The present reality, in which all conditions for leaping higher and faster have been created, demands that we step up the revolutionary advance more boldly to achieve the high objectives of building a powerful socialist state...Building an economic power is an urgent demand of our revolution and social development at present and a worthwhile and historic cause for perfecting the looks of a powerful state. We should concentrate national efforts on solving economic problems, so as to turn the military-first Korea into a prosperous people's paradise. The main task in today's general onward march is to direct primary efforts into rapidly improving the people's living and step up technological updating to put our economy on a modern footing and display its potentials to the fullest…We should successfully realize the noble intention and plan of our party that regards the improvement of the people's living as the supreme principle in its activities.[*]

Whether Pyongyang has sought nuclear weapons in order to conduct a more assertive regional policy is unclear. From a geopolitical perspective, the North may see its nuclear weapons as helping to shift the regional power paradigm more in Pyongyang's favor, enhancing its standing and placing it front and center of the diplomatic agenda. According to an article published in a pro-DPRK Japanese newspaper in December 2006:

The DPRK's nuclear test has shaken the balance of power and mechanical structure in Northeast Asia. In the past, the United States threat of nuclear war and the DPRK's responsible measures for self-defense created tension in the region. As the DPRK and the United States are facing each other as nuclear states, the prevention of their all-out confrontation has now become the most urgent task. A phase is opening where the new order of peace and stability can be established in the region by putting an end to the two countries confrontation and by seeking coexistence by the two countries.[18]

As for inter-Korean relations, some conservative South Koreans believe that a nuclear Pyongyang will feel empowered to conduct a more aggressive, intimidating policy towards South Korea. Nuclear weapons may also give the North new hope that it will be able to achieve reunification of the two Koreas on its own terms. Others disagree, arguing that the North already has sufficient political, military, and economic resources to act provocatively towards the South. And, regardless of its capabilities, Pyongyang cannot hope for reunification on its terms given the strength of political, military, and economic factors arrayed against it.

Pyongyang's nuclear weapons have helped enhance its political leverage, though not its international standing. While the North has been relatively low-key in

---

[*]*Rodong Sinmun*, "Let Us Usher in a Great Heyday Full of Confidence in Victory," January 1, 2007. This is in contrast to an earlier line taken by the Korean Workers' Party to call the nuclear test "a demonstration of its scientific and technological potential" as justification for belt-tightening to give priority to military spending. KCNA, "*Rodong Sinmun* Praises Songun as Great Banner of National Prosperity," November 27, 2006.

boasting of its nuclear prowess, its nuclear stockpile and ballistic missile program have been important sources of political leverage in dealing with other more powerful countries, particularly the United States. These programs have allowed a small, economically devastated country to command international attention and to bolster what otherwise would be a weak bargaining position vis-à-vis the rest of the global community.

Moreover, by sowing mistrust and feeding doubts about its ultimate intentions, the North has skillfully exploited that attention. The North has played to uncertainty about whether it will give up its weapons (including Pyongyang's pledge in the September 2005 Joint Statement to abandon "all nuclear weapons and existing nuclear programs.") By continuing to yield, however grudgingly, to demands that it constrain its nuclear programs, the North has kept alive hopes that it will finally agree to denuclearization.

NUCLEAR PLANS

Little is known about North Korea's plans for the development of a nuclear arsenal and its possible uses. As of the end of 2008, all the components for a small nuclear force appeared to be in place. Pyongyang has sufficient nuclear material, has worked for many years on a weapons design, and has developed ballistic missiles potentially capable of striking targets in the region. But critical questions still remain, particularly about the size and reliability of Pyongyang's nuclear device and whether it can be mated successfully to existing missile delivery systems. Data from its May 2009 test may answer some of those questions.

Over the past 15 years, the North's planning for a nuclear arsenal may have evolved. In the late 1980s, those plans appeared to have been extensive. Pyongyang's plutonium production program, located at the Yongbyon nuclear facility, included an operating five megawatt reactor, two much larger reactors under construction, and a large reprocessing plant near completion. Overall, US intelligence estimates were that by the end of the decade, if all these facilities became operational, the North could produce hundreds of kilograms of plutonium, enough nuclear material to build a large nuclear weapons stockpile.

However, that large stockpile never materialized. As a result of the 1994 US-North Korea Agreed Framework, Pyongyang never completed its two larger nuclear reactors. While the five megawatt reactor and reprocessing plant were "frozen," they were still maintained. Both larger reactors, however, were allowed to atrophy to the point where they were no longer salvageable. A fuel fabrication facility, which had produced fuel rods for all three reactors, fell into a state of serious disrepair even before the 1994 agreement was signed. Efforts to refurbish it were suspended during disabling.

Consequently, North Korea's plan for plutonium production now seems limited. In addition to the small amount US analysts believed was extracted at Yongbyon before the 1994 agreement was signed (some 8.4 kilograms), Pyongyang is thought to have separated approximately 25 kilograms of weapons-grade plutonium in its 2003 reprocessing campaign, following the collapse of the agreement in 2002, and 12 to 14 kilograms in its subsequent campaign in 2005. As a result, the North may have had approximately 40 to 50 kilograms of weapons-grade plutonium, sufficient for roughly six to eight bombs, before using a certain amount of that material in its October 2006 nuclear test.[19] The North also has a bomb's worth or more of plutonium in the spent fuel unloaded from the Yongbyon reactor in 2008 as part of the process of disabling that facility, as agreed to in the Beijing Six Party Talks.

There is some evidence to suggest that North Korea has also periodically explored the possibility of producing highly-enriched uranium (HEU) to build nuclear weapons. The North Koreans have told visiting Americans that they had a pilot uranium enrichment program in the early 1990s which was discontinued. In the late 1990s, US intelligence received reports that Pyongyang had acquired a small number of centrifuges from Pakistan that could be used for enrichment. Acquisitions of technologies useful for uranium enrichment were stepped up in 2001, leading the United States to estimate that the North was "constructing a plant that could produce enough weapons-grade uranium for two or more nuclear weapons per year when fully operational, which could be as soon as mid-decade."[20] However, the US later admitted that it was less certain about the North Korean program and that no such plant had ever been located. The North, meanwhile, unable to acquire components for very many centrifuges, seems to have diverted aluminum tubes acquired for that purpose to other uses. Pyongyang has now threatened to resume its enrichment effort.

Parallel to its plutonium production program, Pyongyang has been developing — albeit in a haphazard manner — ballistic missiles, some potentially able to deliver nuclear weapons. Pyongyang's indigenous program dates back over three decades and is largely based on old Soviet technology. The first missile thought capable of delivering nuclear weapons, the Nodong, was developed during the late 1980s and has a range of about 1500 kilometers, sufficient to reach targets in Japan. During the 1990s, the North unveiled a longer-range missile capable of reaching the United States (Taepodong), albeit only if carrying very small payloads. More recently, Pyongyang is reported to be working on a new family of solid-fuel mobile missiles based on the design of an old Soviet submarine-launched ballistic missile that would presumably be capable of delivering nuclear weapons throughout the region.

A key factor in determining whether these missiles could serve as delivery systems is whether the North had tested them sufficiently so that DPRK leaders could be confident that they would work reliably and with a modicum of accuracy. The North's indigenous test program has been limited. Only two tests of medium- and longer-range missiles were conducted until July 2006, when it launched eight missiles, including a failed Taepodong-2 test, and April 2009, when it tested Taepodong-2 technology with partial success in the guise of trying to put a satellite into orbit. One possibility is that the North has gathered sufficient test information from Iran and Pakistan, both of which also have developed missiles based on the Nodong design. Even if that is the case, test data for the Taepodong and the new family of mobile missiles would seem to be limited.

A closely related consideration is North Korea's nuclear weapons design. The North has been working on a design since at least the early 1980s when US intelligence detected implosion tests of the required high explosive core at the Yongbyon facility. A KGB report issued in 1990 concluded that the North had completed the development of a nuclear device.[21] The following year, the Pentagon estimated that Pyongyang was capable of building a crude device able to fit on a railroad boxcar.[22]

Whether Pyongyang's partially successful nuclear test in 2006 allowed it to further miniaturize its design remains unclear. If North Korea had attempted to test a large, crude nuclear device, some analysts think the detonation demonstrated that it had not mastered the complex timing of high explosives needed to compress the plutonium into a critical mass. Others contend that North Korea was testing a smaller device, one with a lower yield-to-weight ratio that could be mounted on a missile. If so, the North may require another nuclear test to validate the warhead. Without further tests, however, the North may not be sufficiently confident about the reliability of its missiles to risk mounting its few nuclear warheads on them.

Answers to key questions about the North's nuclear capabilities and its plans for employing those weapons remain uncertain. There is no indication that the North Koreans have any illusions about the military utility of nuclear weapons. As Kim Il Sung himself told a visiting member of Congress, Stephen Solarz, chair of the House Subcommittee on Asian and Pacific Affairs, in December 1991:

> What's the use of a few nuclear weapons? In 10,000 years time we couldn't have as many nuclear weapons as you. Assume that we are producing nuclear weapons and have one or two nuclear weapons. What's the point? They'd be useless. If we fire them, they will kill the Korean people.[23]

Instead, the North Koreans have spoken of their weapons capability as a deterrent. Given the retaliatory capabilities arrayed against Pyongyang, the North Koreans would likely consider nuclear use only as a last resort in the event that their country came under attack. A case in point came in announcing its nuclear test, when a

Foreign Ministry spokesman declared its policy to be one of no first use and nonproliferation: "The DPRK will never use nuclear weapons first but strictly prohibit any threat of nuclear weapons and nuclear transfer."[24]

One possibility is that the North is planning a small nuclear force consisting of a few weapons deliverable by missiles and other, larger devices. The main purpose of such a force would be to deter attack against North Korea, perhaps through a combination of detonating "warning shots" during a crisis, as well as using them against military targets and population centers in South Korea and Japan during a conflict. In 1998, Hwang Chang-yop, the most senior North Korean official to have defected, stated that the North "will use them [i.e., nuclear weapons] if South Korea starts a war. For another, they intend to devastate Japan to prevent the United States from participating. Would it still participate even after Japan is devastated? That is how they think."[25]

NORTH KOREA'S PROLIFERATION CONCERNS

While North Korea may have some concerns about the spread of nuclear weapons to neighbors, particularly Japan, its primary focus has been on US hypocrisy in its relationships with proliferating states. Pyongyang has condemned Washington's willingness to condone proliferation by friendly states (evidenced by the 2008 US-India deal), but to exploit the proliferation issue to isolate and attack unfriendly states. A Korean Central News Agency commentary recently noted:

> The US biased nuclear policy is upsetting the general view of the international community on the energy issue. The US is still working hard to completely block the DPRK's nuclear activities for a peaceful purpose although it talks about the provision of nuclear technology and fuel for a civilian purpose and the like to those countries outside the NPT [India]…The US has long shut its eyes to its allies or those countries in which it is interested over the matter of R&D for nuclear weapons and its intensification and covertly helped them, unhesitatingly transferring even nuclear technology to those countries although they are outside the NPT. This notwithstanding, it urged the other countries to strictly observe the NPT and has applied sanctions against them in a coercive manner. The US not only insists that those countries incurring its displeasure including the DPRK be denied access to nuclear technology including that for a civilian use but threatens that it would not rule out a preemptive nuclear attack on them. This proves that the US call for nuclear non-proliferation is nothing but sophism intended to pressurize other countries to meet its own interests. The US biased application of double standards concerning the settlement of major international issues found a clear manifestation in the issue of providing light water reactors (LWRs) to the DPRK.[26]

A different tack was taken by a pro-North Korean newspaper in Japan which was sharply critical of the India deal on nonproliferation grounds:

> The essence of the nuclear agreement concluded at summit talks between President Bush and Prime Minister Singh states that the United States not only acknowledges India's possession of nuclear capability, but also recognizes cooperation in the field of nuclear technology between the two countries…The United States has come out now and ratified India's withdrawal from the N.P.T.[sic] to become a nuclear state, and it has even decided to shower it with 'gifts'…The Bush government's underlying motives are clear. First, it wants to drive a wedge in the tight India-China-Russia relationship, and especially contain China by pulling another great Asian nation – India – over to its side, while at the same time it wants to make large sales of its latest weapons to India, along with state-of-the-art nuclear technology. We do not know if this measure by the Bush government will be a money-maker, but we can say it is a fatal diplomatic blunder that will destroy the basic framework of the N.P.T. built by the United States itself and will hasten the collapse of the already-crumbling [US] policy of unipolar domination.[27]

Pyongyang's commentary may reflect its own policy objectives. For example, there is little doubt that the North's ideal outcome for the Six-Party Talks is both to improve relations with the United States and to hold on to its nuclear arsenal. In short, the North would like to be included in a class of "approved" proliferators. Another possibility is that if North Korea finally agreed to eliminate its nuclear arsenal, it would likely demand nuclear power plants in return, a point its diplomats noted after the India deal. In either case, the proliferation issue is not one that motivates North Korea to do much besides take rhetorical and tactical negotiating positions.

NORTH KOREA'S LIKELY RESPONSE TO GLOBAL ELIMINATION

A serious initiative by leading nuclear weapon states to eliminate nuclear weapons might make it easier for North Korea to rationalize eventual implementation of its commitment to eliminate its own nuclear weapons. But Pyongyang is unlikely to move down that path regardless of what steps other countries take unless there is a fundamental improvement in political relations with long-time enemies, particularly the United States, but also Japan and South Korea. Without such an improvement, the North is likely to see its small nuclear arsenal as vital to defend against the threat posed by these more powerful countries, even if they are armed only with conventional weapons.

That reality would seem to argue for a parallel process of bilateral and multilateral denuclearization and normalization of negotiations with Pyongyang, part of which focuses on steps to improve political relations, even if the international community moves down the road towards the elimination of nuclear arsenals. Such a process is already in place through bilateral contacts between Washington and Seoul, as well as the Beijing Six-Party Talks, which have been ongoing since 2003. While the future of those talks remains unclear given recent differences between Pyongyang and the other participants over verification issues and North Korea's refusal to return to talks in response to the UN Security Council's criticism of its April 2009 missile test, it is well understood that steps towards political and economic normalization of relations with the North must be embedded in any future agreements if denuclearization is to be achieved.

ENDNOTES

[1]Barry M. Blechman, et al., Force without War: US Armed Forces as a Political Instrument (Washington: Brookings Institution, 1978), pages 2, 48, 51, and 128; Richard K. Betts, Nuclear Blackmail and Nuclear Balance (Washington: Brookings Institution, 1974), pages 31-47; Alexander L. George and Richard Smoke, Deterrence in American Foreign Policy: Theory and Practice (New York: Columbia University Press, 1974), pages 238-41; Roger Dingman, "Atomic Diplomacy During the Korean War," International Security, XIII, 3 (Winter 1988-89), pages 60-66, 72, 75, and 79-86; Rosemary Foot, "Nuclear Coercion and the Ending of the Korean Conflict," International Security, XIII, 3 (Winter 1988-89), pages 98-101; Peter Hayes, Pacific Powderkeg: American Nuclear Dilemmas in Korea (Lexington, MA: Lexington Books, 1991), pages 60-62, 127-28, and 131-33; and Leonard S. Spector and Jacqueline R. Smith, "North Korea: The Next Nuclear Nightmare," Arms Control Today, XXI, 2 (March 1991), page 10.

[2]Don Oberdorfer, The Two Koreas: A Contemporary History (New York: Basic Books: 2001), pages 252-53.

[3]US-DPRK Joint Communiqué, October 12, 2000 [www.nautilus.org/archives/library/security/napstreaty.html]

[4] KCNA, "DPRK FM on Its Stand to Suspend Its Participation in Six Party Talks for an Indefinite Period," February 10, 2005.

[5]KCNA, "Statement of Foreign Ministry Spokesman Blasts UNSC's Discussion of Korean Nuclear Issue," April 6, 2003. [All KCNA references can be found at [http://www.kcna.co. jp/index-e.htm.]

[6]KCNA, "DPRK Foreign Ministry on Its Stand," op. cit.

[7]US Department of Defense, Special Briefing on the Nuclear Posture Review (January 9, 2002); White House, President Bush Delivers Graduation Speech at West Point (June 1, 2002).

[8]KCNA, "DPRK Foreign Ministry on Its Stand," op. cit.

[9]KCNA, "DPRK Foreign Minister Clarifies Stand on New Measures to Bolster War Deterrent," October 3, 2006.

[10]Ibid.

[11]KCNA, "DPRK Foreign Ministry Spokesman Dismisses U.S. Wrong Assertion," January 13, 2009.

[12]Axel Berkovsky, "Koizumi under a Nuclear Smokescreen," Asia Times (June 13, 2002).

[13]KCNA, "KCNA on Japan's Undisguised Nuclear Ambition," June 4, 2002.

[14]Ibid.

[15]KCNA, "Japan Denounced for Disturbing Six-Party Talks," April 19, 2007.

[16]KCNA, "Foreign Ministry Spokesman Demands Clarification of S. Korea's Nuclear Issue," October 6, 2004.

[17]KCNA, "Foreign Ministry Spokesman Blasts US and I.A.E.A. Double Standards," December 1, 2004.

[18]Tokyo Chosun Sinbo, "Pro-DPRK Organ In Japan Foresees DPRK-led Changes in Northeast Asia in 2007," December 31, 2006.

[19]Siegfried S. Hecker and William Liou, "North Korea's Nuclear Dealings and the Threat of Nuclear Export to Iran," *Arms Control Today* (March 2007).

[20]Declassified Intelligence Estimate, November 11, 2002, issued in response to request by Senator John Kyl.[www.globalsecurity.org/wmd/world/dprk/nuke-uranium.htm]

[21]"KGB Document Reveals DPRK Nuclear Potential," *Izvestiya* (June 24, 1994), p. 4 as cited in FBIS-SOV-94-122.

[22]Bill Gertz, "North Korea Fortifies Air Defenses, Fears U.S.-Led Strike on Nuclear Arms Plant," Washington Times (November 28, 1991), page A3.

[23]Interview with Stephen Solarz , "Notes of meeting with Kim Il Sung, December 1991," January 16, 1992.

[24]KCNA, "Foreign Ministry Clarifies Stand on New Measure to Bolster War Deterrent," October 3, 2006.

[25]"Defector Hwang Chang-yop Interviewed," as cited in FBIS-EAS-98-191, pages 328-45.

[26]KCNA, "KCNA Urges US to Drop Its Biased Nuclear Policy," March 11, 2006.

[27]*Choso'n Sinbo*, "Pro-DPRK Paper Decries Bush for Recognizing India As a Nuclear Weapons State," *Foreign Broadcast Information Service* (March 7, 2006).

PAKISTAN'S PERSPECTIVE ON THE GLOBAL ELIMINATION OF NUCLEAR WEAPONS

Feroz Hassan Khan[*]

Pakistan approaches nuclear weapons differently than any other nuclear weapon state. In the broad scheme of world politics, Pakistan is a small country. It has neither a decisive say nor a strong belief regarding the role of nuclear weapons in international security. It is, however, a proactive participant in nuclear diplomacy and, as a *de facto* nuclear power, the establishment of global nuclear norms, non-proliferation regimes, and new developments regarding disarmament will have direct bearing on its national security. Pakistani policy makers have called consistently for regional nuclear disarmament and regional arms control regimes as preludes to the global elimination of nuclear weapons.

Pakistan was not the first country to introduce nuclear weapons to South Asia.[†] Pakistani leaders believe that had India not been obsessed with competing against China, the region below the Himalayas may well have remained a nuclear-weapons-free zone.[‡] Pakistan's nuclear capability was thus the third step in nuclear proliferation in Asia. The introduction of nuclear weapons to South Asia's profoundly complicated political and security challenges made resolution of existing

---

[*] The author is currently on the faculty of the US Naval Postgraduate School. He is a former director of Arms Control and Disarmament Affairs in Pakistan's Strategic Plans Division, Joint Services Quarters. The views expressed in this paper are the author's alone and do not necessarily represent those of the United States Government, Department of Defense, or the Government of Pakistan. The author wishes to express thanks to Ms. Kali Shelor for her assistance and research inputs and to Michael Krepon, Moeed Yusuf, Adil Sultan and Rabia Akhtar for their valuable comments on an earlier draft.

[†] Nuclear weapons were formally introduced to South Asia in May 1974 when India conducted a nuclear test, which it called a "Peaceful Nuclear Explosion (PNE)" under an ironic codename "Smiling Buddha." India argues that it did not weaponize its nuclear capabilities after the test, putting the onus on Pakistan for being the first to go nuclear. From Pakistan's viewpoint, however, the 1974 explosion was the first validation of India's nuclear arsenal and galvanized the nascent Pakistani nuclear research into a full-fledged weapons program and triggered the nuclear arms competition. See George Perkovich, *India's Nuclear Bomb: Impact on Global Proliferation* (New York: Oxford University Press, 1999), pages 161-189. In 1983, India embarked on the Integrated Guided Missile Program (IGMP), which again led Pakistan to develop missile options to deliver nuclear weapons. See for details, Rodney W. Jones et. al., *Tracking Nuclear Proliferation: A Guide in Maps and Charts* (Washington, DC: Carnegie Endowment for International Peace, 1998), pages 127-29 and Naeem Salik, "Missiles Issues in South Asia," *The Non-Proliferation Review* (Summer 2002), pages 47-55.

[‡] India's ambitions regarding nuclear weapons date back to the period prior to independence. Indian leader Jawaharlal Nehru in a public speech in 1946 said, "I hope Indian scientists will use the atomic force for constructive purposes, but if India is threatened she will inevitably try to defend herself by all means at her disposal." Quoted in Kamal Matinuddin, *The Nuclearization of South Asia* (New York: Oxford University Press, 2002), page 61. After independence, in 1948 in an address to the Constituent Assembly, Nehru stated, "The atomic bombs that had forced Japan's surrender and ended the Second World War just a few years before had left a powerful impression on the minds of nationalist leaders, reinforcing the power of science for state ends, and India's own shortcomings in this regard." See Constituent Assembly of India, *Legislative Debates*, Second session, Vol. 5 (1948), pages 3328-34. Also, see further details in George Perkovich, *op. cit.*, pages 13-25.

conflicts more difficult and more dangerous, and intensified the competition between India and Pakistan.

Pakistan inherited enormous structural problems when it was granted independence in 1947 and continues to struggle on multiple fronts. One of its many problems is the search to define its national identity—a struggle between the secular ideals of modern leaders (who conceived the idea of Pakistan) and the theocratic aspirations of religious organizations and leaders (who see Pakistan as a platform for rising political Islam). Pakistan's security has been threatened throughout its existence by both external and internal challenges. Today, national security challenges – including internal instability and immense socio-economic issues – are tearing apart the Pakistani state and society. Nuclear weapons in themselves can do little to bring stability within the country.[1]

Although initially reluctant to go nuclear in the 1960s, for most Pakistanis nuclear weapons have now become essential to its national survival and a critical factor in its domestic political culture.[2] The consensus on maintaining a nuclear deterrent capability is a rare symbol of national unity in a country more recognized for lack of a common narrative on most aspects of national policy.

When the US "Atoms for Peace" plan was offered in the 1950s and 1960s, Pakistan complied strictly with the letter and spirit of President Eisenhower's initiative, developing nuclear technology solely for peaceful purposes and supporting nuclear disarmament. Strongly affected by the atomic bombings of Hiroshima and Nagasaki, its leaders were conscious of being a developing country emerging from the yolk of colonialism. Pakistani leaders were eager to embrace modernity and nuclear technology was considered the cutting edge of scientific understanding. Exploring the application of nuclear technology as weapons was a luxury Pakistan could ill afford. It was a new state grappling with abject poverty, deprivation, and general penury; a situation which has remained constant throughout most of its turbulent political history. That struggle continues even after 60 years of survival, despite progress in several areas of national life, and, most importantly, the development and operational deployment of an unspecified number of nuclear weapons and their means of delivery.[3]

The key argument of this paper is that Pakistan is not the primary driver of nuclear weapons proliferation, neither in the world nor in the region in which it resides. Pakistan's acquisition and continuing support of nuclear weapons is the result of its security environment. For a state struggling for national consolidation and survival, a world at peace – with or without nuclear weapons – is the highest aspiration. On its own, Pakistan would be unable to detach itself from the deterrent value it now places on nuclear weapons, which it believes provide it with national security assurances otherwise not available to it.

This paper examines Pakistan's position on the central question of the prospects of global nuclear disarmament in four major parts: the motivating factors that led to Pakistan's acquisition and continued modernization of nuclear weapons; the security parameters upon which Pakistan's nuclear plans are based and possible roles of nuclear weapons in foreign policy; Pakistan's position on global nuclear proliferation; and, potential Pakistani reactions to a global move towards the elimination of all nuclear weapons in all nations.

FACTORS MOTIVATING PAKISTAN TO ACQUIRE AND MODERNIZE ITS NUCLEAR WEAPONS

Few nations in the world today face a security predicament comparable to Pakistan's; the country's history is essentially a story of national survival. Pakistan's attachment to nuclear weapons is best explained through the "realist theory" of nuclear proliferation, which treats a state's decision to build nuclear weapons primarily as a function of its level of insecurity.[4]

Made independent as a result of communal religious violence and the resulting massive migrations of populations, and surrounded by much larger neighbors, Pakistan's insecurity would be understandable even absent the fact that key adjacent countries seem unreconciled to the nation's founding. Afghanistan, for example, questioned Pakistan's existence and quarreled over the contours of the Pak-Afghan border.[§] India was always wary of partition, fearing that the example of Pakistan's independence might inspire other minority groups to seek secession. Pakistan was born "truncated and moth-eaten" as the founder of the country, Muhammad Ali Jinnah, described it, and, as reported in Life Magazine in January 1948, the world doubted that the new Muslim nation, lacking both the institutions and the infrastructure of government, could survive.[5] From the very beginning, the new nation-state depended on the support of the Western nations, which required building and modernizing its armed forces and forging alliances with greater powers.[6]

Pakistan's perspective on nuclear weapons thus is founded on the search for security to ensure the permanence of the Pakistani state. The Pakistan case is analogous to

---

[§] Afghanistan voted against Pakistan's proposed membership in the UN in 1947. In 1949, Afghanistan unilaterally revoked the 1893 agreement signed by Afghanistan and the British Empire that delineated the border between then British India and Afghanistan. This revanchist claim to territories in Pakistan's western provinces (North West Frontier Province and Baluchistan) resulted in the birth of the "Pashtunistan" (land of the Pashtuns) movement, which in turn was nurtured and supported by India and later by the Soviet Union. Pakistan faced a two-front dilemma from its birth.

another state—Israel. Driven by identical fears and concerns, both states were founded by a people who felt persecuted or marginalized when living as a minority in other countries, sought basic religious rights, and eventually won statehood. Both faced immediate political and security dilemmas. Living under the shadow of hostility from powerful neighbors, Pakistan and Israel followed identical strategic policies after having fought wars with their neighbors and facing physical threats of annihilation. Both sought external alliances with great powers. But, also in both cases, such external support failed to alleviate security concerns and "both ultimately concluded that outsiders could not be trusted in a moment of extreme crisis, and this led them to develop nuclear weapons."[**]

SECURITY CONCERNS

Pakistan's initiation of a covert nuclear program and ultimate creation of an operational nuclear deterrent is the outcome of a four-decade long debate about competing threat analyses and conceptions about national security among Pakistani politicians, scientists, and military leaders.[7]

Weak states, like Pakistan, confronting threats to their existence, have several fundamental options to survive. They can "bandwagon" by accepting another's dominance and appease the powers making threats against it. Alternatively, they can seek to balance "internally" by relying on their own military capabilities or "externally" by relying on the military capabilities of allies.[8] A third possibility is to involve international institutions like the UN and World Bank to help alleviate security concerns and resolve conflicts.[9]

Pakistan has pursued each of these potential options in its desire to balance growing Indian power and other regional threats. In Pakistan's experience, however, alliances proved to be unreliable, especially in times of international crises, building sufficient conventional military capabilities was excessively expensive, and international institutions were capricious, at best. After its military defeat by India in the 1971 war that led to the secession of the eastern portion of Pakistan as the independent nation of Bangladesh, Pakistani defense planners concluded that national survival could not be left to the good-will of others. Consequently, Pakistan determined that its security could only be ensured by matching India's conventional and nuclear capabilities. This strategy of internal balancing remains the preferred course of Pakistani military and political leaders as they continue to experience threats from unreconciled neighbors.[10] At a fundamental level, all nuclear weapon development programs constitute a response to insecurity and a

---

[**] One essential difference between Israel and Pakistan, however, is that Pakistan faced annihilation threats from a hostile neighbor with superior conventional and nuclear capabilities, whereas Israel has repeatedly demonstrated its military superiority over its hostile neighbors. Stephen P Cohen, *India: Emerging Power* (Washington, DC: Brookings Institution Press, 2001), page 204.

form of balancing foreign threats. In sum, military insecurity stimulated Pakistan's interest in acquiring and modernizing its nuclear weapons.

The primary purpose of Pakistan's acquisition of nuclear capabilities was (and remains) to offset the larger conventional forces and military threats posed by India. Under the leadership of Zulfikar Ali Bhutto, a modest start in the nuclear program was made in 1972 after the humiliating military defeat in the 1971 war. This initial quest was meant as a hedging strategy to develop an option for "just in case."[11] But the Indian test of a so-called "nuclear device" in 1974 complicated the straight-forward imbalance of conventional forces and meant that a structurally weak and geographically vulnerable Pakistan now faced a combined threat from nuclear and conventional forces. These military imbalances, now in existence for nearly four decades, have been compounded by the emergence of new Indian military doctrines that contemplate fighting and winning either a conventional or a nuclear war in the region.[12]

Pakistani leaders believe that their nuclear weapons deter war and, if deterrence failed, could deny victory, thereby dissuading potential adversaries from initiating a conflict.[13] As the late Sir Michael Quinlan noted, "Pakistan's rejection of no-first-use seems merely a natural refusal to lighten or simplify a stronger adversary's assessment of risk; it implies the retention of an option, not a positive policy of first use as a preferred course."[14]

Relations with India have improved in fits and starts in recent years, but they remain adversarial in nature. The enduring rivalry between India and Pakistan is over several interlinked issues concerning territory and national identity, as well as political influence and relative power in the region.[15] Pakistani fears are compounded by the belief that India seeks to encircle Pakistan geo-politically and that India seeks revenge for what it believes to be decades of Pakistani support to various insurgencies within India.[††] Indian and Pakistani forces have been deployed along the Line of Control (LOC) in the disputed territory of Jammu and Kashmir for over six decades and, despite some progress toward normalization of relations, tensions continue. With the balance of both conventional forces and nuclear capabilities favoring India, Pakistan remains concerned about India's intentions.16 India's modernization of its military forces appears to be primarily oriented against

---

[††] Pakistan's concerns stem from allegations of India's influence and activities through its embassy and consulates in Afghanistan and Iran's support of insurgencies in Pakistan's volatile western provinces of Baluchistan and North West Frontier Province. See Henry D Sokolski ed., *Pakistan's Nuclear Future: Worries Beyond War* (Carlisle Barracks, PA: US Army War College, January 2008), page 3; Barnett R Rubin, "Saving Afghanistan," *Foreign Affairs* (January/ February, 2007), page 73. For a skeptical view of Pakistan's official position, see Ahmad Rashid, *Descent into Chaos: The United States and the Failure of Nation Building in Pakistan, Afghanistan and Central Asia* (New York: Viking, 2008), page 248.

Pakistan and, as noted, its new military doctrine envisages fighting conventional wars under a nuclear umbrella.[17]

India's new military doctrine, "Cold Start," was developed in the wake of military crises in 1999 and 2001-02.[18] During the latter crisis, India and Pakistan had completely mobilized their military forces for war. The United States sought to defuse the crisis through diplomacy, and the counter-mobilizations and risk of a nuclear exchange made the possible cost of war prohibitively high. The crisis de-escalated only after a 10-month stand-off, however, and gave birth to new military scenarios that, from the Indian side, envisage rapid force mobilization, followed by attacks on a broad front with multiple thrusts by mechanized forces in shallow maneuvers that would call, what they consider to be, Pakistan's nuclear bluff. The primary rationale of the concept is to give Indian leaders the possibility of responding militarily to a terrorist event in India that is believed to be sponsored by Pakistan.[‡‡] The underlying objective is to undergird political leaders' decision-making, preempt international diplomatic intervention to defuse the crisis, and beat the Pakistani military's counter-mobilization capability. Although Pakistan normally could respond more quickly due to the relatively short distances to its borders, India assumes it could keep military operations below Pakistani nuclear red-lines. Indian military planners are confident that even if they do not read the Pakistani nuclear red-lines correctly, by acting quickly to defeat Pakistan's conventional forces and by posing the threat of massive Indian retaliatory nuclear strikes, it will be impossible for Pakistan to escalate to the nuclear level.[19]

Pakistani threat perceptions include the risk of a preemptive Indian strike using state of the art conventional air forces or missiles against its leadership, infrastructure, military forces, and even nuclear facilities. Pakistani leaders have warned about the possibility of preventive strikes against Pakistani nuclear installations or strategic assets for some time. These concerns were reinforced after Israel's successful destruction of Iraq's Osiraq reactor in 1981. In 1984, there were revelations in the media of Indian plans to undertake a similar venture against Pakistan. Indian Prime Minister Indira Gandhi rejected such a plan but, after her death, military planners revived the idea during the "Exercise Brass-tacks" military crisis in the winter of 1986-87.[20] Pakistan continues to be concerned about the possibility of such attacks. In May 1998, for example, when it was preparing to respond to India's nuclear tests, Pakistan received "credible reports" that India was contemplating striking Pakistani nuclear test sites.[21] India's growing partnership with the US and Israel in more

---

[‡‡] The terrorist incident in Mumbai on 26 November 2008 which Indian officials allege involved the Pakistani-based militant group Lashkar Tayyaba (also functions as Jamaat–ut–dawa), is precisely the type of incident that the Indian strategy is intended to respond to. The Pakistan-based group denies involvement but allegedly was involved in many incidents in the past – including the 2001-02 attacks on the Indian Parliament -- which led to the subsequent 10-month military stand-off between the two countries. The full consequences of the 2008 Mumbai incident remain uncertain at the time of this writing.

recent years has increased such concerns, but these worries are far from central in Pakistan's military planning.

Pakistani leaders believe strongly that nuclear weapons, aided by the intervention of the international community, have deterred India from repeating the 1971 military incursion. Since the development of Pakistan's nuclear capability, there have been five major military crises in the region that had the potential to escalate, but each crisis was eventually terminated without military conflict; this makes the case, in the minds of Pakistan's leaders, that nuclear deterrence works. [22] The region remains unstable, however, and often on the brink of crises, which simultaneously raises the risk that deterrence may one day fail.

Although India remains Pakistan's primary security threat a decade after Pakistan demonstrated its nuclear capacity, new threats also are emerging in the region. Since September 11, 2001, Pakistan's primary military commitment has been to counter-terrorism and counter-insurgency along its Western borders and neighboring areas within the country. In addition to confronting India, Pakistan's military must now defeat the expanding internal threats of violent extremism and terrorism. Pakistan's western borderlands were never stable, nor were relations with Afghanistan. New security threats have been created by internal conflict and instability in Afghanistan over the past three decades. Currently, there is conflict with the Taliban and al-Qaeda forces, which have penetrated Pakistan's tribal areas and expanded the insurgency in Pakistan's western provinces. Extremist threats and suicide bombers are not deterred by nuclear weapons and require a qualitatively different security response.[23]

For a poor country like Pakistan, balancing its military resources between multiple contingencies is extremely challenging. As Pakistan's conventional forces are reoriented against the internal insurgent and terrorist threats, nuclear deterrence gains strength in the minds of Pakistani leaders and planners as the most reliable factor to defend against India. Pakistani leaders believe Indian threats are real and justify nuclear weapons in a region in which strategic stability is far from assured.

In addition, neighboring Iran's quest for nuclear capabilities has created another potential reason for Pakistan to value its nuclear weapons. Although Iran and Pakistan have good relations currently and no direct problems, if and when Iran acquires a nuclear weapons capability, Pakistan could become concerned that it is being squeezed between India and Iran. The Iranian threat is only hypothetical at present, but Pakistan's reactions to an Iranian nuclear capability could be strong, especially if Iran and Afghanistan became part of India's strategic network against Pakistan.[24]

Pakistan has declared that its nuclear weapons are intended to deter aggression, both conventional and nuclear. By implication, its nuclear weapons are last-resort weapons and will be considered as war-fighting weapons only if physical threats to the country's security are manifested. However, given that the region is full of active conflicts in which future limited wars cannot be ruled out, Pakistani leaders also believe that nuclear weapons have to be configured for war-fighting roles if only to retain their deterrent value. Pakistan therefore has developed and deploys nuclear forces separate from its conventional forces, but has integrated war plans which include targeting policies for conventional and nuclear weapons and a national command authority to make decisions on nuclear use. Unlike India, Pakistan does not have an officially declared nuclear doctrine. Instead, Pakistan has made public its command and control organization (Strategic Plans Division) and elaborated on the professional manner in which it would function.[25] Pakistan does not have an affirmative policy of nuclear first-use, but retains a nuclear use policy option, leaving it to potential aggressors to calculate the risk of the option's implementation.

The final elements in Pakistan's security assessment are evolving relationships among India, Pakistan, Russia, and the United States. The US and Pakistan have been strategic partners and allies for nearly 60 years, but there is growing mistrust between the two states. Reports of US forces directly striking alleged al-Qaeda targets in Pakistani tribal regions has created unprecedented tension.[§§] Moreover, there have been reports in the media alluding to US plans to physically take out Pakistan's nuclear arsenal in some contingencies.[26] The United States has tried many tools to dissuade Pakistan, first, from going nuclear, then pressuring it to give up its weapons, and finally trying unsuccessfully to persuade Pakistan not to join in an arms race with India.[27] Lately, an old idea has been re-floated to buy off the Pakistani nuclear program in return for economic and conventional military aid.[***] These developments have profoundly increased security concerns in Pakistan.

The past 20 years marked the end of strategic competition between the Soviet Union and the United States. The global security landscape, however, was transformed with unresolved regional conflicts and security competitions. Developing countries, such as Pakistan, that lost their great power alliances when

---

[§§] US forces carried out their first attacks on Pakistani territory on 3 September 2008. This and subsequent attacks created a widespread popular uproar, just when Pakistan's new democratic government was finding its feet. Tension in the tribal border is mounting as strikes by unmanned "Predator" drones continue in the area and the public outcry is building a wave of anti-US sentiment.

[***] In the mid-1970s, Henry Kissinger offered similar ideas and, again, in May 1998, Deputy Secretary of State, Strobe Talbott, made a failed attempt to convince Pakistan not to respond to India's nuclear tests in return for economic and military rewards. Bret Stephens, "Lets Buy Pakistan's Nukes," *Wall Street Journal* (December 16, 2008), http://online.wsj.com/article/SB122939093016909205.html?mod=googlenews_ws; Brig-Gen Feroz Khan (ret.) and Christopher Clary, "Dissuasion and Regional Allies: The Case of Pakistan," in *Strategic Insights* (October 2004), http://www.ccc.nps.navy.mil/si/2004/oct/khanOct04.asp.

the Cold War ended were now exposed to powerful regional neighbors with whom there had been a history of wars and crises. Under such circumstances, the rationale for a nuclear deterrent became even more relevant for Pakistan. As far as the major nuclear weapon states were concerned, regional security diminished in value, but the proliferation of nuclear weapons per se was recognized as the principal threat to international security. The United States followed a policy of seeking to prevent the proliferation of nuclear weapons in war-prone countries in order to prevent wars between nuclear weapons-capable countries. This was especially true for South Asia where long-standing conflicts had been shaped into active hostility. Moreover, US policy shifted from initial aversion to any spread of nuclear weapons technology to a policy of selective proliferation—identifying "good" proliferators and "bad" proliferators. For the United States, Israel and India became acceptable proliferators in the Middle East and South Asia, respectively, fueling a sense of discrimination among other nations in both regions.

From Pakistan's perspective, the US-India nuclear deal is the most important example of nuclear weapons discrimination. The foremost implication is that India has been accepted as a de facto nuclear weapon state without accepting the constraints of the Non-Proliferation Treaty (NPT). India is the only state that enjoys the benefit of having no legal obligations under the NPT and yet has been given carte blanche authority to produce nuclear weapons from indigenous sources. The most significant aspect of the nuclear deal is that it confers legitimacy to a state that has defied the regime intended to control nuclear proliferation. It rewards the defiant, whereas virtually all other developing states were held to account. The behavior of the international community, and the United States in particular, in the run-up to the Nuclear Suppliers Group's (NSG) decision to grant a waiver to India, making the US-India deal possible, is a telling illustration that world leaders were not serious about wanting to eliminate nuclear weapons at the time.

The NSG is a supplier's cartel, created outside the folds of the NPT treaty, ironically in reaction to India's 1974 nuclear test. By granting the waiver to India, the cartel has presented itself as a promoter of nuclear trade with an outlier to the NPT regime.[28] Moreover, during the International Atomic Energy Agency (IAEA) meetings held to get the India–specific waiver endorsed, the United States coerced states that had simple objections to the draft waiver. Western countries such as New Zealand, the Netherlands, Norway, and Austria, who simply wanted stronger assurances that India would not conduct additional nuclear tests, were forced by US pressure to back down. The US also pressured Pakistan to back away after the Pakistani delegate raised some objections.[29] The deal shows clearly that political and economic expediencies can trump non-proliferation concerns. Criticizing the NSG waiver for India, Daryl Kimball, director of the US Arms Control Association commented, "The decision is a non-proliferation disaster of historic proportions that will produce harm for decades to come."[30]

REGIONAL AMBITIONS

The most common notion regarding Pakistan's regional ambitions are that it seeks to control Afghanistan for the strategic depth it would provide vis-à-vis any conflict with India. This concept is no longer relevant in the Pakistani security calculus, however, especially after the events of September 11, 2001. Pakistan does not seek Afghanistan's geographic space for any strategic purpose. The Pakistani security concern is to ensure that Afghanistan is not used by hostile powers for mischievous purposes against Pakistan's volatile Western borders. One reason for the bitter history of Afghanistan-Pakistan relations is that Afghanistan, or individuals or groups within it, have at various times acted on behalf of other powers, notably the Soviet Union, India, and Iran, against Pakistan's interests.

At this point in its history, Pakistan's regional ambitions are limited to its own defense and national survival. It has no ambitions to aggrandize its position in Asia or in the Islamic world, and does not view its nuclear capabilities as supporting such goals, either now or in the future. Pakistan is affected, however, by the ambitions of others, primarily because of its geographical position and strategic environment. Instability in Afghanistan and the Afghan government's continuous antagonistic attitude towards Pakistan has caused Pakistani security officials to believe that India is pursuing an encirclement strategy against Pakistan through Afghanistan and Central Asia.[†††] In response, Pakistan believes it has to secure its regional interests through internal and external balancing, which includes restructuring its conventional forces to meet threats from Afghanistan, as well as from India, and to look for strategic partners who share Pakistan's security concerns. China is one country that has had a special relationship with Pakistan since the early 1960s. China understands and sympathizes with Pakistani security concerns, particularly as it, too, is sometimes concerned about the possibility of conflict with India, but it does not necessarily agree with Pakistani responses to its security predicaments.[‡‡‡]

Nuclear weapons have limited influence in this regional context. Except for preventing war with India, they do not play any role in redressing other instabilities.

[†††] Among the Afghan government's hostile acts toward Pakistan are revanchist territorial claims, abetting tribal insurgents in Pakistan western provinces, and accusing Pakistan of supporting the Taliban. Pakistan sees an Indian hand behind much of this and notes also that India is developing a military base called "Ayni" in Dushanbe, Tajikistan. Henry D Sokolski, ed., *Pakistan's Nuclear Future: Worries Beyond War* (Carlisle Barracks, PA: Army War College, January 2008), page 3; also see Stephen Blank, "Russia- Indian Row Over Tajik base Suggests Moscow Caught in Diplomatic Vicious Cycle," *Eurasia Insight* (January 11, 2008), http://www.eurasianet.org/departments/insight/articles/eav011108f_pr.shtml.

[‡‡‡] One such public example was that China did not support Pakistan's position in the 1999 Kargil Conflict. On other issues, China does not publicly chastise Pakistan for upping the ante but advises privately that it is unable to deliver what Pakistan might expect.

To this extent, Pakistan is satisfied that its prime requirement of deterring India from war is served by its nuclear capability. Pakistan has neither desired to provide, nor received request for, the extension of its nuclear umbrella to any of its neighbors or allies in the Persian Gulf or elsewhere in the Middle East. India's smaller neighbors – Sri Lanka, Nepal and Bangladesh – may look to Pakistan to stem India's hegemonic ambitions, but these countries have not sought nuclear guarantees or even explicit security assurances—it would be unrealistic to do so.[31] For the smaller nations of South Asia, stability in Pakistan and its economic progress are more important than Pakistan's nuclear capabilities. An end to the India-Pakistan rivalry will increase the prospects for regional cooperation and, in turn, provide greater benefits to people of all South Asian nations.

GLOBAL AMBITIONS

Pakistan has never expressed global ambitions in any official or unofficial pronouncement. Pakistan has never perceived itself as anything than a smaller neighbor of India. The notion that nuclear weapons might enhance Pakistan's prestige and influence in the world has no particular attraction, except as a rhetorical device to address a particular domestic audience.

The late Zulfiqar Ali Bhutto founded the Pakistani bomb lobby in the early 1960s when he was foreign minister in President Ayub's Cabinet (1963-66). He incubated the idea in Pakistan's Ministry of Foreign Affairs and was supported enthusiastically by some bureaucrats, such as Foreign Secretary Aziz Ahmad and Mr. Agha Shahi, among others.[§§§] Under Bhutto's stewardship from 1963 until 1966, Pakistan's Foreign Office adopted a proactive foreign policy of building a close partnership with China, thereby upping the ante in Kashmir and laying foundations for broadening alliance relationships with countries other than the United States and Europe. At the time, this nuclear lobby promoted an exaggerated image of Pakistan as a bigger player in the region and in Asia more broadly – possibly to attract China as a strategic partner – but, in reality, the primary factor motivating the push for nuclear weapons was India's growing conventional capabilities and nuclear ambitions. By early 1965, when India was reacting to China's nuclear test in 1964 with a program of its own, President Ayub nevertheless continued to reject the bomb option.

When Z.A. Bhutto became president (and then prime minister) from 1971-77, he not only initiated Pakistan's nuclear program, but also reoriented Pakistan's foreign policy toward the Muslim states in the Middle East. Bhutto saw himself in the mold of such revolutionary third world leaders as Egypt's Nasser, Yugoslavia's Tito, and

---

[§§§]Author's interview with Mr Agha Shahi on 19 June 2005 in Islamabad. Pakistan does not have a practice of declassifying documents for public research, hence it is difficult to substantiate if Bhutto intended a nuclear capability for anything other than to counter the Indian threat.

Algeria's Ben Bella.[****]   It was Bhutto's ambition to provide leadership on Islamic causes and the pragmatic necessity of attracting support from oil-rich Arab states which led Bhutto to hold a Summit of the Organization of Islamic countries in Lahore at the peak of the world oil crisis in 1974. Bhutto cleverly embroidered the Pakistani nuclear program with an Islamic identity and attracted support from Saudi Arabia and Libya, in particular.[††††] Bhutto boasted that he would make Pakistan the first Muslim nuclear power, rhetoric that resonated both domestically and among oil-rich Muslim countries. Bhutto had hoped the Middle Eastern states would consider the Pakistani nuclear program as contributing to the collective prestige of Islamic Umaah, and to treat the India nuclear test of 1974 as a threat to all Muslim countries, not just Pakistan. From his death cell in 1979, Z.A. Bhutto wrote how an "imperial conspiracy" was responsible for his ouster from power, because he championed the cause of the "Islamic Civilization bomb."[‡‡‡‡]

Subsequent Pakistani leaders downplayed any notion that Pakistan sought even to become a nuclear power, much less an Islamic nuclear power. Bhutto's successor, President Zia-ul-Haq, kept a low profile with regards to the Pakistani nuclear program, particularly because of the threat of US sanctions and, after the Soviet invasion of Afghanistan in 1979, so as not to jeopardize the renewal of close US–Pakistan relations. Zia, though Islamist himself, never countenanced Bhutto's notion of the Islamic bomb. Zia felt that such a posture would increase the challenge from anti-nuclear forces in the US and Europe and make Pakistan's nuclear program even more controversial. He maintained a strict public posture of denying nuclear weapon ambitions. This stance more or less remained Pakistan's position until May 1998, when Pakistan conducted nuclear tests in response to India's. As Pakistan's permanent representative to the Conference on Disarmament stated on 2 June 1998,

> Pakistan is not interested in an arms race with India nor is Pakistan seeking the status of a nuclear weapon state. Our tests were defense oriented and

---

[****]Author's interview with Mr Tanvir Ahmad Khan on 19 June 2006. When Zulfiqar Ali Bhutto came to power, he shifted the focus of Pakistani foreign policy away from New Delhi and toward the Middle East. This brought him into contact with Muammar Gaddafi and other Middle Eastern leaders. Given his nuclear ambitions, Bhutto could easily impress Middle Eastern leaders and extract financial aid from them. Gaddafi apparently offered to buy uranium ore from Niger for Pakistan, but Bhutto never allowed any note-takers in meetings where he discussed sensitive issues like this one. See Wyn Q. Bowen, *Libya's Nuclear Program: Stepping Back from the Brink*, Adelphi Paper 380 (London: Institute of Strategic Studies, 2006), pages 30-31.

[††††]Bhutto courted Libyan leader Muammar Qaddafi particularly. He renamed the Lahore cricket stadium as Qaddafi Stadium, for example, pleasing the Libyan leader and gaining both financial support and uranium yellow cake resources for Pakistan in return. Author's interview with Tanvir Ahmad Khan on 19 June 2006. See also Wyn Q. Bowen, *Libya and Nuclear Proliferation: Stepping Back from the Brink*, Adelphi Paper 380 (London: International Institute for Strategic Studies, 2006), pages 30-31.

[‡‡‡‡]Bhutto famously wrote, "The Christian, Jewish and Hindu Civilizations have this capability. The Communist powers also possess it. Only the Islamic Civilization was without it, but that position was about to change." Zulfikar Ali Bhutto, *If I am Assassinated…* (New Delhi: Vikas Publishing House, 1979), page 137; Steve Weissman and Herbert Krosney, *The Islamic Bomb* (New Delhi: Vision Books, 1983), page 9; Ashok Kapur, *Pakistan's Nuclear Development* (New York: Croom Helm, 1987), page 56.

meant to restore strategic balance in the region. We will adjust ourselves in the best interest of Pakistan, as developments in various related areas take place.[32]

However, Pakistan's efforts to acquire a latent nuclear capability in the 1970s changed dramatically into a full weapons program after the 1974 India test, which alerted the world to the prospects of nuclear proliferation in South Asia. The US anticipated Pakistani reaction to the Indian test, and pressured Western supplier countries not to deliver contracted nuclear supplies to Pakistan, tightened the nascent nuclear suppliers regime, and, by 1977, passed domestic legislation (Glenn and Symington Amendments to existing US non-proliferation laws) to prevent further proliferation. The United States attempted to persuade Pakistan not to respond to the 1974 India test by promising to bolster its conventional force capabilities, but Pakistan's security predicament was far too great to be persuaded. Instead, Pakistan switched from a bomb design based on plutonium to one based on highly enriched uranium, something the Western countries doubted that a technologically backward state like Pakistan could successfully manage.[33]

It was under these circumstances that Dr. Abdul Qadeer Khan, a metallurgist then working at the URENCO uranium enrichment facility in Holland, offered his services. Motivated to help his home nation, Dr. Khan greatly enhanced Pakistan's efforts to produce highly enriched uranium through a gas centrifuge process, which at the time was a secondary track to national nuclear acquisitions, the primary track being based on plutonium separation: India, Israel, and South Africa, for example, had all acquired nuclear weapons through plutonium separation. With knowledge obtained during his service at URENCO, AQ Khan reorganized Pakistan's fledgling centrifuge program and developed a procurement network in Europe, where willing suppliers were prepared to circumvent laws and help fill those industrial voids that Pakistan's indigenous capacities could not achieve. The 1970s and 1980s saw a race between the establishment of obstacles to prevent technology transfers and the efforts of AQ Khan's network to stay ahead of the curve. Illicit nuclear trafficking and trade in nuclear-related expertise and technologies thrived, not only due to illegal practices, but also by exploiting loopholes in national export control regulations, often with the complicity of willing officials in supplier countries. Dr. AQ Khan had considerable knowledge of this underworld. He established an independent network to help Pakistan procure what it could not get through transparent means. Several countries involved in proliferation were either not party to the global non-proliferation regime or maintained covert state-to-state cooperative activities. There were also private entities doing business in dual-use technologies, which included state actors as recipients. The now infamous AQ Khan nuclear network was eventually established under such circumstances, where the lucrative nuclear business provided great financial returns to businessmen in

Asia, Africa, and Europe willing to ignore the law. As described in a "London Dossier" by the International Institute of Strategic Studies, the Khan network was established with an interconnected set of nodes of suppliers and intermediaries in various countries, often loosely connected. It evolved over time from a state-controlled to a largely private criminal enterprise.[34]

Pakistan clearly benefited from the Khan network and, in fact, it required that the Pakistani nuclear program be characterized by secrecy and compartmentalization. From 1989-99, the Pakistani system of governance was also characterized by a de facto power sharing arrangement among the president, the prime minister, and the Army chief, something intrinsic to the Pakistani system of governance even today.[§§§§] The diffusion of power helped the AQ Khan network to turn from importing for the state to exporting to other aspirant nuclear weapon states, functioning nearly autonomously from the Pakistani government with a functioning office in Dubai and nodes elsewhere. Given the national importance of the Pakistan nuclear program and the premium placed on preserving its secrecy, the lack of oversight and autonomy given to AQ Khan was deliberate. It is possible that several government officials, including some senior military officials, were beneficiaries of this business. In February 2000, Pakistan formally announced the establishment of a Nuclear Command Authority (NCA), which tightened controls after the military regime took power in 1999. Subsequent disclosure of the activities of the global network in 2003- 2004 forced Pakistan to further institutionalize and tighten its command and control system with improved organizational best practices and tighter structures for nuclear safety and security.[35]

The Pakistan nuclear program suffers from the activities of the AQ Khan network. The latter casts a huge shadow and does not reflect on the real reasons for, and meanings of, Pakistan's nuclear capability. AQ Khan's illicit practices with Libya, Iran, and North Korea have brought few benefits to Pakistan and have, in fact, damaged Pakistan's reputation, made it cause for concern around the world, and undermined the achievements of its other scientific organizations, the role of nuclear weapons in its national security policy, and the progress it has made to tighten command and control and nuclear security and safety.[36]

NUCLEAR PLANS

Like many nuclear weapon states, Pakistan's actual nuclear plans are shrouded in secrecy. Pakistan's planning parameters envision a deterrent force consisting of a relatively small number of weapons to be delivered by aircraft and liquid- and solid-fueled ballistic missiles.[37]

[§§§§] During the periods 1977-88 (Zia-ul-Haq) and 1999-2007 (Pervez Musharraf), Pakistan was ruled by military regimes with the offices of the president and the Army chief in the same person. This ensured unity of command, on the one hand, but, on the other hand, undermined the growth of democratic governance.

Generally speaking, Pakistan is satisfied with its progress in developing nuclear capacity. Pakistan has been unwilling, however, to cap its nuclear weapons development and production, as well as the development of more advanced means of delivering those weapons, for several reasons discussed below. Still, as a practical matter, Pakistan's economic situation has been deteriorating rapidly since 2007. Worsening political instability and growth of extremism have stalled Pakistan's impressive economic growth over the previous six years. The economic situation influences Pakistan's nuclear program in the short-term in two ways. First, the financial crunch will slow down the pace at which nuclear weapon development plans are implemented. Second, the rising cost and growing scarcity of oil and gas resources will force Pakistan to try and increase the availability of alternative energy sources, especially nuclear energy.***** In the long run, however, Pakistan can neither ignore India's weapons modernization nor its own energy needs.

India's strategic modernization program includes acquisitions of modern air and naval weapons that can dominate the air space in any conflict and provide options to India for sea-based offensive threats ranging from naval blockades to the destruction of infrastructure along the Pakistani coastline. The Indian army also is being modernized, including the mechanized fighting units that are organized and equipped to fight against Pakistan. India's army modernization has little to do with potential conflicts with China, as the terrain that borders China would make maneuver warfare nearly impossible.[38] India's stocks of nuclear materials and nuclear weapons are also expected to increase at a faster pace as a result of the previously mentioned US-India agreement and the subsequent exceptions to limitations on trade in fissile materials with nations that have not ratified the NPT granted by the IAEA and NSG. India is also developing more advanced ballistic and cruise missiles that will increase India's strategic reach. Finally, India's space systems and ballistic missile defenses will make Pakistan more vulnerable from stand-off distances. Cumulatively, the offense-defense balance in the region is tilting in favor of the offense and eventually may lead to strategic instabilities.[39]

Pakistan's nuclear plans will be directly affected by changes in India's military capabilities. Pakistan will be under greater pressure to maintain even a minimal deterrent, especially if India pursues an interest in ballistic missile defenses.40 One of the primary motivators of Pakistan's quest for nuclear weapons was what Michael Mandelbaum describes as the "orphan state factor."[41] Unlike many nations

---

***** The Pakistani Planning Commission's energy projections are based on growth over the next 25 years of 163,000 megawatts (MW), of which nuclear energy will provide 8,800 MW. This implies a twenty-fold increase in current capacity, which is around 450 MW, at its optimum. This information is based on background briefing given to the author, along with a visiting team from the US Naval Postgraduate School in Monterey by the director of the General Strategic Plans Division, and Secretary of Pakistan National Command Authority at Joint Services Headquarters, Rawalpindi, Pakistan (June 15, 2006). Also see Pak's vision 2030 project
http://www.dailytimes.com.pk/default.asp?page=2008\04\09\story_9-4-2008_pg5_1.

in Europe and Japan, states that enjoy security as a result of the nuclear umbrella extended through NATO by the US, Pakistan and Israel have been left to fend for themselves. For most of its nuclear history, Pakistan was treated the same as Israel and India, the other non-NPT nuclear powers. Pakistani security planners now, however, are increasingly conscious of their solitary status, given the US nuclear deal with India and the United States' official acceptance of Israel's nuclear opacity.[42] This apparent loss of US sympathy for Pakistan's security rationale is now magnifying the country's sense of isolation. Pakistan's security anxiety is compounded by the United States' current insistence that the Pakistani armed forces focus on counter-insurgency on the Afghan frontier, even at the expense of preparing to defend against threats it perceives from India. The US has stepped up pressure for Pakistan to "do more" about threats related to the global war on terror and violent extremism. This means that Pakistan must now find a balance between strategic threats from India, which can turn rapidly into operational threats in the event of a military crisis, while simultaneously focusing on countering the expanding insurgency. For all these reasons, Pakistan is being compelled to rely more heavily on nuclear weapons to counter the growing threat it perceives from India.

FORCE POSTURES

Pakistan's fissile material stockpiles are primarily based on highly enriched uranium (HEU) and, secondarily, plutonium. Though estimates vary in public sources, Pakistan has at least 1,500 kilograms (kg) of HEU and about 60 kg of plutonium. Pakistan continues to produce these two categories of fissile materials at Khan Research Laboratories (KRL), the gas centrifuge facility at Kahuta, and at the Khushab power reactor. The total average annual production capacity is approximately 100 kg HEU and 10 kg plutonium. Pakistan is reportedly constructing another power reactor, Khushab-2, which will have roughly the same capacity (40 - 50 MW). There are also reports of a commercial-scale reprocessing facility under construction at Chashma. Together, these new facilities would at least double Pakistan's plutonium capacity over the next five to ten years.[43] Reports in Western media that Pakistan plutonium capacity will be tripled due to additional power reactors under construction at Khushab were rebutted by Pakistani officials in 2007, but not refuted and no reactions were shown in subsequent reports.[44]

Public estimates of Pakistan's nuclear weapons stockpile vary widely. Based on various sources, at the end of 2008, Pakistan's nuclear stockpile probably consisted of between 80 and 125 weapons, with 100 weapons being the author's best estimate.[45]

Pakistan currently utilizes a combination of aircraft and ballistic missiles for nuclear delivery missions. Two aircraft in Pakistan's inventory, the US-supplied F-16

"Fighting Falcon" multi-role fighter and the French Mirage 5PA are particularly well suited for a nuclear delivery role. At present, Pakistan has about 50 Mirage 5s and 35 1980s-vintage F-16s. However, the United States has agreed to provide mid-life upgrades for Pakistan's existing F-16s and to transfer another 18 aircraft to the Pakistan Air Force.[46]

Pakistan relies primarily, however, on ballistic missiles as its means of delivering nuclear weapons. Today, Pakistan possesses a missile force comprising road and rail mobile solid-fuel missiles (Abdali, Ghaznavi, Shaheen 1 and 2) as its mainstay, and the less accurate liquid-fuel missiles (Ghauri 1 and 2) for long-range strikes against population centers deep inside India. Pakistan is also working on a ground-launched cruise missile called the Babur, which was tested first in August 2005 and again in March 2006. In addition, Pakistan is working to build a sea-based nuclear strike arm, but this is still in the research and development stage. At some point, Pakistan may be able to field a submarine-based cruise missile. Pakistan does not have deep water naval ambitions, but eventually its sea-based deterrent will provide Pakistan an assuredly survivable second-strike capability. Pakistan's eventual force posture will be determined by Indian air force modernization, India's potential deployment of missile defenses, and the modernization of Indian naval platforms. The table below lists the main air and missile delivery systems in Pakistan's inventory.[47]

Aircraft / Missile	Range	Source	Status
F-16 A/B	925 km	United States	35 planes in inventory
Mirage 5 PA	1300 km	France	50 planes in inventory
Hatf 1	80-100 km	Indigenous	In service since mid-1990s
Hatf 2 (Abdali)	180 km	Indigenous/China	Tested in May 2002, in service
Hatf 3 (Ghaznavi)	300 km	Indigenous/China	M-11, tested May 2002, in service
Hatf 4 (Shaheen 1)	600-800 km	Indigenous /China	First tested October 2002, in service
Hatf 5 (Ghauri 1)	1300-1500 km	Indigenous/DPRK	No Dong, tested May 2002, in service
Hatf 5 (Ghauri 2)	2,000 km	Indigenous/DPRK	No Dong, tested April 2002, in development
Hatf 6 (Shaheen 2)	2,000-2500 km	Indigenous/China	First tested March 2004, in development
Hatf 7 (Babur)	500 km GLCM	Indigenous/China?	First tested August 2005, in development

Pakistan's nuclear targeting policy is obviously not in the public domain. Pakistan maintains deliberate ambiguity about its targeting policy, deployment patterns, and the nature of the warheads on its strategic weapons, making it difficult for its adversaries to distinguish between nuclear-tipped delivery systems and conventional weapon systems. Pakistan's nuclear targeting plans, moreover, are integral to its military operational planning and the balancing of strategic requirements for the multi-directional threats described previously.

The expansion of Pakistan's nuclear forces, their improving accuracy, and the emphasis on diverse means of delivery are intended to ensure that in the event of

crisis or conflict, Pakistan could continue to hold Indian cities, defense facilities, and its military-industrial complex, at risk. Pakistani planners believe these improvements are necessary to maintain the credibility of its deterrent. If a situation ever evolved into an actual nuclear exchange, the numbers and identification of targets would depend on the severity of the war situation and the gravity of the threat posed to Pakistan by India's conventional forces. The trend in Pakistani military modernization is to add a mix of forces capable of counter-value, as well as counter-force, targeting.

To date, Pakistan has not contemplated developing and fielding short-range (tactical) nuclear weapons. However, the nature of the competition in the region would indicate that if India fielded such weapons, Pakistan would match it with a countervailing strategy. According to Agha Shahi, Zulfiquar Khan, and Abdul Sattar,

> Obviously, deterrence force will have to be upgraded in proportion to the heightened threat of preemption and interception. Augmentation of the quantum and variety of our strategic arsenal is unavoidable...equally important are questions about adequacy of conventional forces. A nuclear response cannot be involved to deal with local contingencies. Given the consequences, the nuclear threshold should be maintained at a high level. Can Pakistan cope with the budgetary burden?[48]

THE ROLE OF PAKISTAN'S NUCLEAR WEAPONS IN ITS OVERALL FOREIGN POLICY

The role of nuclear weapons in a nation's foreign policy and political-military strategy depends on the balance of two competing potential consequences – whether nuclear weapons make the state's leaders feel more secure or more vulnerable. On one level, leaders may gain a sense of invincibility when they possess the ultimate weapon. Will that confidence cause the nation to act in more aggressive ways than it would otherwise? Alternatively, nuclear weapons may make a nation's leaders feel more vulnerable because of international opprobrium or even the threat of preventive strikes by adversaries. If the state is isolated internationally, it not only loses influence but may pay a price for acquiring nuclear capabilities.

Pakistan's nuclear weapons status has not provided any significant leverage for either its foreign policy or its political-military strategy. Nuclear weapons in and of themselves do not provide any advantage unless they are backed up by other elements of national power. Pakistan's weak economic performance, domestic political instabilities, and role in aiding instability in neighboring countries have created vulnerabilities that far outweigh the potential leverage that might otherwise be associated with its nuclear weapon status.

There are two controversial hypotheses about Pakistan's political and military strategy. The first is whether nuclear weapons emboldened Pakistan to foment insurgencies in Kashmir and Afghanistan. Examination of the regional history reveals that a political–military strategy of supporting insurgencies, followed by military incursions, was adopted by both India and Pakistan well before either acquired nuclear weapons. Pakistan has consistently supported Muslim insurgents in Kashmir since 1948; indeed, the casus belli of the 1965 war with India was Pakistan's active efforts to foment the insurgency (Operation Gibraltar), followed by limited military excursions intended to sever Kashmir from India.[49] These events occurred, of course, well before Pakistan acquired nuclear weapons. Six years later, still well before the advent of nuclear capabilities in South Asia, India followed the same strategy in East Pakistan and succeeded in creating Bangladesh.[†††††] India helped fuel the insurgency in East Pakistan for nine months before assailing the country with conventional military forces.[‡‡‡‡‡] Although India succeeded where Pakistan failed, both strategies were pursued prior to nuclear weapons entering either country's arsenal.

Nor did the support of each other's dissidents and insurgents come to an end with the advent of nuclear capabilities. It was especially pertinent to the crises in 1999 and 2002 that followed the South Asian nuclear tests. These incidents seem to have occurred as a result of continuing business–as–usual, not the result of nuclear capacity. The unresolved problem in Kashmir will continue to embroil the region in crises and, potentially, wars. Nuclear weapons have only hardened the two sides' positions – they have not caused them to resolve this potential source of disaster.[50]

Pakistan's security is linked symbiotically to Afghanistan, and its support of the Taliban has little or nothing to do with its nuclear weapons capability. As explained earlier, the systemic changes in the region since 9/11 have forced Pakistan to undertake a major strategic reorientation. The blowback of the continuing civil war in Afghanistan on Pakistan's internal situation is aggravating already existing anxieties about nuclear security in Pakistan. In this sense, nuclear weapons have again complicated, not resolved, an issue. The terrorists operating in Pakistan and Afghanistan are clearly not deterred by Pakistan's nuclear weapons.[51]

[†††††] India permitted establishment of rebel Awami League Headquarters in Calcutta, established a Bangladesh government in exile and "Radio Free Bangladesh," and established training camps for Bangladesh "liberation forces." See: Richard Sisson and Leo Rose, *War and Secession: Pakistan, India and the Creation of Bangladesh* (New York: Oxford University Press, 1990), pages 142-43.

[‡‡‡‡‡] Influential hardliners in India urged the exploitation of the situation in East Pakistan as Bengali refugees poured into India. See K. Subrahmanyam's highly publicized remark published in the *National Herald* on April 5, 1971 to the effect that the East Pakistan crisis presented India "an opportunity the like of which will never come again." Cited in Dennis Kux, *The United States and Pakistan 1947- 2000: Disenchanted Allies* (Washington DC: The Woodrow Wilson Center Press, 2001), page 206; Richard Sisson and Leo Rose, *op.cit.*, pages 149-50.

The most controversial hypothesis about the role of nuclear weapons in Pakistan's foreign policy concerns its relationship with China and the alleged Pan-Islamic implications.

The special character of relations between Pakistan and China has been a subject of curiosity for nearly five decades, since the India-China crisis began in 1959 and subsequent war in 1962.[52] The basis of Pakistan-China entente is strategic logic—a realistic power calculation based on their respective potential conflicts with India and interest in the strategic balance of the 21st century.[53] Pakistan's strategic location—not just as a rival neighbor to India, but as neighbor to China's volatile Xinjiang province—is of intrinsic interest to China. Pakistan also offers potential trade and energy corridors, as well as important political conduits to China's interests in the Middle East and the Muslim world.[§§§§§] This special relationship is not without concerns, however, especially with regard to issues of terrorism and China's sensitivity about Islamist separatism in Xinjiang. In recent years, China has disengaged somewhat from the India-Pakistan conflict and sought rapprochement with India, causing anxieties in Pakistan, but overall the relationship remains vital and strong. China realizes that India possesses far greater military strength than Pakistan, and has never considered a formal strategic alliance with Pakistan against India or any other country. It strives simply to keep "Pakistan strong and confident enough to remain independent of Indian domination and willing to challenge Indian moves in the South Asian region."[54] For Pakistan, its alliance with the United States, though critical for both nations, is adversely affected by growing distrust and could potentially break down. In 1990, in fact, it broke down over nuclear issues and, with a growing US-India partnership, China is the only major power ally on whom Pakistan can rely.

It is within this context that nuclear cooperation between Pakistan and China began, and it has been a closely kept secret in both countries.[55] It is, however, widely understood that China assisted Pakistan in gaining critical military technologies in significant ways, which included helping overcome technical denials and sanctions by Western nations.[56] The most oft cited Chinese support to Pakistan has been on missile systems and the development of nuclear weapons.[57] In 1982, the first reports appeared about China helping Pakistan overcome technical difficulties at the uranium enrichment plant.[58] The Financial Times reported in 1984 about China's provision of a nuclear weapon design of a type that had been successfully tested as China's fourth nuclear test in 1966.[59] In June 1994, further controversy arose when it was reported that China's Nuclear Energy Industry Corporation (CNEIC) had sold 5000 ring magnets to Khan Research Laboratories, putting China's assistance under

---

[§§§§§] China is helping with massive developments projects in Pakistan and is constructing Gwadar Port in Western Baluchistan as a key transit point for Central Asian energy supplies. This port provides Pakistan a second seaport 450 kilometers away from Karachi, providing some strategic depth to Pakistan's Navy.

a spotlight.****** Another report suggested China had provided uranium hexafluoride to Pakistan before the latter had gained the capability to produce its own.[60] China came under US pressure as a result of these reports and that same year ceased to provide both nuclear and missile support to Pakistan.[61] China also came to Pakistan's rescue in the late 1980s when Pakistan worried about the Indian Integrated Guided Missile Development Program that had commenced in 1983.[62] The Chinese assisted Pakistan in launching two short-range ballistic missiles—Hatf-1 (80 km) and Hatf-II (150–180 km). Later, Pakistan acquired M-11s from China – a solid fuel missile with a 290 kilometer range. China helped establish a missile manufacturing plant as well as training personnel, which enabled Pakistan to field longer range (600- 800) solid fuel missiles (purportedly derived from the Chinese M-9 missile) and, more importantly, helped establish an indigenous base for solid fuel technologies. It was only in November 1994 that China agreed with the United States to abide by the Missile Technology Control Regime (MTCR) and promised to halt this assistance.[63] US analysts and intelligence reports, however, allege that Pakistan and China continued missile technology cooperation until the early 2000s.[64]

A nuclear-armed Pakistan is relatively more confident to stand up to hegemonic pressures and, because of that, China saw logic in balancing India by supporting Pakistan. China does not encourage Pakistan, however, to proactively challenge India, either through asymmetric means or by upping the ante in a direct confrontation. Nuclear proliferation, crises, violent extremism, and terrorism emanating from in and around Pakistan are sources of concern and China has actively cautioned Pakistan and sought Pakistani cooperation to control these dangers, both bilaterally and through its membership in the Shanghai Cooperation Organization.

As regards the alleged Pan-Islamic role, Pakistan has consistently denied that its nuclear program reflects any aspirations to lead a broad Islamic coalition, insisting instead that the program is focused strictly on its South Asian security challenges.[65] Saudi Arabia is cited most often as a potential beneficiary of Pakistan's nuclear capability.[66] Western sources have alleged a secret deal between Pakistan and Saudi Arabia, supposedly a quid pro quo for Saudi financial support; these allegations remain unsubstantiated.†††††† Both Libya and Saudi Arabia have contributed to Pakistan's nuclear program in some way.[67] As noted, Libya provided financial assistance and uranium from Niger in the 1970s.[68] But AQ Khan's assistance to

---

****** Ring magnets are used to stabilize and balance the cascading centrifuges spinning at extraordinarily high speeds. See *London Dossier*, *op.cit.*, page 26.
†††††† Saudi Arabia has contributed financially during critical periods of Pakistani economic downturns, particularly at times when Pakistan was being sanctioned by the United States and other nations for its nuclear developments. In 1999, a visit by the Saudi Defense Minister to the AQ Khan Research Laboratories reinforced such allegations. See: Bruno Tertrais, "Khan's Nuclear Exports: Was there a State Strategy?" in Henry D Sokolski, *op. cit.*, pages 26-27.

Libya's nuclear program in the 1990s and later was not connected to Libyan cooperation in the 1970s. Relations between Pakistan and Libya went cold after ZA Bhutto was hanged and never returned to the same level again.[69] Libya contacted the Khan network in 1997, when there were no ideological or military connections between the two governments.[70]

At least one religious scholar and current Senator, Khurshid Ahmad, who belongs to a major religious party, Jama'at-e-Islami, is reported to have expressed the view that Pakistan's nuclear weapons have a role beyond deterring India. He stated that,

> Pakistan as an Islamic state has a responsibility to the broader Umma…Pakistan's nuclear weapons will inevitably be seen as a threat by Israel, and therefore Pakistan must include Israel in its defense planning. Under the circumstances, the future of the Muslim world depends on Pakistan.[71]

It is unclear if the contention of Senator Ahmad is intended to provide extended deterrence to Muslim countries or if he has some other objective in mind. To date, however, there have been no official public statements, serious policy planning, or military strategies adopted in Pakistan that includes consideration of influence in other nations resulting from its nuclear weapons, whether through extension of a "nuclear umbrella" or help with their nuclear weapon programs. There is, of course, the popular rhetoric and pride that has resulted from Pakistan becoming the first Muslim country to acquire nuclear weapons, and this resonates strongly within the domestic political culture.

The instabilities in South Asia make Pakistan's nuclear program a cause of worry for the international community. Except for possibly contributing to the avoidance of a new war between Pakistan and India, nuclear weapons have brought little benefit to South Asia. There is close to a consensus in Pakistan in support of the concept that nuclear weapons provide the ultimate insurance for a nation's security. Its is, however, unclear how nuclear weapons in Pakistan might affect NATO forces operating in Afghanistan on Pakistan's western borders or Indian forces exercising on its eastern borders.[72] These factors, along with complications caused by recent US military activity inside Pakistani borders, call into question the continuing capability of Pakistan's nuclear weapons to succeed in their role as a deterrent of outside threats.

PAKISTANI VIEWS ON PROLIFERATION, ARMS CONTROL, AND DISARMAMENT

Nuclear proliferation has never been in Pakistan's interest. Even though diffusion of nuclear technology helped Pakistan to acquire its nuclear weapons capability, it gained little as a result in terms of its international position. Pakistan was better off in the 1960s, before it acquired nuclear weapons, in all aspects of national life— political, economic, and in the relative capabilities of its conventional armed forces. The military regime of Ayub Khan in the early 1960s was a leading proponent of disarmament and global non-proliferation. In an address to the United Nations General Assembly in 1962, President Ayub Khan outlined Pakistan's preference stating:

> An aspect of disarmament which is of deep concern to Pakistan is the clear and present danger of the spread of nuclear weapons and the knowledge of their technology to States which do not now possess them…This imminent peril demands that the General Assembly give urgent consideration to the conclusion of a treaty to outlaw the further spread of nuclear weapons and the knowledge of their manufacture, whether by acquisition from the present nuclear powers or by any other means.[73]

For Pakistan, the primary cost of acquiring nuclear capabilities has been the deterioration of its relations with the United States. Pakistan complained of India's nuclear ambitions to its Western allies in the 1960s, but to no avail. When India declined to join the Non-Proliferation Treaty, it became impossible for Pakistan to become a member, even if it had wanted to. Nor was India the only hold-out; Pakistan and India were joined by Argentina, Brazil, Israel, and South Africa in opposing the Treaty, to name a few. Pakistan acquired its nuclear capabilities in a global proliferation environment. Most of the other hold-outs have since renounced a weapons capability, but only after major systemic shifts occurred domestically or in their regional security situations.

These days, Pakistan's official position of concern about nuclear proliferation, no matter how sincerely expressed by Pakistani officials, lacks credibility in the eyes of the international community. Pakistan's record of acquiring nuclear weapon technologies and materials from the grey market and then allowing this technology to slip out of the country to others is a scarlet letter that Pakistan has been unable to overcome. It is the direct result of the AQ Khan network. In an effort to counter this opprobrium, Pakistan has undertaken extraordinary efforts to shut down the network, reorganize its command of the nuclear security regime, and pass stringent export control legislation. Pakistan also has sought help from the US and other Western countries to modernize its nuclear management capabilities. The general perception of Pakistan's role in nuclear proliferation, however, is still dominated by the legacy of the AQ Khan network.[74]

Pakistan's position on nuclear arms control and disarmament has been proactive and supportive from the beginning. Based on this author's interviews with Pakistani officials who served in the 1960s under President Ayub Khan, the military and civil bureaucracy believed firmly that preserving the alliance with the United States was critical for balancing a weak Pakistan against a stronger India. Under Ayub Khan's leadership, the scientific community did not want to jeopardize its reach by exceeding acceptable limits, either in terms of its knowledge base or its nuclear energy building capacity. Similarly, the bureaucracy, as well as the military, were benefiting from Western military technologies and aid and concessions from the World Bank and International Monetary Fund. Consequently, Ayub rejected the rhetorical and political push by the bomb lobby as a matter of deliberate policy.[75]

Since the mid-1970s, even after Pakistan embarked on a nuclear weapons program and especially after the 1974 Indian nuclear test, Pakistan has proposed regional arms control and disarmament agreements that would directly complement global disarmament objectives and conform to the letter and spirit of Article VI of the NPT. It is difficult to classify the real from the rhetoric in a nation's diplomatic position, especially when proposed in formal plenary sessions of the United Nations' Committee on Disarmament or General Assembly; all nations engage in rhetorical excess on these occasions. But bilateral papers exchanged for purposes of negotiations can be considered serious endeavors by a state. Pakistan's actual position, as expressed in these papers, has been to seek to arrest nuclear proliferation in South Asia—both to be on the right side of the international community and to avoid a strategic arms race with India. It makes logical sense that Pakistan would want to avoid an arms race with India—economically it cannot afford such an endeavor and, in proposing not to do so, gains the favor of the international community.

The initiatives taken by Pakistan to arrest nuclear proliferation in South Asia are a matter of historical record. After India's 1974 nuclear test, Pakistan proposed a joint Indo-Pakistan declaration renouncing the acquisition or manufacture of nuclear weapons. In 1978, Pakistan proposed mutual inspections by India and Pakistan of each other's nuclear facilities. In 1979, Pakistan proposed simultaneous adherence to the NPT by India and Pakistan. Also that year, Pakistan proposed simultaneous acceptance of full-scope IAEA safeguards by the two rivals. In 1987, it proposed a bilateral or regional nuclear test-ban treaty. And, finally, in 1994, it proposed a South Asia Zero-Missile Zone.[76]

In addition to these specific initiatives, Pakistan has suggested various modalities for negotiations, including bilateral talks with India, 5-nation regional talks, and even multilateral conferences to support initiatives suggested by the United States in the early 1990s. For example, the US has offered 5-nation talks and, later, 9-nation consultations on nonproliferation in South Asia and Pakistan agreed to participate. Pakistan continued faithfully to negotiate the CTBT until 1996, when India made clear it would not participate in the treaty. Depending upon one's position, these Pakistani initiatives could either be considered rhetorical, as Pakistan could assume that they inevitably would be rejected by India; or be viewed as genuine, as Pakistan could sincerely hope the proposals would lead the international community to pay greater attention to the situation in South Asia and the threats posed by India. More importantly, Pakistan hoped through these efforts to mitigate or undo the series of nuclear sanctions it had been subjected to, as they were having detrimental effects domestically. In the wake of the 1998 nuclear tests and intense US diplomacy, a mutual restraint agreement between India and Pakistan was designed to stabilize proliferation in the region and to insulate South Asian proliferation from the rest of the world. The first such initiative was proposed on 2 June 1998 when the UN contemplated nuclear sanctions against India and Pakistan. This was followed up in several United Nations forums, seeking to balance conventional arms control and nuclear arms control in the region, enabling India and Pakistan to resist engaging in an intensified arms race. During bilateral negotiations, Pakistan formally presented a "Strategic Restraint Regime for South Asia" to the United States and India, separately.[‡‡‡‡‡‡] The model presented in that paper showed how to contain nuclear capabilities at an acceptable level, as well as to prevent vertical proliferation. Unfortunately, India rejected the proposal. To India, the Pakistani proposal would have limited it to a regional context, which would have undermined India's goal to emerge as a global power.

Pakistan is aware that energy needs are growing among the industrialized countries in Asia and that there will be growing demand for peaceful uses of nuclear energy. From a proliferation standpoint, when any country develops its own nuclear energy capability, there is always a latent risk that such technologies and materials could be applied to develop weapons. In anticipation of this possibility, Pakistan put forward a proposal at an IAEA conference which would establish "nuclear energy parks," a direct effort to alleviate proliferation stemming from civilian nuclear programs.[77]

[‡‡‡‡‡‡] This author was primarily responsible for conceiving the Strategic Restraint Regime proposal in 1998 which was a non-paper proposal submitted by Pakistan during the strategic dialogue with the United States (Strobe Talbott and Robert J Einhorn) in July-September 1998 and subsequently the same concept was put forward to India on 16 October 1998 (Foreign Secretary level Composite Dialogue on Peace, Security and Confidence Building Measures). The peace process culminated in a summit between the prime ministers of India and Pakistan in Lahore on 20-21 February 1999 which ended with a Lahore Declaration. One part of the peace security and CBM was the Lahore Memorandum of Understanding (MOU) of 21 February 1999. The Lahore MOU is the founding document based on which India and Pakistan were to bilaterally negotiate and consult on security concepts, nuclear doctrine, and confidence building measures in the nuclear and conventional weapons fields. India and Pakistan were to undertake national measures to reduce the risks of accidental or unauthorized use of nuclear weapons; abide by their respective unilateral moratoriums on conducting further nuclear test explosions; review the implementation of existing Confidence Building Measures (CBMs); review the existing communication links; engage in bilateral consultations on security, disarmament and non-proliferation issues; and work on technical details at the expert level. Text of the Lahore Declaration and Lahore MOU is available at http://www.stimson.org/southasia/?sn=sa20020109215, last accessed March 12, 2009.

Pakistan's primary proliferation concern, however, is the growth of Indian and Pakistani nuclear arsenals, resulting indirectly from the cascading effect of competition between India and China. That competition will likely directly affect Pakistan or, at least, change the dynamics of the balance of power in the region. None of the non-nuclear-weapon countries in South Asia or Central Asia have nuclear ambitions, except Iran. However, Pakistan's secondary proliferation concern is that if peaceful uses of nuclear energy become more wide-spread, the proliferation of nuclear materials in a region where borders are insecure, local wars of secession are not rare, and violent ideological extremism is the norm, would be dangerous in terms of the possibility of seizures by extremists.

Pakistan's third proliferation concern stems from the prospect of a nuclear-armed Iran. While Iran poses no direct threat to Pakistan, the relationship between the two countries could deteriorate for three main reasons. First, Sunni fundamentalism in Pakistan has been influenced by Pakistan's close relationship with its Arab neighbors, particularly Saudi Arabia. A nuclear Iran would almost certainly be more assertive in encouraging its preferred strain of Islam within the Shia population of neighboring countries. Especially given the recent shift in its leadership, Pakistan does not want to see greater sectarian divisiveness in the region. Second, Iran and Pakistan compete for influence in Afghanistan. In the 1990s, Iran supported the Northern Alliance against the Pakistan- and Saudi-backed Taliban. The continuing conflict in that country could cause problems again between Iran and Pakistan. Third, India has courted Iran in recent years. If Iran and India were to work in concert against Pakistan, it would have huge implications for Pakistan's security situation, posing a second-front threat.

In general, given recent history and the Khan network, nuclear proliferation anywhere in the world evokes fear in Islamabad of allegations against Pakistan. Nuclear ambitions that emerge anywhere in the Islamic world will make Pakistan a suspect by default, until proven otherwise. For this reason alone, Pakistan looks nervously upon the risk of additional proliferation or any nuclear smuggling incident. The porous borders in Central and South Asia add another layer to proliferation anxieties. Trafficking of all sorts is widely acknowledged in this area and any incident rings alarms in the Pakistani polity for fear of charges of complicity. Pakistan today is the last country to desire additional nuclear proliferation. It is struggling hard to move beyond its reputation, especially after the favor bestowed upon India by the US-India nuclear agreement.

MOVING TO ZERO

Pakistan would respond positively to any genuine move by the leading nuclear weapon states to negotiate a treaty to eliminate nuclear weapons on a global basis by a date certain. This would be in keeping with Pakistan's long-held position that the best non-proliferation policy is disarmament. Pakistani officials point to the position of other nuclear weapon states—Britain, especially—that have stated that they would consider reducing their arsenals further once the major nuclear powers come down to "reasonable numbers." This means that a disarmament treaty would become a realistic prospect only when it spells out, not a quantum leap to zero, but a sequence of obligations or stages to progressively lower numbers. France and Britain can set the standard. Today, it appears that these two nuclear weapon states have the least rationale to retain their arsenals. A treaty which, after reducing US and Russian arsenals, eventually brought in France and Britain as a second stage, would then create conditions for the remaining four nuclear weapon states (China, India, Israel, and Pakistan) to eliminate their arsenals—along with the weapons remaining in the larger powers' arsenals—in the third stage. Should such momentum develop, countries like Pakistan would likely seek to resolve outstanding conflicts so as to eliminate the conditions that led them to develop nuclear weapons in the first place.

However, Pakistan's experience during decades of disarmament negotiations gives it little confidence in the sincerity of Western powers when they state that they wish to eliminate nuclear weapons. There are three main reasons for this lack of trust. First, Pakistan has observed the US negotiate multilateral treaties with the intent of denying a capability to some while making it available to "like-minded" countries. One example occurred during the Conference on Disarmament in the United Nations in Geneva, notably during the Comprehensive Test Ban Treaty (CTBT) deliberations. Throughout the proceedings in the mid-1990s, Western countries formed an exclusive consultative group to support each other's positions against the developing countries' interests; the latter had formed its own grouping, called the G-21. During the CTBT negotiations, France conducted nuclear tests in the Muroroa Islands, clearly undermining the basic objectives of the treaty. In 1995, however, when India's imminent preparations for a nuclear test were discovered, India was pressured to forgo the explosions. By 1996, it became evident to India and Pakistan that the CTBT was designed to prevent nascent nuclear powers from developing reliable deterrents.[§§§§§§]

The US and Pakistan have a bitter history when it comes to nuclear issues, alternating between sanctions and partnership. US policy goals are often neglected for expediency. The sanctions imposed in the 1970s were lifted to persuade Pakistan to help defeat the Soviet Union in Afghanistan, only to be put back in place

---

[§§§§§§] The author was present at several Conference on Disarmament debates in the mid-1990s in support of the Pakistan permanent missions. Observation of the nuclear powers' behavior during the debates was a significant factor in persuading both India and Pakistan to refrain from signing the CTBT.

when the job was done.[*******] The US coerced Pakistan to roll back its program unilaterally in the early 1990s, hoping to break Pakistani resolve under sanctions. That policy did not work, instead causing Pakistan to seek help from other sources, namely China.[78] New layers of sanctions were again applied after the 1998 tests, only to be reversed when the US again needed Pakistan's help after the 9/11 attack. Lastly, the manner in which the US abandoned its long-standing position in order to make possible nuclear trade with India has reinforced the belief in Pakistan and many other nations that disarmament is a utopian notion used for cynical national purposes.[††††††]

In short, if the United States wishes to create a serious disarmament initiative, it must provide a clear concept of what it is proposing. It will need to persuade many countries, not only Pakistan, that the initiative is not another self-serving 'catch them' trick disguised as disarmament. It will have to demonstrate that it is sincere in its proposals. There is a belief in Pakistan that the US and other major powers keep moving the goal posts mid-play. A set of principles and commitments that would assure fair play would be essential. The main players would enter a disarmament negotiation with wide disparities in capabilities relative to each other. There would need to be an assurance that the approach would not be "bottom-up," i.e. the smaller nuclear states cannot be expected to accept far-reaching obligations unless there is first some leveling of capabilities. Pakistan would not want to find itself in a position in which it freezes its options while others keep their capabilities operational.

Pakistan fears the consequence of continuing competition between China and India. Pakistan would prefer to see rapprochement among the major powers in Asia, so that an arms competition between India and China does not force Pakistan to make excessive expenditures to keep up its minimal deterrent vis-à-vis India. Any conflict that brings the US, Japan, and India into a strategic alliance against China

---

[*******] The Carter Administration had applied nuclear sanctions against Pakistan in 1977. The Soviet invasion of Afghanistan forced a change in US policy. US National Security Advisor Zbigniew Brzezinski concluded that the Afghan policy, "will require a review of our policy toward Pakistan…Our national security policy toward Pakistan cannot be dictated by our non-proliferation policy." Cited in Steve Coll, *The Ghost War: The Secret History of the CIA, Afghanistan and Bin Laden* (New York: Penguin Books, 2004), page 51. When the Reagan Administration came to power, Pakistan negotiated new terms of its relations with the US, which relegated the nuclear issue to the back burner. Throughout the 1980s, to avoid imposing sanctions on Pakistan, as was required by the Pressler Amendment, the US government certified that Pakistan's nuclear program was for peaceful purposes. This waiver was not given in 1990, when the Soviet Union had left Afghanistan and the Cold War had ended, and the US then applied the sanctions required by the Pressler Amendment. See Dennis Kux, *op. cit.,* page 257.

[††††††] Author's discussions with Pakistani officials on 19 August 2008 on the implications of the US-India deal revealed two opposite reactions: The first was concern about the US double standard of arming India while lecturing Pakistan and, especially, anger at the arm-twisting for Pakistan not to register its protest at the IAEA Board of Governors. A second reaction was that Pakistan prudently stepped aside seeing that the action for India set an obvious precedent for an agreement with Pakistan. See Adil Sultan, "Nuclear Double Standard," *The NEWS, Pakistan* (September 20, 2008).

would force Pakistan to join one side or the other. On the other hand, a serious disarmament initiative, one that eschews an arms race in Asia, would help Pakistan in the long run.

Pakistan seeks an end to its rivalry with India and to resolve conflicts with India and Afghanistan. Pakistan would gain a great deal if it were able to open up an energy corridor between Central Asia and South Asia. Further, Pakistan's reaction to a disarmament initiative would not be so much a question of response, as it would be about timing. The time frame of a global disarmament treaty must be preceded by progress toward conflict resolution and threat reduction. Pakistan would need assurances about conventional military forces and progress in bilateral relations with India. If these were attained, Pakistan would certainly look more favorably upon the ultimate goals of a disarmament initiative and reduce the time it believed necessary to achieve that end-state.

END-STATES

Developments in the Far East are not fundamental to Pakistan's security calculus, which has always focused narrowly on South Asia. However, should Japan develop nuclear weapon capabilities, it could be a tipping point in Asia, giving birth to a new proliferation environment. The ensuing tension in Asia would seep through to South Asia as well. Since India is being propped up by the United States as counter-weight to China, Pakistan sees the trajectory moving in a negative direction. The disarmament of North Korea is also of interest to Pakistan. Regardless of whether or not Korea is eventually unified, Pakistan would want North Korea to disarm and erase that country's history of proliferation—that has involved Pakistan as well.

In all probability, Pakistan should be expected to play an active role in seeking to reverse any new proliferation trend in Asia. From history, it can be surmised that Pakistan's competition with India and partnership with China places it in a position where avoiding the impact of any further proliferation would be impossible, thus Pakistan should be expected to discourage any proliferation of nuclear weapons to its east or west. It would not serve Pakistan's interest. If anything, it would focus additional negative scrutiny on Pakistan.

Realistically, in the event of nuclear disarmament, the big powers would retain conventional military superiority and there would be a significant risk of a conventional arms race amongst the great powers. Pakistan would be concerned for several reasons. First, its primary threat, India, would be building up its conventional forces in competition with China. Also, unlike the case of nuclear weapons, there is no taboo on the use of conventional forces. Despite the devastation caused in Europe and Asia during the Second World War, conventional forces have been used frequently for decades. Today, conventional weapons are sophisticated and future conventional wars could be even more lethal. Second, Pakistan's fundamental reason to acquire nuclear weapons was to offset India's superior conventional forces. If Pakistan's example is considered the standard, conventional force superiority could cause other affected countries to seek to develop nuclear capabilities and undermine any disarmament treaty that was in effect—unless there was an effective enforcement regime. Third, the US, Israel, India, and Iraq under Saddam Hussein in the 1990s, have demonstrated that even when a nation has nuclear capabilities, the aggressive use of conventional forces against it cannot be ruled out. Nuclear weapon capabilities have not reduced expenditures on conventional forces. Rather, it allowed states to enhance conventional force capabilities, making use of conventional forces more feasible under the nuclear umbrella.

Thus, three interrelated steps are required if nuclear disarmament is to be successful. Regional conflict resolution, conventional forces arms control, and nuclear arms restraints should be the first stage to build confidence; they may take years. A paradigm shift is required from confrontation and use of force to cooperation and conflict resolution and disarmament. Such an environment is hard to achieve, but in regions where there is structural asymmetry, it should be recognized and not exploited. For such a regime to flourish, the bigger powers would have to take the initiative and be more magnanimous and accommodative.

ENDNOTES

[1] Feroz Hassan Khan and Peter R Lavoy, "Pakistan: The Dilemma of Deterrence," in Muthiah Alagappa, ed., *The Long Shadow: Nuclear Weapons and Security in 21st Century Asia* (Stanford: Stanford University Press, 2008), page 219.

[2] Peter R Lavoy, "Nuclear Proliferation Over the Next Decade: Causes, Warning Signs, and Policy Responses," *The Nonproliferation Review* (November 2006), page 441.

[3] For estimates of Pakistan's nuclear weapons inventory, see Peter R Lavoy, "Islamabad's Nuclear Posture: Its Premises and Implementation," in Henry D. Sokolski, *Pakistan's Nuclear Future: Worries Beyond War* (Carlisle PA: Strategic Studies Institute, US Army War College, January 2008), pages 141-143; Institute for Science and International Security, "Global Stocks of Nuclear Explosive Materials," revised 7 September 2005, http://www.isis-online.org/global_stocks/end2003/tableofcontents.html.

A separate study by a team of Indian and Pakistani analysts puts Pakistan's plutonium inventory slightly higher and its HEU holding slightly lower. Zia Mian, A. H. Nayyar, R. Rajaraman, and M. V. Ramanna, "Fissile Materials in South Asia: The Implications of the U.S.-India Nuclear Deal," *International Panel on Fissile Materials Research Report No. 1* (September 2006), page 3, http://www.fissilematerials.org/ipfm/site_down/ipfmresearchreport01.pdf.

[4] Benjamin Frankel, "The Brooding Shadow: Systemic Incentives and Nuclear Weapons Proliferation," in *The Proliferation Puzzle: Why Nuclear Weapons Spread and What Results*, edited by Zachary S. Davis and Benjamin Frankel (London: Frank Cass, 1993), pages 37-78; Bradley A. Thayer, "The Causes of Nuclear Proliferation and the Utility of the Nuclear Nonproliferation Regime," *Security Studies* (Spring 1995), pages 463-519.

[5] "Pakistan Struggles For Survival: Religious Warfare and Economic Chaos Threaten the Newly Born Nation of 70 Million Moslems," *Life* (January 5, 1948), pages 16-23.

[6] Shuja Nawaz, *Cross Swords: Its Army, and the Wars Within* (New York: Oxford University Press, 2008), pages 92-121.

[7] See Peter R. Lavoy, "Nuclear Myths and the Causes of Nuclear Proliferation," *Security Studies* (Spring/Summer 1993), pages 192-212. Also see Feroz Hassan Khan and Peter R Lavoy, "Pakistan: The Dilemma of Deterrence," in Muthiah Alagappa, ed. *The Long Shadow: Nuclear Weapons and Security in 21st Century Asia* (Stanford: Stanford University Press, 2008), page 217.

[8] Scott D. Sagan, "The Origins of Military Doctrine," in Peter R Lavoy, Scott D Sagan, and James J Wirtz, eds. *Planning the Unthinkable: How New Powers Will Use Nuclear, Biological, and Chemical Weapons* (Ithaca: Cornell University Press, 2000), page 23.

[9] Kenneth N Waltz, *Theory of International Politics* (New York: Random House, 1979), page 168.

[10] Scott D. Sagan, "Why do States Build Nuclear Weapons? Three Models in Search of a Bomb," *International Security* (Winter 1996/97), pages 73-85.

[11] Feroz Hassan Khan, "Nuclear Weapons Motivations: Lessons from Pakistan," in Peter R Lavoy ed., *Nuclear Weapons Proliferation in the Next Decade* (New York: Routledge, Taylor and Francis Group, 2006), page 71.

[12] John H. Gill, "India and Pakistan: A Shift in Military Calculus," in Ashley Tellis and Michael Wells, eds. *Strategic Asia 2005-06, Military Modernization in Era of Uncertainty,"* (Seattle: The National Bureau of Asian Research, 2005), pages 257-67; Walter Carl Ladwig III, "A Cold Start for Hot Wars? The Indian Army's New Limited War Doctrine," *International Security* (Winter 2007/08), pages 158- 190; Gurmeet Kanwal, "Cold Start and Battle Groups for Offensive Operations," *ORF Strategic Trends* (June 2006), http://www.observerindia.com/cms/sites/orfonline/modules/strategictrend/StrategicTrendDetail.html?cmaid=1504&mmacmaid=1505.

[13] Agha Shahi, Zulifiqar Ali Khan and Abdul Sattar, "Securing Nuclear Peace," *The News International* (October 4, 1999).

[14] Michael Quinlan, "How Robust is India-Pakistan Deterrence," *Survival* (Winter 2000-2001), pages 149-50.

[15] T.V. Paul, ed., *The India- Pakistan Conflict: An Enduring Rivalry* (New York: Cambridge University Press, 2005), page 8.

[16] See John H Gill, "India and Pakistan: A Shift in Military Calculus," in Tellis and Wells, *op. cit.*, pages 257-67.

[17] For India's armed forces' size and disposition in peace time, see Brigadier Agha M. U. Farooq, "Nuclear Deterrence in South Asia: A Strategic Failure or Beginning of Regional Stability," *US War College Strategy Paper* (Carlisle Barracks, PA: US Army War College, 19 March 2004). Also see: John Gill, *op. cit.*, pages 257-67.

[18] Walter Carl Ladwig III, "A Cold Start for Hot Wars? The Indian Army's New Limited War Doctrine," *International Security* (Winter 2007/08), page 158; S. Paul Kapur, "India and Pakistan's Unstable Peace: Why Nuclear South Asia Is Not Like Cold War Europe," *International Security* (Fall 2005), pages 138-139; Firdaus Ahmed, "The Calculus of 'Cold Start,'" *India Together* (May 2004), http://www.indiatogether.org/2004/may/fah-coldstart.htm.; Subhash Kapila, "Indian Army's New 'Cold Start' War Doctrine Strategically Reviewed—Part II (Additional Imperatives)," Paper No. 1013 (Noida, India: South Asia Analysis Group, June 1, 2004), http://www.saag.org/papers11/paper1013.html.

[19] Walter Carl Ladwig III, op. cit., page 164.

[20] Scott D. Sagan and Kenneth Waltz, *The Spread of Nuclear Weapons: A Debate Renewed* (New York: WW. Norton and Company, 2003), pages 92-95.

[21] Statement of Ambassador Munir Akram, Pakistan's permanent representative to the Conference on Disarmament in Geneva, Switzerland (June 2, 1998).

[22] Feroz Hassan Khan, "The Independence-Dependence Paradox: Stability Dilemma in South Asia," *Arms Control Today* (October 2003), pages 15-19.

[23] Khan and Lavoy, *op. cit.,* pages 217-222.

[24] *Ibid.,* page 219.

[25] For a detailed explanation of Pakistani nuclear command and controls, see International Institute for Strategic Studies, *Nuclear Black Markets: Pakistan, A.Q. Khan and the Rise of Proliferation Networks, a Net Assessment* (London: IISS Dossier, 2007).

[26] Allegedly, a US Special Forces unit was training with Israel's most trusted anti-terrorist unit. See: Ben Fenton, "US Special Unit Stands by to Steal Atomic Warheads," *The Telegraph* (29 October 2001), http://portal.telegraph.co.uk/core/Content/displayPrintable.jtml;$sesssionid$XTAR4U; see also, Seymour Hersh, "Watching the Warheads: The Risks to Pakistan's Nuclear Arsenal," *The New Yorker Magazine* (November 5, 2001), pages 48-54. According to Hersh, the US had prepared, "an elite Pentagon undercover unit trained to slip into foreign countries and find suspected nuclear weapons, and disarm them if necessary, [and] has explored plans for an operation in Pakistan.;" David Albright, "Securing Pakistan's Nuclear Weapons' Complex," Paper commissioned and sponsored by Stanley Foundation for the 42nd Strategy for Peace Conference, *Strategies for Regional Security (South Asia Working Group),* October 25-27, 2001; Nigel Hawkes, "The Nuclear Threat: Pakistan Could Lose Control Of Its Arsenal," *Times Online* (September 20, 2001), http://www.timesonline.co.uk/article/o,,28-114933,00.html.

[27] Peter R. Lavoy, "Nuclear Proliferation Over the Next Decade: Causes, Warning Signs, and Policy Responses," *The Non-Proliferation Review* (November 2006), pages 441-442; Also see in the same issue Feroz Hassan Khan, "Nuclear Proliferation Motivations: Lessons from Pakistan," pages 501-17.

[28] Adil Sultan,"Nuclear Double Standard," *The NEWS* (September 20, 2008), page x.

[29] Author conversations with Pakistani officials during visit to Islamabad in August 2008.

[30] Daryl Kimball on C-Span on 9 September 2008 available at http://www.c-spanarchives.org/library/index.php?main_page=product_video_info&products_id=280986-6.

[31] Feroz Hassan Khan and Peter R Lavoy, *op. cit.,* pages 223-224.

[32] Statement by Ambassador Munir Akram at the Special Session of the Conference on Disarmament on 02 June 1998.

[33] Feroz Hassan Khan, "Nuclear Proliferation Motivations: Lessons From Pakistan," *The Nonproliferation Review* (November 2006), pages 501-17.

[34] "Nuclear Black Markets," *op. cit.,* page 9.

[35] "Nuclear Black Markets, *op. cit.,* pages 107-18.

[36] Feroz Hassan Khan and Peter R Lavoy, *op. cit.,* pages 215-40.

[37] Andrew C. Winner and Toshi Yoshihara, *Nuclear Stability in South Asia* (Boston: The Institute for Foreign Policy Analysis, 2001), pages 47-48.

[38] Rodney Jones*, Conventional Force Imbalance and Strategic Stability in South Asia* (Bradford, UK: South Asia Strategic Stability Unit, 2004); Zawar Abidi, *Threat Reduction in South Asia* (Washington, DC: Henry L Stimson Center, November 2003).

[39] Rodney Jones, *op. cit.*; John Gill, *op. cit.*, pages 257-67; *Military Balance: 2007-2008* (London: International Institute for Strategic Studies, 2007), pages 329- 362.

[40] The Pakistan Nuclear Command Authority (NCA) met on April 12, 2006 and announced that it had reviewed the minimum deterrence requirement; "Concern Expressed at Indo-US Deal: Deterrence Satisfactory, NCA," *Dawn (Karachi)*, April 13, 2006, http://www.dawn.com/2006/04/13/top5.htm.

[41] Michael Mandelbaum "Lessons of the Next Nuclear War," *Foreign Affairs* (March/ April 1995), pages 22- 37.

[42] Israel's special status was legitimized as early as 1969 when President Nixon agreed secretly with Prime Minister Golda Mier on a "don't ask, don't tell" pledge. See Avner Cohen, *Israel and the Bomb* (New York: Columbia University Press, 1998), pages 336-338; Joseph Cirincione et al, *Deadly Arsenal* (Washington, DC: Carnegie Endowment for International Peace, 2005), pages 225- 226.

[43] For estimates of Pakistan's nuclear materials production capabilities, see Muthiah Alagappa, *op. cit.,* pages 5-16. Also see London Dossier*, op. cit.*

[44] The most famous report was written by David Albright and Paul Brennan, "Second Khushab Plutonium Production Reactor Nears Completion," Institute for Science and International Security (September 18, 2008), available at http://www.isis-online.org/publications/southasia/Khushab_18September2008.pdf. For Pakistan's official rebuttal to an earlier report see http://www.pakistanlink.com/Headlines/June07/23/07.htm.

[45] Based on the author's calculations from public sources, particularly the IISS *London Dossier, op. cit.,* published in 2007. Also, see estimates in Muthiah Alagappa, *op. cit.*

[46] John Grevatt, "USAF Awards Lockheed Martin Pakistan's F-16 Upgrade," *Jane's Defence Industry* (January 1, 2007). Cited in Peter R Lavoy "Islamabad's Nuclear Posture: Its Premises and Implementation" in Henry D Sokolski ed. *Pakistan Nuclear Future: Worries Beyond War* (Carlisle Barracks, PA: Strategic Studies Institute, January 2008), page 141.

[47] Information contained in the table is taken from various sources, including, "Pakistan: Air Force," *Jane's World Air Forces* (28 November 2006), and "Pakistan: Armed Forces," *Jane's Sentinel Security Assessment: South Asia* (22 November 2006) – both sources are subscription websites. Also see, Rodney Jones, *op. cit.*, pages 16-18.

[48] Agha Shahi, Zulfiqar Khan and Abdul Sattar, *"Securing Nuclear Peace,"* The News International Pakistan (5 October 1999), page 4.

[49] Shuja Nawaz, *Cross Swords: Pakistan, Its Army, and the Wars Within* (New York: Oxford University Press, 2008), pages 219-48; Brian Cloughley, *A History of the Pakistan Army: Wars and Insurrections* (New York: Oxford University Press, 1999), pages 63-78.

[50] Peter R. Lavoy, "The Costs of Nuclear Weapons in South Asia?," in D.R. SarDesai and Raju G.C. Thomas, eds., *Nuclear India in the Twenty-First Century* (New York: Palgrave- Macmillan, 2002), pages 259-61.

[51] For a detailed discussion see, Feroz Hassan Khan and Peter R Lavoy, *op. cit.,* page 219.

[52] John Garver, *Protracted Contest: Sino-Indian Rivalry in the Twentieth Century* (Seattle: University of Washington Press, 2001), page 187.

[53] For China's apprehensions about India's role as an expansionist power, see Shao Zhiyong, "India's Big Power Dream," *Beijing Review* (April 12, 2001), cited in Andrew Scobell, "Cult of Defense and Great Power Dreams: The Influence of Strategic Culture on China's Relationship with India," in Michael Chambers, ed. *South Asia in 2020: Future Strategic Balances and Alliances* (Carlisle Barracks, PA: US Army War College, 2002), pages 344-45; John Garver, *op .cit.,* page 188.

[54] John Garver, *op. cit.,* page 189.

[55] London Dossier, *op. cit.*, page 25.

[56] John Garver, "The Future of the Sino- Pakistani Entente Cordiale," in Michael Chambers, *op. cit.,* pages 344-45; John Garver, *op. cit.,* pages 402-05.

[57] US Assistant Secretary of State Robert Einhorn in testimony before the US Senate in 1997 alleged strong evidence of Chinese support to Pakistan. See *Proliferation: Chinese Case Studies*, Hearing Before the Subcommittee on International Security, Proliferation, and Federal Services of the Committee on Governmental Affairs, United States Senate, 105th Congress, 1st Session (April 10, 1997), pages 8, 12.

[58] Judith Miller, "U.S. Is Holding Up Peking Atom Talks," *New York Times* (September 19, 1982), page 11.

[59] Simon Henderson, "Why Pakistan May Not Need to Test a Nuclear Device," *Financial Times* (August 14, 1984), page 3; also see Mark Hibbs, "Despite U.S. Alarm over Algeria, Europeans Won't Blacklist China," *Nucleonics Week* (May 23, 1991), page 1.

[60] *Ibid.*

[61] *Ibid.;* John Garver, *op. cit.*, pages 404-05.

[62] Joseph Cirincione with Jon Wolfsthal and Miriam Rajkumar, *Deadly Arsenals: Tracking Weapons of Mass Destruction* (Washington, DC: Carnegie Endowment for International Peace, 2005), pages 213-15.

[63] John Garver, *op. cit.,* page 404; Joseph Cirincione, *op. cit.,* page 215.

[64] John Garver, *op. cit.*, page 407.

[65] Former Foreign Minister Gauhar Ayub Khan, cited in, "Pakistan: Beware Indian, Israeli Propaganda on 'Islamic Bomb,'" FBIS-NES-98-167 (June 16, 1998), cited in *Ethics and Weapons of Mass Destruction: Religious and Secular Perspectives*, edited by Sohail H. Hashmi and Steven P. Lee (New York: Cambridge University Press, 2004), page 341.

[66] "Saudi Nuclear Pact," *Washington Post* (January 18, 1981) cited in Henry D Sokolski ed. *Pakistan Nuclear Future: Worries Beyond War* (Carlisle Barracks, PA: Strategic Studies Institute, January 2008), pages 26- 28; Mohammad Al- Khilewi, "Saudi Arabia is Trying to Kill Me," *Middle East Quarterly* (September 1998), page 74.

[67] London Dossier, *op. cit.,* page 83.

[68] Wyn Q. Bowen, *op. cit.*, pages 30-31.

[69] London Dossier. *op.cit.*, page 30.

[70] Malfrid Braut-Hegghammer, "Libya's Nuclear Turnaround: Perspectives from Tripoli," *Middle East Journal* (Winter 2008), page 69.

[71] Khurshid Ahmad, "Nuclear Deterrence, CTBT, IMF Bail-outs and Debt Dependence," *Tarjuman al-Qur'an* (December 1980), cited in Sohail H. Hashmi, "Islamic Ethics: An Argument for Nonproliferation," in Hashmi and Lee, *op. cit.,* page 341.

[72] Feroz Hassan Khan and Peter R Lavoy, *op. cit.*, pages 221-23.

[73] Address by Mr Mohammad Ayub Khan, President of Pakistan, 26 September 1962, in General Assembly Official Records, 17th Session 1133rd Plenary Meeting, 26 September 1962, page 150. Quoted in Bhumitra Chakma, "Pakistan's Nuclear Weapons," (New York: Routledge, 2009), page 14.

[74] For a detailed analysis of the AQ Khan network's activities and Pakistani efforts to strengthen its system of controls, see *London Dossier, op. cit.*

[75] See Ashok Kapur, *Pakistan's Nuclear Development* (New York: Croom Helm, 1987); Ziba Moshaver, *Nuclear Weapons Proliferation in the Indian Subcontinent* (New York: St. Martin's, 1991).

[76] Statement by Ambassador Munir Akram, Permanent Representative of Pakistan to the United Nations, Conference on Disarmament, Geneva, 14 May 1998.

[77] See Pak's vision 2030 project, available at http://www.dailytimes.com.pk/default.asp?page=2008\04\09\story_9-4-2008, page 5.

[78] John Garver, *op. cit.*, pages 403-408.

RUSSIAN PERSPECTIVES ON THE GLOBAL ELIMINATION OF NUCLEAR WEAPONS

Dmitri Trenin[*]

As the self-perceived isolated great power in a highly competitive global environment, Russia regards nuclear weapons as the mainstay of both its security posture and status among the major powers of the 21st century. Even though the likelihood of a war with its ex-Cold War adversaries—America, its European allies, and China—is extremely low, nuclear deterrence gives a measure of comfort to the Kremlin that Russia's vital interests will be respected under all circumstances by Washington and Beijing, whose military power and "combined national might," respectively, are now far greater than Russia's.

Moscow's prime interest lies in regulating the major-power competition through arms control, not in abolishing nuclear weapons altogether and thus ending nuclear deterrence. Russia's resources are not nearly great enough to match NATO's or China's conventional arsenals. Making the world safe for US global conventional superiority, or allowing China to dominate Eastern Eurasia militarily, is anathema to Russian strategists. On the other hand, engaging with Washington and eventually Beijing in nuclear arms control negotiations, strategic dialogue, and the non-proliferation regime gives Russia both strategic confidence and elevated status. Russia has embraced, in principle, the goal of nuclear disarmament in its National Security Strategy (approved in May 2009), but real progress toward that goal is only possible if there are first major improvements in the strategic offensive and defensive arms area (both nuclear and non-nuclear), as well as conventional arms relationships. Most important, it would require a fundamental change of its security perceptions of other major powers to acquire a comfortable degree of mutual confidence and trust.

FACTORS MOTIVATING RUSSIA'S RELIANCE ON NUCLEAR WEAPONS

Already a central element of the military and foreign policies of the Soviet Union, Russian Federation officials see nuclear weapons as playing even more important roles—protecting Russia's security and supporting its regional and global political ambitions.

[*] Dr. Trenin is director of the Moscow Center of the Carnegie Endowment for International Peace. The views expressed in this paper are his and not necessarily those of the Center.

Security concerns

Russia has been afflicted by a plethora of security concerns following the end of the Cold War. Early hopes for integration into the West as a second-among-equals after the United States were dashed soon after the Cold War's peaceful end and Russia's leaders adopted a crass *Realpolitik* view of the world. Big powers, they are convinced, inevitably compete for global supremacy and regional spheres of influence. Russia faces new threats: terrorism, ethnic and religious conflicts, and transnational crime. Moreover, Moscow has to admit that the Russian Federation is a substantially weaker player compared to the Soviet Union. While the danger of a global nuclear war may have dramatically receded with the end of the Cold War, Russia's territorial integrity, domestic stability, strategic status, access to vital economic and strategic zones and lines of communications, and even its sovereignty, are all being challenged. Russia's military leaders argue that the country's post-Cold War attempts at cooperation with the West "have done nothing" to strengthen its military security. If anything, they maintain, Russian national security has suffered as a result of NATO's eastward enlargement and new US military deployments. Only one element of Soviet military power has survived virtually intact: nuclear weapons. As a result, not only Russia's security, but its status and self-image throughout the 1990s relied heavily, even disproportionately, on Moscow's possession of a massive nuclear arsenal.[†]

Since great-power relations remain of paramount importance to national security, Moscow has been eyeing two countries in particular—one overtly (the United States); the other, covertly (China).

America's global supremacy, its ubiquitous presence, and forceful foreign policy activism not only jar the sentiments of a former superpower, but directly affect Russian interests in what Moscow regards as its zones of concern, particularly in the now independent states of the former USSR. During the past decade, three developments were particularly important in this regard: (1) the expansion of NATO to include the countries of Central Europe, the Baltic region, and the Balkans; (2) NATO's air war against Yugoslavia over Kosovo, eventually leading to that province's forced separation from Serbia; and (3) US support for the so-called "color revolutions" in Georgia, Ukraine, and Kyrgyzstan and, subsequently, the prospect of awarding NATO membership action plans to Kiev and Tbilisi. The Kremlin also suspects the West of exploiting the conflicts within the Russian Federation, particularly in the North Caucasus, to contain and weaken Russia. In the Kremlin's view, Georgia's move against the Ossetians in August 2008 was a

---

[†] The writer's understanding of the views of Russian leaders is based on his experience as a staff member of the USSR delegation to the US-Soviet Nuclear and Space Talks in Geneva (1985-91), and on numerous personal conversations with diplomats, military officials, and political leaders over the past twenty years.

war by proxy launched by "certain quarters" in Washington (then-Vice President Dick Cheney's name is often mentioned) to "test" the Russian leadership and to help the Republican presidential nominee, John McCain, in the US elections. There is a near-consensus among Russian leaders that the one thing that protects Russia from direct US intervention is its nuclear weapons. According to this way of thinking, nuclear weapons made all the difference in restraining the United States from supporting Chechen independence the way it supported independence for Kosovo.

Next to geo-political worries, Russia is concerned about the growth and evolution of American military power. The US fiscal year 2009 defense budget is one-half of Russia's gross domestic product, even in purchasing power parity (PPP) terms. Meanwhile, US military technology is well ahead of Russia's and virtually in a race with itself. The Bush Administration withdrew from the 30-year-old treaty restricting missile defenses (ABM Treaty) and signed agreements with Poland and the Czech Republic to deploy ballistic missile defense (BMD) interceptors and radar. Virtually no one in Moscow's governing circles believed this was done in order to protect the US and its allies from an emerging Iranian missile threat, as US officials maintained. The choice of sites for the US "Global BMD Third Positioning Area," as the sites in Central Europe are known, add insult to the injury because of the inclusion of these former Soviet allies in NATO. Again, the predictable Russian response to this situation is to further develop its nuclear arsenal.

Not that Russia is dismissive of the dangers of nuclear proliferation. It shares with the United States the overriding interest of preventing more states from acquiring nuclear weapons. Nor can it ignore the facts that even though some of the would-be proliferators, such as Iran and North Korea, are virulently anti-American, they are geographically much closer to Russia's territory.

Like the United States, however, Moscow is discriminating in its approach to proliferation, distinguishing "acceptable" proliferators from those it opposes. Russia has tacitly accepted India's quest for nuclear weapons, for example. India, Moscow has reasoned, is a great power and cannot be seriously denied what other great powers take for granted. Moreover, India is the one great power that is totally unproblematic from the Russian perspective. Similarly, Israel, which was considered a potential adversary during the Cold War, has now won Russia's respect as a responsible player: Its nuclear arsenal is seen as a weapon of last resort and thus a factor helping to stabilize the Middle East. On the contrary, Russia had been very concerned about the Pakistani nuclear program even before Islamabad tested its nuclear weapons in 1998. To Moscow, Pakistan, unlike India, had been historically more of an adversary than a friend: It provided crucial support to the

United States proxy war against Soviet forces in Afghanistan; it has been and still is a hotbed of Islamist radicalism; and its political regime, infested with Islamist sympathizers, is believed by Moscow to be inherently unstable.

Russia also has been concerned about North Korea's nuclear program. It fears that Pyongyang's provocative policies could lead to a war, and possible nuclear fall-out, right on Russia's Far Eastern doorstep. Moscow has participated in the "Six-Party Talks" and supports Washington's current approach to solving the issue, which it wishes to be a model for other potential proliferators, above all, Iran. In the case of Iran, an important and growing neighbor across the Caspian Sea, Moscow favors a negotiated solution that would prevent Tehran from becoming a nuclear weapons state even as it takes Iranian security and economic interests into account.

Unlike the United States, China is never mentioned publicly by Russian officials as a security concern. Moscow believes that China will remain friendly toward Russia, at least in the medium-term, and that the current relationship, described as a "strategic partnership," will continue. Yet, beyond the 15-20 year horizon, many alternative scenarios are possible, especially if China turns more nationalistic. This raises the problem of Russian arms sales to China. In the 1990s, selling arms to Beijing was one of the very few means available to Moscow to keep the Russian defense industrial base afloat. In the current decade, these arms transfers are more difficult to defend. Basically, Russians see China through the same prism of *Realpolitik* which they use to watch America. In fact, the Sino-Russian power relationship has changed more dramatically in the last two decades than the US-Russian one. Until recently, Russia never had to live with a strong China. Russian leaders are perfectly aware of the vulnerabilities of their eastern flank, which they have been trying to bolster through various development programs and energy projects. Indeed, former President Vladimir Putin regards the 2004 agreement fixing the entire Sino-Russian border as his top foreign policy accomplishment.[‡]

Although a full-scale military conflict with China would be an absolute disaster for Russia, a combination of vested interests, anti-Americanism, and sheer complacency keeps the policy of arming China intact. Moscow, of course, imposes certain restrictions on what can be sold to China's military, but essentially it assumes that a Russian refusal to sell military hardware would motivate China to look for other suppliers, including Ukraine, and, at least potentially, Western Europe. Also, arms transfers, some Russian officials hope, have the potential to create special relationships and make the buyer's arsenal more or less transparent to

---

[‡] Putin made the comment during an informal meeting with members of the Valdai Club, which brings together Russian and international academics, experts and journalists for private discussions. http://www.kremlin.ru/text/appears/2006/09/111114.shtml

the seller. Others see this as a gamble, and point to the Soviet Union's support of post-Versailles Germany to build its armored forces and chemical weapons arsenal, later inherited by Adolf Hitler. All agree, however, that in order to deter China militarily, if it ever has to, Moscow has no better option than nuclear weapons.[1]

As is evident from the above analysis, for Russia to support an initiative to eliminate nuclear weapons, it would need to find ways to resolve both its perceived American security problem and its potential China problem, too. The former could be achieved, in principle, along the lines of a new Euro-Atlantic security compact that includes Russia alongside the United States, the European Union, and Russia's neighbors, such as Ukraine. This possibility looks remote, but is essentially the only means of ensuring Europe's security—and Russia's too. As to the latter, this can be achieved, again in principle, along the lines of a US-China-Russia security dialogue which effectively removes Russia's fear of a strong and assertive China. Needless to say, the latter appears even more remote than the former.

Deterrence vs. war-fighting

Russia has declared that, in order to defend its own sovereignty, territorial security, and the territorial security of its allies, it would use nuclear weapons, even if it were the first nation in the conflict to use of them. This is a striking departure from the Soviet declaratory stance which proclaimed a "no-first-use" doctrine. This declaratory change of heart is attributable to the dramatic change in its own condition and resources, including its military capabilities, rather than Russia's strategic environment. Russia's conventional forces have been redeployed from the forward positions they previously occupied in Central and Eastern Europe, Central Asia and the Caucasus, Afghanistan, and Mongolia. Russia's defense perimeter has moved closer to Moscow, reducing its strategic depth in the west by about 1,000 kilometers (km). Russia's conventional forces, also reduced to about one-third of their Soviet size, have still not been restructured for modern warfare and their quality has deteriorated drastically. Russia's military has a top-heavy structure, with an outsized overhang of flag officers and colonels, a pathetic shortage of company officers, and a complete lack of professional non-commissioned officers (NCOs). Its weapons and equipment are obsolete, with virtually no combat systems purchased since the collapse of the Soviet Union. Its training exercises have only been resumed recently, after a break of a decade and a half. Russia took a long time and a lot of effort to defeat the insurgency in Chechnya, and although it did defeat Georgia in the short war in 2008, its conventional forces are no match for the forces of its principal neighbors—NATO in the west and China in the east.

As a result, Russia has adopted a version of NATO's 1970s doctrine, which envisaged the first use of nuclear weapons in response to a massive conventional attack by much larger enemy forces. Occasionally, Russia points to the continuing presence of US tactical nuclear weapons (TNW) in Europe as justification for its new policy and maintenance of TNW in support of it, but Moscow has no interest in eliminating TNW altogether.

The likelihood of any attack on Russia is judged to be minimal in the west and – for now – very low in the east. In 1990, the Conventional Forces in Europe Treaty eliminated the material possibility that NATO could potentially launch a surprise attack. However, the version of the treaty negotiated in 1999 to reflect the changed political-military situation following the end of the Cold War, and ratified by Russia, has not entered into force, pending its ratification by NATO countries. The latter have delayed, calling on Moscow to first withdraw its military units from Georgia and Moldova. In response, Moscow has suspended its participation in the original 1990 agreement. Even though there are no signs of a return to military confrontation in Europe, Russia is troubled by new US deployments in Romania and Bulgaria, the US missile defense sites and potentially additional forces in Poland and the Czech Republic, and the "blank area" created by the Baltic States' non-participation in the CFE Treaty. Meanwhile, Western concerns have been heightened by the recent Russian-Georgian war.

Although Moscow signed an agreement with Beijing on a set of confidence building measures along the Russo-China border in 1996, it is fully aware of its weaknesses and vulnerabilities. Should the Sino-Russian relationship turn sour, Moscow's only logical answer would be nuclear threats, both to deter war and, if necessary, to fight it, both at the strategic and tactical levels.

Hardly anyone in Russia today envisions fighting a nuclear war in the west and virtually everyone hopes Russia will not have to fight one in the east. There is no public discussion of the use of nuclear weapons against other nuclear powers in specific scenarios. Russian military and political thought has evolved since the nuclear war-fighting strategies of the 1950s. One can only speculate that, in case of an existential crisis, after the outbreak of hostilities and in the face of a realistic prospect of military defeat, the Russian leadership could order a nuclear demonstration, e.g., an air burst over a body of water or a desert, to bring home to the enemy the seriousness of the stakes involved.

Prompted by the doctrinal innovations and technical experimentation by the George W. Bush Administration, Russia has also hinted at preventive uses of nuclear weapons directed at sub-state groups, such as well-entrenched insurgents, rebels, or terrorists, which may differ from the "first-use" concept. For three decades now, it is the south, rather than the west or the east, which has confronted Russian strategists with a set of real military security contingencies, from Afghanistan to the North Caucasus. Given the dearth of high-precision conventional munitions in the

Russian arsenal, miniature nuclear weapons could be an attractive means of dealing with deeply entrenched enemies. It seems, however, that this is still a controversial option.[2]

Support for Russia's security position in specific regions and for its regional ambitions

The "region" in which Russia operates is geographical Eurasia. Historically, Russia has been a major power in Europe, Asia, and the Middle East. The current Russian leadership considers much of the former Soviet Union its "zone of privileged interests." Moscow aspires to a hegemonic role in the post-Soviet area. It has pursued economic integration with Kazakhstan and Belarus and, at a lower level, with Kyrgyzstan, Tajikistan, and Uzbekistan. So far, the results have been limited. It turned the loose 1992 Collective Security Treaty into a smaller, but potentially more effective security organization with members in Eastern Europe (Belarus), the South Caucasus (Armenia), and Central Asia (all countries minus Turkmenistan). It used the economic crisis to give Kyrgyzstan an offer Bishkek could not refuse: Financial aid in exchange for the termination of US base rights in that country.[§] Russia does not want to undercut the US/NATO effort in Afghanistan: it simply wants Washington to recognize Moscow's primacy in the region and to deal with the Central Asian states through Russia.

Central Asia is also the geographical focus of the Shanghai Cooperation Organization (SCO), a mostly Chinese-designed security and development forum in which Moscow enjoys de facto co-leadership status alongside Beijing. As an organization, the SCO is still in a formative stage; as a forum, it draws many of Asia's leading countries, including India, Pakistan, and Iran. The value of the SCO to Russia lies in the China connection. However, Beijing's flat refusal—supported by all of Russia's own nominal allies—to recognize Abkhazia and South Ossetia, has brought home to the Kremlin that China will never compromise its own interests for the sake of supporting Russia: a most useful insight.

Many Russian leaders believe that their nuclear arsenal both enhances these regional security interests and prevents the US from gaining global dominance. As Chief of the General Staff Yuri Baluevsky contended, "Washington's policy is aimed at attaining global military superiority. The only real barrier to that dream coming true is Russia's strategic nuclear forces."[**] Russians are reading US government

---

[§] Editor's note: Since the writing of this paper, Kyrgyzstan has reconsidered its decision to terminate US base rights at Manas and on June 25, 2009 its parliament agreed to the US use of the base at nearly triple the previous annual rent. Russian President Medvedev has stated his support for this agreement.
Anne Gearhan, "Relieved US keeps base key to Afghan war," *The Washington Post*, June 26, 2009.
http://www.washingtonpost.com/wp-dyn/content/article/2009/06/26/AR2009062600785.html
[**] Author's translation

documents closely, especially those coming from the Pentagon and the intelligence community, for any indication of US strategic policy toward Russia. Even though these documents are usually written in a circumspect manner, the audience in Moscow has formed a habit of reading too much into what they see. Any official US statement of "concern" about Russia's nuclear arsenal, or any verbal placement of Russia as being too close to an avowed US adversary, such as Iran or North Korea, is viewed suspiciously. Russian leaders notoriously do not trust appearances and seek to penetrate the "hidden thoughts" of others, especially the United States. In that effort, they expose themselves as being too clever by half: Even innocuous phrases can acquire ominous meaning when over-interpreted. These perceptions, however, fit into the general concept of the world as seen by the security wing of the Kremlin; namely, that the principal foreign policy goal of the United States is to contain, dominate, and, ultimately, dismember Russia as its one implacable rival.[3]

Since the turn of the century, Russians taking this point-of-view have seen their suspicions confirmed: In the US public debate on security issues, according to many American writers, including former Bush Administration officials, Russia and China have emerged as major problem countries. To Moscow, these statements read as "potential adversaries" or even "future enemies." Since US statements often refer to the existential threat to America posed by Russian nuclear weapons, many Russian security analysts infer that the denuclearization of Russia is a supreme US security interest. As a first step toward that goal, they claim, the United States seeks to impose its "control" over the Russian nuclear arsenal under the guise of programs aimed at enhancing nuclear security and safety.[4]

Russian leaders are impressed by the sheer size of the US military establishment, its growth since the end of the Cold War, and Washington's willingness to use that immense power in various parts of the world. During the Cold War, the Russian concept of military security rested very much on the notion of rough equality of US and Russian global military capabilities. With that equality gone, and no alliance-type, or even cooperative, relationship to replace it, Moscow feels uncomfortable. It perceives the stated US resolve to prevent the emergence of a military competitor as a claim to perpetual military superiority, which leaves the rest of the world, including Russia, at the mercy of Washington decision-making.

US actions since the end of the Cold War have generated and intensified these threat perceptions. Russians, generally, blame US administrations for believing the West "won" the Cold War and for their condescending attitudes in the 1990s toward a "defeated" Russia. The first wave of NATO enlargement in the mid-to-late 1990s, which resulted in the accession of Poland, Hungary, and the Czech Republic, was seen as a US vote of no-confidence in a post-Communist Russia, an extension of the US zone of influence, a bridgehead for further reducing Russia's influence, and, very importantly, as a breach of faith with regard to US and West European promises to then-President Mikhail Gorbachev that NATO would not expand eastward following the reunification of Germany within the alliance. The fact that the latter were not written promises, and may have been misinterpreted, changes little: Most Russian leaders and officials believe the West deceived Gorbachev and took advantage of Russia's enormous difficulties at the start of the 1990s.[5]

NATO's second enlargement wave in 2004 led to the inclusion of the three Baltic States, whose relations with Moscow are particularly strained over those nations' historical grudges against Russia and Moscow's anger over Estonia's and Latvia's refusal to extend automatic citizenship to their sizeable Russian minorities. With the admission of Romania and Bulgaria, the Black Sea, like the Baltic, became dominated by NATO. Although it did not present a direct military threat, NATO's enlargement came to signify a fundamental geo-political rebalancing west of Russia's borders. Gone was the neutral cushion of Central Europe that separated Russia from the West historically and which, in the past, was a battleground for competing Russian and German influence. The West was now virtually at Russia's doorstep, projecting its influence into parts of what the Russians believe is the core of their historical proto-state, i.e. Ukraine and Belarus.[6]

Former President Putin's unfortunate involvement in the 2004 Ukrainian presidential election, with current President Medvedev at his side as the then-Kremlin chief of staff, had the principal objective of preventing the victory of pro-Western Ukrainian forces that, it was feared, would bring Ukraine into NATO and host US bases there. The so-called "Orange Revolution," however, ousted instead the corrupt clique with whom Moscow had aligned itself. In the Kremlin's mind, the revolution was little more than a special operation conceived and conducted by the United States, aimed at achieving geo-political, rather than democratic goals. When, four years later, the pro-Western Ukrainian President Viktor Yushchenko applied for NATO's Membership Action Plan, widely considered a virtual guarantee of eventual accession to the alliance, Moscow decided to do everything in its power to prevent its acceptance. Putin warned the Ukrainians of the dire consequences of joining with the West against Russia and played the pragmatic Ukrainian Prime Minister Yuliya Tymoshenko against her ideological president. He also personally cautioned NATO leaders against accepting an unstable country and counted on German and French understanding of, and concern about, Russia's position on this issue and ability to stand up to US pressure, and thus prevented the needed consensus within the alliance.[7]

Faced with a similar situation in Georgia—a pro-Western leadership succeeding a corrupt post-Soviet regime through a near-revolutionary situation—Russia used the conflicts in Abkhazia and South Ossetia to place insurmountable obstacles in the way of Georgia's NATO ambitions. When Georgia launched a surprise attack against the South Ossetian capital in August 2008 and killed a number of Russian peacekeepers, Moscow initially interpreted that move as a war by proxy, waged by the Georgian president Mikheil Saakashvili on behalf of the Bush Administration in Washington. Russia's armed response was aimed as much at Georgia's patron, the United States, as it was aimed at Georgia itself. The Georgian crisis not only marked the lowest point in Russian-US and Russian-Western relations since the start of Gorbachev's perestroika in the mid-1980s, but also the most dangerous period for European and world security. Moscow did not immediately believe the US would take the defeat of its client calmly; it saw the humanitarian mission of the US Sixth Fleet in the Black Sea as an exercise in re-supplying and rearming Georgia for a war of revenge, and interpreted the Ukrainian president's decree restricting the movements of Russia's own Black Sea Fleet as potentially an intolerable provocation, designed to bog Russia down in another conflict, this time in the Crimea. Had it not been for the advent of the world financial and economic crisis the following month, a serious US-Russian collision could have been unavoidable.[8]

Neither the Georgian nor the Ukrainian NATO issues have been resolved. Both have been postponed, but both remain on the agenda. If NATO chooses to reactivate either issue, however, the consequences could be deadly. In Ukraine's case, the NATO issue is extremely divisive as it touches the country's identity, with a majority of its people wishing neither to be part of Russia nor to part with Russia. Russia's concerns need to be taken seriously; everywhere east of Berlin, NATO is perceived to be not about Afghanistan, but still about Russia. In Georgia's case, where the elites and the public are pro-NATO and anti-Russian, the issue is the state's borders. Admitting Georgia in its *de facto* borders (i.e. minus Abkhazia and South Ossetia) would be unproblematic for Moscow, but totally unacceptable for the Georgians. Admitting Georgia in its internationally recognized boundaries, however, would mean that NATO would run a significant risk of a military conflict with Russia. Even those Georgians who point to the fact that the Federal Republic of Germany was admitted to NATO in 1954, while East Germany remained in the Soviet sphere of influence, would have to admit that Germany was the central issue in Cold War East-West relations, while Georgia is a very much off-center item in current global politics.

Russia recognized Abkhazia and South Ossetia not as a belated response to the Western recognition of Kosovo, as has been suggested by some, but as a means to deploy regular forces in both breakaway republics in order to deter a fresh US-supported Georgian attempt to retake them. As for Kosovo itself, from Moscow's perspective, it came as the culmination of a broader Western intervention in the Balkans, through which the US and its allies picked the winners, appointed the villains, and redrew the borders—all without Moscow's consent and often against its protests. The issue for Russia was not the vaunted Slav solidarity, as so often is maintained in the West, which is a chimera, but its demonstration of complete US/NATO dominance in matters of European security. Not only did Russia no longer count diplomatically, even though its leaders believed it remained a great power, but the United States and its allies went into a war of choice in Europe— despite Moscow's most vehement, but also impotent, protests. From Kosovo in 1999 and again in 2008, Moscow heard resoundingly that Russia was now safe to be ignored.[9]

Moscow's other complaints include the lack of any apparent US appreciation for Putin's early conciliatory actions, such as closing the electronic intelligence station at Lourdes, Cuba, and the Danang naval facility in Vietnam in 2000. Russia also tolerated a US military presence in parts of the former Soviet Union, including Central Asia and Georgia, in the wake of the 9/11 incident, not to speak of Russia's strong support for the United States following that attack, including its material help in defeating the Taliban in 2001.

The Obama Administration has entered office with a different set of priorities than its predecessor. It has signaled to Moscow that while NATO's promise of membership to Ukraine and Georgia stands, it will not be a priority, and will not be "pushed." It has also softened its approach to the issue of ballistic missile defenses in Central Europe, linking it to progress toward resolving the Iranian nuclear issue, and indicating willingness to explore the potential for US-Russian collaboration on missile defenses.

This has quelled the Kremlin's early fears about the new Democratic administration. Initially, Moscow was concerned by the number of hold-overs from the Clinton era that were taking positions on Team Obama: the Clinton years are remembered in Moscow mainly for the humiliation that Russia felt due to its weakness and dependency on the West. Within months of the new administration taking office, however, the Russian leadership discovered that the new US governing team was actually very pragmatic, and decided they could do business with them.

The Obama Administration's early policies on nuclear disarmament have received a generally positive, though not a raving, reaction in Moscow. The Russian leadership welcomed the re-launch of strategic arms control negotiations in April 2009. These will allow Moscow to reduce its nuclear arsenal in tandem with Washington, rather than to face the prospect of unilateral cuts and growing disparity in strategic offensive arsenals, which would damage the Kremlin's self-image. At the same time, the Russian leaders take a rather skeptical view of both the feasibility and desirability of full nuclear disarmament. They have taken note, however, that, in his

April 2009 Prague speech, Barack Obama envisioned this as "perhaps" not happening "in his lifetime."

Reacting to Obama's vision, President Medvedev agreed with the US President's "conditions" for phasing out nuclear weapons and added three of his own: Preventing deployment of weapons in outer space, preventing a build-up of non-nuclear strategic systems to compensate for reductions in nuclear forces, and a guarantee that a "nuclear return potential" would not be created (i.e. addressing the issue of non-deployed nuclear weapons).[10]

Thus, one is tempted to say that in the Kremlin's view, "movement (toward disarmament) is everything; the end goal (i.e. nuclear abolition) is nothing." Yet, there are limits to how far Russia would be prepared to go in reducing its nuclear arsenal. A thousand nuclear weapons is a psychological barrier below which the Russian leadership believes any further reductions could be destabilizing. These numbers are also dependent on the scope and efficacy of future US ballistic missile defenses. Moreover, whatever Moscow's willingness to cut its strategic nuclear forces, it also believes in the utility of deterrence at sub-strategic levels. Although its officials would never admit it publicly, Russia is reluctant to eliminate shorter-range nuclear weapons for fear of undermining the credibility of its deterrent vis-à-vis China.

Support for Russia's global ambitions

After a period of weakness and withdrawal, Russia has again emerged as a global actor, although a relatively weak one. Moscow aspires to become a member of a self-selected group of independent "power centers," alongside the United States and China. (Moscow considers the European Union to be less of a strategic player, due to its lack of unity on a number of political issues and its dependency on the United States for its security). Moreover, recently, Russia has been trying to present itself as the only global military power next to the United States: After a 15-year break, it resumed global air and naval patrols in 2007 and has conducted a number of major military exercises on land. Russian nuclear-capable strategic bombers have been flying over the Atlantic and the Pacific, coming close to the eastern and western coasts of the United States and to the territories of its allies, Britain, Norway, and Japan. The Russian Navy has resumed cruises in the Mediterranean and has sent a ship to the Somali coast to protect shipping against pirates. There has been talk that Russia is considering expanding its presence at the naval facility at Tartus in Syria, and even a return to the Yemeni island of Sokotra in the Gulf of Aden. The economic and financial crunch, however, may trim these ambitions. Indeed, in terms of global naval activity, Russia in 2008 ceded its perennial second place to the fast-growing Chinese Navy.[11]

In order to send a message to Washington not to involve itself militarily in what Russia regards as its sphere of "privileged interests," Moscow sent two Tu-160 strategic bombers in 2008 to Venezuela; within weeks, a squadron of ships from the Russian Northern Fleet followed. Russia has been trying to profit from the strained relations between the United States and several Latin American countries, including Venezuela, Bolivia, Nicaragua, and the former Soviet client Cuba, but its objectives, besides making a point in a public relations contest, are mostly economic. Unlike the Soviet Union, Russia is not thinking of creating a global anti-US coalition.

For almost a decade, its nuclear arsenal, together with its UN Security Council seat, were the two major arguments supporting Russia's claim to great-power status. While Russia's nuclear deterrent has always stayed in the background, its existence gave the Kremlin a degree of self-confidence that, despite the country's weakness in the 1990s and its near-isolation in the first decade of this century, core Russian interests would be sufficiently protected against anyone, including the reigning world hegemon, the United States, and the rising power of China. It is likely that Russian leaders will continue to see value in this role for nuclear forces. Despite the plan for sweeping military reform announced in 2008, Russia, especially given the economic crisis which is hitting the country hard, can not be expected to modernize its conventional military forces quickly or sufficiently in the mid-term to match US global capabilities. Even when and if it succeeds in its conventional modernization program, Russia's resources—financial, economic, and not least demographic—will prevent Moscow from claiming an equal military status with the United States and, in conventional terms, also with China. For this reason alone, Russian leaders will likely always see value in nuclear forces as defining Russia's claim to a seat at the table with the other world powers.

RUSSIA'S NUCLEAR PLANS

As of January 1, 2007, under the counting rules enshrined in the START I Treaty between the US and the Soviet Union, the Russian strategic nuclear forces included a triad of 530 intercontinental ballistic missiles (ICBMs), 16 nuclear-powered strategic submarines (SSBNs) armed with 272 submarine-launched ballistic missiles (SLBMs), and 78 nuclear-capable heavy bombers, for a total of 4,162 warheads. Maintaining and optimizing this nuclear triad is considered a supreme national priority. The stated mission of the strategic nuclear arsenal is to deter large-scale aggression against Russia and its allies (presumably in the Collective Security Treaty Organization), including under the worst possible conditions—i.e. by retaining a capability to withstand a first nuclear strike and retaliate with profound effects against the attacker.

Russia's ICBMs are being modernized substantially. In an effort to increase the survivability of these forces and their capability to penetrate the defensive systems being acquired by the United States, Russia is deploying mobile "Topol-M" ICBMs with single warheads (these are also known as RS-12M2). Alongside the existing silo-based RS-24, which is equipped with multiple independently targetable reentry vehicles (MIRVs), Topol-M should increase the Russian missile force's survivability and penetration capabilities and thus counter US BMD plans. Russia is also introducing maneuvering warheads (MARVs) and plans to deploy a hypersonic gliding warhead. The older ICBMs (RS-12M, RS-18 and RS-20) are going through extensive modernization to extend their life cycles to 23, 30, and 25 years respectively. Existing ICBM development plans foresee a smaller, but more modern and more capable force, by 2016.

The sea-based element of Russia's strategic nuclear forces is expected to deploy a new SSBN (the *Yuri Dolgoruky*, *Borey*-class) in 2009. This submarine will be armed with a new MIRVed SLBM (*Bulava*), which is completing its flight tests and is expected to go into serial production soon. Two more *Borey*-class SSBNs may become operational in 2010. At the same time, older submarines are being overhauled and equipped with the modernized RSM-54 SLBM (*Sineva*).

After a long break, three TU-160 heavy bombers have been produced since 2001. The emphasis, however, is not so much on producing new aircraft as on modernizing the existing ones, extending their life cycles to 30-35 years. The bombers are being equipped with a new air-launched cruise missile (ALCM), the X-102. A decision to build a new heavy bomber is expected by 2011-12.

Shorter-range non-strategic nuclear forces (tactical and operational-tactical forces in Russian classification) are considered indispensable for deterring conflicts at the regional level. The emphasis is on extending the life-cycles of the existing systems. Tu-22M3 and SU-24 nuclear-capable strike aircraft are being modernized. Only one new short-range missile system, the *Iskander*, has been deployed since the break-up of the Soviet Union.[12]

Under the terms of the 2002 US-Russia SORT Agreement, by the end of 2012 Russia would have 220-260 ICBMs with 810-980 warheads; eight to nine SSBNs with 136-148 SLBMs and 592-664 warheads, and up to 50 heavy bombers with 400 weapons, a grand total of 1,800-2,000 weapons. After that, the Russian strategic nuclear arsenal would be maintained within the range of 1,700 – 2,200 operationally deployed weapons (ie. excluding shorter-range systems and warheads held in reserve).

In the more distant future, the size of the Russian arsenal will depend on the fate of arms control negotiations, the state of nuclear weapons proliferation, global progress in military technologies, and the prospects for ballistic missile defenses. The leaders of the Russian armed forces are confident that Russia could live under the terms of the SORT Agreement until 2015-20, regardless of the anticipated progress of the US BMD program. Beyond 2020, however, it is felt that Russia would need to raise the penetration capability of its strategic systems substantially, increase their survivability, and improve the effectiveness of the Armed Forces' command, control, communications, and intelligence components. [13]

Following the Cold War, Russia was forced to adjust its nuclear strategy. Strategic nuclear *parity* with the US, the Soviet Union's main achievement in the nuclear arms race, is no longer considered necessary. Instead, Russia's current deterrence strategy talks of maintaining a US-Russian *balance* of nuclear capabilities and, increasingly, neutralizing the impact of the US global BMD system. The importance of this distinction is that rather than seeking numerical equality or, better, preponderance in nuclear warheads and delivery systems, as it did in Soviet times, Moscow could abstain from a nuclear arms race it could not win, and focus on building capabilities which would give it enough confidence that any US lead would not translate into a capability to blackmail Russia.

Proliferation concerns

Russia's proliferation concerns are real. Fundamentally, they are similar to those of the United States (even though the proliferators do not see Russia as their prime adversary), but there are important differences in how the two countries' deal with those concerns.

Moscow abhors unilateral US military actions to prevent or roll back proliferation. From Moscow's perspective, a war in Korea or Iran to destroy those countries' emerging nuclear weapon capabilities would be nearly as bad as living with nuclear-armed regimes in Pyongyang or Tehran. Russia strongly prefers multilateral decisions reached and implemented by the leadership of the UN Security Council, where it has a permanent seat and enjoys veto rights. Russia is also a solid supporter of the International Atomic Energy Agency (IAEA), another check on unilateralism.

In North Korea, Russia sees an embattled Stalinist dictatorship that resorts to nuclear and missile blackmail of its neighbors, South Korea and Japan, and the United States, as its only means of ensuring its security from outside attack and its domestic survival—the latter both through permanent political mobilization against the "imperialist enemy" and through the acquisition of scarce food and fuel from that same enemy. Moscow sees Pyongyang as an essentially untrustworthy and unreliable, but a generally rational, if abhorrent, actor. The best way of dealing with such a regime is not to pressure it, but to quell its fears of outside aggression, and mellow its regime through engagement. Russian leaders believe that a natural process of regime decay will do the rest. Thus, Russia supports a US-North Korean understanding as a key element of any solution to the North Korean nuclear program; it also supports China's role as the principal facilitator of North Korea's acceptance of the deal and the agreement's informal guarantor, and the hammering out of the agreement in a wider international setting (the Six-Party Talks), of which Russia is an integral part.[14]

In principle, Russia would want to see a similar framework applied to Iran: A US-Iran deal, Russian-EU "massaging" of Tehran to accept and stick by it, and ratification of the agreement in a wider context (in this case the permanent members of the UN Security Council plus Germany). In the Russian view, the IAEA and the UNSC are the relevant bodies to monitor compliance and act upon the arrangement. Russia appreciates Iran's role as a regional power and has managed to have a productive relationship with Tehran. Its view of Iranian politics and foreign policy is markedly different from that of the United States. Russia does not dispute Iran's right to engage in peaceful nuclear research and has been helping Iran to build its first nuclear reactor. Russia, however, would want to present Iran with a set of incentives to drop any nuclear weapon ambitions in exchange for an opportunity to pursue peaceful nuclear energy under international supervision in a greatly improved regional security situation.[15]

In contrast to Iran, whom the Russians see as an essentially stable geopolitical actor, Pakistan had been a major cause for concern in Moscow long before it tested its first nuclear weapons in 1998. The specter of a political meltdown in Pakistan, ultimately affecting its nuclear weapons, is a bigger nightmare for Moscow than a conceivable Iranian nuclear strike at Israel. Another concern is a new war between Pakistan and India over Kashmir or resulting from a terrorist attack inside India. Recognizing the limits of any historical analogy, Moscow supports India and Pakistan working to stabilize their nuclear relationship through confidence building measures and agreements in the image of the steps taken by the US and Soviet Union after the Cuban missile crisis in 1962.

Use of nuclear weapons by sub-state groups, including Islamist terrorists, is also a real concern for Moscow. Following the 9/11 attack on Washington and New York, Russia has initiated and participated in a variety of high-level international meetings and programs, both within the G-8 format and in other forums, to prevent such a threat from materializing, and has been cooperating with the United States and other countries to keep nuclear weapons and materials out of reach of terrorists.[††]

[††] As early as 1997, Russia initiated a draft convention on nuclear terrorism; the document was finally approved in 2005. At the 2006 G-8 Summit in St. Petersburg, Russia promoted a Global Initiative to Combat Nuclear Terrorism.

Since the days of the Cold War, Russia has lived at the epicenter of a nuclear confrontation that has outlived its original cause. Yet Russia is less worried about the nuclear forces of the United States and China, not to speak of France and Britain, India and Israel, than about proliferation involving unstable regimes and sub-state actors. Resisting proliferation is done more effectively if there is close cooperation among the major nuclear powers than if those powers focus primarily on just phasing out their stockpiles, which favors those with more advanced non-nuclear weapons.

In its newly-regained global status, Russia's neighborhood extends way beyond its borders. A future world with perhaps as many as three dozen nuclear states is unacceptable from Moscow's perspective. Such a world would be teetering constantly on the brink of nuclear war, and may eventually fall off the cliff. This horror vision forms a solid basis for renewed Russian-American cooperation to bar nuclear proliferation and to move, eventually, to a world free of nuclear weapons.

MOVING TO ZERO

Mikhail Gorbachev outlined the vision of a nuclear-free world in 1986 and actually discussed a time-table for bringing that vision into reality with President Ronald Reagan at Reykjavik. In present-day Russia, such ideas are mostly considered Utopian. US conventional capabilities have reached the level that many missions which previously demanded nuclear strikes can now be performed more effectively by non-nuclear systems. The lack of such conventional systems in the Russian arsenal has caused Moscow to continue to firmly base its overall security strategy on nuclear deterrence.

Toward the end of his second term, for example, President Putin talked about a new technological arms race in both offensive and defensive systems. Though he didn't mention it by name, he was clearly referring to the United States. As Moscow has discovered, nuclear weapons are a relatively cheap way of ensuring one's security vis-à-vis a much stronger, richer, and technologically accomplished counterpart. Nuclear weapons are considered the great equalizer in a situation of US global dominance, conventional military supremacy, and active interventionism.[16] Both Vladimir Putin and Dmitri Medvedev have come out in support of nuclear disarmament. This is not just rhetoric, but support for disarmament as a principle and a process, within safe limits; it does not constitute a wholehearted embrace, à la Gorbachev, of the actual goal of zero nuclear weapons.[17]

There exists, however, a small group of prominent Russians who would like to see nuclear weapons abolished once and for all, for the same reasons as those campaigning for eliminating nuclear weapons in the United States. To make a serious case in the councils of the Russian state, they need to be able to prove that moving toward nuclear abolition would not endanger Russia's security and would not "make the world safe for US conventional military dominance." Whether or not they would be able to get that proof would depend heavily on the actions that other nations, in particular the United States, would be prepared to undertake.

Actions like the following might improve the prospects for a positive response from Russia to a serious US initiative to eliminate nuclear weapons:

- If the US were to agree to the basic rules of engagement proposed by Vladimir Putin in Munich in 2007: Accept us as we are; treat us as equals, and cooperate on the basis of shared interests;
- If a gradual, but steady, build-up of confidence, leading eventually to genuine mutual trust, co-leadership on security issues in which Russia can play an important role, with an emphasis on WMD proliferation was introduced into US-Russian relations;
- If a new Euro-Atlantic security system were created in which Russia belonged as a full member (Medvedev's call for a new treaty on European security), anchoring Russia in Europe (Putin's idea of an energy community linking Russia and the EU);[18]
- If the US were to invite Russia to join it as an equal partner in building and operating global/regional ballistic missile defenses;
- If verifiable curbs on advanced, non-nuclear military technologies and non-nuclear strategic weaponry were negotiated;
- If "weaponization of space" (the meaning of this Russian term itself needs to be clarified) were safely barred;
- If a new US-Russian strategic arms agreement were concluded, leading not only to reductions of offensive systems, but to a genuine strategic dialogue between the two countries, addressing such issues as strategic defenses, WMD non-proliferation, and nuclear disarmament;
- If the US/NATO and Russia were to cooperate more closely on Afghanistan;
- If the US and Russia were able to cooperate to resolve the Iranian nuclear issue;
- If the US and Russia were able to cooperate in stemming long-range missile proliferation in the greater Middle East and elsewhere;
- If China were to join the US-Russian strategic arms control talks and resulting mechanisms, and if India showed an interest in at least becoming an observer in that process;
- If NATO were to formally forego any further enlargement into the former Soviet space and if the NATO-Russia Council were transformed

into a decision-making body on all matters pertaining to Euro-Atlantic security. The Council, for example, could serve as venue for negotiating, outside of the NATO structure, a new Euro-Atlantic security compact, which would embrace both NATO and non-NATO countries in Europe, including, besides Russia, also Ukraine, Georgia, Kazakhstan and others.

While not each and every one of these conditions needs to be fulfilled, of particular importance are the concerns over US conventional military superiority. These perceptions can only be put to rest through a fundamental change in US-Russian relations, leading from stronger confidence to mutual trust to a new and lasting partnership. This security partnership needs to be strengthened by a revived economic relationship.[‡‡] At the same time, Russia needs to be anchored in Europe through a closer relationship with the European Union, including membership in a free-trade area, visa-free travel, and a serious energy partnership. Finally, the United States, the European Union, Russia, and other non-NATO, non-EU countries of Europe need to come together to form a new security system for the 21st century, not to replace NATO and the EU, but to form their functional equivalent for a much wider and more diverse membership.

As noted previously, President Medvedev has come up with an initiative for a new Euro-Atlantic architecture. Moscow's thinking, for the time being, revolves, sadly, around a new-look Organization for Security and Cooperation in Europe (an OSCE plus, Medevdev called it), a Cold War construct, which would ideally include a UN-style Security Council. This is a non-starter. Rather than prod Moscow for the details it does not have, the United States and its European partners need to engage with Russia in a common thinking about the future relationship that would finally make Europe secure. This is also a *sine qua non* for attaining the objective of a world free of nuclear weapons, at least as far as Russia is concerned. If the United States adopts a foreign policy personality of a global leader by consent, a *primus inter pares*, and a consensus builder, neither goal seems out of reach.

[‡‡] Finalizing the WTO membership process for Russia, granting it "preferred nation" status as America's trading partner, and ratification and implementation of the "123 agreement" on peaceful nuclear cooperation would serve as a good beginning.

Endnotes

[1] See, e.g., my public debate with Vitaly Tsygichko, a leading military expert, in *Security Index, 2007*, Issue 2 (82), vol. 13, page 147-156.

[2] See, e.g., Nestrategicheskoe Yadernoe Oruzhie. Problemy Kontrolya I Sokrashcheniya. Centr po Izucheniyu Problem Razoruzheniya, Energetiki I Ekologii (Moscow: MFTI, 2004).

[3] Cf, e.g., Vadim Solovyov, "Reforma Ovoennaya Rbyavlena Bessrochnoy." *Nezavisimoe Voennoe Obozrenie (NVO)* (January 26, 2007); Gen. Makhmut Gareev. "Novye Usloviya – Novaya Voennaya Doktrina," *NVO* (February 2, 2007).

[4] Cf., e.g., the many fairly strident writings and interviews on the subject by Gen. (Ret.) Leonid Ivashov. For a more serious analysis, see Gen. (Ret.) Pavel Zolotarev, "USA Rashiryayut Control Nad Rsossiyskimi Yadernymi Obyektami," *NVO* (March 4, 2005).

[5] See, e.g., Remarks by Foreign Minister Sergey Lavrov at the Brussels Forum-2009, convened by the German Marshall Fund of the United States. www.mid.ru, document 488-31-03-2009.

[6] Sergey Lavrov, Vneshnya Politika Rossii I Novoe Kachestvo Geopoliticheskoy Situatsii. www.mid.ru (Posted on December 29, 2008).

[7] Sergei Tolstov, "Ukraina Mezhdu Krizisom I Vyborami," *Nezavisimaya Gazeta*, April 20, 2009; James Sherr, "NATO Strengthens Ukraine and Itself," *Zerkalo Nedeli* (April 12-18, 2008).

[8] Sergey Markedonov, *Pro Gruziyu s lyubov'yu*. www.apn.ru (Posted October 28, 2008). See also my article, "Russia in the Caucasus: Reversing the Tide," *Brown Journal of World Affairs* (Spring/Summer 2009), pages 143-155.

[9] Cf. Dmitri Trenin, "The Kosovo Casus," *Pro et Contra, 2006*, Issue 5-6. On the implications of the Kosovo casus for Russia's foreign policy, see Dmitri Medvedev's interview with Russia Today TV (August 26, 2008), www.president.kremlin.ru.

[10] "President Dmitri Medvedev's Remarks at the University of Helsinki" (April 20, 2009), www.president.kremlin.ru

[11] *Kommersant* (September 24, 2008); www.newsru.com/arch/world/29jan2009/yemenbases.html.

[12] Alexei Arbatov and Vladimir Dvorkin, editors, *Nuclear Weapons After the Cold War* (Moscow: Carnegie Moscow Center, R.Elinin Publishing House, 2008), pages 43-45.

[13] C.f. "Round Table: Nuclear Arsenals in 25 Years," *Security Index*, Vol. 1, 86 (Winter 2008/09), pages 69-74; for a highly skeptical view of the prospects for nuclear disarmament, and a vision of a future Russian nuclear posture, see: Opasnost Yadernogo Razoruzheniya. Perspektivy Sozdaniya Novykh Rossiyskikh Yadernykh Sil (A Report by the Institute for National Strategy, 2009); www.apn.ru Document 2009-03-31 INS.

[14] Vassili Mikheyev et. al., in Arbatov and Dvorkin, *op.cit.*, pages 352-387.

[15] Vitaly Naumkin et. al., in *Ibid*, pages 388-429.

[16] President Putin's annual address to the Federal Assembly, May 2006, www.president.kremlin.ru.

[17] See "The National Security Strategy of the Russian Federation to 2020," approved by President Medvedev on May 13, 2009; http://www.kremlin.ru/text/docs/2009/05/216229.shtml.

[18] President Medvedev's made his proposal in Berlin on June 5, 2008, and in Helsinki on April 20, 2009; www.president.kremlin.ru; Putin made his remarks at Davos in January 2009. Cf. http://www.government.ru/content/rfgovernment/rfgovernmentchairman/chronicle/archive/2009/01/28/5825465.htm.

TURKEY'S PERSPECTIVES ON NUCLEAR WEAPONS AND DISARMAMENT

Henri J. Barkey

In principle, Turkey would welcome the global elimination of nuclear weapons. For the current government, the possession of nuclear weapons by other states is a factor that, indirectly at least, reduces Turkey's regional (if not global) aspirations and power. However, in the medium term, it remains deeply ambivalent on the future of nuclear weapons and its own plans regarding nuclear energy and weapons development.

Turkey lacks a coherently articulated national policy vis-à-vis nuclear weapons. This is partly due to the fact that as a member of NATO it is a direct beneficiary of the US nuclear umbrella and because the United States maintains a number of nuclear weapons at the Incirlik Air Force base in southern Turkey.[1] The absence of such a policy is also the result of the unclear demarcation of lines of authority between civilian and military leaders on issues of national defense. While this may not have been a problem in the past, civil-military relations have been strained under the current ruling government, led by the Justice and Development Party (AKP). Until recently, when it came to setting national priorities, the military establishment's role could best be described as *primus inter pares*. The AKP's preoccupation with expanding Turkey's role in the region and its push to reform Turkish state structures, including the military's prerogatives, are radically challenging the military's control of the national security agenda.

WHAT FACTORS MIGHT MOTIVATE TURKEY TO ACQUIRE NUCLEAR WEAPONS?

Any discussion of Turkey's approach to nuclear weapons—whether it is to support an initiative such as "Global Zero" or to acquire them—has to be studied in the context of the transformation it is undergoing: Turkey is not just a dynamic emerging market economy, but one that contains deep divisions among domestic political forces that are battling for the very essence of the country, its identity, and future direction. Aggravating the current divide between arch-secularists and a coalition of liberals and more religiously conservative groups is a deepening ethnic cleavage—Kurds against majority Turks. For some or all protagonists involved, the issues at hand are existential in nature and compromise is difficult to achieve.

Parallel to these is the fact that Turkey's immediate security environment has been, and continues to be, in a state of flux. The war in Iraq has had a direct impact on

Turkey, in part due to Turkey's past policies with regards to its own Kurdish minority. Ankara feels threatened by the emergence of a federal (if not bi-national) Iraq that contains a robust Kurdish component. Most Turkish military thinking has been dominated by the threat posed by Kurdish developments and the domestic Kurdistan Workers' Party (PKK)-led insurgency which, after 20 years, shows few signs of dying out. In fact, until a new foreign policy was formed by the AKP government, much of Turkey's foreign policy considerations were dominated by the Kurdish question and the need to combat the PKK.

Another important transformational development is Turkey's ongoing application to join the European Union (EU). The EU membership process has already forced Turkey to make significant changes to its domestic institutions, including on issues of the rule of law and minority rights. However, Ankara has a long road ahead to comply fully with EU requirements including, perhaps most importantly, far more sweeping changes to Turkey's organizational structure, including civil-military relations. The EU membership process, with close scrutiny of Ankara's behavior, is one of several factors acting as a constraint on potential Turkish nuclear ambitions.

Security Concerns

As a NATO member and US ally, Turkey has enjoyed the protection extended by US nuclear guarantees—the so-called "nuclear umbrella." Extended nuclear deterrence was primarily designed to protect Turkey from the Soviet Union, and with the collapse of the Soviet state, the nuclear issue lost its relevance. In fact, even before the end of the Soviet Union, the US had begun to progressively reduce its nuclear weaponry in Europe and to withdraw from installations that had housed these weapons. Turkey, along with four other European countries, maintain US nuclear weapons; some 90 tactical weapons are stored at the Incirlik Air Force base near the southern city of Adana pursuant to the 1999 NATO strategic concept that envisaged a "minimum level sufficient to preserve peace and stability."[2]

How credible today are the US and NATO's nuclear guarantees to Ankara? After the demise of the Soviet Union, Turkey's security threat perceptions shifted away from the Cold War calculations of the threat posed by the Warsaw Pact to its immediate neighborhood and specifically the Middle East. Even Turkey's age-old conflict with Greece has eased as Athens made a strategic choice to support Turkey's EU application as a means to contain, if not eliminate, the perceived Turkish threat. Ironically, Ankara sees its primary threat to be an internal one with foreign linkages. The possibility of Kurdish secession, as difficult as this may be to imagine, is the primary threat that drives Turkey's security policies. This has become even more pronounced in the aftermath of the 2003 Iraq War, as Iraqi Kurds, who had already enjoyed a *de facto* quasi-independent status since the 1991 crisis with Iraq over Kuwait, gained official recognition within Iraq with the creation of a federal Iraqi state.

In recent years, some Turks have begun to question the effectiveness of the NATO/US security umbrella. In part, this is due to the reluctance and sluggishness with which some NATO members responded to Turkey's request for military deployments during the 1991 Iraq/Kuwait crisis. Then "some NATO allies questioned the need to deploy even token reinforcements to Turkey."[3] Growing anti-Americanism in Turkey has also exacerbated the general lack of confidence in Western (specifically American) security guarantees.[*] Some leading Turkish military officials have even suggested that Turkey ought to rethink its alliance commitments.[4] Anti-Western sentiment is also reinforced by the constant drumbeat of reports that Europeans and Americans are not doing enough to combat the PKK.

In contemplating conventionally armed foes, the Turkish armed forces are quite competent. For example, the first post-Cold War demonstration of Turkish military prowess occurred in 1998 when the Turks threatened Syria with military intervention unless it stopped providing the PKK's leader, Abdullah Öcalan, with refuge in Damascus and Syrian-controlled parts of Lebanon. With most of its divisions facing south against Israel, Syria quickly capitulated and sent Öcalan on his way—a decision that ended with his capture and imprisonment by Turkish officials. With the capture of Öcalan and further political changes in both Turkey and Syria, relations between the two governments have improved significantly.[5]

However, in the absence of any nuclear weapons of its own, when it comes to contemplating threats from nuclear-armed nations, Turkey has little else to rely on other than NATO's guarantees. This might be relevant in considering the possibility of a revanchist Russia, or scenarios in which Iran and/or Syria acquire nuclear weapons. Hence, despite the discordant voices emanating from various groups, Turks continue to rely on the American security umbrella. Ankara has always stressed the importance of its NATO commitments. Moreover, as will be discussed below, there is no easy way for Turkey to obtain such weapons, even assuming it was willing to forsake its alliance and treaty pledges. It currently has no nuclear power plants and only the beginnings of a research/technical infrastructure. What has made the Turkish military a potent force has been its NATO links. The combination of NATO, a robust army, and a willingness to take security seriously has served effectively as Turkey's primary form of deterrence.

In considering the possibility of a nuclear-armed Iran, Turkey has often stressed that it has enjoyed a peaceful border with Iran dating back to the Qasr-i Shirin Treaty of

---

[*] A Pew poll in 2007 had found that with only 12 percent of the respondents in favor, Turkish support for America was the lowest among most countries. http://pewglobal.org/reports/display.php?ReportID=252.

1639. Although Ankara routinely complained in the 1990s that Tehran was aiding and abetting the PKK's activities in Turkey, the two nations actively collaborated politically to contain the *de facto* Kurdish entity in northern Iraq that the Gulf War allies protected. In more recent years, moreover, Turkey and Iran claim to have made common cause against both the PKK and its Iranian affiliate, The Party of Free Life of Iranian Kurdistan (PJAK), occasionally even coordinating artillery strikes.[†] Unlike Israel and Saudi Arabia, no one in Turkey perceives Iran as representing an existential threat to Turkey. As Turkish columnist Cüneyt Ülsever argued, Turkey and Iran are two imperial powers with leadership ambitions in the Middle East, but if they have not fought much between them, it is because neither can decisively defeat the other.[6]

Iran's acquisition of nuclear weapons, of course, could alter this deterrent balance and the Turkish secular establishment harbors serious reservations about Iran's intentions. The 1979 Iranian Islamic Revolution was an eye opener for many in Turkey who feared that their own Islamists would emulate this path. Indeed, Turkish authorities accused Iran of trying to foment domestic unrest by encouraging Turkish Islamic groups to even engage in violent activities. The advent of AKP and the election of its leader, Recep Tayyip Erdogan, as Turkey's Prime Minister, however, have dramatically changed the relationship. The current government in Ankara, as opposed to establishment Turks, has a more benign view of Tehran. It has gone out of its way to accommodate Iranian concerns and sought to increase trade and deepen bilateral relations. As a result, Turkish-Iranian relations are enjoying their best period since 1979.[7] AKP's self-confidence has also manifested itself in a desire to become an intermediary between the West and Tehran on all matters, but especially on the nuclear file.[‡]

That said, Turkey is opposed to a nuclear Iran. A nuclear Iran would be likely to upset the regional balance of power. Already, by removing one of Tehran's most bitter enemies, Saddam Hussein, and by bringing to power a Sh'ia regime in Baghdad, the war in Iraq has drastically improved Iran's geopolitical standing in the region. Because Iran is a revisionist power, some Turks fear that its acquisition of

---

[†] Turkey's willingness to acknowledge such cooperation publicly is designed to send Washington a message that even the military is willing to deal with the much-disliked regime in Tehran when it comes to the Kurdish question. The Turkish military had been frustrated until the end of 2007 by American unwillingness to allow Turkish forces to target PKK encampments in northern Iraq. The PKK has been fighting the Turkish authorities since 1984; it reached its zenith in 1991. Based initially in Syria, the PKK also established rear bases in Iran and Iraq. While its effectiveness has been severely curtailed by years of Turkish counterinsurgency operations, it remains a potent force able to harass security forces. PJAK, the Iranian offshoot of the PKK, is far smaller and extremely dependent on the PKK. It has benefited from the absence of other Kurdish insurgent groups in Iran, but it too has faced a growing Iranian military counterinsurgency campaign. For a detailed analysis of the Turkish-Kurdish relations please see Henri J. Barkey, *Preventing Conflict over Kurdistan* (Washington, DC: Carnegie Endowment for International Peace, 2009).

[‡] In seeking support for Turkish diplomatic overtures towards Iran, a high-ranking Turkish foreign policy official has often stressed in private communications to his American interlocutors that "no one knows Iran better than Turkey."

nuclear weapons would be likely to make it far more self-confident and, therefore, adventurous in its regional relations.[§]

There is, however, a division between the government and the security establishment regarding Iranian intentions. The government and most of the Turkish public do not perceive the Iranian nuclear program as a serious threat to Turkey. This, in large measure, is due to the fact that the US has taken the lead in admonishing Iran and trying to force it to comply with IAEA regulations and NPT agreements. Both the government and public are completely opposed to an American (or possibly Israeli) strike on Iranian nuclear installations.[**] One other factor bearing on Turkish decision-making and policy formulation is the absence of independent Turkish capabilities to collect, analyze, and assess intelligence on nuclear issues. As a result, Turkey is dependent on outside sources, namely the US, IAEA, and NATO for its information. This both helps and constrains US influence; to the degree that the US provides the information, Turks develop an aversion to the US agenda on the issue. Moreover, the United States' credibility problem following the WMD debacle in Iraq and the general lack of sympathy for the US in Turkey has made it difficult for the government, assuming it is alarmed by developments in Iran, to assume a vocal and pro-American stance in this issue.

The AKP and much of its leadership rose through the ranks of more hard-line Islamist movements. Even though Prime Minister Erdogan and company broke with the old guard, represented by Necmettin Erbakan, a former prime minister and father of the Islamist movement in Turkey, the current AKP leadership still perceives the world through a religiously tinted lens. Erbakan, during his short stint as prime minister, tried very hard to create a grouping of Islamic states, called the D-8, which was intended to rival the G-8 assemblage of economically advanced Western nations. Erbakan and his lieutenants extolled the virtues of an Islamic NATO and Islamic Union, complete with its own currency. Not surprisingly, Erbakan and his supporters, though much diminished in size and influence, fully support Iran's quest for nuclear power and weaponry. While this justification is couched in the form of Iran's need to deter the United States, underlying this wish is also their perception of a civilizational struggle between East and West.[††]

[§] Three Turkish parliamentarians told a Congressional staff delegation visiting Turkey that were Iran to go nuclear, Turkey would follow suit. How representative this sample might be, however, is debatable. See: *Chain Reaction: Avoiding a Nuclear Arms Race in the Middle East* (Washington, DC: Committee on the Foreign Relations of the United States, Senate, February 2008), page 41.

[**] Interestingly, the Turkish government took a very low-key approach to the September 2007 Israeli raid on Syria's nuclear installation. In part because the Syrians decided to underplay the event themselves, and despite stories that Israeli jets had ditched their empty fuel tanks over Turkish territory, when asked about it Prime Minister Erdogan simply said, "we talked to both sides and they both denied that there was a violation of our airspace," *HaberX* (April 26, 2008).

[††] The mouthpiece of the current party established by Erbakan, the Felicity party, is the daily *Milli Gazete*, which published a long analytical article supporting the Iranian quest for nuclear capabilities on November 24, 2005.

Current Turkish political leaders often respond to concerns expressed about Iran with a similar refrain: Iran has the right to access nuclear technology provided it is for peaceful purposes.[‡‡] Often, Turkish political leaders raise the issue of Israeli nuclear weapons; in 2006 then foreign and deputy prime minister, Abdulah Gül, in his party's annual meeting, argued that if Iranian nuclear weapons are dangerous, then so are the Israeli ones.[8] When asked about the Iranian nuclear effort, Prime Minister Erdogan, on a visit to Washington in late 2008, responded by being as critical of the United States as he was of Iran. He said that "those who counsel Iran not to acquire nuclear weapons, should themselves not have these weapons in the first place."[9]

On the other hand, Turkey wants a quiet and stable neighborhood in order to accomplish its developmental goals— after decades of economic ups and downs it has finally managed to put together a consistent record of economic growth—and EU accession. Turkey has tried hard to become an energy (especially gas) conduit between the energy-rich producers of Azerbaijan, Iran, Turkmenistan, and Russia, on the one hand, and an energy-hungry Europe, on the other. Its own domestic needs are being supplied in part by Iran.

An Iranian nuclear weapons program might stand in the way of both Turkish economic development and EU accession if the Middle East were plunged into a serious arms competition. This is why the Turks have stated their support for the UN process and in August 2005 allowed Britain, speaking on behalf of the EU, to issue a statement for Turkey, as one of the prospective member countries, at the IAEA board of governors meeting supporting the EU diplomatic initiative to contain the Iranian uranium enrichment process, known as the E-3. Iran was quite displeased by Turkey's action.[10]

The security establishment, by contrast, has a more jaundiced view of Iran. In 2005, as he was about to leave his post as Turkish Ambassador to Washington, Faruk Logoglu, a former Ministry of Foreign Affairs undersecretary, pointedly argued that Iran is inexorably moving towards the acquisition of nuclear weapons and that the European efforts at containing this development would fail.[11] Turkish military officials have also been blunt about their concerns regarding the Iranian nuclear program. The Turkish General Staff perceives Iran as an ideological enemy; a theocratic state bent on undermining the secular basis of Turkey and of the region. In a speech in Washington, given while he was deputy chief of staff, the current chief of the armed forces, General Ilker Basbug, argued that Turkey, just as the United States, was following Iran's nuclear activities with apprehension.[12] In his

---

[‡‡] Occasionally, there are expressions to the contrary, as was the case with the AKP chairman of the parliamentary foreign policy committee, Murat Mercan, who on a trip to Israel suggested that Iran was first and foremost a threat to Turkey, *Haaretz* (December 12, 2008). Two days later, the Iranian News Agency, IRNA, posted a correction by Mercan on its Turkish website, http://www1.irna.ir/tr/news/view/line-6/0812128992144327.htm.

departure speech, a former chief of staff, General Hilmi Özkök, without mentioning Iran by name, warned that "unless the crisis over nuclear weapons is not resolved diplomatically, [Turkey] would soon be faced with important strategic choices. Otherwise, we would be faced with the possibility of losing our strategic superiority in the region."[13] This sentiment is echoed by voices associated with the nationalist camp in Turkey who fret about Iran's increased influence, not only in the Middle East but also in Central Asia and the Caucasus, and especially in Azerbaijan.[14]

Like the politicians, though, the security establishment opposes any military action to forcibly eliminate Iran's nuclear weapons. Of most concern to them is the possibility of a repeat of the after-effects of the Iraq War, which completely undermined the status quo in the region and gave further momentum to the Kurdish issue. Similarly, a US strike against Iranian installations is likely to upset domestic balances in Iran and unleash a series of unpredictable consequences that would likely further undermine regional stability. Hence, the Turkish military is caught between its desire to see a diplomatic initiative succeed and the very real prospect that such an endeavor will fail and Iran will ultimately achieve nuclear weapons status.

This may also explain why Turkey has not experienced the public debates on the removal of nuclear weapons from its territory. Of the four other non-nuclear European states—Italy, Germany, Belgium, and the Netherlands—that continue to store US nuclear weapons, only Belgium and Germany have had extensive parliamentary debates on the pros and cons of maintaining them.[15]

The advent of an Iranian nuclear device would not automatically change Turkey's approach to nuclear weapons. However, it would certainly unleash a brand new debate in the country because, to date, the discussion in Turkey has remained conjectural and, with few real specialists on the subject, has had a somewhat unreal quality to it. Two factors will determine the future course of action: first, regional development pursuant to Iran's nuclearization and, second, which of Turkey's domestic political parties is in power at the time.

Turkey's reaction would not be solely contingent on Iran's behavior. After all, Turkey benefits—and presumably will continue to do so for some time in the future—from the nuclear umbrella offered by the United States. However, there are indications that an Iranian bomb would lead to a regional nuclear arms race, which could trigger a Turkish nuclear program.

The Saudis, who feel the most threatened by Iran's nuclear, conventional, and revolutionary ambitions, are likely to try to follow Iran if it develops nuclear weapons. Saudi Arabia has already intimated that it would seek its own warheads in the event Iran goes nuclear.[16] Turkey could also be encouraged by the Saudis to seek its own path to nuclear weaponry. Even though Turkey has recently sided with the more radical elements in the region over Gaza, the Turks would also be worried about the burgeoning 'Shia Crescent,' stretching from the Palestinian territories to Pakistan. Turkey considers such a division dangerous for the security and stability of the region as a whole, and aims to bridge the gap between Sunni Arab states and Iran.[17]

Moreover, an Iranian bomb may compel Israel to come out of its nuclear closet to deter Iran. In turn, as Robert Einhorn has argued, such a development would undermine the unspoken arrangement that has ruled the Egyptian-Israeli relationship to date. Despite its boisterous denunciations of the Israeli nuclear program, Egypt has put its nuclear ambitions on a back-burner as long as Israel maintains its ambiguous stand about its program. If Israel were to go public with its arsenal in response to an Iranian bomb, it would risk reigniting Egypt's nuclear effort.[18] An Iranian nuclear weapon would certainly set back the cause of creating a Nuclear Weapon Free Zone in the Middle East for decades and might even trigger a rush to emulate Tehran. Even in the event of a Palestinian-Israeli peace agreement, Iran's quest would represent a sufficient shock to the system to engender such a reaction.

The likelihood that Turkey would seek its own path to a nuclear capability, however long this might take, would increase in the event of such a regional nuclear arms race. Domestic political pressure and the region's anarchic character would be sufficient to propel any Turkish government to begin its own program. In the meantime, the presence of US weapons on its soil would serve as a security bridge.

On the other hand, were the United States to remove its nuclear weapons from Europe altogether, Turkish calculations would be altered drastically. Their presence, as David Yost points out, has helped Europe, especially Turkey, to connect to NATO strategy and contribute to collective decision-making.[19] Their removal therefore could severely shake confidence in the concept of extended deterrence. In the eyes of experts and European security officials, weapons based in Europe are considered far more important to maintaining a deterrent posture than weapons on US soil or at sea.[20]

The second factor that could encourage Turkey to develop a nuclear capability would be its domestic politics. The AKP has tried hard to position itself as a regional leader; it takes pride in its ability to intervene in regional conflicts and offer its services as a state imbued with soft power to help resolve them. It has even offered its services to the United States and Iran. AKP's bid for regional influence has struck a chord with the Turkish public. Prime Minister Erdogan has been its primary beneficiary and has carefully tailored these diplomatic initiatives to a rise in

Turkish nationalism. He and his current government have done much to stoke and ride the nationalist wave. This was most evident in the dramatic theater he engineered over Israel's Gaza incursion.

A nuclear arms race in the region in which Turkey remained on the sidelines, lost influence, and relied on American security guarantees raises the prospect of a strong nationalist backlash. If this were coupled with disillusionment over the prospects for membership in the European Union, the government might be unable to withstand a groundswell for nuclearization. Fundamentally, predicting how Turkey would react to a future Iranian nuclear weapon depends in part in the direction Turkey takes in the near future: Will it endure the difficult transition to a modern European-like state while getting ever so close to membership in the EU, or will it be tempted by opportunities to make a bid for regional leadership? As an EU member it would have much less reason to worry about the changing regional balance of power—and the powerful constraints on its ability to break current commitments in the NPT and other agreements to remain non-nuclear.

Were Iran to cross the nuclear threshold one day, what would Turkey do? On the assumption that it cannot stand still and do nothing, it has three choices:

1. Multilateral defense option: It could strengthen its ties with the US. Turkey is already part of the NATO alliance and therefore Ankara benefits from the US nuclear umbrella and already has nuclear weapons on its soil.[21] In order to improve its deterrent capacities, it might seek to reinforce these ties, seeking extra diplomatic and political assurances and asking for more advanced weaponry from the US, including state-of-the-art anti-missile technology and advanced aircraft. It might also appeal to the EU to strengthen its defense-related institutions and even speed up the accession negotiations. In other words, under this option, Turkey would seek to bolster its existing defense agreements and might even push the US to declare publicly and officially the presence of nuclear weapons on Turkish soil.

2. Go nuclear option: This could not be achieved quickly. As will be described below, Turkey does not have the technical wherewithal to produce nuclear weapons anytime soon. It can decide to make the necessary investments, but it would take time and resources to reach fruition. Moreover, Turkey does not have the possibility of pursuing this option clandestinely because of the close relationships it has developed with the United States and Europe over the years, making the country fairly transparent. An open nuclear endeavor would risk alienating the Europeans and Americans, but a covert program would do so even more. During the Reagan Administration,

the United States was very concerned about the existence of a nuclear supply relationship between Pakistan and Turkey. President Reagan and his aides warned the Turks in a number of different settings about this relationship until means for greater cooperation between the two countries were instituted.[22] Ankara is intent on being far more cautious on this front; in June 2008, Turkish officials met a visiting Syrian energy minister's suggestion for nuclear cooperation between Turkey and Syria with silence.[23]

3. Regional diplomatic attack option: The Turkish ruling party has a great deal of confidence in its own standing in the region. Hence, it may choose to pursue an active diplomatic route designed to isolate Iran. This could be done in concert with the first option. The desired goal of isolating Iran would be to help trigger a change in regime or orientation that would reverse the nuclear decision.

None of these choices are particularly appealing or realistic, which suggest that the best outcome for Turkey would be for the current multilateral effort under UN auspices aimed at convincing Iran not to proceed with nuclearization to succeed.

Regional and Global Ambitions

Turkey has been experiencing a wave of nationalism and prickliness. The public has become more xenophobic. The call for Turkey to be an unrivalled power in the region and beyond is often heard. An Iranian bomb is likely to galvanize and mobilize those who would like to see Turkey go nuclear.

The AKP government came to power arguing that Turkey punched far below its weight in international affairs. Previous governments (with the notable exception of Prime Minister, and later President, Turgut Özal) had avoided engagement with its immediate region assiduously. The AKP, by contrast, trading on its more pious roots and opposition to Turkey's secular establishment, decided to engage the region. While it took care to maintain good relations with Israel, a fact that provided it with clout both in the immediate region and in Europe and America, the AKP government also signaled that its foreign policy approach would be more encompassing and that it expected to have a seat at the table. Among its goals was greater representation in international institutions, including the UN Security Council, where for the first time since the early 1960s, it gained the chance to occupy one of the non-permanent seats for the two-year term.

Under Prime Minister Erdogan, Turkey has had several recent diplomatic ventures. The prime minister invited himself into the Russian-Georgian crisis without any consultations with the NATO allies or the EU. Following the 2006 Lebanon war, he also convinced Turkey's military to send troops to Lebanon as part of a UN monitoring mission. Finally, Turkey became an important intermediary between Israel and Syria at a time when the Bush Administration seemed to have created a vacuum through its refusal to forcefully engage in the region. Underlying the AKP approach is a conceptualization of Turkey's role as gateway between East and West. Ahmet Davutoglu, the eminence grise behind this approach, who until his recent elevation to Minister of Foreign Affairs served as an advisor to both the prime minister and the president, formulated a vision for Turkey that has its two legs anchored in Europe and America, while reaching over to Asia and beyond as a means of balancing its traditional alliances. In his vision, Turkey deserves to be, and ought to be, a global player.[24] Moreover, Davutoglu has also pushed for a policy of "zero problems" with neighbors that commits Turkey to maintaining good relations at the highest levels with neighboring states. In fact, Turkey was one of the few countries to immediately congratulate Iranian President Ahmedinejad following his disputed 2009 reelection "victory." This may prove to be a problematic relationship for Turkey if the Iranian leadership, anxious to buttress its domestic base after these tainted elections, were to decide to harden its position on the nuclear question triggering an even deeper crisis with the international community.

Ironically, it is Prime Minister Erdogan's criticisms of Israel, especially following the January 2009 Gaza operation, which elicited the greatest acclaim in the Arab street. While he and Turkey have achieved greater visibility as a result, it is not altogether clear that Turkey has limitless possibilities and that it does not make mistakes that can be costly over time.

Moreover, there are limits to Turkish influence deriving from its own domestic inconsistencies and clashing ideas regarding its identity and place in the world. These will undoubtedly be accentuated both physically and psychologically by Iran becoming a nuclear power. Iran's achievement on the nuclear front, it must be remembered, comes with a whole panoply of other military-industrial accoutrements. For the Iranian nuclear deterrent or threat to be effective, the weapon has to be accompanied by a delivery infrastructure. When it comes to long-range missiles, the Iranians, with North Korean support and advice from Russian engineers, have already built an impressive array of potential delivery means. This was demonstrated recently by Iran's successful launch of a satellite into space. Turkey is far from achieving such capabilities.

All of these developments have catapulted Iran into the forefront of a regional balance of power game. Iran's progress on these fronts has made up for its relative weakness in the conventional weapons arena. By contrast, the Turks have no indigenous capability to manufacture missiles, much less launch satellites. For both of these, Ankara relies on the United States or the European Arianne program.

One of the consequences of the Iranian nuclear program has been an increased interest in nuclear power. Although Turkey has no nuclear power plants, global concerns over climate change and the growing realization of Turkey's dependence on imported hydrocarbons to satisfy its growing energy demands has spurred the government to seek tenders to build the first nuclear power plants. As Ilter Türkmen, a former foreign minister, pointed out, Turkey has fallen behind in nuclear knowledge and technical expertise. This, he argued, "was incompatible with Turkey's geopolitical standing and economic potential. If neighbors were intent on developing nuclear weapon technology, it behooved Turkey, at the very least, to acquire peaceful forms of nuclear technology."[25] In March 2007, the government passed legislation approving the construction and operation of nuclear power plants. Strong opposition to such plants exists, however, which makes it difficult politically for the government to go forward without paying a high political price.

TURKEY'S NUCLEAR INFRASTRUCTURE

Turkey is a signatory to the NPT and signed on to the Additional Protocol in 2006. Turkey has one research and two small experimental nuclear facilities. The main such installation is on the outskirts of Istanbul at Küçük Çekmece. Built in 1962 and upgraded subsequently to a 5 megawatt research reactor, it provides isotopes and other services to the medical industry. The other two experimental facilities are situated near Ankara are straightforward research laboratories.[26]

However, Turkey has no nuclear power plants, despite studies that were started as early as 1965 to explore building one such plant.[27] Turkey has in the past expressed interest in developing a nuclear industry, but despite discussions with a variety of countries to forge a way to collaborate, it has never managed to translate these efforts into concrete action. Nuclear energy is an attractive source for Turkey given that it has to import almost all of its energy needs from abroad. It has a tiny amount of oil and can rely on hydropower for some of its needs. However, both the discussion of climate change and the potential unreliability of its energy partners, including Iraq, Russia, Azerbaijan and Iran, have spurred Turkey to take a new look at nuclear power. In 2006, the Turkish Prime Minister announced that Turkey would soon start building three nuclear plants that would become fully operational by 2015. However, these hopes are unlikely to materialize because of domestic opposition; the costs are high and there seems to be a lack of interest on the part of would-be investors. In September 2008, the government received only one bid for its Akkuyu tender on the Mediterranean coast. The one bid, from a Russian company undermined the very notion of reducing Ankara's energy dependence on Russia from which it purchases most of its gas.[28] The government subsequently decided to postpone its decision to whether to cancel the tender until after the March 2009 local elections. The AKP is nonetheless determined to go ahead with nuclear energy because, as Prime Minister Erdogan has argued, this is vital for Turkey's industrial competitiveness.[29] The government took a modest step in that direction in August 2009. As part of a broader set of agreements on energy projects, Turkey and Russia agreed to reopen talks on civilian nuclear cooperation.

The nuclear cooperation agreement Turkey signed with the United States on June 2, 2008 is designed to enhance the exchange of information, technology, research, and nuclear power production and could give a boost to Ankara's nascent efforts.[30] President George W. Bush, when sending the bill to Congress, commented that the agreement would "serve as a strong incentive for Turkey to continue its support for nonproliferation objectives and enact future sound nonproliferation policies and practices. It will also promote closer political and economic ties with a NATO ally, and provide the necessary legal framework for US industry to make nuclear exports to Turkey's planned civil nuclear sector."[31] President Bill Clinton had initiated this deal; however, its consideration had been delayed by proliferation concerns. Its reemergence may be due to American concerns that Turkey, pressured by growing domestic energy demand, will increasingly be tempted to seek Iranian gas sources.

TURKISH ATTITUDES TOWARD NUCLEAR DISARMAMENT

There is not enough public information to evaluate Turkey's likely stance if there were a serious effort by the United States and other nuclear weapon states to eliminate all nuclear weapons on a global basis. However, what can be surmised from the discussion above is that Turkey would welcome such an initiative precisely because, in the absence of nuclear-armed countries, its industrial and conventional military prowess would help increase its influence in its immediate region and beyond. The Turkish political leadership—as distinct from its military leadership—is far more at ease with what it perceives to be Turkey's "soft power." Much of Turkey's opening to the region and its attempt at mediating international disputes comes from its conviction that it can tap its "soft power" reservoir. Provided that all countries embark on such an initiative, Turkey can rightfully calculate that it stands to benefit, especially if Iran and Israel are de-nuclearized.

One of Turkey's foremost researchers on the nuclear question has even suggested that the time had come for Turkey to rethink the presence of American nuclear weapons on Turkish soil. Mustafa Kibaroglu argues that the benefits derived from these weapons (deterrence and, more importantly, the traditional argument that they represent an investment in good relations with the United States) would be exceeded by the benefits of their removal. The weapons not only represent a hazard, he maintains, and represent a roadblock to a greater, region-wide nuclear free zone initiative, but more importantly permit the Iranian regime to use the nuclear weapons stored at the Incirlik base as a justification for their own program.[32]

Furthermore, in the absence of a genuine disarmament agreement, should Iran develop nuclear weapons and Turkey decided that it had to follow suit, it would face significant obstacles in the pursuit of nuclear capabilities. It not only would jeopardize relations with the United States, but it would also have a negative impact on its NATO links. Moreover, such a decision would almost certainly deal a fatal blow to Turkey's aspirations to join the European Union. Olivier Roy argued that were Iran to go nuclear, Turkey would face a hard choice: It can either rely on the EU and NATO nuclear umbrella or go for its own nuclear weapons. However, were it not to trust the Europeans, then it would also forsake its place within Europe.[33]

Finally, there is the question of domestic opposition. Turkish civil society groups have expanded dramatically in recent years. Many of them work in the environmental arena. Opposition to nuclear power plants has already led to the cancellation of one proposed project. The fact that Turkey spans an earthquake prone zone adds further momentum to these groups' efforts and there is no question that they have been influential in this regard. A PIPA poll conducted in December 2008 found that in Turkey, 55 percent of the population was strongly in favor of eliminating nuclear weapons and another 10 percent somewhat in favor of this proposition. Comparable figures for Egypt are 39 and 43 percent; Iran has 50 and 18 percent; and a world-wide average of 50 and 26 percent respectively. While these figures for Turkey are above the mean, interestingly, the percentage of the Turkish population who are in strongly opposed to a treaty abolishing nuclear weapons (5 percent) are among the lowest in the world.[34]

The growing momentum around the world towards eliminating nuclear weapons is overshadowed in Turkey by the perception of declining American influence in Turkey's immediate region. As a result, it is not evident what consequences there will be if additional countries are willing to make their own deals on nuclear power and weapons, as suggested by James Russell.[35] It could prove to be an impetus for nuclearization. Turkey might also interpret the waning of American power as a reason to pursue a nuclear option, particularly in the face of an Iranian bomb and additional proliferation in the Middle East. For now, however, Turkey's commitments to the EU and NATO and the long and costly gestation period necessary to develop nuclear technologies and related weapons, are likely to incline Turkey to favor a disarmament agreement. How long that sentiment will last remains to be seen.

ENDNOTES

[1] Hans M. Kristensen, *US Nuclear Weapons in Europe* (Washington, D.C. Natural Resources Defense Council, February 2005).

[2] Of these 90 weapons, 50 are to be delivered by the American and 40 by the Turkish air forces, Kristensen, *US Nuclear Weapons in Europe*, page 9.

[3] F. Stephen Larrabee and Ian O. Lesser, *Turkish Foreign Policy in an Age of Uncertainty* (Santa Monica, CA.: RAND, 2003), page 150.

[4] Mustafa Kibaroglu and Baris Çaglar, "Implications of a Nuclear Iran for Turkey," *Middle East Policy,* XV: 4 (Winter 2008), pages 68-69.

[5] Melek Firat and Ömer Kürkçüoglu, "Orta Dogu'yla Iliskiler" in Baskin Oran (ed.)*Türk Dis Politikasi: Kurtulus Savasindan Bugüne Olgular, Belgeler, Yorumlar* (Istanbul: Iletisim Yayinlari, 2002), Volume II, pages 565-567.

[6] Cüneyt Ülsever, "Ahmedinejad ne Yapmak Istiyor?" *Hürriyet* (February 8, 2006).

[7] Gökhan Çetinsaya "Nükleer Kriz Eşiğinde İran ve Türkiye," *Cumhuriyet Strateji* (June 5, 2006).

[8] *Hürriyet* (March 13, 2006).

[9] *Radikal* (November 15, 2008).

[10] For the UK statement, please see http://www.iaea.org/About/Policy/GC/GC49/Statements/UKforEU.pdf.

[11] "Logoglu: Iran Nükleer Silah Yolunda," *NTV* television channel, Istanbul (December 20, 2005).

[12] Fikret Bila, "Org. Basbug'un ABD'ye verdigi mesajlar," *Milliyet* (June 8, 2008). The full text of his comments can be found at http://www.tsk.mil.tr/10_ARSIV/10_1_Basin_Yayin_Faaliyetleri/10_1_7_Konusmalar/2005/gnk urIIncibsk_atckonusmasi_060605.html .

[13] Author's translation. "Genelkurmay Baskani Hilmi Özkök'ün Devir-Teslim Töreni Konusmasi," (August 28, 2006), http://www.tsk.mil.tr/10_ARSIV/10_1_Basin_Yayin_Faaliyetleri/10_1_7_Konusmalar/2006/orgh ilmiozkokdvrtslkonusmasi_28082006.html.

[14] Ümit Özdag, "Iran Nükleer Silah Sahibi Olmali mi?" *Aksam* (March 7, 2005).

[15] Lale Sariibrahimoglu, "Incirlik'teki Nükleer Silahlar Yine Gündemde," *Taraf* (May 6, 2009).

[16] Thomas W. Lippman, "Saudi Arabia: The Calculations of Uncertainty," in Kurt Campbell, Robert J. Einhorn and Mitchell B. Reis (eds.), *The Nuclear Tipping Point: Why States Reconsider their Nuclear Choices* (Washington, DC: The Brookings Institution, 2004), page 129.

[17] Hakki Uygur, "Iran's Nuclear Ambitions and Turkey," *SETA Policy Brief* (February 2008, No. 7), page 5.

[18] Robert J. Einhorn, "Egypt: Frustrated but still on a Non-Nuclear Course," in Campbell, Einhorn and Reiss, *op. cit.*. pages 73-74.

[19] David S. Yost, "Assurance and US Extended Deterrence," *International Affairs* 85:4 (2009), page 770.

[20] *Ibid.,* page 764.

[21] Sariibrahimoglu, *op.cit.*

[22] Leon Fuerth, "Turkey: Nuclear Choices amongst Dangerous Neighbors," in Campbell, Einhorn and Reiss, *op. cit.*. pages 160-162.

[23] Gareth Jenkins, "Syria Proposes Nuclear Cooperation with Turkey," *Eurasia Daily Monitor* (Jamestown Foundation), June 16, 2008.

[24] Ahmet Davutoglu has put forward what has become AKP's vision foreign policy vision in *Stratejik Derinlik: Türkiye'nin Uluslararasi Konumu* (Istanbul: Küre Yayinlari, 2001). See also Philip H. Gordon and Omer Taspinar, *Winning Turkey* (Washington, DC: Brookings, 2008).

[25] Ilter Türkmen, "Nükleer Santrallar Meselesi," *Hürriyet* (July 31, 2004).

[26] Mustafa Kibaroglu, "Turkey's Quest for Peaceful Nuclear Power," *Nonproliferation Review* (Spring-Summer 1997), pages 33-44.

[27] Erkan Erdogdu, "Nuclear Power in Open Energy markets: A Case Study of Turkey," *Energy Policy* 37 (2007), page 3069.

[28] Gareth Jenkins, "More Speed, Less Haste Results in Turkish Nuclear Tender Fiasco," *Eurasian Daily Monitor* (Jamestown Foundation), September 28, 2008.

[29] *Milliyet*, (May 21, 2006).

[30] *Zaman*, (June 4, 2006).

[31] "Bush pushes US-Turkey nuclear cooperation," *Reuters*, January 23, 2008.

[32] Mustafa Kibaroglu, "Isn't it Time to Say farewell to Nukes in Turkey?" *European Security* 14:4 (December 2005), pages 450-53.

[33] *HaberX*, (September 3, 2006).

[34] World Public Opinion Poll Organization, "Publics around the World Favor International Agreement To Eliminate All Nuclear Weapons," http://www.worldpublicopinion.org/pipa/articles/international_security_bt/577.php?nid=&id=&pnt=577&lb=btis.

[35] James A. Russell, "A Tipping Point Realized? Nuclear Proliferation in the Persian Gulf and the Middle East," *Contemporary Security Policy* 29:3 (December 2008), pages 521-537.

BRITISH PERSPECTIVES ON NUCLEAR WEAPONS AND NUCLEAR DISARMAMENT

Sir Lawrence Freedman

Of all the established nuclear powers, Britain has appeared for some time to be the best placed to abandon its nuclear status. It has achieved this through its strategy of a minimum deterrent with a marginal strategic rationale. Here, "minimum" is defined as the smallest force sufficient to threaten retaliation credibly in the event of an attack on the United Kingdom. Credibility is never a truly objective test, so there will always be debate about how low it is prudent to go, but at some point there will be no more scope for further cuts before the force's implausability is undeniable. The choice is no longer one of an increasingly smaller force, but any force at all. Britain's nuclear capabilities now consist solely of a fleet of ballistic-missile carrying submarines (SSBNs). These have the requisite second-strike capability, but are also subject to block obsolescence. Regular opportunities do therefore arise for a clean break with the country's nuclear arsenal. Although a decision to replace the current SSBNs has been taken in principle, it will not be until 2012 that the most substantial investment decisions will need to be taken. It would therefore be more straightforward for Britain to cease to be a nuclear power than for any other of the first five weapon states.

Not only could Britain abandon its nuclear capability with less trouble than others, but its sole rationale for retention depends on continuing to live in a world of actual and potential nuclear powers, some of which may become hostile. Without a national nuclear strike force at some future point, the country's most vital security interests might be endangered by an unspecified antagonist. Actual scenarios in which Britain's status as a nuclear state might make the difference have been left vague. Arguments of this sort create a potential internal responsiveness to changes in the strategic environment greater than those for other established nuclear powers. There are no overriding rationales for Britain's nuclear forces geared to non-nuclear contingencies, other than possibly chemical or biological warfare. British governments also have been wary about arguing that a nuclear status translates readily into greater political status, for example by confirming the country's standing as a great power or creating a special position in discussions on alliance or disarmament issues. Successive governments have accepted, at least in public statements, that even if nuclear status does create special negotiating rights and privileges, it would not be sufficient grounds to justify the expense of maintaining the forces or give credibility to operational preparations. Lastly, British governments have asserted officially a readiness to abandon nuclear weapons in the event of an international nuclear disarmament agreement.

THE EVOLUTION OF BRITISH NUCLEAR CAPABILITIES

The question of Britain's nuclear status tends to come to the fore when decisions have to be made about future capabilities. After Britain opted for a submarine-based force in the early 1960s, it reevaluated its nuclear status when options for the replacement of the Polaris fleet were considered at the start of the 1980s and again when options for the future of Trident were evaluated in the mid-2000s. The only time when changes in the strategic environment prompted a major review of nuclear policies came after the end of the Cold War. In this section, I review the key decisions taken over the past three decades.

During the Cold War: Polaris to Trident

The first occasion when Britain had cause to consider its role in the nuclear business came in 1962 when the Kennedy Administration abruptly cancelled the Skybolt air-launched missile upon which the future of Britain's V-bomber force had come to depend.[1] President Kennedy bailed out his ally, Prime Minister Harold Macmillan, by providing instead the Polaris submarine-launched missile, which turned out to be a far more reliable basis for a long-term deterrent, as it was relatively invulnerable to a surprise attack and was posed few problems by Soviet defenses.

Although the Labour Party in opposition had questioned the Polaris agreement, in government in 1964 it did no more than abandon an option to build a fifth SSBN, keeping the force at four boats. This was considered sufficient to ensure that, taking into account of long refits and rests between patrols, there was always one submarine on patrol at any time. This has remained the standard for a minimum national deterrent. After a couple of inconclusive nuclear debates in Parliament—in 1964 and 1965—there was no full debate on the nuclear force until 1980 and little parliamentary scrutiny of the Polaris program. With regard to the future, both Labour and Conservative governments confined themselves to statements to the effect that the effectiveness of the force would be maintained and that there would be no move to a new generation of weapons. Both parties thus supported the decision not to follow the US and buy the Poseidon missile to replace Polaris, but instead chose to upgrade the Polaris front-end to make it more capable of penetrating Soviet ballistic missile defenses. This was the Chevaline program, which placed two warheads plus decoys atop each Polaris missile.[*] Otherwise, the Polaris force did not appear to be excessively expensive, as the main costs were

---

[*] During this period of silence, little was written by the strategic studies community in Britain on national nuclear policy. For rare examples see, John Groom's, *British Thinking about Nuclear Weapons* (London: Frances Pinter, 1974) and Emanuel de Kadt, *British Defence Policy and Nuclear War* (London: Frank Cass, 1964). In 1970, Ian Smart analysed the possibility for Anglo-French nuclear cooperation in *Future Conditional: The Prospect for Anglo-French Nuclear Cooperation* (London: IISS, 1970). In 1974, two Adelphi Papers by Geoffrey Kemp analysed some of the policy options although without relating them directly to the broad issues of British policy: *Nuclear forces for Medium Powers, Part I, Targets and Weapons Systems, Parts II and III, Strategic Requirements and Options*, Adelphi Papers 106 and 107 (London: IISS, 1974).

those of operations and maintenance and so did not raise questions of priorities in an acute form.

The question of replacement of the Polaris force again arose toward the end of the 1970s. True to tradition, Prime Minister James Callaghan explored the options for replacement by means of small unofficial committees of responsible—and reliable—ministers. He also had preliminary discussions with President Carter at the Guadeloupe summit of January 1979. In his memoirs, he makes it clear that he would have opted for the system chosen by the incoming government—the Trident C4.[2] For Margaret Thatcher, prime minister from May 1979, as for Callaghan, the issue of Polaris replacement was more one of how rather than whether. The approach was to exploit American economies of scale and the infrastructure originally created for Polaris, relying still on the relative invulnerability of sea-based systems to surprise attack and the ability of multiple warheads to penetrate Soviet defenses. In July 1980, the British government announced that Britain's nuclear deterrent of four nuclear-powered submarines, each carrying 16 Polaris missiles, would be replaced by a similar number of missiles on a similar number of submarines, but the new missiles would be the most modern in the American arsenal—the Trident C4—and they would be accommodated on new and larger submarines. In March 1982, it was further announced that Britain would continue to follow American nuclear policy by upgrading from the C4 version of Trident to the even more modern D5.[3] This would allow for longer range (up to 6,000 miles) and even more warheads, although the government took care to stress that it was not anxious to maximize the warhead potential. The missiles would be American: Britain would build its own submarines and nuclear warheads. One American estimate suggested that without US help, the cost of the missile part of the program would rise from $2.5 billion to $6.5 billion.[4]

After this decision was announced there was a public debate about whether Britain, no longer such a great power, really needed a nuclear arsenal at all. The argument that it did not was picked up by the Labour Party in opposition. For most of the 1980s, the "defense" issue in British politics was the future of the country's nuclear deterrent. Labour provided a functional, as much as a moral, critique. Trident was criticized for being excessively sophisticated, with its long-range and accurate multiple-warheads, and far too expensive. In practice, there was no obvious successor to Polaris other than Trident that would be less expensive. The main alternatives debated tended to be based on Polaris itself (cloning the old system or upgrading it to take advantage of technological advances), or cruise missiles, to be either ground-launched or submarine-launched. The financial savings offered by these alternatives appeared less than might be expected, as large proportions of the costs were in the launch platform and the warhead, and were qualified by the risk of expensive delays in any indigenous development effort or by the lower life-expectancy of systems based on obsolescent technology. Where savings could be achieved (particularly with ground-launched cruise missiles), it was largely by relaxing the survivability criterion and the threat this posed to the Soviet Union, which could mean a less-than-minimum deterrent.

In the harsh economic conditions of the early 1980s, Trident's price-tag, which initially was put at £5 billion and soon went up to £7.5 billion, could be presented as a gross extravagance, even inimical to the wider defense effort, for it would use up a large chunk of the available funds for new conventional military equipment. At a time when NATO was talking of relying more on conventional and less on nuclear forces, Britain would be moving its defense priorities in exactly the opposite direction.[†] The government's position, as stated by Secretary of Defence Nott, was that while "money spent on Trident is money that is not spent on something else," Trident could be justified on the question of priorities.

> I find it hard to understand those who argue against Trident on the utilitarian ground of deterrent cost-effectiveness. If one asks which will give more pause to an adversary contemplating aggression—Trident or an increase in our conventional forces—the answer is plain.[5]

The difficulty with the economic critique was that it was most powerful during the early stages of the program. As money was spent and committed, the potential for savings gradually declined. Eventually, a point was reached at which it would cost almost as much to get out of the nuclear business as to stay in it. Here, the government was helped by Trident staying on schedule and within budget. If the Trident program were abandoned then, additional money in the form of cancellation charges, the costs of converting the new submarines to something other than the carriage of ballistic missiles, and the de-commissioning of Polaris and its nuclear warheads would have to be factored in. The result would have been to make the short-term budgetary burden of Britain's nuclear forces more severe than if it continued as planned. There would have been savings over the longer term, but in defense terms they would not have been large.[6] In a "leak" during the 1987 campaign, it was reported that Ministry of Defence (MoD) estimated of the cost of implementing the Labour Party program to decommission Polaris and other UK nuclear systems at £2 billion.[7] Estimates suggested that it would take some three to five years to disarm the nuclear warheads in the stockpile and recycle the fissile materials. Even then, the secrets of nuclear weapons would remain. However, once

---

[†] The expenditure was made up of 12 percent on missiles, 30 percent on submarines (less weapon systems equipment), 16 percent on weapon systems equipment (including tactical weapons), 12 percent on shared construction and 30 percent on warhead design and production, and contingency. Fourth Report from the Defence Committee, Session 1980–81, *Strategic Nuclear Weapons Policy*, June 1981, p. xiv.

the design teams at Aldermaston had disbanded, it would be extremely difficult to rebuild Britain's nuclear capability.[8]

After the Conservatives returned to office with another large majority in the June 1987 general election, Britain was confirmed as a nuclear power. Had the result had been different and the Labour Party won, the Polaris submarines then on patrol would have been called back and the Trident program would have been cancelled, at least according to official policy. What would have happened to American nuclear forces based in Britain we will never know, for the party manifesto, issued at the start of an election campaign and the closest thing a new government has to a mandate, was ambiguous on that point. In any event, with the Conservatives re-elected, Britain's nuclear status was more securely based than ever before. In addition, the opposition parties were obliged to rethink their nuclear policies because of their evident unpopularity during the election campaign and in response to the momentum behind the Trident program. Labour Party internal appraisals of its performance in the 1987 election suggested that its anti-nuclear defense policy lost the support of up to five percent of the electorate.

Over this period, Britain became even more dependent on its SSBN force. The 56 Vulcan bombers were phased out in the early 1980s, thereby removing the last alternative strategic nuclear capability. The Vulcans were already old and expensive to run in terms of both men and fuel, and the RAF replaced them with Tornado aircraft. Although nuclear-capable, Tornados lacked the range of Vulcans and could not be considered for serious operations against the Soviet Union. The Tornados also replaced three of the five squadrons of Buccaneer aircraft, which, with four squadrons of Jaguars, could deliver free-fall nuclear bombs (as well as conventional weapons) from bases in Britain and Germany. At this time, the Royal Navy also operated maritime helicopters capable of delivering nuclear depth-bombs. The Sea Harrier aircraft squadrons, which operated from the new Invincible-class carriers, were also capable of delivering free-fall nuclear bombs.

At this time, Britain also maintained systems of smaller yield and lesser range that were variously described as "tactical," "theatre," or "sub-strategic" nuclear systems. By the end of the Cold War in 1989, this arsenal was made up of the WE-177 "family," with different characteristics having come in at different dates, including the nuclear depth-charge (WE-177C) as well as the RAF's free-fall bombs (WE-177A and B). The weapon was developed in the early 1960s and the first WE-177s were delivered to the RAF in 1966–67. Thereafter, more than 180 were produced up to 1982, of which 20-30 were "C" variants. Production continued at Aldermaston and Burghfield until 1978, when manufacturing lines began to produce warheads for Chevaline.[9] Their yields were between 10 and 200 kilotons. The yield was probably closer to the lower end than to the upper number, if only because of German concerns about the use of high-yield weapons in their defense. Tornados were normally assumed to carry two WE-177 bombs. A 1989 estimate put the total number of sub-strategic weapons at 180.[10] Britain also operated American systems under 'dual-key' control arrangements: Four squadrons of Nimrod maritime patrol aircraft equipped with nuclear depth-bombs and four Army regiments in Germany, one of Lance missiles, and three of dual-capable artillery, all employing American warheads.

After the Cold War

Retention but Retrenchment

If the Polaris replacement decision had come a decade later, it is by no means clear, given the optimism of the early 1990s, that a decision would have been made in favor of Trident. By this time, however, the major investments had been made and the first SSBNs would soon be ready to deploy. Instead, the government decided to find a new minimum level for its deterrent.

Because of the capacity of the Trident missiles, the number of warheads in the British strategic nuclear arsenal was scheduled to rise over the 1990s. The government promised to keep warhead numbers down as an informal response to the changing political climate. This promise may also have been influenced by production problems with the warheads. Just before it entered service, Secretary of Defence Tom King confirmed that Trident would not "carry the maximum" number of warheads:

> We have long emphasized that each Trident submarine would carry no more than 128 warheads. This has always been an upper limit, not a specification: the number to be deployed in the mid-1990s onwards will be decided in the light of circumstances at the time.[11]

His successor, Sir Malcolm Rifkind, later indicated that the new force would not carry the maximum number of warheads, but would be closer in total destructive power to the Polaris capability. In practice, this still meant more warheads than Polaris, as each was of lower yield.[12]

The post-Cold War pressures for a minimal deterrent were reflected much more in the non-strategic arsenal than the strategic arsenal. All short-range, land-based systems (which were dual-key) were abandoned.‡ In the autumn of 1991, it was

---

‡These included four batteries of three Lance short-range missiles, plus 16 M-110 203mm self-propelled howitzer and 101 M-109 155mm self-propelled howitzer. The M-110 launched a shell of 2 kilotons to a distance of 14 kilometres with accuracy from 0.04 to 0.17 kilometres depending on the range. The M-109 had comparable accuracy and a slightly longer range with a yield of 2 kilotons. The 50 Missile Regiment and the 56 Special Weapons Battery Royal Artillery were disbanded.

announced that nuclear weapons would no longer be deployed on Royal Navy ships "in normal circumstances." This was made more permanent in 1992.[13] The 20-30 nuclear depth bombs, intended for use at sea with Lynx and Sea King helicopters, were destroyed, and RAF Nimrod maritime patrols with American nuclear depth charges were terminated.[14] Reductions also were announced from 11 Tornado and 4 Buccaneer squadrons to four Tornado squadrons based in the United Kingdom and four in Germany. The number of WE-177 free-fall bombs available for these aircraft was cut by half.[15] Plans to develop up to 200 new stand-off missiles with a range of up to 600km to succeed the WE-177 were also abandoned. (In addition, the WE-177 was scrapped in 1998.)

The Labour Party's 1997 manifesto promised retention of Trident, strength in "defense through NATO," and "a strategic defense and security review to reassess our essential security interests and defense needs."[16] After a resounding win in the general election, the Labour government under Prime Minister Tony Blair set in motion a strategic defence review (SDR). This was never intended to reappraise the Trident program, although it did provide the fullest account of UK nuclear capabilities yet published. The bill for Trident had been largely paid: A significant portion of future nuclear expenditure would be used to decommission old weapons and facilities and would have had to be spent even if Trident itself was abandoned. Nonetheless, the drive to push down numbers continued. It was decided that each of the four Trident submarines would now carry no more than 48 warheads, down from 96. This reduced the explosive power of the warheads on a new SSBN to "one third less than a Polaris submarine armed with Chevaline," although individually the warheads would be more lethal as they could destroy individual targets.

During the 1980s, the number of operationally available warheads was around 400. Under the previous Conservative government, this was to have gone down to 300. As a result of Labour's SDR, the number of operationally available warheads was to be less than 200. The chart below, taken from the 1998 SDR, compares the explosive power of the UK's operationally available weapons during the 1970s and 1980s with previous plans for 1999 and the SDR decisions.[17] Thirty percent of the 1970s figures would suggest something equivalent to about 20-30 megatons (million tons of TNT). This would leave Britain with the smallest stockpile of all the established nuclear powers, with a total yield representing less than 1 percent of the global total.

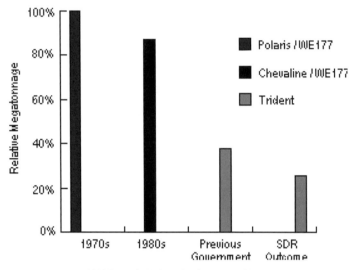

1998 Strategic Defence Review, para. 64.

After looking at a range of alternatives, in the end it was decided to configure Trident for possible use in a sub-strategic role, though this would be an enormously expensive method of delivering a small warhead. The 1998 Strategic Defence Review defined a "sub-strategic" role as, "an option for a limited strike that would not automatically lead to a full scale nuclear exchange."[18] Uniquely for an established nuclear state, Britain relies on only one weapon system. Although, according to one report, in 2000 President Clinton authorized 110 bombs to be retained at the American operated based at RAF Lakenheath, following a 2004 decision to reduce all stocks held in Europe, the last US nuclear weapons were removed from Britain in 2008.[19]

In a move to identify the minimum in operational terms, the policy would remain to keep one submarine always on patrol. It would, however, operate on a "reduced day-to-day alert state." The government argued for maintaining a continual operational patrol largely on the grounds that if it did not do so, then a sudden return to sea could aggravate a crisis by appearing provocative. The full possible meaning of a "minimum" deterrent was explored further by not running the submarines intensively and by operating with only one crew per boat (compared with two during the Cold War). The missiles would not be on quick reaction alert but kept days away from operational readiness and not targeted against anyone in particular.

The 2007 Decisions

The HMS Vanguard entered service in December 1994, the HMS Victorious a year later, the HMS Vigilant in June 1998, and the HMS Vengeance in February 2001.[§] Although the new boats had not been long in service, by the Labour government's third term it was arguing that early preparations were needed for replacement submarines lest the system become obsolete by the 2020s. Although the government claimed to be investigating all options, there was never much doubt that any replacement would follow the same path as before with a submarine-based system. There was no longer a serious air-based option and ground-based options all failed tests of survivability to first strikes.[20] Following a familiar path also strengthened confidence in cost estimates, which could be assumed to be comparable to the Trident program, taking account of inflation, and coming in at £15 billion for research, development and production, with a further £10 billion to cover the rest of the costs over the subsequent twenty years of operations. These estimates depended on continuing cooperation with the United States.[**] There were obvious opportunity costs, but it would be hard to argue that a country of Britain's economic strength could not afford this amount if it considered nuclear weapons essential to its security. At the end of 2006, the Labour government produced a White Paper setting out the case for retention of the nuclear deterrent.[21]

This led to a debate that previous generations of Labour leaders would have avoided at all costs, but it was surprisingly muted. The best argument in favor remained uncertainty and continuity. With the background noise of North Korea's and Iran's nuclear exertions, it was politically challenging to argue that this was the moment for Britain, alone among the nuclear powers, to abandon its nuclear status. The best argument against modernizing Trident appeared to be that the expenditure would be wasteful and meet no evident security purpose. As both sets of arguments were speculative, the debate was conducted with little passion and scant public interest. Labour dissidence was not as high as with the 2003 Iraq vote, although when the vote came in March 2007, Conservative support was still necessary for a majority.[††]

To mollify his backbenchers, Prime Minister Blair indicated that, "it is always open to us to come back and look at these issues." Blair spoke of a "gateway stage-between 2012 and 2014," after the design and concept phase for the new program was completed and when the main contracts for design and construction would have to be let. Furthermore, the renewal program could be cancelled, "should there be a

---

[§] Each submarine weighs approximately 16,000 tonnes, is 150 metres in length, is powered by a Rolls Royce PWR2 nuclear reactor, and has 16 independently-controlled missile tubes which house the missiles.
[**] In 2004, President Bush and Prime Minister Blair signed an agreement extending US/UK nuclear cooperation for another ten years.
[††] 409 MPs supported the proposals, and 161 were against, including 88 Labour backbenchers, a majority of 248. In 2003, 138 Labor MPs voted against the Iraq war. http://news.bbc.co.uk/go/pr/fr/-/1/hi/uk_politics/6448173.stm.

fundamental change for the better in the strategic environment."[22]   According to Foreign Secretary Margaret Beckett,

> Today's decision does not mean that we are committing ourselves irreversibly to maintaining a nuclear deterrent for the next 50 years, no matter what others do and no matter what happens in the rest of the world. That would be absurd, unnecessary and, indeed, incompatible with the nuclear proliferation treaty.[23]

She indicated that there were future decisions to be made about whether to renew or replace the warhead, whether to participate in any American programs to develop a successor to the D5 missile, and the precise design of the submarine and whether four or three should be procured.[24]

There is one interesting angle on future nuclear decisions that is worth noting. Britain's Trident fleet is largely run out of Scotland's nuclear base, Her Majesty's Naval Base Clyde. Scottish opinion, including the Scottish National Party, which runs the devolved Scottish government in Edinburgh, has always been more skeptical about the need for nuclear deterrence than the rest of the UK. On 14 June 2007, the Scottish Parliament voted against renewing Trident by a 71 to 16 vote, with only the Conservatives in favor and most Labour members abstaining, other than five who voted with the opponents. A working group, chaired by Bruce Crawford, the Minister for Parliamentary Business, was established with an extremely broad remit, which includes questions of the legality of nuclear weapons and how to promote international peace and reconciliation, as well as more mundane but potentially significant issues, such as the licensing and regulatory framework relating to the main nuclear submarine base on the Clyde and the economic impact of ending its nuclear weapons role.[25]   At least one member of the group (Professor William Walker) is an acknowledged academic authority on nuclear weapons issues, and there is one leading anti-nuclear campaigner from an NGO (Dr. Rebecca Johnson). The other members are largely from trade unions and religious groups.   In practice, little could be done about this issue by a devolved government, because defense and foreign policy are reserved powers under the 1998 Scotland Act. However, it would be an issue that an independent Scotland would undoubtedly address. There are questions of transport and planning over which it has some influence, but any attempt to use these to frustrate the policies of central government with regard to fundamental questions of national security would create a constitutional crisis.

NUCLEAR MODERNIZATION PLANS

The three components of the remaining British nuclear system—warheads, missiles, and submarines—each have its own timetable. We consider each in turn.

Warheads

The Atomic Weapons Establishment (AWE) at Aldermaston is required to build, maintain, and certify the existing weapons stockpile, as well as to ensure good stewardship of nuclear weapons knowledge. It is managed by a consortium, in which one-third of the shares are held by the US firm Lockheed Martin. The UK's current nuclear warhead is based on the American W76 design. In July 2005, the government announced an "extensive research programme to assure the safety and effectiveness of the warhead stockpile," and an investment program at Aldermaston, amounting to some £350 million over three years. This would allow the current warhead to be maintained in service into the 2020s, with any necessary upgrading and refurbishment, but also ensure that the core skills and facilities were available to develop a successor warhead.[26] The skilled workforce was by this time down to about one-third of its peak Cold War levels. The government was anticipating substantial further investment, with the cost of AWE rising by over 20 percent, up from an equivalent of 2.5 to 3 percent of the defense budget. A decision on whether to go for a new warhead would be taken in the early 2010s following "a detailed review of the optimum life of the existing warhead stockpile and analysis of the range of replacement options that might be available."[27] It may be that the UK will follow the American Reliable Replacement Warhead program (RRW), geared to producing warheads that are relatively simple in design and cost-effective, not dependent on testing to ensure their reliability, and able to deliver as small or large a blast as required.[28]

Missiles

By the time of the 1998 SDR, 58 Trident D5 missiles had been purchased. There was an option to purchase an additional seven missiles but this was exercised. Occasional test firings reduced the inventory to 50, but the government concluded that no further procurement of D5 missiles would be necessary. It was decided, however, to participate in the US life extension program for the D5 missile, at a cost of some £250 million. This will add another twenty years to their operational life and enable them to stay in-service until the early 2040s. The modernization of existing missiles would focus on the components most at risk of obsolescence, especially the electronics in the flight control systems, but not payload, range, or accuracy.[29] Any decision on a successor missile would therefore not be needed until the 2020s, and assurances had been sought and received that in the event the US decided to develop a successor to the D5 missile, the UK would have the option of participating in the program and that this missile would be compatible with the launch system in the UK's SSBNs.[‡‡]

[‡‡] See exchange of letters between Prime Minister Tony Blair and President George W Bush, 7 December 2006, Cm 6994. The reply from the US President stated that the United States "continues to attach great importance to the maintenance of an operationally independent nuclear deterrent capability by the United Kingdom." It also said

Submarines

The SSBNs are based at Faslane in Scotland, which is also a home for Britain's conventionally-armed submarines. The nuclear warheads carried onboard the SSBNs are stored and fitted to the UK's Trident missiles at the Royal Naval Armaments Depot at Coulport, near Faslane. Submarines are built at Barrow-in-Furness, Cumbria, by BAe Systems. The operational and refit and support site is at Devonport, Plymouth. This is run by DML (a consortium of which fifty-one per cent is owned by the US firm Halliburton). As can be seen, the UK lacks redundant capabilities. If any of these facilities with its specialized infrastructure and highly-skilled workforce was lost, it would be extremely difficult and expensive to recreate over the long-term.

The key factor influencing replacement decisions in 2007 was the SSBNs. The logic was as follows: The first of class entered service in 1994; their life expectancy would be 20 years, though this could be extended by about five years; they will therefore start leaving service at the latest in the early 2020s. Once the second boat has left service, continuous patrols cannot be guaranteed; it will take around 17 years to develop and build a replacement. The major issue with the submarines appears to be the steam generators and other elements of the nuclear propulsion system. The timetable would call for two years for the concept stage, seven years for design, and another seven to build, with the final period devoted to sea trials and other tests, training the crew, putting the missiles in, test-firing the missile, and then getting the submarine on operational patrol.

The MoD's timetable has been challenged by American Professor Richard Garwin, who argued that the decision to replace the Vanguard-class submarines was "highly premature."[30] He argued that the Vanguards could last as long as the US boats, which were worked much harder, and that steam generator life could be extended by "improved management of their water chemistry."[31] Garwin also argued that SSBNs could be built at a rate of one every four years, rather than one every two years, and still maintain an adequate skills base. MoD disagreed with this assessment and warned that it would be a high-risk strategy. Unlike the Americans, who built the potential for a substantial life extension into the design of their Ohio-class SSBNs and now plan to run them for as long as 40 years, the British do not

---

that the United States "fully supports and welcomes the intention of the United Kingdom to participate in the life-extension program for the Trident II D5 missile. We will work to ensure that the necessary components of the overall system are made available to the United Kingdom to support life-extended D5 missiles...For the longer term...I would invite the United Kingdom to participate, at an early state, in any program to replace the D5 missiles or to discuss a further life extension—for your purposes—of the D5 missile to match the potential out-of-service date of your new submarines. In this respect, any successor to the D5 system should be compatible with, or be capable of being made compatible with, the launch system for the D5 missile, which you will be installing into your new submarines. The United States will also ensure...that the United Kingdom has the option to sustain an effective nuclear delivery system for at least the life of your successor submarine force as was done with the Polaris system."

have this option. With the British boats, MoD said, changes to the propulsion unit would require penetrating into the hulls which would require taking individual boats out of service for extended periods of time and with only limited gain. With 14 SSBNs, the US also has more flexibility and British officials deny that the US boats are run harder. Further, if problems developed in the refits there would be no redundancy. British officials still recall a whole class of long-range bombers—the Valiants—suddenly having to be removed from service because of metal fatigue. The experience with the Resolution-class, moreover, was that it was a struggle to maintain a continuous patrol in the later stages of their lives. On the other hand, relaxing the criterion of continual patrols could clearly make it possible to put off the decision.

One potential advantage of the decision is that the new SSBNs could be designed to maintain a continual patrol with only three boats. In the past, four boats have been necessary to keep one on patrol because one is normally preparing to enter refit, in refit, or leaving refit and preparing to re-enter service, while another is in maintenance between patrols, and another is either on its way to take up patrol or returning from patrol. One reason for the timing may be concern about the UK's submarine industrial base, which might decline if there were a long gap before new submarine development and construction were to begin. The current program for Astute-class nuclear attack submarines (SSNs), for example, has experienced some difficulties because of the loss of key design skills.[32]

The House of Commons Defence Committee set out the following decision timetable:

- **2006-2007** Decision on investment to sustain the industrial and basing infrastructure and specialist skills base pending a decision on the future of the nuclear deterrent;
- **2007-2010** Decision on whether or not to begin a Service Life Extension Program for the current Trident system, which would affect the rest of the timetable;
- **2010-2014** Decision on whether to retain a strategic nuclear deterrent and extend the life of the Trident submarines, and evaluation of options for potential successor platforms;
- **2014** Decision on the exact form of the future platform and whether to make the investment commitment, thereby making the decision to retain the force harder to reverse.

A successor platform must be ready by 2020 without an extension program for existing SSBNs. With an extension program, the successor platform would need to be ready by 2025 if continuous patrols are to be maintained. In short, over the next six years or so Britain must confirm that it wishes to retain a nuclear deterrent.

BRITISH RATIONALES FOR MAINTAINING NUCLEAR WEAPONS

Although it might have been expected that there were would be major shifts in rationale, along with changes in the wider strategic environment, there has been considerable continuity in Britain's rationale for maintaining nuclear forces. This has meant that rationales have been sustained at a rather general level of security against unknown dangers, while the specific issues of how to deter the Soviet Union were seen to have been rendered irrelevant by the end of the Cold War.

During the Cold War

By way of contrast with France, Britain has never associated an independent nuclear deterrent with any deep sense of national destiny. Little patriotic symbolism was generated around the nuclear force and no extravagant claims were made as to its military value. For example, in 1980, Defence Secretary Francis Pym dismissed justifications for the British nuclear capability such as "political prestige, our status in the Alliance, or a comparison with France ... the concept of a 'Fortress Britain'- some kind of insurance policy concept, should the United States go isolationist or the Alliance collapse."[33] Far more decisive was the view that, "Britain needs to be a nuclear power primarily because of what this contributes to NATO's strategy of deterrence and, through that, to our own security." His successor, John Nott, also remarked that he had "little time for arguments based on prestige, seats at top table and the like."[§§]

The challenge for Britain was to develop a strategic rationale without repudiating the US nuclear guarantee to Europe, along with NATO itself. This was particularly difficult in the early 1960s, when the United States was raising objections to small nuclear forces, famously described by Secretary of Defense Robert McNamara as "dangerous, expensive, prone to obsolescence and lacking in credibility as a deterrent."[34] Some of the American complaints were met by moving Britain's nuclear deterrent from air-launched bombs and missiles to more survivable submarine-launched missiles, which were less likely to prompt the premature outbreak of nuclear war. The problem of explaining how NATO could benefit from a separate British nuclear force was solved by adopting the concept of multiple decision centers, usually associated with the French strategist, Andre Beaufre.[35]

[§§] *Official Record*, 3 March 1981, col. 139. The 'top table' is a reference to Prime Minister Sir Alec Douglas-Home's promotion of an independent nuclear force as a "ticket of admission to the top table" during the 1964 General Election. Nott did, however, add "that I would feel more than a touch of discomfort if France, with her clear policy of non-commitment to Alliance strategy, were the only West European nuclear power."

This formula was adopted in the mid-1960s and was maintained thereafter without amendment, through governments of both parties, and also through the end of the Cold War. While the United States went through regular twists and turns in its nuclear doctrine, Britain's view was remarkably consistent. Neither changes in the strategic environment nor did doctrinal shifts by allies influence this formula. The reason was less one of intellectual conviction than diplomatic convenience. The official version stressed the British government's complete confidence in the US guarantee but recognised that, mistakenly, the adversary might be less impressed. A second center of nuclear decision, particularly one close to the likely conflict, would add extra uncertainty to the adversary's calculations. To a determined enemy, the risk of calling the American bluff might just about be tolerable, but not necessarily that of calling the British and French bluffs as well.[36]

In the 1980s, unexpected difficulties were caused when President Reagan entered his "anti-nuclear phase." This began with the Strategic Defense Initiative (SDI) of 1983, and reached its peak with the Reykjavik Summit with Soviet President Mikhail Gorbachev in October 1986. Reagan's tendency towards an absolutist critique of nuclear deterrence during this period caused a series of problems for Prime Minister Margaret Thatcher. With SDI, Reagan was arguing that the world would be safer if both sides were able to defend themselves against ballistic missile attack. There was thus a natural question to ask as to whether Britain could expect to be protected by the US defensive shield, given its proximity to the Soviet Union, while its own missiles might not be able to penetrate the Soviet defensive shield, and so fail to function as a deterrent. The government's analysts convinced themselves that the Trident system would be able to cope with any shield that the Soviet Union would be able to put up during its life-time, but if a "strategic-defense race" had developed, then the government would have been hard put to convince Parliament and the electorate that it was worth bothering with Trident, without casting doubt on Reagan's whole enterprise.

With US-Soviet strategic arms control negotiations ongoing, there also was a risk that the United States would agree to measures that would limit its ability to provide Trident missiles to the UK. In the early 1980s, this seemed unlikely as submarine-based systems were preferred by the US and thus there was virtually no risk of that the program would be cancelled. However, as President Reagan zeroed in on ballistic missiles as the targets for the SDI, his proposals for strategic arms control began to focus on missiles, as well. In fact, in the summer of 1986, he proposed a ban on all ballistic missiles. The disastrous consequences of such a prohibition for the British program resulted in an anxious letter from Prime Minister Thatcher to President Reagan. British officials believed the letter led to rejection of the heresy and so were horrified to see a missile ban return so publicly to the US position during the Reykjavik summit later in the year. In both December 1984, as a result of SDI, and in December 1986, after Reykjavik, Prime Minister Thatcher scuttled across the Atlantic to encourage the President to correct the anti-nuclear impression he had created. She had argued that nuclear deterrence based on the threat of devastating retaliation was moral, durable, and essential for security. It was alarming to hear her close ally, President Reagan, suggest that it was none of those things.

Despite the fact that Britain's nuclear policies were closely linked to those of its allies and the disavowal of nationalistic and prestige rationales, much of the debate on the need for a British nuclear force has been bound up with the claim of "independence," which has been a theme in writings about Britain's nuclear forces from the 1950s through the present time.[37] Analysts have explored repeatedly whether Britain really could sustain, let alone operate, its nuclear forces without American assistance.[38] Critics of British nuclear forces considered that they were making a telling point against it by pointing to the impossibility of imagining circumstances in which a British prime minister would use nuclear weapons even though an American president had declined to do so. This point was often made by Lord Carver, former Chief of the Defence Staff, for example, who was cited by the Labour Party in its 1986 statement on defense policy as authority for the observation that, "It is inconceivable that a British politician would use these missiles, knowing with complete certainty that doing so would be followed by obliteration of our country."[39]

Carver was not arguing against nuclear deterrence—only questioning whether Britain needed to make a contribution. The circumstances in which national nuclear use might be contemplated by Britain are almost always bound up with a European crisis in which the key question is the role of the United States. Britain had never attempted to argue that its own forces could substitute for those of the United States: At most, the existence of British national forces could add uncertainty to Soviet (and American) decision-making.

By hosting American nuclear forces on its territory, Britain's commitment to sustaining the American nuclear guarantee was underlined. There has always been some domestic political opposition to the bases and governmental nervousness at times over the use that the Americans might make of them. Contentious in the 1950s, they were not a prominent political issue from the early 1960s to the 1980s. To the extent that they were, it was the US Polaris (and later Poseidon) base at Holy Loch that attracted the greatest criticism, rather than the air bases.[***] As late as 1976, the Labour Government had agreed that about 90 F-111 aircraft could be

---

[***] In the 1950s anti-Americanism in the Labour Party was used to support the case for a national force. See Leon Epstein, "Britain and the H-Bomb, 1955-1958," *Review of Politics*, XXI (1959), pages 522-533.

added to the 70 that had been based in Britain since 1971 (the result of an earlier negotiation undertaken by a Labour government). These F-111s had ranges sufficient to reach the Soviet Union and could each carry two weapons of up to 800 kilotons. When the aircraft arrived in 1977, there was neither public debate nor protest. During the late 1970s, Labour ministers were far more nervous about being seen to contemplate the replacement of Polaris than tolerating the possible entry of American cruise missiles.

During the 1980s, however, opposition to American bases struck a responsive political chord. The arrival of 96 Tomahawk ground-launched cruise missiles at Greenham Common and another 64 at Molesworth was the result of NATO's December 1979 "double-track decision," combining new nuclear deployments with an arms control initiative. This decision had taken on a more controversial aspect than anticipated because of widespread concern over the apparent trend in American strategic thinking, beginning in 1981, which seemed to take concepts of nuclear war-fighting seriously because of the deterioration in East-West relations following the Soviet invasion of Afghanistan. The issue of US bases raised questions of sovereignty, as well as of nuclear weapons. There was now anxiety that not only might American bases draw fire, but also that they would be used to initiate a major war, and that little notice would be taken of British views if the government sought to protest. In 1983, there was a heated debate over the nature of the "joint decision" that would have to be taken if US nuclear forces were to be launched from Britain. This debate was prompted by the imminent arrival of cruise missiles, which were to be operated solely by the US, and by the apparent lack of consultation over the US intervention in Grenada earlier that year. The debate produced one of the most massive opinion poll majorities ever recorded against government policy. Ninety-four percent of the British people declared themselves in favor of dual keys for all US nuclear weapons based in the UK.[40]

In the 1980s, therefore, there were more doubts in the electorate over the advisability of American nuclear bases than there were over the desirability of Britain remaining a nuclear power, for which there was a consistent and substantial majority.[41] This created difficulty for the Labour leadership, which did not wish to appear anti-NATO. The most respectable argument against a British nuclear capability was that the existence of an American capability rendered it largely irrelevant. If, however, the American nuclear capability was also to be rejected, then the Labour Party risked the appearance of offering no form of deterrence to Soviet nuclear capabilities. Nonetheless, this was the path pursued by the Labour Party leading up to the 1987 election. It did not reject one aspect of nuclear deterrence: It rejected nuclear deterrence in toto. Instead of making choices within the framework of a minimalist approach to nuclear deterrence, it decided to abandon deterrence altogether—both British forces and the American guarantee, the threat of second use and the threat of first use.

By 1987, moreover, there was no longer the sense of an imminent international crisis to add urgency to the defense debate, as there had been earlier in the decade. The resumption and progress in arms control negotiations suggested that current policies were working perfectly well, obviating the need for radical corrective actions. Prime Minister Thatcher endorsed the "double zero" in the negotiations on Intermediate-range Nuclear Forces (INF), as proposed by the Soviet Union and received sympathetically by the United States, despite her own and West German misgivings, ensuring that she was not vulnerable to the charge of dragging her feet on arms control. The nuclear issue lost the sense of imminent danger and therefore its political salience.

The collapse of European communism and the evaporation of the Soviet threat and hegemony in 1989 raised a new question mark against the established rationale. In the discussion document accompanying the July 1980 decision on Trident, the only hint that history might move on was a vague reference to a future Soviet leadership "much changed in character from today, perhaps operating amid the pressures of turbulent internal or external circumstances."[42]

Targeting doctrine was geared to the Soviet threat, particularly in view of the introduction of a missile defense system around Moscow. The introduction of Chevaline, which began operational service in the summer of 1982, did not mandate an attack on the Moscow area as the only targeting option. It appears, however, to have committed Britain to an attack on a few, and possibly no more than one, large target(s). In 1980, it was acknowledged officially that, "There is a concept which Chevaline makes clear, that Governments did not want to have a situation where the adversary could have a sanctuary for his capital and a large area around it."[43] With Polaris' old A-3 warhead, all missiles on a submarine would have to be committed and yet the authorities would be without complete confidence of success. With Chevaline, a similar number of missiles would be launched, but with a much greater chance of success. The concept was to rain a series of warheads and decoys simultaneously over the target, gaining its effect not from the contents of a single missile, but from the combined contents of a number of missiles–probably the full complement of one SSBN. With the Soviet Union gone and Russia not considered an enemy, Britain's targeting concept and strategic rationales had lost its footing.

After the Cold War

When the Cold War ended, it became necessary to disentangle the SSBN system to enable it to take on a number of targets at once. Until Trident became operational, Britain had little flexibility in targeting. With Trident, however, each submarine could carry as many as 16 missiles, each with eight warheads. If three boats were on station there could be maximum coverage of 384 targets. As already noted, successive governments committed themselves to reduced numbers of warheads, until a base level of around 160 was reached. The numbers carried at sea could be varied according to the perceived strategic situation. In an individual boat, some missiles could carry loads geared to a strategic exchange, while others would carry smaller packages.

With the end of the Cold War, it became even more difficult to stress prestige arguments for retaining a nuclear arsenal as Ukraine, Belarus, and Kazakhstan were being told that they had little to gain by retaining the pieces of the old Soviet nuclear arsenal still residing in their territory. Moreover, a major plank of policy towards the third world was to prevent the further spread of weapons of mass destruction. In another sense, the case for a national nuclear force was strengthened, as the key strategic issues shifted away from old questions about the durability of the US nuclear guarantee.[44] With Europeans no longer preoccupied with the credibility of the US umbrella against the Soviet threat, many of the provisions established to reassure Europeans about extended deterrence were withdrawn. In December 1990, for example, NATO's Nuclear Planning Group spoke of reduced reliance on nuclear systems as influencing both "Alliance nuclear force levels and structures," and promised "further dramatic reductions in the number of NATO's nuclear weapons retained in Europe."[45]

Reflecting on this situation, Secretary of Defence Malcolm Rifkind warned against "any tendency towards thinking that there could be a major conflict in Europe in which the question of nuclear use arose which did not involve the vital interests of all the allies, including the US."[46] However, circumstances could be envisaged in which the US nuclear guarantee might be called into question by the limited stake the Americans might perceive in the particular issues that had created the crisis. On this basis, the old second center of decision-making argument from the Cold War era still had some "validity."

The critical focus also stuck with the former Soviet Union. Even taking into account planned reductions, Moscow would still have a capacity to inflict unacceptable damage on Western nations and its integration into the Western economic and political system was likely to be tenuous at best. Russia would still have a substantial nuclear arsenal well into the next century. Thus, Rifkind argued, "Our strategy makes military recidivism by any future Russian leadership a pointless option for them."[47]

Nor was there much support for the view that an alternative guarantee could be based on France and Britain. This was always assumed to lack the credibility of an

American guarantee, both because of French policy and the balance of forces. With the Alliance rationales looking dated, the official rationale reverted to basics:

> Our defence strategy will continue to be underpinned by nuclear forces as the ultimate guarantee of our country's security. Nuclear weapons guard against any attempt by an adversary to gain advantage by threat or coercion. They are also uniquely able to ensure that aggression is not a realistic option, by presenting to a potential aggressor the prospect of a cost that would far outweigh any hoped-for-gain.[48]

Rifkind reported that nuclear use would only be credible, justifiable and proportionate when, "vital national interests were at stake," and that the most vital of interests were narrowly national—"the most obvious hypothesis being a direct homeland threat from an aggressor equipped with weapons of mass destruction."[49]

Increasingly, the risks of third-world proliferation were used to reinforce the case for the British deterrent. This rarely went much further than the rhetorical, "what if [whoever happened to be the most menacing dictator at the time–Galtieri, Gaddafi, Saddam, etc] had nuclear weapons and we did not?"[†††] A nuclear capability might neutralise nuclear threats posed by a rogue state, though this implied a readiness to make nuclear commitments to other countries—a policy that would go well beyond anything contemplated since the 1960s, when there had been some suggestions that UK nuclear capabilities might be relevant to Indian attempts to deter China. Such possibilities might be the context for the supposed sub-strategic use of Trident, in some sort of warning-shot function. With Trident, however, the "sub-strategic" nature of the shot would have to be made clear by the choice of target. At the same time, because of both past practice and international declarations, it could be no part of policy to use nuclear weapons to intimidate non-nuclear powers armed with only conventional forces.[‡‡‡]

There was a degree of ambiguity regarding the relevance of nuclear forces with regard to deterring the use of other terror (i.e. chemical and biological) weapons. At no stage, however, were explicit nuclear threats issued by the US during the 1991 Persian Gulf War. The coalition's capacity for severe retaliation with conventional air power (as well as defensive measures against chemical use), plus a

---

[†††] Eg. *Rifkind Speech*: "The thought of what might have happened had Saddam Hussein been able to build a nuclear weapon before the invasion of Kuwait is a sobering one indeed."

[‡‡‡] In 1978, the Head of the UK Delegation to the UN Special session on Disarmament made the following statement:
I accordingly give the following assurances on behalf of my Government to non-nuclear weapon States which are parties to the Non-Proliferation Treaty or other internationally binding commitments not to manufacture or acquire nuclear explosive devices: Britain undertakes not to use nuclear weapons against such states except in the case of an attack on the United Kingdom, its dependent territories, its armed forces or its allies by such a state in association or in alliance with a nuclear weapons State.
Annex Q, *The United Nations Special Session on Disarmament*, Cmnd 7267 (London: HMSO, 1978).

deterrent threat based on the extension of political objectives to threaten the Iraqi regime itself, appeared sufficient. When John Major was questioned on the possibility of nuclear use in retaliation for Iraqi chemical use while visiting troops just before the start of the war, he replied, "We have plenty of weapons short of that. We have no plans of the sort you envisage."[50]

Rifkind, in fact, queried rogue state rationales. If deterrence relied on rationality and caution in an aggressor, would it would work with a "tyrant with little regard for the safety and welfare of his own country and people? If he is a gambler or an adventurer? If his judgement is unbalanced or clouded by isolation?"[51] He also expressed concern that public opinion would always think nuclear use disproportionate against a "small country, or an economically weak one." Nor would more "usable" low-yield nuclear weapons be effective as a deterrent — "There is a horror associated with nuclear weapons which we should not attempt to mitigate." The preference was to place hope in the non-proliferation regime, plus the threatened use of conventional weapons with precision strike technologies and also precision intelligence. In addition, "Pre-emptive conventional strikes against clearly-identifiable targets under appropriate international sanction are a conceivable option, given the capability of modern conventional weapons, and given the availability of good intelligence."[52]

The 2007 Decision

Nuclear capabilities do not have to be threat-specific in their design, but could be targeted against any potential enemy should the need arise. Such capabilities could evidently be of scant value in terms of current threats, but perhaps could become truly relevant in the event of the emergence of more extreme threats to national security. If the UK's nuclear capabilities serve any current strategic purpose, it is in reinforcing the presumption, established during the Cold War, that great power warfare would be catastrophic. In the December 2006 White Paper, the government used the minimalist argument. It could not be argued that "a major nuclear threat to our strategic interests will not emerge." By the time of the 2007 decision on whether to begin the Trident replacement program, the rationale had become essentially a generalised worry about the future.

Prime Minister Blair's introduction to the December 2006 White Paper stated that,

> The future is uncertain: accurately predicting events over the period 2020 to 2050 is extremely hard. There are worrying trends: nuclear proliferation continues; large nuclear arsenals remain, and some are being enlarged and modernised; and there is a potential risk from state-sponsored terrorists armed with nuclear weapons.[53]

A "minimum nuclear deterrent" was presented as insurance against such risks. Other than the fact that a decision was needed to prepare for a new generation of SSBNs, this was not an obvious time to abandon the capability, he continued. "None of the present recognised nuclear weapons States intends to renounce nuclear weapons, in the absence of an agreement to disarm multilaterally, and we cannot be sure that a major nuclear threat to our vital interests will not emerge over the longer term." It was up to those arguing for what would be unilateral disarmament to explain how this "gesture" would change "the minds of hardliners and extremists" in proliferating countries and how the UK's "capacity to act would not be constrained by nuclear blackmail by others." The "enduring principles underpinning the UK's approach to nuclear deterrence" that are cited in the White Paper could have been offered at any time over the previous forty years. The focus would be on preventing nuclear attack, rather than military use during conflict, although the reference to what was being deterred was not just, "nuclear blackmail," but also, "acts of aggression against our vital interests that cannot be countered by other means." There would be no specificity about "precisely when, how and at what scale we would contemplate use of our nuclear deterrent," as that would "simplify the calculations of a potential aggressor." The national deterrent was also held to support "collective security through NATO for the Euro-Atlantic area," which might be considered significant by the absence of mention of the Middle East. Lastly, the independent center of decision-making rationale was repeated:

> Potential adversaries could gamble that the US or France might not put themselves at risk of a nuclear attack in order to deter an attack on the UK or our allies. Our retention of an independent centre of nuclear decision-making makes clear to any adversary that the costs of an attack on UK vital interests will outweigh any benefits. Separately controlled but mutually supporting nuclear forces therefore create an enhanced overall deterrent effect.[54]

The Secretary of Defence answered the question of why a nuclear deterrent was needed with "because it works." The evidence was cited in the negative: The absence of nuclear use or great-power conflict since the advent of the nuclear age. He stressed concerns about proliferation in unstable regions rather than just uncertainty. The UK's nuclear capabilities would only be used to deter extreme threats and not to provoke or coerce. He added that it had been decided to stop using the term "sub-strategic Trident" as this implied the possibility of limited use during a conflict.[55]

Critics of the decision have argued that maintaining Britain's nuclear capabilities is unnecessary and complicates non-proliferation efforts. Whereas in the past the arguments might have been related more to arms races and aggravation of the Cold

War, contemporary critiques point to the irrelevance of nuclear weapons in most of the conflicts in which the UK has been engaged, the potential illegality of nuclear capabilities, and the bad example being set at a time when the government claims to wish to reinforce the non-proliferation treaty and promote multilateral disarmament.[56] A major feature of the attack is that the British force is not truly independent. This is directly contradicted by the government which insists that the system's operations are fully independent of the US, including all the command and control procedures, that all decision-making remains under sovereign control, and that only the prime minister could authorize nuclear use, even in a NATO context. Any "instruction to fire would be transmitted to the submarine using only UK codes and UK equipment." Moreover, the government maintains, the SSBNs do not require the US Global Positioning by Satellite (GPS) system to function, while the missile—with its own inertial guidance system—does not use GPS at all. Finally, the government states, that while a decision by the US to withdraw all cooperation, which would be a breach of treaty commitments, would over time degrade the ability of the UK to maintain the SSBNs and the missiles, an abrupt break with the UK during a crisis would not have much impact (unless an adversary perceived it to have made an impact).[57]

THE BRITISH APPROACH TO NUCLEAR ARMS CONTROL AND DISARMAMENT

One of the justifications for Britain's continued retention of a nuclear capability is that it has given the country a guaranteed presence and influential position when nuclear issues are discussed, including disarmament. In this section, we consider the evolving UK policy on disarmament.

During the Cold War

From the 1950s, British governments have always declared themselves in favor of eventual general and complete disarmament and supportive of more modest arms control efforts. Britain was involved in the direct negotiations of the 1963 Limited Test-ban Treaty and the 1968 Non-Proliferation Treaty. Though in the 1980s, arms control might have been an obvious candidate for some Thatcherite revisionism, challenging its interventionist, regulatory ethos, and pointing to the contrived conclusions reached by the negotiations, no such critique was ever launched. However, there has always been a clear determination to protect the British nuclear force from arms control. During the Cold War, the country's basic attitude towards strategic arms control combined enthusiasm in principle with wariness in practice. This was explained as follows:

> The US and the Soviet Union between them have about 95% of the world's nuclear weapons. The clear priority is to get these huge stockpiles reduced.

Even when the UK's nuclear deterrent is modernised with Trident, it will remain less than 3% of the Russians' nuclear potential - at the minimum level for effective deterrence. But the British Government has never said 'never' to including UK nuclear weapons in the negotiations. If Soviet and American strategic arsenals are very substantially reduced, and if no new significant changes have occurred in Soviet defences against them, we will be ready to consider how the UK can best contribute to arms control talks in that new situation.[58]

After the Cold War

With the Cold War ended, and the United States and Russia promising major cuts in nuclear forces, the British government became somewhat more candid about the slight room for manoeuvre allowed by a nuclear force already at a minimum level:

We have always made it clear that the United Kingdom would deploy only the minimum deterrent required for our security needs. These are not determined by the scale of the offensive capabilities of the super-powers. We did not seek to match them in the large build-up in their strategic forces in the 1970s and 1980s, and the reductions they have now agreed - though very welcome in themselves - are not a determinant in sizing our own deterrent. The superpowers have now charted a course which, if all goes well, will lead after another seven to eleven years to substantially smaller strategic stockpiles, reflecting a much improved strategic environment. We very much hope that this improvement will continue; but the course of international events cannot be predicted with certainty. At the same time there is increasing interest in the improvement of ballistic missile defences, and their deployment on a limited basis.[59]

Such statements suggest that the transformation of the European security scene as a result of the end of the Cold War was of slight relevance. As Britain already had a minimum deterrent, there was no scope for further reductions if it was to have any deterrent at all. Those cuts undertaken by the United States and Russia still left them with a substantial deterrent capability. If Russia, in particular, intended to go down to a minimum force, it would still have some capability and so unilateral deterrence by Britain, or even a contribution to a NATO deterrent, also still required some capability above the practical minimum. There was even a suggestion that the required level could grow rather than decline, should Russia develop effective ballistic missile defenses.

In January 1992, Boris Yeltsin visited London as the head of the newly independent Russian Federation. Both the Labour and Liberal Democrat parties were calling for a commitment to limit the number of British warheads on the Trident missiles to the levels currently held on Polaris. Labour also indicated that it would be prepared to negotiate a further reduction in the number of warheads, though it was taking care not to commit itself to negotiating away the whole nuclear deterrent.[60] Yeltsin had called for Britain, along with France and China, to put their forces into international disarmament talks. Prime Minister John Major insisted that this path would not be followed.

Yeltsin also made a promise to Britain along similar lines made to the United States—its cities would be spared in Russian nuclear targeting: "In the past, the United States, Britain and Europe in general were regarded as our potential enemy. That doctrine has to be changed, and the missiles retargeted." A degree of skepticism was expressed with regard to the retargeting of Russian missiles—they could quickly be retargeted back again. One British official was reported to have remarked: "Targeting can be punched in and out at will. Weapons can easily be retargeted. Most of them simply point up into the sky." Major was successful in persuading Yeltsin not to push the question of British participation in a disarmament regime. When pressed by reporters, the Russian leader played down the issue: "The number of nuclear weapons at Britain's disposal is not comparable with ours, and therefore the matter is not really worth discussion."[61]

A few days later, speaking in Washington, General Colin Powell, chairman of the Joint Chiefs of Staff, observed that the strategic arms negotiations had always been bilateral and should remain so. He was "not inclined" to pull the allies in, he said, "and I don't suspect they wished to be pulled in." He added that the Russians should not "feel any particular concern over these non-US systems but they do, and that's a matter for them to take up with the other Western nuclear powers."[62] This statement effectively removed the issue from the British domestic political agenda.

Meanwhile, the government sought to reinforce its arms control credentials by drawing attention to initiatives outside the strategic arms area, such as chemical weapons and arms transfers. In claiming credit for the cuts in sub-strategic nuclear forces, the benefit was described in terms of the objective of confidence building, rather than "stability" or "balance." As Defence Minister Rifkind put it,

> All these measures to reduce nuclear force levels not only have obvious attraction for tax-payers and for finance ministers: they also reduce, as a matter of simple mathematics, the risk of an error or a accident; and they contribute to the building of greater confidence, facilitating the development of co-operative relations.[63]

Confidence-building measures that did not impinge directly on force structure raised few problems for British planners. Thus, London had its own "hot-line" with Moscow, and there was approval for American efforts to add to the locks and safety catches safeguarding nuclear arsenals by strengthening command and control procedures, the end of quick-reaction alerts, dismantling of warheads, and the separation of nuclear weapons from general purpose forces. This established as a central theme a policy of reducing nuclear risk as a supplement, and for countries such as Britain, an alternative, to simple disarmament.

Where possible Britain has always sought to comply with arms control agreements. An example of this is nuclear testing. As would be expected from the minimalist approach, Britain's underground nuclear test program was very much smaller than those of other nuclear powers, with a few tests geared either to safety or to checking new weapon designs. After the Limited Test-ban Treaty of 1963, which precluded atmospheric tests and which Britain had helped negotiate, Britain conducted only 21 tests. Britain also supported the negotiations for a comprehensive test ban (although some of its scientists agreed with their American counterparts that the reliability of warheads could not be guaranteed without tests), but kept open the option of further underground tests until such a treaty was in place. This option depended on the US allowing continued use of its Nevada test site, as Britain lacked its own facility. In September 1992, Congress, against the wishes of President George H.W. Bush, enforced a nine-month moratorium on US nuclear testing, which was intended (at least by Congress) to lead to a complete ban by 1996. Britain would be allowed one test per year up to 1996, and the Pentagon was reported to have made provision for this number (that is three out of 15 in total). The British Embassy lobbied against the moratorium on the grounds that, "we still need to carry our minimum test program for reasons of safety, reliability and effectiveness." The Ministry of Defence's response to the prospect of a complete ban after September 1996 was that it would, "use the intervening time to ensure our deterrent is on good order for the 21st century."[64]

The Clinton Administration came to power in 1993 under considerable pressure to accept a complete ban on nuclear testing. Officially, the position remained that tests were necessary to "maintain the safety and credibility of our deterrent."[§§§] And, indeed, as with a number of issues, President Clinton did not find the test ban issue as straightforward as had candidate Clinton. The Department of Energy, responsible for testing, argued that nine tests would be needed up to 1996, largely for safety purposes, though the Pentagon had maintained that these would be unnecessary. Britain's last nuclear test took place in 1991. The Trident warhead was fully tested and any future tests would have been geared to the WE-177 replacement, but Britain had never put much stress on future proof-testing. MoD officials, in explaining why

---

[§§§] *The Observer* (14 March 1993). The shadow cabinet agreed on 3 March 1993, `that no further testing is needed for Britain's Trident programme and that any further work can be adequately conducted under laboratory conditions.' *The Times* (4 March 1993).

they wanted to continue testing, have largely concentrated on the value in new warhead design as providing "an opportunity to touch reality, to relate the predictions of your theoretical calculations to empirical results."[65]

Unlike the United States, Britain has ratified the Comprehensive Test Ban Treaty, which was completed in 1998, but has not yet entered into force because only 33 of 44 named states that are required to ratify the Treaty have done so. Since 1995, Britain has also followed a moratorium on the production of fissile material for nuclear weapon purposes and placed excess defense material under international safeguards. The US, France, and Russia have made similar arrangements, although these steps have yet to be consolidated into a treaty.

A more challenging question has been the nuclear Non-Proliferation Treaty (NPT). On the one hand, the Treaty recognises the UK's status as a nuclear weapon state; on the other, it carries a requirement "to pursue negotiations in good faith on effective measures relating to the cessation of the nuclear arms race at an early date, and on a treaty on general and complete disarmament under strict and effective international control."[66] This provision is short of a legal obligation. Nor does it preclude maintaining or improving nuclear arsenals so long as some effort is made to negotiate disarmament. Against the argument that abandoning, or at least not renewing the nuclear strike force, would be an exemplary act and encourage others not to aspire to nuclear status, the official line has always been that there is no evidence to justify such a claim. It is argued that nuclear policies are too important to be influenced by the example of others.[67] Against the argument of hypocrisy in opposing the efforts of such countries as India, Pakistan, North Korea, and Iran to acquire nuclear weapons, while insisting on retaining a national arsenal, successive British governments have pointed to the basis of the NPT in distinguishing between nuclear and non-nuclear states and demanding that the non-nuclear do not seek to acquire weapons.

Britain has agreed not to deploy or use or threaten to use nuclear weapons in nuclear-weapons free zones covering Africa, Latin America, and the South Pacific. The abandonment of the "sub-strategic" category of weapon and insistence on use only in extreme circumstances reflects the 1996 International Court of Justice (ICJ) Advisory Opinion on the "Legality of the Threat or Use of Nuclear Weapons." This opinion aimed to fit nuclear weapons use in with the normal laws of armed conflict, that any use should be proportional, distinguish between combatants and non-combatants as much as possible, and not cause unnecessary suffering. The ICJ concluded that "the threat or use of nuclear weapons would generally be contrary to the rules of international law applicable in armed conflict, and in particular the principles and rules of humanitarian law." The destructiveness would be such that any use "seems scarcely reconcilable," with this law. The ICJ would not, however "conclude definitively whether the threat or use of nuclear weapons would be lawful or unlawful in an extreme circumstance of self-defense, in which the very survival of the state would be stake."[68] The British government accepted this ruling.

The 2007 Decision

One of the features of the 2007 decision, coming as it did when pressure was building up to look again at the abolition of all nuclear weapons, was a strong reaffirmation of support for this goal. "We stand by our unequivocal undertaking to accomplish the total elimination of nuclear weapons."[69] The issue was addressed in the White Paper and then again in two major speeches, one by Foreign Secretary Margaret Beckett in the summer of 2007, and then another by Defence Secretary Des Browne to the Geneva Conference on Disarmament in February 2008. Between these two statements, the new Prime Minister Gordon Brown affirmed, in a speech in New Delhi in January 2008, his government's commitment "in the run up to the Non-Proliferation Treaty review conference in 2010 to accelerate disarmament amongst possessor states, to prevent proliferation to new states, and to ultimately achieve a world that is free from nuclear weapons."[70]

Beckett's starting point was the article by George Shultz, William Perry, Henry Kissinger, and Sam Nunn in the Wall Street Journal that made the case for "a bold initiative consistent with America's moral heritage."[71] That initiative was to re-ignite the vision of a world free of nuclear weapons and to redouble efforts on a number of practical measures towards it. Beckett agreed on the need for both "vision—a scenario for a world free of nuclear weapons," and also "action—progressive steps to reduce warhead numbers and to limit the role of nuclear weapons in security policy."[72] Though these two strands were separate they should be mutually reinforcing, she maintained, "Both are necessary, both at the moment too weak." She argued for an unappealing and unequivocal vision. Taking her cue from William Wilberforce and the slave trade, she asked, "Would he have achieved half as much, would he have inspired the same fervour in others if he had set out to 'regulate' or 'reduce' the slave trade rather than abolish it?"[73]

The bold vision was combined, however, with very modest expectations of what might be achieved. Progress would be at best "steady and incremental." She did not argue that the nuclear weapon states should make "immediate and unrealistic promises—committing to speedy abolition, setting a timetable to zero." The reason for her caution was that abolition would require much more than effective disarmament diplomacy, but also, "a much more secure and predictable global political context."[74]

As for Britain, there was no middle way between maintaining a minimum force and abolition. It would therefore be "only towards the end" of the process leading to total elimination that it will "be helpful and useful for us to include our own small fraction of the global stockpile in treaty-based reductions." She acknowledged that the dilemma "between our genuine commitment to abolition and our considered judgement that now was not the time to take a unilateral step to disarm,"[75] was a difficult one to resolve, but she claimed this has been done by not upgrading Britain's nuclear capability and by looking for ways to keep the numbers to the minimum.

Foreign Minister Beckett stated that the process that might lead to the abolitionist goal in the first instance were matters for the Americans and Russians, as they held between them 96 percent of the world's remaining 20,000 nuclear warheads. There was plenty of scope for reducing numbers and this did not necessarily always require treaty negotiations. Britain had shown that it was possible to make cuts through an independent examination of actual strategic needs. The Comprehensive Test Ban Treaty and the Fissile Material Cut-Off Treaty also could play valuable roles in limiting the ability of countries to develop and expand their nuclear capabilities, she pointed out. Margaret Beckett also argued the need to reappraise "how we manage global transparency and global verification," which she wanted to take beyond bilateral arrangements between Russia and the US. She argued that a verification regime geared to a nuclear-free world would need to be tried and tested before complete abolition, and geared to warheads more than delivery systems. She concluded with a hope that Britain could be to the fore in preparing for global nuclear disarmament as a "disarmament laboratory." Practical work would involve looking at techniques of verification and authentication, at chain of custody issues, and at ensuring that the dismantled components of nuclear warheads do not return in new warheads.

The main addition to these positions articulated by Des Browne in his 2008 speech in Geneva was to offer to host a technical conference of nuclear laboratories from the permanent five Security Council countries (P5) on the verification of nuclear disarmament for purposes of both technical analysis and confidence building. This conference would take place before the 2010 NPT Review Conference. He also expressed interest in developing other confidence-building measures on nuclear disarmament with the P5 throughout the NPT Review Cycle.

British objectives for the 2010 NPT Review Conference are to "promote consensus around key measures encompassing the treaty's three pillars—zero tolerance of proliferation; safe, secure and peaceful use of nuclear technology; and a reinvigorated commitment to a world free from nuclear weapons."[76] Particular measures would include raising the cost of withdrawal from the treaty, with automatic referral to the UN Security Council, and to ensure that all material, equipment, technology, and facilities acquired under NPT membership be restricted to peaceful uses even after withdrawal from the Treaty.[77]

The trend in British opinion in favor of abolition was confirmed by a newspaper article published by three former foreign secretaries and a defence secretary, following the American example of senior figures coming out in favor of abolition. They warned that the combination of widespread proliferation with extremism and geopolitical tensions meant that the benefits associated with nuclear weapons during the Cold War—greater stability among the great powers—no longer applied. They pointed to the danger of rogue states or terrorists with access to these weapons. Rather than calling for unilateral disarmament, however, they argued for "working alongside other nations towards a shared goal, using commonly agreed procedures and strategies."[78] Their starting point, as with Foreign Minister Beckett, were the excessive arsenals of the US and Russia. They also stressed the importance of monitoring and accounting for nuclear materials and setting up domestic controls to prevent security breaches, especially in the former Soviet Union. They also proposed strengthening the NPT's provisions on monitoring compliance, bringing the Comprehensive Test Ban Treaty into effect, and providing assistance to those trying to develop civilian nuclear capabilities in a secure manner. As for Britain's and France's contributions, however, they were rather vague. "If we are able to enter into a period of significant multilateral disarmament Britain, along with France and other existing nuclear powers, will need to consider what further contribution it might be able to make to help to achieve the common objective." This did not represent a challenge to government policy. It shared the focus on limiting proliferation and containing the nuclear danger, rather than eliminating it altogether, even while asserting abolition as a long-term goal.[79]

CONCLUSION

In terms of the dangers associated with a nuclear-armed world, successive British governments have never strayed too far from mainstream opinion. It is accepted that the nuclear danger has helped underline the foolishness and futility of great power war and in that respect has contributed to international stability. The end of the Cold War has removed the political triggers to a great power conflict, and while relations with Russia, and, to a lesser extent, with China, go through tense moments, there is no evident dynamic pointing to a revival of the daunting confrontations of the past. The concern therefore has shifted to the potential for new nuclear states, especially if they seem to lack internal stability or are likely to get caught up in serious conflicts.

On proliferation, British policy has been consistent. It has not considered itself a proliferators, since it was the first country to identify a practical path to the construction of a nuclear weapon and was closely involved in the war-time

Manhattan project. Once it became a nuclear power, it consistently opposed additions to the nuclear club. It also rationalized its nuclear status by insisting on the special role this gave the country in disarmament negotiations. It was active in pushing for a test ban treaty from the late 1950s and then for a non-proliferation treaty. In both cases, it played a significant part in the negotiations and was a depository power. It has consistently deplored every move by other states to acquire nuclear weapons and then taken a pragmatic view towards these states once the weapons have been acquired. Only in the case of Iraq in 2003 did a British government make the case that the risks of proliferation were sufficiently great to justify drastic action, and even then, Iraq's potential nuclear status was only one of many factors shaping the government's position. The evidence on the actual state of Iraq's nuclear program at the time was far too tentative to justify military action on its own. In the case of Libya, Britain worked closely with the US, at times taking the lead, in weaning the regime away from both support for terrorism and its nuclear program, and claimed this as a great diplomatic success when the breakthrough agreements were reached in late 2003. In the North Korean case, the British role has been marginal in a crowded field of interested parties.

In the case of Iran, Britain has been part of the "Euro-3," along with France and Germany, pressing for a diplomatic solution and relying on sanctions as the main coercive instrument. It has given no indication that it believes that a nuclear Iran would be so dangerous that military action would be warranted to prevent this from coming about. If Iran becomes a nuclear power, past practice suggests that Britain would work to remind the country of the responsibilities that come with nuclear status, and seek generally to discourage it from aggressive behaviour towards its neighbours, or sharing its nuclear technology with others. This is the approach that Britain has taken with Pakistan and where its limits have already been most severely tested. The combination of the discovery of the A. Q. Khan network and the risk-taking demonstrated by elements of the Pakistani elite sympathetic to Islamic extremism and hostile to India has at times been alarming. Nonetheless, the argument that will be made will be that there is no alternative to engagement with new nuclear powers, and that isolation is more likely to turn them into rogues. In this way, British practice has always been to seek to mitigate the effects of proliferation rather than assume that it will be for the worst. There is certainly no sign of panic when it comes to proliferation. The approach is more "glass half full" than "glass half empty." Every new nuclear power introduces new risks into the situation, but overall there have been far fewer new powers than once anticipated and so far those who have acquired the bomb have not appeared reckless when contemplating its use. It is evident that if they become confirmed nuclear powers, North Korea and Iran could stimulate further proliferation in their regions, but this is seen as a problem for the long-term. As a political matter, proliferation is seen as reflecting tense regional environments and therefore the question of British nuclear status is sui generis. The greatest anxiety is about terrorist groups getting hold of weapons of mass destruction. This is not unrelated to general problems of proliferation—insofar as established nuclear powers are likely to be the source of fissile material or even complete weapons—but the methods used to deal with a potential terrorist bomb are different, with a premium on intelligence and police work.

Because of the often-expressed belief that whether or not Britain remains a nuclear power is of minor relevance to the decisions of other states on their own nuclear status, it can be assumed that the risk of further proliferation would only reinforce Britain's determination to remain a nuclear power. Britain's case for nuclear retention is that it is a mature democracy of honourable intent with the need for an insurance policy. Nuclear weapons remain a hedge against an uncertain future. They can play the role that they have always played—of reminding of the folly of total war—but in circumstances less demanding than before. The government has argued that there is nothing inconsistent with holding onto its own nuclear force and to a commitment to eventual abolition. Over the years, the attempt to demonstrate that Britain's nuclear needs were modest left the country with a force that could be abolished far easier than those of other nuclear powers, although this would be easier still if abolition came at one of those moments of anticipated block obsolescence when a decision has to be taken on whether to move to a new generation of nuclear weapons. Over time, Britain has come to rely on one system only, dispensing with strategic aircraft to concentrate on SSBNs, abandoning shorter-range systems and the so-called "sub-strategic" role. There is now an effort to identify the minimum configuration of SSBNs, in terms of the number of submarines, missiles carried, and warheads available. In addition, the government has set out ideas for preparing the way for abolition should appropriate political conditions emerge at some point. In the event of a general move towards abolition, particularly if led by the US and Russia, Britain would pose few obstacles to success.

In this move, Britain would see itself as a facilitator, rather than a leader. The government argues the need to develop practical, technical aids to encourage moves towards disarmament through improved monitoring of compliance with provisions of any agreement. Having gone so far unilaterally, it does not really see its own forces as being relevant to a disarmament package until at quite a late stage. In this respect, signing up to visionary statements on abolition is non-problematic. All such schemes would find the first eighty percent of reductions straightforward, consisting largely of cuts in US and Russian arsenals. It is only as the lower numbers are reached that deterrence might be said to be put at risk, or discrepancies in the numbers of weapons held by different countries really start to matter. The point at which British—and French—forces would be an unavoidable part of the mix is well down the line, when progress to a truly nuclear-free world will depend not only on the goodwill created by the earlier negotiations, and on the technical fixes developed for problems of decommissioning, verification, and potential reconstitution, but also on an extraordinary favorable international political climate.

ENDNOTES

[1] Lawrence Freedman and John Gearson, "Interdependence and Independence: Nassau and the British Nuclear deterrent", in Kathleen Burke and Melvyn Stokes, ed, *The United States and the European Alliance since 1945* (New York: Berg, 1999).

[2] James Callaghan, *Time and Chance* (London: Collins, 1987).

[3] *The United Kingdom* TridentTrident *Programme,* Defence Open Government Document 1982/1 (London: Ministry of Defence: March 1982).

[4] White House Background Briefing, *U.S. Sale of* TridentTrident *One Missiles to U.K.* (US International Communications Agency, 17 July 1980).

[5] House of Commons, *Official Record*, 19 May 1981, Col. 168.

[6] House of Commons, Third Report from the Defence Committee, Session 1986-87, *The Progress of the Trident Programme* (May 1987).

[7] *The Independent*, 5 June 1987.

[8] Lawrence Freedman, 'Britain: The First Ex-Nuclear Power', *International Security*, vol. 6, no. 2 (Fall 1981), pages 80-104.

[9] *Independent,* 16 May 1988; 23 June 1989.

[10] *Independent*, 23 June 1989; Fieldhouse et al, *SIPRI Yearbook 1992*, p. 80.

[11] Secretary of State for Defence, *Statement on the Defence Estimates 1983*, Vol 1, Cmnd 1981-1 (London: HMSO, July 1992), page 22.

[12] See speech by Malcolm Rifkind to Centre for Defence Studies, 15 November 1993, reprinted in *Brasseys Defence Yearbook 1994*, (London, Brasseys, 1994). Hereinafter referred to as Rifkind speech.

[13] *Financial Times,* 16 June 1992; *Independent,* 16 June 1992. The non-UK weapons were returned to the United States.

[14] *Independent,* 23 June 1989. Their yield was put at 5-10KT.

[15] *Defence Estimates 1992*, page 28.

[16] *New Labour because Britain deserves better*, Labour Party manifesto, May 1997.

[17] *The Strategic Defence Review*, (London: Ministry of Defence, July 1998), para 64.

[18] *The Strategic Defence Review*, para 63; Select Committee on Defence, *Defence—Eighth Report* (London: House of Commons, 20 June 2006).

[19] Hans M. Kristensen, <u>U.S. Nuclear Weapons Withdrawn From the United Kingdom</u>, Federation of American Scientists Strategic Security Blog, 26 June 2008, http://www.fas.org/blog/ssp/2008/06/us-nuclear-weapons-withdrawn-from-the-united-kingdom.php.

[20] Tim Youngs and Claire Taylor, TridentTrident *and the Future of the British Nuclear Deterrent* (London: International Affairs and Defense Section, House of Commons Library, July 5, 2005).

[21] Secretary of State for Defence and The Secretary of State for Foreign and Commonwealth Affairs, *The Future of the United Kingdom's Nuclear Deterrent*, Cmnd 6994, (December 2006).

[22] *Official Record*, Written Answers, 14 March 2007.

[23] *Official Record*, Column 309, 14 March 2007.

[24] *Ibid.*

[25] Working Group: Scotland without nuclear Weapons, http://www.scotland.gov.uk/Topics/People/swnw-working-group.

[26] Select Committee on Defence, *Defence—Eighth Report* (London: House of Commons, 20 June 2006), paras 118-9.

[27] Cmnd 6994, p. 31.

[28] Michael Smith, "Focus: Britain's secret nuclear blueprint," *Sunday Times*, March 12, 2006.

[29] Cmnd 6994, p. 26.

[30] House of Commons Defence Committee, Ninth Report of Session 2006–07, *The Future of the UK's Strategic Nuclear Deterrent: the White Paper*, Volume I, Report, together with formal minutes, HC 225-I, 7 March 2007, para 28.

[31] *Ibid.*

[32] House of Commons Defence Committee, Ninth Report of Session 2006–07.

[33] *Official Record*, January 29, 1980, col. 678.

[34] Robert S. McNamara, Address at the Commencement Exercises, University of Michigan, Ann Arbor, Michigan, 16 June 1962.

[35] Andre Beaufre, The Sharing of Nuclear Responsibilities: A Problem in Need of a Solution', *International Affairs*, vol. 31, no. 3 (July 1965).

[36] See statement by Secretary of Defence Francis Pym, House of Commons, Official Record, 24 January 1980, cols. 678-9.

[37] For examples, see, Margaret Gowing, *Independence and Deterrence: Britain and Atomic Energy, 1945-1952, Vol. 1, Policy-Making*, (London: Macmillan, 1974);
G.M.Dillon, *Dependence and Deterrence* (London: Gower, 1983);
John Simpson, *The Independent Nuclear State: The United States, Britain and the Atom*, (London: Macmillan, 1983);
Andrew Pierre, *Nuclear Politics: The British Experience with an Independent Strategic Nuclear Force*, (London: OUP, 1972).

[38] See, for example, Shaun Gregory, *The Command and Control of British Nuclear Weapons*, (University of Bradford School of Peace Studies, Peace Research Report No. 13., December 1986).

[39] The Labour Party, *Modern Britain in a Modern World: The Power to Defend our Country*, (December 1986), page 6. The next sentence mentions 'this so-called independent nuclear weapon.'

[40] National Opinion Poll based on a representative quote of 1060 electors in 53 constituencies across Great Britain on 4-7 November 1983. *Daily Mail* (9 November 1983).

[41] David Capitanchik and Richard Eichenberg, *Defence and Public Opinion*, Chatham House Papers No. 20 (London: RKP, 1983), Chapter Three.

[42] *The Future United Kingdom Strategic Deterrent Force*, Defence Open Government Document 80/23. (London: Ministry of Defence, July 1980).
I noted at the time: `There is no discussion of the possibility that the superpowers' strategic relationship might undergo a critical transformation before Trident is in service, or that the dispersion of the relevant technology around the world will lead to the emergence of new nuclear threats'. Lawrence Freedman, `Trident: Will it still work in 2020 AD?' *The Sunday Times*, 20 July 1980.

[43] HC 36 of 1980- 81, page107.

[44] The old rationale is discussed in Lawrence Freedman, *Britain and Nuclear Weapons* (London: Macmillans, 1980).

[45] Nuclear Planning Group, *Final Communiqué* (7 December 1990), para 14; *Rifkind Speech*, page 6.

[46] *Rifkind Speech*, page 17.

[47] *Ibid*, page 5.

[48] *Defence Estimates 1992*, page 9.

[49] *Rifkind Speech*, page 14.

[50] *Independent* (9 January 1991).

[51] *Rifkind Speech*, page 28.

[52] *Rifkind Speech*, pages 10-12.

[53] Tony Blair, "Foreword to the White Paper by the Prime Minister," *The Future of the United Kingdom's Nuclear Deterrent: Presented to Parliament by The Secretary of State for Defence and The Secretary of State for Foreign and Commonwealth Affairs,* December 2006, page 5.

[54] Cmnd 6994, page 18.

[55] Speech by Des Browne MP, Secretary of State for Defence, "The United Kingdom's Nuclear Deterrent in the 21st Century" (25 January 2007), at Kings College, London.

[56] Rebecca Johnson, Nicola Butler and Stephen Pullinger, *Worse than Irrelevant? British Nuclear Weapons in the 21st Century*, (London: Acronym Institute for Disarmament Diplomacy, 2006).

[57] Cmnd 6994

[58] Questions on Arms Control, Foreign and Commonwealth Office and Ministry of Defence: (February 1988), cited in John Poole (ed), *Independence and Interdependence: A Reader on British Nuclear Weapons Policy* (London: Brassey's, 1990), page 261.

[59] Secretary of State for Defence, *Statement on the Defence Estimates 1992*, Vol. 1, Cmnd 1981, (London: HMSO, July 1992), page 22.

[60] *Independent* (30 January 1992).

[61] *Independent* (31 January 1992); *Financial Times* (31 January 1992).

[62] *Arms Control Reporter 1992*, 408.B.137.

[63] *Rifkind Speech*, page 7.

[64] *Times* (26 September 1992); *Independent* (3 October 1992).

[65] House of Commons Defence Committee, Ninth Report of Session 2006–07.

[66] Article VI of The Treaty on the Non-Proliferation of Nuclear Weapons.

[67] Rebecca Johnson, Nicola Butler and Stephen Pullinger, *Worse Than Irrelevant? British Nuclear Weapons in the 21st Century* (London: Acronym Institute for Disarmament Diplomacy, 2006), page 10;
Julian Lewis, "Nuclear Disarmament versus Peace in the Twenty-First Century," *International Affairs* 82, no. 4 (July 2006), 670;
Michael Quinlan, "The Future of UK Nuclear Weapons: Shaping the Debate," *International Affairs* 82, no. 4 (July 2006), page 629;
Keith Hartley, "The Economics of UK Nuclear Weapons Policy," *International Affairs* 82, no. 4 (July 2006), page 675.

[68] International Court of Justice (ICJ) Advisory Opinion at the request of the UN General Assembly, "Legality of the Threat or Use of Nuclear weapons" ICJ Reports, 8 July 1996, para 95

[69] *The Future of the United Kingdom's Nuclear Deterrent: Presented to Parliament by The Secretary of State for Defence and The Secretary of State for Foreign and Commonwealth Affairs,* December 2006, page 13.

[70] Margaret Beckett, "A World Free of Nuclear Weapons?" Carnegie International Nonproliferation Conference, Keynote Address (Washington, DC: 25 June 2007);
Gordon Brown, Speech to the Chamber of Commerce in Delhi, (New Delhi: 21 January 2008);
Des Browne, "Laying the Foundations for Multilateral Disarmament," Geneva Conference on Disarmament (Geneva: 5 February 2008).

[71] George Shultz, William Perry, Henry Kissinger, Sam Nunn, "A World Free of Nuclear Weapons," *Wall Street Journal* (4 January 2007).

[72] Margaret Beckett, "A World Free of Nuclear Weapons?" Carnegie International Nonproliferation Conference, Keynote Address (Washington, DC: 25 June 2007).

[73] *Ibid.*

[74] *Ibid.*

[75] *Ibid.*

[76] Foreign Secretary, Written Answers, *Official Record*, 18 February 2008, cols 176-7W.

[77] *Ibid.*

[78] Douglas Hurd, Malcolm Rifkind, David Owen and George Robertson, "Start worrying and learn to ditch the bomb: It won't be easy, but a world free of nuclear weapons is possible," *The Times* (20 June 2008).

[79] *Ibid.*

US Perspectives on the Global Elimination of Nuclear Weapons

Barry Blechman, Alexander Bollfrass, and Frank Valliere

The United States was the first nation to build nuclear arms and is the only nation to have used such a weapon in warfare. It has relied on the threat of nuclear devastation as a central element in its national security policies for most of the sixty-plus years these weapons have existed, during which it issued explicit nuclear threats in several international crises. With the end of the Cold War in 1989, however, and particularly with growing recognition of the dangers posed by terrorist organizations after the September 11, 2001 attacks, many American citizens and the US government began to re-evaluate the benefits and risks of nuclear weapons. As a result, the US in recent years has downplayed both its rhetorical and policy attachment to issuing nuclear threats, sharply reduced the size of its nuclear arsenal and supporting infrastructure, and has begun to discuss seriously the possibilities of eliminating nuclear weapons completely or, at least, the necessary prerequisite of further dramatic reductions in the number and salience of these weapons. Indeed, there is great hope that the US could become a serious and leading proponent of a world-wide treaty to eliminate nuclear weapons from all nations by a date certain.

US Motivations for Acquiring and Modernizing Nuclear Weapons

The US has acquired and maintained large nuclear forces for reasons associated both with military planning and with its political relations with other nations, friend and foe alike. Military motivations for investing in nuclear weapons tended to be more prominent earlier in the nuclear era and pertained to specific opponents and conflicts. Political motivations, however, have persisted through to the current period. Throughout the Cold War, nuclear weapons played a prominent role in US national security policies, not only vis-à-vis the Soviet Union, but with regard to US policies toward China and other nations in Asia. During this period, the US was motivated to develop and continually modernize its nuclear arsenal because of a belief that the threat of nuclear devastation served to encourage prudent behavior on the part of the great powers and deterred conventional conflicts among them.

The US was also concerned that, even with its allies, it would be unable to match the great size of the armed forces of the Soviet Union and China. In order to deter conventional attacks on its own forces and those of its allies, the US maintained, as a central element in its security policy, the threat that it would initiate the use of nuclear weapons in a conflict that it might otherwise lose. US leaders also believed that third parties viewed the balance of nuclear forces as an important indicator of the relative strength and commitment of the superpowers, and thus it was essential to maintain nuclear forces second to none to avoid the political consequences of being seen as the weaker power. Finally, beginning in the 1960s, the US stressed the need to maintain a balance of nuclear capabilities with potential adversaries in order to "extend nuclear deterrence" to certain allies, preventing decisions on their part to develop nuclear weapons of their own. This final motivation gained added currency with the emergence of new nuclear powers in recent years and, with them, a renewed threat of accelerated proliferation.

Military/security motivations

The United States was driven to develop nuclear weapons because of a deep concern that Hitler's Germany was close to developing such a weapon in World War II. Moreover, the desire to end the war without suffering the massive American casualties that were expected to result from an invasion of the Japanese home islands prompted the first, and, so far, only, uses of nuclear weapons in warfare. Although we know now that the atomic bombings of Hiroshima and Nagasaki were not the most important factors in Japan's surrender, the US entered the nuclear age convinced that atomic bombs were usable as weapons of war and could be decisive.[1]

As the post-war euphoria of the late 1940s turned into the bitter acknowledgment of continuing challenges in Europe from the Soviet Union and in Asia from the new Communist government of China, the US, having rapidly demobilized the armed forces it had built up for World War II, began to rely on nuclear weapons to offset military threats it perceived from both countries. President Harry Truman embraced the nuclear instrument reluctantly, partially deterred by his self-awareness that he had authorized the use of the weapon against the Japanese and its consequences in human terms, and partially constrained by the very small size of the US arsenal in the early years. Truman resisted pressures from both military leaders and political figures to utilize nuclear weapons in the Korean War, for example.* His successor, President Dwight Eisenhower, however, was not nearly so reluctant and, encouraged by Secretary of State John Foster Dulles, made the use of nuclear

---

* Following General Douglas MacArthur's numerous public repudiations of official presidential policies during the Korean War, advancing instead policies that called for the unrestricted use of American military power in Asia that would likely directly involve China in the war, President Truman relieved MacArthur of his command, stating, "A number of events have made it evident that General MacArthur did not agree with that policy. I have therefore considered it essential to relieve General MacArthur so that there would be no doubt or confusion as to the real purpose and aim of our policy…We do not want to widen the conflict. We will use every effort to prevent that disaster. And in so doing, we know that we are following the great principles of peace, freedom, and justice." President Harry S. Truman, Radio Report to the American People on Korea and on U.S. Policy in the Far East (April 11, 1951), http://www.trumanlibrary.org/publicpapers/index.php?pid=290&st=&st1=;.For a detailed account of the Truman-MacArthur controversy, see: John W. Spanier, *The Truman-MacArthur Controversy and the Korean War* (Cambridge: Belknap Press, 1959).

weapons a central element of US foreign and security policies throughout his two terms in office. Eisenhower was motivated by a determination to restrain federal spending; he was unwilling to increase the defense budget sufficiently to match either Soviet or Chinese conventional armed forces, believing that such budgets could not be sustained.

The US deployed nuclear weapons at its bases in Asia early in the 1950s and made explicit nuclear threats on several occasions. The first was President Eisenhower's message to Chinese leaders, passed through India, that if the stalled negotiations to end the Korean War were not brought rapidly to a conclusion, the United States would "move decisively without inhibition in our use of weapons, and would no longer be responsible for confining hostilities to the Korean peninsula."[2] The negotiations and the war ended soon thereafter, but the importance of Eisenhower's threat is debatable. The Soviet leader, Josef Stalin, had died a few months prior to the close of the negotiations and his successors, seeking a respite in tensions with the West, may have brought pressure on China, then a close ally, to end the conflict prior to the threat being made.[3] When crises recurred between the US and China, over the Tachen Islands in 1954 and Quemoy/Matsu in 1957-58, Eisenhower again threatened the use of nuclear weapons, in the first instance rushing new weapons into the theater and making fairly explicit allusions to their possible use. These threats seemed to have clear effects on the Chinese leaders. When their Soviet ally stated bluntly that it would not risk nuclear war with the US to support China's position on the islands, China backed down. At the same time, however, Chairman Mao Tse Tung decided that China could not depend on the USSR and needed to acquire its own nuclear capabilities—a feat accomplished within a few years in 1964.[4]

Eisenhower did show nuclear restraint in Asia on one important occasion. When pressed by the Joint Chiefs of Staff under Chairman Arthur Radford to utilize atomic bombs to relieve the French forces besieged at Dien Bien Phu in Vietnam, Eisenhower demurred, stating, "You boys must be crazy. We can't use those awful things against Asians for a second time in less than ten years. My God."[5]

It was Europe, however, that was the focus of US nuclear strategy and the primary manifestation of the role Eisenhower and Dulles foresaw for nuclear weapons in support of national security policy. As early as 1947-48, Secretary of Defense James Forrestal, one of the leading proponents of the need for a firm stance against Soviet expansion in Europe, deployed US B-29 bombers (previously used to deliver the atomic bombs on Hiroshima and Nagasaki) to bases in England and Germany as warnings to the USSR that the US had means of resisting Soviet encroachments. The bombers were not carrying nuclear weapons, as the US had very few, if any, in its arsenal at the time, but they seemed to have bolstered the allies' morale, as well as making an impact on the Russians. This was the beginning, of course, of the US extended deterrence guarantee, the so-called "nuclear umbrella" that the US eventually placed over all the members of the North Atlantic Treaty Organization (NATO).[6]

The central role of nuclear weapons in US military strategy to counter Soviet expansion in Europe was outlined in an official US government document in 1953. The so-called "NSC 162/2" stated, "The major deterrent to aggression against Western Europe is the manifest determination of the United States to use its atomic capability and massive retaliatory striking power if the area is attacked."[7] This strategy was sealed at the NATO meeting on December 17, 1954 in Paris, when the allies decided explicitly not to match Soviet conventional armed strength. With 22 Soviet divisions in eastern Germany, 60 in East European satellite states and the western USSR, and another 93 elsewhere in the USSR, the task was far too daunting from both a manpower and budgetary point-of-view.[8] Instead, NATO adopted Secretary Dulles' doctrine of "massive retaliation," stating that if Soviet forces invaded and NATO was unable to defeat them conventionally, the alliance would make use of nuclear weapons to end the conflict. This doctrine envisioned the use of short-range, or tactical, weapons initially, but included the commitment to escalate the conflict as necessary, up to and including the possibility of a strategic nuclear exchange between the US and Soviet homelands.[9]

To make the doctrine credible, the US deployed many kinds of tactical weapons to Europe beginning in 1955, nearing 3000 nuclear weapons deployed in seven European states by the end of 1960.[10] Additionally, the US reorganized its ground forces to fight on "atomic battlefields" and built up its strategic forces. President John F. Kennedy continued this policy and even accelerated the nuclear build-up, at the same time adopting a more flexible strategy that put greater emphasis on keeping any conflict on the conventional level. For example, during the Berlin Crisis of 1958-59, the Eisenhower Administration seemed to relish the West's conventional inferiority, implementing Secretary Dulles' policy of "brinksmanship" and highlighting its determination to respond to any outbreak of war with "massive retaliation." As Eisenhower asserted, "…if resort to arms should become necessary, our troops in Berlin would be quickly overrun, and the conflict would almost inevitably be global war. For this type of war our nuclear forces were more than adequate."[11] During the 1961-62 Berlin Crisis, on the other hand, President Kennedy called up military reserve forces to bolster US conventional capabilities and indicated to his military planners the need to find conventional means to end the Soviet pressures on Berlin. In a televised speech announcing this call up and his request of "some $1.8 billion…for the procurement of non-nuclear weapons, ammunition and equipment," President Kennedy asserted, "We intend to have a wider choice than humiliation or all-out nuclear action."[12]

The stalemate over Berlin was followed quickly by the Soviet gambit to emplace nuclear-armed missiles in Cuba and the ensuing crisis—the riskiest nuclear confrontation to have ever taken place—seemed to have sobered both sides. Although the US/NATO policy remained unchanged from the mid-1960s to the end of the Cold War, throughout this period American planners sought means of either countering quantitatively superior Soviet conventional forces with superior Western conventional military technology or controlling the Soviet advantage through arms control agreements. Additionally, the US continually modified its nuclear forces, seeking greater flexibility and means of containing a nuclear war, should one begin.[13]

The US/NATO willingness to stand by its first nuclear use policy persists to this day, now motivated primarily by the post-Cold War Russian emphasis on its tactical nuclear forces as substitutes for its now clearly inferior conventional military capabilities. Although, following the dissolution of the Soviet Union, the US and Russia solemnly declared that they no longer considered each other to be enemies, each nation remains wary of the other. NATO's expansion to include the former members of the Warsaw Pact, as well as some former parts of the Soviet Union, raised concerns in Russia, while NATO, and especially its new members, remain wary of their former Russian masters. Although relations are more cooperative and peaceful than during the Cold War, the potential remains for crises and confrontations, as seen in Georgia during the summer of 2008. As a result, the US retains some, if many fewer, tactical nuclear weapons in Europe in support of NATO, and Russia deploys large numbers of tactical nuclear weapons on its territory and maintains a doctrine that stresses their potential use in the event of war.[14]

During the contemporary period, the US has also flirted with a new security-related motivation for nuclear weapons. Greatly concerned about the possibility that a terrorist organization might acquire, or be given, nuclear weapons that it could use to attack US cities, the George W. Bush Administration attempted to deter such actions in support of terrorist organizations by hostile governments. Hence, following North Korea's nuclear test in 2006, President Bush warned, "the transfer of nuclear weapons or material by North Korea to states or non-state entities would be considered a grave threat to the United States, and [the United States] would hold North Korea fully accountable of the consequences of such action."[15] Subsequently, National Security Advisor Stephen Hadley broadened the warning to other governments stating,

> The United States has made clear for many years that it reserves the right to respond with overwhelming force to the use of weapons of mass destruction against the United States, our people, our forces and our friends

and allies. Additionally, the United States will hold any state, terrorist group, or other non-state actor fully accountable for supporting or enabling terrorist efforts to obtain or use weapons of mass destruction, whether by facilitating, financing, or providing expertise or safe haven for such efforts."[16]

Although the threat of nuclear retaliation was not made explicitly in either statement, the words, "overwhelming force," are normally taken as an allusion to nuclear capabilities.

Political motivations

The US strategic policy of extended deterrence and the resulting forward deployment of nuclear weapons in Europe and East Asia served political, as well as security, functions. In the 1940s and 1950s, the deployments were part of the many actions taken by the Truman, Eisenhower, and Kennedy administrations to "draw the line" in Europe. Its goal was to make it clear to the Soviet Union that although the West would not contest Soviet control of the countries it had occupied during World War II, the West would not permit the USSR to extend its influence into Western Europe and especially into the portions of Germany occupied by US, UK, and French forces; indeed, these actions signaled that the US and its allies were prepared to go to war, if necessary, to stop the Soviet advance. Moscow tested this determination on several occasions between 1947 and 1962, and the West responded each time with a variety of diplomatic and military actions, including changes in the disposition and alert status of nuclear forces to signal the ultimate danger of a crisis getting out of hand. Although these dramatic incidents ceased after 1962 (with the partial exception of a contained confrontation following the Soviet re-occupation of Czechoslovakia in 1968), nuclear policies and forces were believed by Western policymakers to play a continuing, positive role in stabilizing the European divide and providing incentives to both sides to reach cooperative arrangements, such as arms control treaties, to reduce the risk of war.

Extended deterrence in Europe also helped to ensure cohesion within the NATO alliance, at least during most of the Cold War period. By placing US troops on the front-lines in Germany, by stating that if those forces were unsuccessful in stopping a Soviet invasion that NATO would utilize tactical nuclear weapons (and by making that threat credible through the deployment of weapons and development and rehearsal of procedures indicating that their use would be almost automatic), and by committing itself to continuing to escalate a nuclear war up to and including an all-out strategic exchange between the US and Soviet homelands, the United States made clear its willingness "to share the risk" of the confrontation with its European partners. Although the US and its European allies sometimes differed over the military requirements to keep the NATO deterrent viable, such as the debate over the deployment of theater-range missiles in the early 1980s, the physical placement of military capabilities (conventional and nuclear) in Europe, and adoption of the policies and procedures which governed their use, made the US security commitment credible in ways that a treaty alone, or even the most forceful statements by US presidents, never could.

US nuclear policies and force deployments strengthened NATO's cohesion in more subtle ways as well, particularly among those nations who accepted nuclear weapons on their soil or dedicated some of their aircraft to deliver those weapons if the need arose. Officials of these states maintain that their nuclear roles permitted them to participate in NATO decision-making more fully and to have influence on those decisions beyond their relative weight in the alliance.† They were also assured a voice in NATO decision-making on war and peace issues that otherwise might have been reserved only for the largest West European powers. In the latter part of the Cold War, this decision-making role extended to NATO's positions on arms control initiatives and negotiations.

In Asia, the political consequences of US nuclear doctrine and deployments were not so stark, but probably helped to stabilize regional relationships—at least during the 1950s. Repeated confrontations between the US and China over Korea and Taiwan, often with a nuclear tinge to them, probably had a sobering effect on Communist China's initial appetite for immediate resolution of outstanding disputes through the use of force, if necessary. Following the Korean War, the US deployed nuclear weapons to Korea and adopted a first use policy to offset North Korea's apparent superiority in conventional forces. Secretary Dulles' effort to replicate NATO's success in Europe by creating a Southeast Asia Treaty Organization was never effective. Moreover, nuclear weapons played no role in the Vietnam conflict and the US suffered a humiliating and costly defeat despite its vast nuclear arsenal. Indeed, following the fall of Saigon in 1975, then-Secretary of Defense James R. Schlesinger reminded Pyongyang of the US nuclear commitment: "If circumstances were to require the use of tactical nuclear weapons...I think that would be carefully considered," adding, "I do not think it would be wise to test (American) reactions."[17] Schlesinger made the statement to deter what was feared to be North Korean intent to test US resolve on the Peninsula, as a result of Washington's willingness to accept the fall of its ally in South Vietnam.

The US also extended its nuclear deterrent to Japan in the 1950s, making clear that if the US-Japan Mutual Security Treaty were challenged and Japan attacked, the US

---

† For instance, in Germany's current coalition government, conservative-run ministries make the participation argument, while the center-left foreign minister has called for their unilateral removal. See, for example, "Yankee Bombs Go Home: Foreign Minister Wants US Nukes out of Germany," *Spiegel Online* (April, 10, 2009) http://www.spiegel.de/international/germany/0,1518,618550,00.html.

would utilize all means at its disposal to defend its ally.[‡] For most of the post-World War II period, these commitments were aimed at the Soviet Union, which disputed Japanese retention of the southern half of Sakhalin Island and some other island territories. After the Cold War, however, extended deterrence to Japan has gained importance as a means of offsetting increasing Chinese military capabilities. Unlike the situation in Europe, the Japanese have never fully reconciled with their World War II enemies and tensions between Japan and China, and Japan and Korea, have ebbed and flowed over issues stemming from the war. Now that both China and North Korea have nuclear weapons, in view of this continuing tension, many Japanese and American leaders believe that the US nuclear guarantee continues to be essential to keep Japan from developing nuclear weapons of its own (see below).

Throughout the nuclear age, most US leaders have also believed that the American nuclear posture serves an even more fundamental political purpose. Along with US economic strength, conventional military power, and the vitality of its culture and international political leadership, US nuclear forces are believed to contribute to the world-wide perception of the United States as a "superpower;" one of two superpowers during the Cold War, and now the only superpower.

To maintain this position during the Cold War, the US continually modernized its strategic nuclear forces to ensure that they would be seen as at least equivalent to those of the Soviet Union—particularly in the capacity to withstand a first-strike and retaliate against the attacker. Many debates over US strategic weapons modernization, such as the so-called "window of vulnerability" in the 1970s, hinged on differing perceptions of what was required to maintain this parity of survivable forces.[18] According to US strategic doctrine, maintaining such parity was essential to avoid providing any incentive to the USSR to launch a first-strike during a crisis. However, fundamental political consequences were also believed to hinge on maintaining parity. Proponents of highly capable nuclear forces proclaimed that third nations viewed trends in the strategic balance of forces as indicators of the two superpowers' resolve. If the US was seen to be declining, as during the Carter Administration, it encouraged greater aggressiveness on the part of hostile nations, not only the USSR, but countries like North Korea, and also caused allied or neutral nations to be less willing to take a stand in support of US interests.[§]

[‡] "In the event of an armed attack against these islands, the United States Government will consult at once with the Government of Japan and intends to take the necessary measures for the defense of the islands, and to do its utmost to secure the welfare of the islanders." Statement by the US Plenipotentiary, Secretary of State Christian Herter, Ambassador to Japan Douglas MacArthur, and Assistant Secretary of State for Far Eastern Affairs J. Graham Parsons. "Texts of U.S.-Japanese Treaty and Communique," *New York Times,* (January 20, 1960), page 4.

[§] Paul Nitze, then Chairman of the Committee on the Present Danger, arguing in favor of a renewed US nuclear expansion in 1980 stated, "[T]he danger that the Soviets might seek to exploit their temporary advantages in terms of military power cannot be dismissed. Crises may indeed arise a little sooner than they would otherwise have done…But what is clear beyond doubt is that if the United States does not act along the lines proposed here, the kind of Soviet gains and threats to world peace that have arisen in the last five years will multiply inexorably and perhaps,

Since the end of the Cold War, elaborate calculations of survivable second strike capabilities have gone out of fashion, but most US leaders continue to believe that fundamental political benefits result from maintaining strategic nuclear forces at least equal to those of any other nation—in effect, Russia. Although several influential analysts urged the Obama Administration to make unilateral reductions in the US strategic arsenal, maintaining that the US had far too many weapons—more than were necessary to deter nuclear use—and that such a gesture would strengthen the US position with respect to proliferation issues, such moves were not undertaken during the administration's early months, with the administration preferring to negotiate bilateral reductions with Russia.[19] The recent Congressional Commission on the US Strategic Posture endorsed this view explicitly, stating, "Substantial stockpile reductions would need to be done bilaterally with the Russians."[20]

Some US leaders also believe that there is a political advantage in maintaining a significant lead in nuclear strength over other countries. The George W. Bush Administration, for example, in its 2001 Nuclear Posture Review, argued that a significant US lead "dissuaded" other states from even thinking about investing the resources that would be needed to match US capabilities and thus prevented an arms race from developing.[**]

Finally, there is a broad consensus among US leaders and nuclear strategists that by extending the US nuclear umbrella to other nations, the United States has greatly curtailed the number of nuclear powers in the world. Following the French and Chinese tests of nuclear weapons in the early 1960s, there was great concern that there would soon be a "cascade" of proliferation, as nuclear technology was spreading widely for civilian purposes, and the knowledge of how to convert such civilian expertise and materials to military applications was also proliferating. In Europe, the US sought to persuade its allies that there was no need to develop their own weapons by discussing a variety of means by which US nuclear forces might be "shared" by the allies. The most seriously discussed proposal was the so-called

---

in the end, irretrievably." Paul H. Nitze, "Strategy in the Decade of the 1980s," *Foreign Affairs*, 59 (Fall 1980), page 97.

[**] This idea was first alluded to in the Bush Administration's 2001 Nuclear Posture Review: "The capacity of the infrastructure to upgrade existing weapon systems, surge production of weapons, or develop and field entirely new systems for the New Triad can discourage other countries from competing militarily with the United States." The White House, *Nuclear Posture Review [Excerpts]* (January 8, 2002), page 14. http://www.globalsecurity.org/wmd/library/policy/dod/npr.htm. Subsequent Bush doctrine reiterated this view: "It is time to reaffirm the essential role of American military strength. We must build and maintain our defenses beyond challenge. Our military's highest priority is to defend the United States. To do so effectively, our military must dissuade future military competition." The White House, *The National Security Strategy of the United States of America*, (September 2002). http://georgewbush-whitehouse.archives.gov/nsc/nss/2002/nss.pdf. "We will work to dissuade potential adversaries from adopting threatening capabilities, methods, and ambitions, particularly by sustaining and developing our own key military advantages." The White House, *The National Defense Strategy of the United States of America*, (March 2005). http://www.defenselink.mil/news/Mar2005/d20050318nds1.pdf.

"Multilateral Force," a ship equipped with nuclear-armed missiles that would be manned by military personnel from several NATO nations. In the end, this and related schemes appeared unwieldy and the alliance settled on the current system in which nuclear bombs are maintained in Europe under US control, but would be made available for delivery by the air forces of several allied nations if authorized by NATO.[21]

The US umbrella was also extended to Asia, as noted previously, particularly to persuade Japan not to develop nuclear weapons in response to China's growing capabilities, but also to Australia, New Zealand, South Korea, and Taiwan. Indeed, in the early 1970s, it came to light that both the latter two nations were developing latent nuclear weapon capabilities. When the US made clear that continuation of these programs would mean loss of the US nuclear guarantee, the weapon programs were stopped immediately.[22] Japan's advanced civilian nuclear capabilities and abundance of nuclear materials means that the possibility that it might develop a weapons capability of its own remains a serious concern to US decision-makers. The role that US nuclear capabilities and guarantees might play in preventing such a step is an important political motivation for maintaining a significant US nuclear arsenal.

The US also utilized vaguely promised nuclear guarantees to help persuade Belarus, Kazakhstan, and Ukraine to give up the nuclear weapons they had inherited when the Soviet Union collapsed, and to sign the NPT as non-nuclear weapon states. Although no formal commitment has been made to these states, then-Secretary of Defense William Perry asserted in 1996, the Ukraine, "can achieve its security interests through a vigorous role in the Partnership for Peace and through a strong bilateral security relationship with the United States – both of which exist now."[23]

Currently, a theory holds that if Iran develops nuclear weapons, a wave of proliferation might engulf the Middle East. Turkey, Saudi Arabia, Egypt, and Algeria are often mentioned as nations that might feel compelled to emulate an Iranian bomb. The US nuclear guarantee to NATO presumably would reassure Turkey, but there is speculation that to prevent proliferation in the region the US would have to extend its deterrent to additional nations. Whether such a step is possible or not—either because the presumed recipients would not like to have such close and public security ties to the US or because the US public might balk at a commitment to risk their own lives in defense of nations that are seen by many as foreign cultures that do not share American values, if not as enemies—remains to be seen.

NUCLEAR PLANS

The priority role of nuclear weapons in US security policy during the Cold War led to a massive investment in nuclear weapon systems and the infrastructure necessary to maintain it. Contemporary doctrine foresees a more circumscribed role for these weapons and the posture has been cut back sharply as a result. Similarly, the infrastructure has been permitted to wither.

US posture during the Cold War

"Only by the end of the 1950s, following fifteen years of nuclear weapon stockpiling and, most important, after the Soviet Union had developed similar weapons and delivery systems, did the concept of deterrence occupy center stage in American military and political strategy."[24] Though the declared US nuclear posture has remained based on the theory of deterrence since the 1950s, the approach to deterring adversarial aggression has undergone many transformations, usually in response to a call for greater flexibility in how nuclear weapons are to be used. Furthermore, the reality of US nuclear planning has not always coincided with the declared deterrent posture.

In 1954, Secretary Dulles suggested, "The heart of the problem is how to deter attack. This, we believe, requires that a potential aggressor be left in no doubt that he would be certain to suffer damage outweighing any possible gains from aggression."[25] The Eisenhower Administration's so-called "New Look" policy, a way to balance the Soviet conventional superiority with the threat of "massive retaliation," formed the beginning of a US strategy based on deterrence. The "New Look" policy threatened a major escalation in response to any Soviet aggression.

Where the Eisenhower Administration had threatened an escalation to nuclear use in response to any Soviet aggression, President Kennedy and Secretary of Defense Robert McNamara looked to provide greater flexibility and discrimination in nuclear targeting. Initially, Secretary McNamara called for a "counter-force" strategy, focusing the US nuclear arsenal on enemy forces, not cities. But with the Cuban Missile Crisis in 1962, the closest the Cold War came to turning hot, "the [counter-force] strategy had proven to be irrelevant," and the declaratory policy shifted to a strategy of "assured destruction," with American nuclear weapons focused predominantly on cities "adopted to warn of the dangers of nuclear war rather than to describe how a nuclear war should be fought if it had to be fought."[26] Thus began a declaratory posture of maintaining a second-strike capability, the ability for nuclear retaliation should an adversary decide to make first-use of nuclear weapons. Maintaining a second-strike capability required an increase in the manufacture of nuclear weapons, as Secretary McNamara testified before the House Armed Services Committee in 1963, "Because since no force can be completely invulnerable…we must buy more than we otherwise would buy."[27] But at the same time, as Soviet nuclear forces achieved parity with US nuclear forces, the Kennedy Administration chose not to impede Soviet realization of their own "assured destruction" capability, in hopes of achieving "mutual deterrence," a nuclear stalemate in which neither side could risk the use of nuclear weapons.

With a rapid build-up of delivery vehicles in the late 1960s, the Soviet missile inventory had surpassed that of the United States by 1971.[28] During this period, interest grew in counteracting the missile threat through Anti-Ballistic Missile (ABM) systems. Yet there was also a growing realization that an ABM system would be costly, probably ineffective, and lead to increased production of offensive counter-measures, escalating the arms race without real military gains. In response to the continued build-up of strategic nuclear offensive and defensive forces, Washington and Moscow announced the commencement of "Strategic Arms Limitation Talks" (SALT I) in 1969.[29] Following two and a half years of negotiations, the first round of SALT concluded with President Nixon and General Secretary Brezhnev signing the ABM Treaty, which included limiting the US and the Soviet Union to "two ABM deployment areas, so restricted and so located that they cannot provide a nationwide ABM defense or become the basis for developing one," and an Interim Agreement on Strategic Offensive Arms, a five year agreement freezing the number of missile launchers, and committing the two sides to continue talks on limiting strategic offensive arms.[30] Praising the ABM Treaty as one "without precedent in the nuclear age; indeed, in all relevant modern history," US Assistant for National Security Affairs Henry Kissinger stated, "We are compelled to coexist. We have an inescapable obligation to build jointly a structure for peace. Recognition of this reality is the beginning of wisdom for a sane and effective foreign policy today."[31] Similarly, Minister of Defense Marshal Andrei A. Grechko and Chief of the General Staff General Viktor G. Kulikov noted the ABM Treaty's significance in "preventing the emergence of a chain reaction of competition between offensive and defensive arms." [32] By providing limitations on strategic arms and limiting defensive capabilities to ensure each side retained its retaliatory capability, the Strategic Arms Limitation Talks slowed the arms race between the US and the USSR and provided a base for greater stability and predictability in the relationship of the two superpowers.

But the Nixon Administration, too, would look to change the US approach to deterrence, complaining that "Mutual Assured Destruction" failed to provide sufficient flexibility in response options. President Nixon posited, "Should a President, in the event of a nuclear attack, be left with the single option of ordering the mass destruction of enemy civilians, in the face of certainty that it would be followed by the mass slaughter of Americans?"[33] In 1974, Secretary of Defense James Schlesinger outlined the Nixon Administration's new approach to deterrence, focusing on maintaining "essential equivalence" in strategic forces, and a "flexibility of response" with a variety of limited, preplanned options available.[34] In planning for the availability of nuclear weapons in more limited roles than an all-out attack and "assured destruction" of enemy cities, including options to target military forces, the Nixon Administration claimed that the new US posture enhanced the deterrent ability of the US nuclear arsenal. The so-called "Schlesinger Doctrine" remained the basis of US nuclear planning for the next 25 years.

Regardless of the approach to deterrence, maintaining a second-strike capability played an important role in the declaratory policy of the Soviet Union and the United States throughout the Cold War and beyond. But despite the persistence of this declaratory posture, the reality is that US war-fighting plans were not always geared solely toward retaliation and deterrence. While US declaratory policy has consistently focused on retaliatory nuclear use, official doctrine has implied the possibility of disarming "first-strike" capabilities. The Kennedy Administration's initial "counter-force" strategy sought "to deter war by [the strategic retaliatory forces] capability to destroy the enemy's war-making capabilities," though many realized the implications of a first-strike in such a strategy.[35] The Nixon Administration's "Schlesinger Doctrine" stated that the primary deterrent objective "does not preclude US use of nuclear weapons in response to conventional aggression."[36] Additionally, the return of a counterforce option in the Nixon Administration's "flexible" nuclear planning once again implied the possibility of a first-strike, necessary to carry out such a strategy. While the reality persisted that a disarming first-strike was highly improbable from the late 1950s onward, planning remained in place to ensure that should the situation change, US forces would be ready to take advantage. US administrations have also sought ways out of the deterrent relationship through defensive measures. Early on, the Nixon Administration considered the creation of an ABM system to counteract the growing Soviet missile threat, before realizing that the prohibitive costs and likely ineffectiveness made the ABM Treaty a better option. The Reagan Administration similarly sought a missile defense system, the Strategic Defense Initiative, which the USSR feared could have provided the US with a credible first-strike capability and an escape from the deterrent relationship of the Cold War.

The US posture in the post-Cold War world

The end of the Cold War brought the beginning of dramatic reductions in the US and Soviet nuclear arsenals and improved relations between the two nations, if not immediate changes in nuclear policy. Since the early 1990s, the nuclear arsenals of both countries have decreased significantly. In September 1991, stating that the end of the Cold War brought with it "an unparalleled opportunity to change the nuclear posture of both the United States and the Soviet Union," President George H. W. Bush called for deep reductions in tactical nuclear weapons (TNW), "the most fundamental change in nuclear forces in over 40 years."[37]   In October, Soviet President Gorbachev similarly pledged the reduction of Soviet TNWs, a pledge that was reasserted in January 1992 by the new Russian President Boris Yeltsin. The so-called Presidential Nuclear Initiatives (PNI), a series of unilateral actions undertaken by the two superpowers, "led to perhaps 17,000 TNWs being withdrawn from service, the deepest reductions in nuclear arsenals to date."[38] In addition to limiting TNWs, President Bush also negotiated and signed the Strategic Arms Reduction Treaties (START) I and II. START I mandated each party to reduce and limit its deployed delivery vehicles to 1,600 and deployed warheads to 6,000. START II called for further reductions, but following years of being held up in the Russian Duma, never entered into force. Still, through the negotiation of START I and the PNIs, President Bush helped achieve significant reductions in deployed nuclear weapons, both strategic and tactical.

The most recent change in US nuclear posture came with the Bush Administration's 2001 Nuclear Posture Review (NPR), which, again recognizing the need for greater flexibility in nuclear planning, called for "Nuclear attack options that vary in scale, scope, and purpose [to] complement other military capabilities."[39] To provide this greater flexibility, the Bush Administration proposed the creation of new nuclear weapons; in particular, earth-penetrating "bunker busters" that could reach "hard and deeply-buried targets." The initiative was rejected by Congress, as was a subsequent proposal to build a more reliable warhead that would not require explosive testing, to replace existing weapons as they wore out. The NPR also sought to reduce reliance on nuclear weapons in some scenarios by positing the possibility of prompt, long-range strikes with conventionally armed missiles. The administration sought to implement this new policy by placing conventionally armed missiles on US strategic submarines, but this initiative, too, was rejected by the Congress.

To support modernization of the nuclear arsenal, the NPR called for, "A revitalized defense infrastructure that will provide new capabilities in a timely fashion to meet emerging threats."[40]   But this initiative also was never fully embraced, and infrastructure modernization has not approached the scope envisioned in the NPR. The NPR also called for reinvigorated development of ballistic missile defenses "to protect all 50 states, our deployed forces, and our friends and allies against ballistic missile attacks."[41]   With this new posture, President Bush announced the US withdrawal from the ABM Treaty, stating, "…we are on the path to a fundamentally different relationship. The Cold War is long gone. Today we leave behind one of its last vestiges."[42]   Russian responses varied, from the mild response of Russian President Putin, who, not surprised by the decision, called it, "mistaken," to the strong responses of Deputy Speaker of the Duma Vladimir Lukin, who called the decision, "worse than a crime," and Duma member Alexei Arbatov, who stated,

"Russia extended its hand full-length to meet the United States in the spirit of cooperation and even mutual alliance. And yesterday and today, the United States has spat into that extended hand." US development of a defensive missile shield remained a primary US focus and primary Russian concern throughout the Bush presidency.

Despite domestic and international concerns raised by the Bush Administration's focus on the creation of new offensive nuclear weapons, defensive ABM systems, and the mistaken perception that the new US nuclear posture increased the possibility of nuclear use by the US, the Bush nuclear posture brought coherence to the US declaratory posture and the reality of US nuclear planning. The 2001 NPR sought to narrow the role of nuclear weapons in US deterrent planning by integrating conventional weapons into the offensive deterrent and bringing a renewed focus on defensive capabilities. The idea that the US no longer views Russia as an adversary allowed for significant cuts in deployed nuclear weapons and resulted in the May 2002 signing of the "Strategic Offensive Reductions Treaty," limiting each side to between 1700-2200 deployed nuclear warheads. Similarly, attempts to integrate long range, conventional strike capabilities as a replacement for nuclear weapons in deterrence planning could justify a further decrease in the nuclear arsenal but, to date, Congress has refused to fund such projects.[43]

At the time this monograph went to press, the future direction of the US nuclear force was unknown. The Obama Administration is required by legislation to complete a review of the nuclear posture by the end of the year. It is likely that President Obama will continue the trend begun under President Bush, as he stated in April, "To put an end to Cold War thinking, we will reduce the role of nuclear weapons in our national security strategy, and urge others to do the same."[44] But in that same speech, President Obama went on to say, "Make no mistake: As long as these weapons exist, the United States will maintain a safe, secure and effective arsenal to deter any adversary, and guarantee that defense to our allies." If this is any indication of the upcoming policy decisions, nuclear weapons will likely continue to play a prominent, if not central, role in US strategic planning for the foreseeable future.

PROLIFERATION CONCERNS

The US has expressed great concern about nuclear proliferation virtually from the beginning of the nuclear age. After a single and perhaps not-so-serious attempt to eliminate nuclear weapons in the 1940s, the US has reacted to each addition to the nuclear club individually, depending on its relationship with the new nuclear power. The few exceptions include the initiative to negotiate the NPT following China's test of a nuclear device in 1964, establishment of the Nuclear Suppliers' Group to constrain trade in nuclear-related exports after India's misuse of reactors and special materials provided for civilian purposes by Canada and other nations in 1974, and efforts during the George W. Bush Administration to forge new types of informal multinational arrangements to constrain trade in nuclear-related items—the Proliferation Security Initiative and UNSC 1540. Generally, however, the US has tended to drag its feet when confronted by international efforts to impose more far-ranging solutions to the proliferation issue.

Global nonproliferation initiatives

On March 16, 1946, less than a year after the bombings of Nagasaki and Hiroshima and while the US was still the sole possessor of nuclear weapons, the US government published the first plan to address the prospect of nuclear proliferation, *The Report on the International Control of Atomic Energy*. Commonly known as the Acheson-Lilienthal Report, it advocated the creation of an International Atomic Development Authority to assume control over the most "dangerous" fuel cycle processes, i.e. uranium enrichment and reprocessing, and apply safeguards to them. Once the internationalized civilian energy infrastructure was operational, the plan asserted, the US would transfer its nuclear weapon components (fissile materials, laboratories, and warheads) to the international authority.

With several modifications that made the plan less attractive to the international community, President Truman's special advisor Bernard Baruch presented the report to the United Nations Atomic Energy Commission on June 14, 1946. In his speech to the UN, Baruch emphasized that the United States, still the world's only nuclear weapons power, would only stop warhead production and disarm once it was satisfied that the new internationalized fuel cycle controls had been implemented effectively, and when it was certain that the United States would not be threatened with biological or chemical weapons. The Baruch proposal could even be understood as suggesting that the US would need to be confident that the threat of warfare had been abolished before it would relinquish its nuclear weapons. In a more constructive addition, Baruch suggested that the UN Security Council should be the enforcing body for the nuclear ban, and that the permanent members of the Council should be stripped of their veto power when it came to these questions. The Baruch Plan was rejected by the Soviet Union and others as a disingenuous attempt by the US to institutionalize its nuclear arms monopoly.[45]

The next major global approach to stemming nuclear proliferation came two decades later in the form of the Treaty on the Non-Proliferation of Nuclear Weapons (NPT). The NPT's procedural origin was a 1961 UN General Assembly resolution that called for the negotiation of a treaty that would bar the proliferation of weapons, as well as the control of those weapons and relevant knowledge about them. Initial attempts to enlist the Soviet Union in negotiations to implement the resolution were unsuccessful, but the US was not really enthusiastic either. After China tested a nuclear weapon in 1964, however, President Lyndon Johnson established the Gilpatric Committee to examine alternative means of stemming proliferation. As previously noted, one idea that had been discussed for some time was to establish a multi-national nuclear force (MNF) within NATO. The arrangement was intended to persuade countries like Germany that it was not necessary for them to develop their own nuclear weapons, but in Soviet eyes, establishing the MNF conflicted with the principle of nonproliferation. In the end, the US decided against the MNF and the Soviet Union agreed to talks on a non-proliferation treaty.[46] A US-Soviet draft was subsequently presented to the Conference on Disarmament and the completed treaty was signed by the US on July 1, 1968. As one of five nuclear-weapon-states recognized by the NPT, the US committed itself "to pursue negotiations in good faith on effective measures relating to cessation of the nuclear arms race at an early date and to nuclear disarmament, and on a treaty on general and complete disarmament under strict and effective international control."[47]

In order to coordinate observance and enforcement of the NPT's Article III, which prohibits the transfer of nuclear equipment and materials for peaceful uses unless the transferred materials were safeguarded against diversion for military purposes, the signatory states with the potential to export such materials formed the Zangger Committee, also known as the NPT Exporters Committee, and sought to compel non-signatories to accept International Atomic Energy Agency (IAEA) safeguards before receiving relevant imports.[††] Following India's 1974 nuclear detonation, France, which was not yet an NPT signatory, joined the US and other Zangger Committee members in establishing a more robust export control regime known as the Nuclear Suppliers Group (NSG). The NSG restricts both materials and technologies (fissile materials, reactors, and so forth) that are directly usable in the production of nuclear weapons, as well as so-called "dual-use items," that have legitimate non-nuclear applications but can also be used for producing fissile materials or warheads.[48] Examples are certain types of aluminum tubes that have many innocent uses, but that also could be used to make centrifuges for enriching uranium.

The nuclear export regime was also strengthened in 1992 when the US led an effort to require so-called "full scope safeguards" before nuclear materials and equipment could be transferred to a country, meaning that not only the reactor for which the materials were intended needed to be safeguarded, but all nuclear facilities in the purchasing country had to have such safeguards.[49]

[††]"Each State Party to the Treaty undertakes not to provide: (a) source or special fissionable material, or (b) equipment or material especially designed or prepared for the processing, use, or production of special fissionable material, to any non-nuclear-weapon State for peaceful purposes, unless the source or special fissionable material shall be subject to the safeguards required by this article." NPT, Article III, paragraph 2. *Ibid.*

Although the US played a key role in strengthening the non-proliferation regime for many years, Washington significantly weakened it in 2008 with a campaign to waive the prohibition on nuclear exports to states that had not signed the NPT for India. Though packaged as a nonproliferation initiative by US officials, it clearly reflected US perceptions that developing a strategic partnership with India, as well as certain commercial interests, were more important than the integrity of the nonproliferation regime. On September 6, 2008, following the United States' intense lobbying of fellow member-states, the Nuclear Suppliers' Group reluctantly exempted India from its requirement that recipient states must have their entire nuclear complex safeguarded.[50] While both governments claimed the agreement would bring India into the "nonproliferation mainstream," it allowed favorable conditions in the nuclear trade with a country that had developed a nuclear arsenal outside the NPT, much to the consternation of countries that had remained within the NPT framework and therefore foregone developing weapons. To other NSG members, it was peculiar that one of only three states that never signed the NPT and, indeed, whose misuse of imported civilian nuclear materials for a nuclear test had inspired the export group's founding, would be selected for such an exemption. Pakistan and Israel, the two other nuclear, yet non-signatory states to the NPT, have continued to push for a "criteria-based approach" to determining a state's eligibility to engage in nuclear trade, hoping that they might be in line to receive a similar deal.[51]

The US, like all the other nuclear weapon states, has paid greater lip-service than serious attention to the NPT's Article VI commitment to disarmament. The carefully hedged formulation of the Article has been interpreted by the US, as by the other nuclear weapon states, as a mandate for negotiations toward arms reductions, rather than as a mandate to act seriously and promptly to eliminate nuclear weapons. The nuclear weapon states also see the link stated in the Article between nuclear disarmament and "general and complete disarmament" as an acknowledgement that radical changes in the international environment would be necessary before it would become possible to eliminate nuclear weapons.

The NPT includes a provision requiring periodic reviews of the Treaty with the possibility that it would be permitted to expire after 25 years, or in 1995. The United States lobbied heavily and successfully for the indefinite extension of the Treaty during that year's review conference. To secure the consent of the non-weapon states displeased by the slow progress that had been made toward disarmament, the US and the other weapon states made a series of commitments, including completion of a comprehensive test ban treaty (CTBT) and a treaty to cut-off the production of fissile materials, as well as further reductions in the size of nuclear arsenals. At the 2000 Review Conference, under President Clinton, the United States and the other weapon states agreed to 13 "practical steps" toward implementing Article VI, which address these three issues more specifically, and added retention of the Anti-Ballistic Missile Treaty, the de-alerting of nuclear forces, the beginning of negotiations for complete disarmament, and declarations of excess fissile materials, among other measures. However, two years later the Bush Administration indicated that the US no longer supported the 13 steps.[52] US refusal to follow through on this agreement was a major contributing factor to the 2005 Review Conference's acrimonious failure; the conference was unable to agree on any joint statement. Instead, the "Final Document" essentially said the NPT signatories had met.[53]

Generally speaking, the Bush Administration preferred greater flexibility through informal arrangements among like-minded states than formal treaties. Throughout the president's two terms, the administration was inclined to respond to problems by assembling informal coalitions to work specific issues. On the nuclear front, this inclination manifested itself through the Proliferation Security Initiative and the Global Initiative to Combat Nuclear Terrorism. Both initiatives were part of an overarching drive to "enhance the capabilities of our military, intelligence, technical, and law enforcement communities to prevent the movement of WMD materials, technology, and expertise to hostile states and terrorist organizations."[54]

The 2003 Proliferation Security Initiative is "an activity, not an organization," which aims to enhance cooperation among states to interdict the movement of materials related to weapons of mass destruction (WMD) across international borders, particularly shipping routes.[55] The Initiative has conducted several dozen exercises with partner nations and, according to US officials, has successfully interdicted a number of shipments related to WMD or their delivery systems.[‡‡]

Born in 2005 under joint US-Russian chairmanship, the Global Initiative to Combat Nuclear Terrorism aims to "prevent the acquisition, transport, or use by terrorists of nuclear materials and radioactive substances or improvised explosive devices using such materials, as well as hostile actions against nuclear facilities." This goal is to be accomplished by cooperative capacity-building in other states and assist in the implementation of UNSCR 1540. Introduced by the United States, the Resolution requires all states to enact anti-proliferation measures to secure all relevant materials. For those states unable to fulfill their obligations, the US has offered assistance to build that capacity.[56]

[‡‡] Robert G. Joseph, "Broadening and Deepening Our Proliferation Security Initiative Cooperation," Warsaw Poland (June 23, 2006). http://poland.usembassy.gov/poland/joseph_remarks.html. The PSI is credited with the seizure of the ship, *BBC China*, which was carrying nuclear materials from Pakistan to Libya, thus revealing both Libya's nuclear program and the AQ Khan nuclear smuggling operation.

President Obama seems to prefer a return to the more formal treaty route and has suggested turning "efforts such as the Proliferation Security Initiative and the Global Initiative to Combat Nuclear Terrorism into durable international institutions," a process he plans to initiate by hosting a global summit.[57]

Responses to individual proliferators

As the first nuclear-armed nation, the United States reacted to those that followed based on the threat level that US policymakers believed the proliferator posed to US interests. The Soviet Union's first detonation in 1948 yielded a nuclear arms race in which both sides attempted to out-produce one another with massive increases in nuclear arsenals. After the Cuban Missile Crisis, diplomatic means were sought to mutually constrain capabilities and the US stockpile steadily declined after its 1966 peak.[58] The next major nuclear breakthroughs by potential adversaries were met by the establishment and strengthening of the global non-proliferation regime. After US intelligence was surprised by China's sooner-than-expected development of a nuclear weapon, the United States prioritized the pursuit of a nonproliferation ban with universal reach, as described previously. US defense planners also announced the deployment of a missile defense system, aimed at neutralizing China's small ballistic missile force.[59] After India's first explosion in 1974, the US sought to develop curbs on trade in nuclear materials and supporting equipment so as to prevent countries from diverting civilian nuclear materials into weapon programs.

Allied countries' weapons programs have provoked less concern in the US government, though responses have ranged from complicity to reluctant acceptance to vigorous opposition. The US was fully complicit in the United Kingdom's development of an arsenal, which has never been fully autonomous from the US despite British insistence on calling it an "independent deterrent." British scientists participated in the Manhattan Project and its current nuclear-armed submarine fleet depends on US provision of Trident missiles. The French weapons project was largely undertaken in an effort to gain independence from the United States, both symbolically and operationally. The French deterrent assumed a key role in the unfolding acrimonious relationship between De Gaulle's France and the United States, even though the United States was more concerned about the broader political symbolism of the French nuclear force than proliferation itself. Indeed, the US even offered its NATO ally the nuclear-capable Polaris missiles as a way to mend the relationship at the time, and eventually helped the French to develop the technology for multiple independently targetable reentry vehicles.[60]

France, in turn, provided Israel with the foundation of its nuclear capability. The United States was kept in the dark by the Israelis about their intentions, but formed its Middle East policy on the assumption that Israel was at the very least capable of quickly assembling a nuclear weapon beginning in 1970.[61] Presented with a covert *fait accomplis*, however, the United States did not react in any significant way, even though it occurred after negotiation and implementation of the NPT, which Israel has not signed to this day. The US posture vis-à-vis the Israeli bomb was worked out in secret discussions between President Richard Nixon and Israeli Prime Minister Golda Meir in 1969 and has more or less remained in place ever since.[62] Many suspect that the Israelis even tested a nuclear bomb in the atmosphere with the help of South Africa in 1979 and that the US helped to cover up the incident.

Despite its displeasure with both the Indian and Pakistani nuclear programs, the US deliberately avoided making a public issue of them for years, and exerted some private pressure to keep the capability ambiguous, for instance by lobbying against further tests after India's 1974 "peaceful" nuclear explosion.[63] The initial impulse among US officials was a lead-by-example unilateral trade restriction. Secretary of State Henry Kissinger instead convened the founding meeting of what was to become the Nuclear Suppliers Group in April 1975 in order to prevent other countries from filling the supply gap.[64] Congress also enacted legislation to require a US vote against World Bank assistance for India, but no efforts were made to enlist other countries to vote similarly.[65]

In Pakistan, the development of nuclear weapons beginning in the late 1970s made an uncomfortable fit for US policy, as the country was home to several US facilities used to monitor military activities in the Soviet Union and became an essential conduit for US support to the Mujaheddin opposing the Soviet Union's occupation of neighboring Afghanistan during the 1980s. As a result, the US found ways around the automatic cut-off of military and financial assistance that was required by law. For example, beginning in 1982, "Congress created eight Presidential waiver authorities exclusively on Pakistan's behalf, and five of these were exercised." Later on, the Pakistani program had become so visible that the country could no longer be certified not to possess nuclear weapons, but by that time US restraint had allowed the creation of "a fairly unimpeded Pakistani weapons program that led to nuclear tests in 1998."[66] The Carter Administration's National Security Advisor Zbigniew Brzezinski made it clear that this was fully intended: "Our national security policy toward Pakistan cannot be dictated by our non-proliferation policy."[67] The harsh sanctions imposed on India and Pakistan after the 1998 tests were also whittled away with waivers and changes within a matter of months. Even revelation of A.Q. Khan's nuclear black market activities did not produce a substantive response by the United States, in large part due to the need for Pakistan's support for US and NATO forces in Afghanistan.

On the other hand, South Africa's covert development of a small arsenal became a priority in US relations with that country. This was in part by design, given that the arsenal's raison d'être was to attract the attention of the United States and Great

Britain during a crisis. A contributing factor was the lack of information on the true capabilities of the South Africans, in particular the controversy over the possible Israeli – South African nuclear test in the late 1970s. As the signals became clearer, however, the United States devoted considerable high-level resources to tempering the apartheid regime's nuclear ambitions. The most notable instance was the Soviet Union's revelation of South Africa's test preparations in 1977, which prompted cooperation among the two Cold War rivals to pressure South Africa to refrain. Given US discomfort with the domestic political arrangements of the proliferator, the South African case again shows the US habit of coming down harder on proliferators that it finds distasteful or threatening.

However, US tolerance for allied proliferation also has had its limits. South Korea and Taiwan started on the path of developing nuclear weapons capabilities in the 1970s, but were threatened with the withdrawal of military protection if they continued. Indeed, Taiwan attempted to create a weapons capability twice, once in the late 1970s and then again a decade later. The United States forced Taiwan to accept verification procedures and asked for the return of separated plutonium from US-origin fuels. The US was responsible for ending Taiwan's drive for a reprocessing capability on both occasions.[68] A similar effort by South Korea was stopped by US pressure on France not to supply reprocessing technology. The US government also strongly pressured its East Asian ally to sign the NPT, which it did in 1975, even though South Korea's clandestine activities continued for several years.[69] In both these cases, the strong US response was probably motivated by concern that the programs would provoke China and destabilize East Asia.

In the cases of states that are non-compliant with their non-proliferation obligations, with which the US already has a hostile relationship, the US has taken hawkish positions to ensure compliance. The most extreme expression of this has been the US overthrow of the Saddam Hussein regime in Iraq, ostensibly because of that government's pursuit of weapons of mass destruction. The United States also led the so-far unsuccessful international effort against Iran's violations of its NPT safeguards. With the 2002 revelation of Iran's clandestine uranium enrichment, the United States has attempted to ensure Iranian compliance and, more broadly, tried to prevent Iran from acquiring a weapon capability. Toward this end, the US has pushed in the UN Security Council for increasingly harsh sanctions but, until 2009, refused to participate directly in European diplomatic efforts to gain Iranian compliance through a package of economic and political incentives. Many observers believe that the US refusal to negotiate directly with Iran, as well as its hostility to the government itself and military presence in the region, has made negotiations much more difficult.[70]

The US has also led the effort to stop the North Korean weapons program. Of course, North Korea's primary motivation for breaking out of the NPT and acquiring nuclear weapons is assumed to be to deter a US attack. The US successfully negotiated a freeze of North Korea's nuclear program bilaterally in 1994, the so-called "Agreed Framework," bringing the first nuclear crisis between the US and North Korea to an end. When the Bush Administration terminated the Agreement as a result of its discovery of a covert North Korean uranium enrichment program in 2002, the North Koreans resumed building plutonium-based weapons and eventually tested one in 2006. After first refusing to negotiate with Pyongyang, the United States organized the so-called "Six Party Talks" to resolve the situation. These talks resulted in a North Koran commitment to dismantle its nuclear weapons and production complex, but the agreement has yet to be implemented and, at the time this paper was written, North Korea had just conducted its second nuclear test and was threatening to resume production of plutonium.[71]

As the only country to have initiated a war chiefly on counter-proliferation grounds, it would seem that US concerns about nuclear proliferation are sincere.[§§] US reactions to individual proliferators, however, show that although US administrations are willing to devote resources and high-level attention to the problem, they often will subsume misgivings about the spread of nuclear weapons to other significant and competing geopolitical interests. Still, when it decides to promote a universal, rule-based solution to the problem—as was the case with the NPT and the subsequent Nuclear Suppliers Group—the United States takes the process seriously and works to advance its interests through it. If a US administration agreed to a disarmament agreement, it could be expected behave in the same way.

US DISARMAMENT DIPLOMACY

Early in its first term, the Reagan Administration's public discourse on expanding the US nuclear arsenal and fighting protracted nuclear wars led to a public backlash that found expression in the "nuclear freeze movement." The movement gained significant domestic and international support and had important effects on the president's policy formation, particularly when it proved to be a potent political force in the 1982 mid-term elections. In that year, President Reagan publicly expressed his own abhorrence for nuclear weapons, stating, "a nuclear war cannot be won and must never be fought."[72] He reiterated this sentiment many times over the following years, including in his 1984 State of the Union address, in which he

---

[§§] The proliferation case for the war was made by then Secretary of State Colin Powell in a presentation to the UN Security Council on February 6th, 2003. In addition to concerns about alleged biological and chemical weapons, he identified a nuclear casus belli: "We have no indication that Saddam Hussein has ever abandoned his nuclear weapons program. On the contrary, we have more than a decade of proof that he remains determined to acquire nuclear weapons." Colin L. Powell, "Remarks to the United Nations Security Council" (February 5, 2003). http://www.globalsecurity.org/wmd/library/news/iraq/2003/iraq-030205-powell-un-17300pf.htm.

stated, "The only value in our two nations possessing nuclear weapons is to make sure they will never be used. But then would it not be better to do away with them entirely?"[73]

However, discussing the possibility of disarmament was only half of the Reagan Administration's approach to ending the threat of nuclear war. In a televised speech on March 23, 1983, President Reagan introduced his idea for a defensive approach to countering the nuclear threat, the Strategic Defense Initiative (SDI), calling upon the American scientific community "to give us the means of rendering these nuclear weapons impotent and obsolete" through the creation of a missile defense shield to counter incoming missiles.[74] But the Soviets feared a US missile defense system would upset the deterrent balance, and though negotiations between the two sides led to agreement to ban an entire class of intermediate-range missiles, President Reagan's and General Secretary Mikhail Gorbachev's talks on disarmament were unable to move beyond the two leaders general agreement on the desirability of the goal.

As the enmities of the Cold War faded later in the 1980s, the United States and the Soviet Union were able to quickly reach agreement on deeper reductions in their long-range strategic forces in the START Treaty, and, once the Soviet Union fell in 1991, President George H.W. Bush and Russian President Boris Yeltsin were able to agree to unilaterally remove nuclear weapons from naval vessels and make other reductions in shorter range weapons.[75]

During the Clinton years, US-Russia progress halted and the United States seemed to focus more on multilateral forums. From 1993-1996, for example, the United States assumed a leadership role in the successful negotiation of a comprehensive test ban at the Conference on Disarmament. This accomplishment was a crucial contributor to the 1995 agreement to extend the NPT indefinitely. Subsequently, however, the Senate declined to provide its consent to ratification. Most observers believe that political factors, rather than the merits of the treaty, determined the Senate's vote. Opponents of the treaty argued that the US needed to maintain its option to test in order to retain confidence in its stockpile and that it was impossible to verify (let alone enforce) compliance with the test ban. Subsequent scientific investigations into these objections have rejected the validity of these concerns to the satisfaction of mainstream observers, even if a core of treaty opponents remains unconvinced.[76] President Obama has promised to "immediately and aggressively pursue US ratification of the Comprehensive Test Ban Treaty," and has appointed Vice President Biden to oversee the task.[77]

President Obama also has promised to "seek a new treaty that verifiably ends the production of fissile materials intended for use in state nuclear weapons."[78] Limits on the production of fissile material for weapons purposes have long been sought by the United States. In his "Atoms for Peace" speech to the UN in 1953, President Eisenhower stated, "The United States would seek more than the mere reduction or elimination of atomic materials for military purposes."[79] A US-drafted resolution passed by the UN General Assembly in 1957 called on the Conference on Disarmament (CD) to pursue a disarmament agreement providing for "the cessation of the production of fissionable materials for weapons purposes..."[80] In 1964, President Lyndon Johnson renewed the call for an end to fissile material production in his State of the Union Address, stating, "Even in the absence of agreement, we must not stockpile arms beyond our needs...."[81] Later that year, President Johnson followed through on this call with a unilateral cut in US production of fissile materials for weapon purposes. While unilateral moves over the next three decades limited production of fissile materials for weapon purposes, the US push for an international agreement banning production faded.

In 1993, President Clinton renewed the call for negotiations of a Fissile Materials Cut-off Treaty (FMCT) in an address to the UN General Assembly, leading to a UN Resolution that recommended "a non-discriminatory, multilateral and internationally and effectively verifiable treaty banning the production of fissile material for nuclear weapons or other nuclear explosive devices."[82] In 1996, President Clinton again called on the CD to negotiate a freeze on fissile materials production, stating it "should take up this challenge immediately." The CD established a committee to begin discussions in 1998, but the talks quickly deadlocked, as China linked the FMCT discussions to limits on military uses of space.[83] In 2006, the Bush Administration presented a draft FMCT to the CD, calling for an end to the production of "fissile material for use in nuclear weapons or other nuclear explosive devices."[84] But the proposal was lacking, as its scope was limited to future production, did not require ratification by key states with unsafeguarded enrichment and reprocessing plants, such as Israel, India, and Pakistan to enter into force, and it contained no provisions for verification.[85] This reflected the Bush Administration's stance that verification was impossible, a belief the Obama Administration does not share.

MOVING TO ZERO

Concerns about proliferation and nuclear terrorism have prompted renewed unofficial, bipartisan, mainstream calls for the elimination of nuclear weapons. For the first time, senior statesmen in the United States, the UK, Russia, China, and India have talked seriously about the need to eliminate all nuclear weapons, from all nations. The trend began with two *Wall Street Journal* op-eds in 2007 and 2008 by former Secretaries of State George Schultz and Henry Kissinger, former Secretary of Defense William Perry, and former senator Sam Nunn. In the articles, these respected voices on national security issues called on the US to provide leadership in reversing the global dependence on nuclear weapons and ultimately moving the world toward the elimination of nuclear weapons, calling this a "bold initiative consistent with America's moral heritage." Although the overall tone of the articles suggested that these four statesmen believe eliminating nuclear weapons to be a realistic goal, as a practical matter they argue that attention should be paid first to measures that could be implemented in the near-term, establishing "paving stones" on the "road to zero."[86]

Esteemed foreign policy experts in other countries have echoed these path-breaking calls for eliminating nuclear weapons. In the UK, for example, former Foreign Ministers Douglas Hurd, Malcolm Rifkind, and David Owen, and former Secretary of State for Defense and Secretary General of NATO George Robertson wrote in the London Times, "The ultimate aspiration should be to have a world free of nuclear weapons. It will take time, but with political will and improvements in monitoring, the goal is achievable."[87] In Germany, former Chancellor Helmut Schmidt, former President Richard von Weizsäcker, former Foreign Minister Hans-Dietrich Genscher, and former Socialist Party leader Egon Bahr wrote a parallel piece.[88] India's venerable grand master of national security strategy, K. Subrahmanyan, has written similarly, "India should attempt to regain its earlier reputation as a champion of a nuclear weapon free world."[89] Finally, in Paris in December 2008, more than 100 leaders from 23 countries came together under the banner of "Global Zero" to kick off a world-wide campaign to persuade the governments of the nuclear weapon states to negotiate a treaty to eliminate nuclear weapons by a date certain.[90]

Many governments have also expressed their desire to attain the "goal" of eliminating nuclear weapons, or have discussed the "vision" of a nuclear-free world. Russian Prime Minister Putin, for example, has said, "I believe it is now quite possible to liberate humanity from nuclear weapons…"[91] Similarly, China has stated that it, "stands for the comprehensive prohibition and complete elimination of nuclear weapons."[92]

US leaders have been equally vocal on the desirability of a nuclear-free world, which became a conspicuous point of agreement during the 2008 presidential campaign. Candidate Barack Obama stated, "A world without nuclear weapons is profoundly in America's interest and the world's interest. It is our responsibility to make the commitment, and to do the hard work to make this vision a reality. That's what I've done as a Senator and a candidate, and that's what I'll do as President."[93] Interestingly, his conservative Republican opponent, Senator John McCain, made a similar statement, "A quarter of a century ago, President Ronald Reagan declared, 'our dream is to see the day when nuclear weapons will be banished from the face of the Earth.' That is my dream, too."[94]

On his first transatlantic trip, President Obama set out his nuclear agenda, identifying as its centerpiece "America's commitment to seek the peace and security of a world without nuclear weapons," though with the caveat that it, "will not be reached quickly – perhaps not in my lifetime." He outlined his view of how the goal could be achieved, beginning with the pursuit of CTBT ratification, the negotiation of a fissile materials cut-off treaty, a "new framework for civil nuclear cooperation, including an international fuel bank," a reduction of, "the role of nuclear weapons in our national security strategy," and a "legally binding and sufficiently bold" strategic arms reductions treaty with Russia. These reductions would then "set the stage for further cuts" that would "include all nuclear weapons states."[95]

Whether US-Russian strategic reductions and the pursuit of CTBT ratification and a fissile materials treaty will translate into tangible movement toward eliminating nuclear weapons as envisioned by the president remains to be seen and will depend on how rapidly progress might be made toward these near-term steps and on broader trends in international relationships. It is evident that the United States will have to take the lead if progress is to be made. Together, the US and Russia own roughly 95 percent of the world's nuclear arsenal, having perhaps ten thousand weapons each, including inactive warheads, while no other nation is believed to have more than a few hundred.[96] Each of the smaller powers, with some justification, point to the need for the US and Russia to make further reductions in their weapon stocks before multinational negotiations for eliminating nuclear weapons could even be considered.[97] Moreover, although Prime Minister Putin has expressed support for the goal of zero weapons, as noted above, in recent years, Russian military doctrine has placed new emphasis on these weapons. Facing sharp deterioration in the quality of its conventional military forces, Russia has taken a page from NATO's book and ended the Soviet Union's long-standing "no-first nuclear use" policy. Although this policy was never reflected in Soviet war plans or equipment, and despite the slow pace of Russian modernization of its nuclear forces, the doctrinal change suggests that while further reductions in Russian forces are possible, Moscow will be reluctant to move seriously into a negotiation aimed at eliminating all nuclear weapons until outstanding issues between it and the West are resolved.[98] However, the surprising joint statement by presidents Obama and Medvedev in April 2009, announcing that they had "committed our two countries to achieving a nuclear free world," is an encouraging sign of the potential for progress in that direction.[99]

Writing in the Obama Administration's earliest days, it is difficult to predict how seriously the president's rhetorical support for eliminating nuclear weapons will be taken. It is certainly good politics—domestic and international—to support zero weapons as a goal or vision; actually seeking to begin negotiations toward that end is something else. The administration would certainly be split on such a political initiative internally. Secretary of Defense Robert Gates, for example, a hold-over from the Bush Administration, has indicated he doesn't believe the goal to be a realistic policy option, stating, "… the power of nuclear weapons and their strategic impact is a genie that cannot be put back in the bottle, at least for a very long time. While we have a long-term goal of abolishing nuclear weapons once and for all, given the world in which we live, we have to be realistic about that proposition."[100] Secretary of State Hillary Clinton reaffirmed the Obama Administration's nuclear elimination goal during her nomination hearing before the Senate Foreign Relations Committee, but key appointments at Defense, State, and the National Security Council have tended to favor incremental approaches to arms reductions in their writings and previous government service.***

The issue will probably be discussed in the context of the "Nuclear Posture Review," which the administration is required by legislation to submit in December, 2009. Proponents of a more visionary approach will not be helped by the Congressional Commission on the Strategic Posture of the United States, which the same legislation also established. In its final report, and despite the fact that its chairman is former Secretary of Defense William Perry, one of the four senior statesmen who kicked off the new attention to nuclear elimination, the Commission stated that, "The conditions that might make the elimination of nuclear weapons possible are not present today and establishing such conditions would require a fundamental transformation of the world political order."[101] This phrase may be interpreted to mean that the current international system would have to morph into some sort of world government before nuclear weapons could eliminated, meaning that the "vision of a nuclear-free world," will always remain just that, a "vision."

In all likelihood, the Obama Administration will continue to pay rhetorical obeisance to the goal of nuclear elimination, if for no other reason than to help reduce problems at the NPT Review Conference to be held in June 2010, but will focus on four tangible actions:

- Attempting to persuade Iran to halt its nuclear weapons program short of an overt capability;
- Attempting to cajole North Korea into resuming progress toward fulfillment of its commitment to dismantle its nuclear weapons and supporting infrastructure;

*** "I take to heart what the chairman said about trying to reduce our numbers even lower. This incoming president, like all presidents, has been committed to the end of nuclear weapons, as long as we can be assured that we have adequate deterrents and that we are protected going forward. So we're going to enter it with that frame of mind, which is quite a change." Hillary Rodham Clinton, "Confirmation Hearing," (January 13, 2009). http://www.cfr.org/publication/18225/transcript_of_hillary_clintons_confirmation_hearing.html

- Negotiating a new, verifiable agreement with Russia for deeper reductions in the two nations' nuclear arsenals, perhaps broadening the limits from their past focus on so-called "strategic" or long-range weapons to encapsulate shorter range weapons, as well as reserve warheads; and
- Seeking ratification of the Comprehensive Test Ban Treaty by the US Senate and, if successful, persuading other key states, especially China, India, Israel, and Pakistan to follow suit.

The first three items on this agenda, of course, are interlinked with a broader range of issues between the United States and the government in question. One would be hard-pressed to predict success in all three. The fourth depends largely on the ebb and flow of politics in the US, for example, whether Republicans will see it in their interest to present a united front against the president as a matter of principal. Nonetheless, should President Obama indeed live up to his reputation of deftly achieving difficult goals and manages to achieve most of the short-term agenda above, the possibility of a far-reaching initiative to start multinational discussions about the elimination of nuclear weapons could be a distinct possibility in the president's second term.

ENDNOTES

[1] Ward Wilson, "The Winning Weapon?," *International Security*, 31 (Spring, 2007), pages 162-79.

[2] Dwight D. Eisenhower, *The Whitehouse Years: Mandate for Change, 1953-1956* (Garden City, NY: Doubleday, 1963), page 181.

[3] Barry M. Blechman and Robert Powell, "What in the Name of God is Strategic Superiority?," *Political Science Quarterly*, 97 (Winter 1982-83), pages 589-602.

[4] Morton H. Halperin, "Chinese Nuclear Strategy," *The China Quarterly*, 21 (March, 1965), pages 77-78.

[5] Eisenhower's recollection as recounted in Stephen E. Ambrose, *Eisenhower, vol. 2* (New York; Simon & Schuster, 1983), page 184.

[6] Barry M. Blechman and Stephen S. Kaplan, *Force Without War: U.S. Armed Forces as a Political Instrument* (Washington, D.C.: Brookings Institution Press, 1978), page 193. There are currently over 30 states under the US nuclear umbrella.

[7] U.S. Department of State, *Foreign Relations of the United States, 1952-1954: Volume II. National Security Affairs* (Washington, D.C.: GPO, 1984), page 126.

[8] Hastings L. Ismay, *NATO: The First Five Years, 1949-1954* (Paris: North Atlantic Treaty Organization, 1954). http://www.nato.int/archives/1st5years/annexes/b5.htm

[9] NATO Military Committee. *The Most Effective Pattern of NATO Military Strength for the Next Few Years (MC 48)* (North Atlantic Treaty Organization, 1954). http://www.nato.int/docu/stratdoc/eng/a541122a.pdf

[10] Robert S. Norris, William M. Arkin and William Burr, "Where They Were," *The Bulletin of the Atomic Scientists* 55 (November/December, 1999), pages 29-30.

[11] Dwight D. Eisenhower, *op.cit.,* page 336.

[12] John F. Kennedy, "Radio and Television Report to the American People on the Berlin Crisis," http://www.jfklibrary.org/Historical+Resources/Archives/Reference+Desk/Speeches/JFK/003POF 03BerlinCrisis07251961.htm

[13] Richard G. Head, "Technology and the Military Balance," *Foreign Affairs*, 56 (April 1978), pages 550-51, 558-59.

[14] Robert S. Norris and Hans M. Kristensen, "U.S. Nuclear Forces, 2008," *The Bulletin of the Atomic Scientists*, 64, no. 1 (March/April 2008), pages 50-58; Robert S. Norris and Hans M. Kristensen, "Russian Nuclear Forces, 2008," *The Bulletin of the Atomic Scientists*, 64, no. 2 (May/June 2008), pages 54-57.

[15] Warren Hoge and Sheryl Gay Stolberg, "Bush Rebukes North Korea; U.S. Seeks New U.N. Sanctions," *New York Times* (October 10, 2006), page A1.

[16]The White House, "Remarks by the National Security Advisor, Stephen Hadley, to the Center for International Security and Cooperation," (February 8, 2008). http://georgewbush-whitehouse.archives.gov/news/releases/2008/02/20080211-6.html

[17]Quoted in Don Oberdorfer, *The Two Koreas: A Contemporary History* (New York: Basic Books, 2001), page 257.

[18] For the debate on the "window of vulnerability," see Paul H. Nitze, "Assuring Strategic Stability in an Era of Detente," *Foreign Affairs*, 54 (January 1976): pages 207-32; Jan M. Lodal, "Assuring Strategic Stability: An Alternative View," *Foreign Affairs*, 54 (April 1976): pages 462-481; Paul H. Nitze, "Strategic Stability," *Foreign Affairs*, 54 (July 1976); pages 820-23.

[19] Ivo Daalder and Jan Lodal, "The Logic of Zero: Toward a World Without Nuclear Weapons," *Foreign Affairs*, 87, no. 6 (November/December 2008), pages 80-95; Arnold Kanter, Morton Halperin, and Barry Blechman. "How Many Nuclear Weapons Do We Need?" (Washington, DC, New America Foundation, May 7, 2008).

[20] Congressional Commission on the Strategic Posture of the United States, *America's Strategic Posture: The Final Report of the Congressional Commission on the Strategic Posture of the United States* (United States Institute of Peace, 2009), page 29.

[21] Martin Butcher et al., *NATO Nuclear Sharing and the NPT - Questions to be Answered,* (The Project on European Nuclear Non-Proliferation, June 1997). http://www.bits.de/public/researchnote/rn97-3.htm.

Currently, 180 of the approximately 480 US nuclear bombs forward deployed in NATO countries are set aside for delivery by non-nuclear NATO states. Hans M. Kristensen, *U.S. Nuclear Weapons in Europe: A Review of Post-Cold War Policy, Force Levels, and War Planning,* (National Resources Defense Council, February 2005), page 11.

[22] Jonathan D. Pollack and Mitchell B. Reiss, "South Korea: The Tyranny of Geography and the Vexations of History," in *The Nuclear Tipping Point: Why States Reconsider Their Nuclear Choices,* edited by Kurt M. Campbell, Robert J. Einhorn, and Mitchell B. Reiss (Washington, DC: The Brookings Institution, 2004) page 263; Derek J. Mitchell, "Taiwan's Hsin Chu Program: Deterrence, Abandonment, and Honor," in *The Nuclear Tipping Point: Why States Reconsider Their Nuclear Choices, op.cit.,* page 301.

[23] *Economist*, February 1996.

[24] Alekseĭ Georgievich Arbatov, Vladimir Dvorkin, Vladimir Evseev, and John D. Steinbruner, *Beyond Nuclear Deterrence* (Carnegie Endowment, 2006), page 17.

[25] John Foster Dulles, "Policy for Security and Peace," *Foreign Affairs* 32 (April 1954), page 358.

[26] Lawrence Freedman, *The Evolution of Nuclear Strategy* (International Institute for Strategic Studies, 1989), pages 244-246.

[27] Quoted in Lawrence Freedman, *Ibid,* page 241.

[28] Martin McGuire, "A Quantitative Study of the Strategic Arms Race in the Missile Age," *The Review of Economics and Statistics* 59 (August 1977) page 329.

[29] US Department of State, *Strategic Arms Limitation Talks (SALT I)*, http://www.state.gov/www/global/arms/treaties/salt1.html

[30] Treaty Between the United States of America and the Union of Soviet Socialist Republics on the Limitation of Anti-Ballistic Missile Systems, 23 UST 3435, TIAS 7503 (1972) http://www.state.gov/www/global/arms/treaties/abm/abm2.html; Interim Agreement Between the United States of America and the Union of Soviet Socialist Republics on Certain Measures with Respect to The Limitation of Strategic Offensive Arms, 23 UST 3462, TIAS 7504 (1972). http://www.fas.org/nuke/control/salt1/text/salt1.htm

[31] Henry Kissinger, "Briefing by the President's Assistant for National Security Affairs for the Senate Foreign Relations Committee," *Strategic Arms Limitations Agreements: Hearings Before the Committee on Foreign Relations, United States Senate, Ninety-second Congress, Second Session* (Washington, 1972). http://www.state.gov/r/pa/ho/frus/nixon/i/20706.htm

[32] Quoted in Raymond L. Garthoff, "Mutual Deterrence and Strategic Arms Limitation in Soviet Policy," *International Security,* (Vol. 3: Summer, 1978), page 137.

[33] Quoted in James R. Schlesinger, "Strategic Forces," *Defense Department Annual Report* (March 4, 1974), page 6. http://www.airforcemagazine.com/MagazineArchive/Documents/2006/February%202006/0206ke eperfull.pdf

[34] *Ibid.*

[35] Quoted in Matthew G. McKinzie et al., *The U.S. Nuclear War Plan: A Time for Change* (Natural Resources Defense Council, 2001), page 6. http://www.nrdc.org/nuclear/warplan/warplan_start.pdf

[36] US National Security Council, *National Security Decision Memorandum 242* (January 17, 1974), page 2. http://www.gwu.edu/~nsarchiv/NSAEBB/NSAEBB173/SIOP-24b.pdf

[37] George H. W. Bush, "Address to the Nation on Reducing United States and Soviet Nuclear Weapons" (September 9, 1991). http://bushlibrary.tamu.edu/research/public_papers.php?id=3438&year=1991&month=9

[38] Eli Corin, "Presidential Nuclear Initiatives: An Alternative Paradigm for Arms Control," (Nuclear Threat Initiative Issue Brief, March 2004). http://www.nti.org/e_research/e3_41a.html

[39] The White House, *Nuclear Posture Review [Excerpts]* (January 8, 2002), page 7. http://www.globalsecurity.org/wmd/library/policy/dod/npr.htm

[40] *Ibid.*, Foreword.

[41] *Ibid.*, page 25.

[42] George W. Bush, "U.S. Withdrawal from the ABM Treaty: President Bush's Remarks" (December 13, 2001). http://www.armscontrol.org/act/2002_01-02/docjanfeb02

[43] "The Air Force and Navy have both studied the possible deployment of conventional warheads

on their long-range ballistic missiles." See Amy F. Woolf, "Conventional Warheads for Long-Range Ballistic Missile: Background and Issues for Congress," (Congressional Research Service report, 2006). http://digital.library.unt.edu/govdocs/crs/permalink/meta-crs-9819:1

[44] Barack Obama, speech at Hradčany Square, Prague, Czech Republic, (April 5, 2009). http://www.whitehouse.gov/the_press_office/Remarks-By-President-Barack-Obama-In-Prague-As-Delivered/

[45] Peter R. Lavoy, "The Enduring Effects of Atoms for Peace," *Arms Control Today* (December 2003). http://www.armscontrol.org/act/2003_12/Lavoy.asp

[46] George Bunn and John B. Rhinelander, "Looking Back: The Nuclear Nonproliferation Treaty Then and Now," *Arms Control Today* (July/August 2008). http://www.armscontrol.org/act/2008_07-08/lookingback

[47] Treaty on the Non-Proliferation of Nuclear Weapons, 21 UST 483, TIAS 6839 (1968), Article VI. http://www.iaea.org/Publications/Documents/Infcircs/Others/infcirc140.pdf

[48] Nuclear Suppliers Group, "What are the Guidelines?" http://www.nuclearsuppliersgroup.org/Leng/02-guide.htm

[49] IAEA, "Statement on Full-Scope Safeguards Adopted by the Adherents to the Nuclear Suppliers Guidelines," (May 1992). http://www.iaea.org/Publications/Documents/Infcircs/Others/inf405.shtml

[50] Wade Boese, "NSG, Congress Approve Nuclear Trade with India," *Arms Control Today* (October 2008). http://www.armscontrol.org/act/2008_10/NSGapprove

[51] Indrani Bagachi, "Israel's Plea to NSG May Hit India," *The Times of India* (September 29, 2007). http://timesofindia.indiatimes.com/India/Israels_plea_to_NSG_may_hit_India_/articleshow/2413008.cms; M S Tanvir, *PM Rules Out IAEA Access to Qadeer, Wants India Type Waiver for Civil Nuclear Programme*, Pakistan Observer (January 18, 2009).http://pakobserver.net/200901/18/news/topstories01.asp

[52] McGinnis said, "We made clear last year that the United States no longer supports all 13 steps." J. Sherwood McGinnis, "Article VI of the NPT: Remarks to the Second Session of the Preparatory Committee for the 2005 NPT Review Conference," Geneva, Switzerland, (May 1, 2003). http://www.state.gov/t/isn/npt/122735.htm

[53] 2005 Review Conference of the Parties to the Treaty on the Non-Proliferation of Nuclear Weapons, "Final Document," (New York, 2005). http://www.nti.org/h_learnmore/npttutorial/2005NPTRCofficial%20documents/2005NPTRCFinal Report.pdf

[54] White House, *National Strategy to Combat Weapons of Mass Destruction (WMD)* (December 2002), page 2. http://www.fas.org/irp/offdocs/nspd/nspd-wmd.pdf

[55] United Kingdom Foreign and Commonwealth Office, "Proliferation Security Initiative: Chairman's Conclusions at the Fourth Meeting," London, UK (October 10, 2003). http://www.state.gov/t/isn/115305.htm

[56] U.S. Department of State, "The Global Initiative to Combat Nuclear Terrorism," 15 July 2006. http://www.state.gov/t/isn/c18406.htm

[57] Barack Obama, speech at Hradčany Square, Prague, Czech Republic. *op.cit.*

[58] Natural Resources Defense Council, *Table of Global Nuclear Weapons Stockpiles, 1945-2002* (November 2002). http://www.nrdc.org/nuclear/nudb/datab19.asp

[59] "Text of McNamara Speech on Anti-China Missile Defense and U.S. Nuclear Strategy," *New York Times,* (September 19, 1967), page 18.

[60] Constantine A. Pagedas, *Anglo-American Strategic Relations and the French Problem, 1960-1963* (Routledge, 2000), page 260; Richard H. Ullman, "The Covert French Connection," *Foreign Policy* (Summer 1989), pages 13, 16.

[61] Jeffrey T. Richelson, *Spying on the Bomb: American Nuclear Intelligence from Nazi Germany to Iran and North Korea* (Norton, 2006), page 264.

[62] Avner Cohen and William Burr, "Israel Crosses the Threshold," *Bulletin of the Atomic Scientists,* (May/June 2006), pages 27-28.

[63] George Perkovich, *India's Nuclear Bomb* (Berkeley: University of California Press, 2002), page 185.

[64] *Ibid.,* page 191.

[65] Richard H. Speier, Brian G. Chow, S. Rae Starr, *Nonproliferation Sanctions* (Santa Monica: RAND, 2001), page 51.

[66] *Ibid.,* page 46.

[67] Steve Coll, *Ghost Wars: The Secret History of the CIA, Afghanistan and Bin Laden* (New York: Penguin Books, 2004), page 51.

[68] Derek J. Mitchell, *op.cit.*, pages 296-301.

[69] Jonathan D. Pollack and Mitchell B. Reiss, *op.cit.,* pages 262-263.

[70] Anoush Ehteshami, "Iranian Perspectives on the Global Elimination of Nuclear Weapons," in *Unblocking the Road to Zero: Perspectives of Advanced Nuclear Nations*, ed. Barry M. Blechman (Washington, DC: The Henry L. Stimson Center, 2009).

[71] Leon V. Sigal and Joel Wit, "North Korea's Perspectives on the Global Elimination of Nuclear Weapons," in *Unblocking the Road to Zero: Perspectives of Advanced Nuclear Nations*, ed. Barry M. Blechman, op.cit.

[72] Ronald Reagan, "Radio Address to the Nation on Nuclear Weapons," (April 17, 1982). http://www.presidency.ucsb.edu/ws/index.php?pid=42414

[73] Ronald Reagan, "Address Before a Joint Session of the Congress on the State of the Union," (January 25, 1984). http://www.presidency.ucsb.edu/ws/index.php?pid=40205

[74] Ronald Reagan, "Address to the Nation on Defense and National Security" (March 23, 1983). http://www.reagan.utexas.edu/archives/speeches/1983/32383d.htm

[75] Eli Corin, *Op.cit.*

[76] See for instance General John M. Shalikashvili (USA, Ret.), "Findings and Recommendations Concerning the Comprehensive Nuclear Test Ban Treaty," Washington, DC, January 2001 and Committee on Technical Issues Related to Ratification of the Comprehensive Nuclear Test Ban Treaty, Technical Issues Related to the Comprehensive Nuclear Test Ban Treaty (Washington, DC: National Academy Press, 2002).

[77] Barack Obama, speech at Hradčany Square, Prague, Czech Republic, *op.cit.*.

[78] *Ibid.*

[79] Dwight D. Eisenhower, "Atoms for Peace," (December 8, 1953). http://www.iaea.org/About/history_speech.html

[80] United Nations General Assembly, Resolution 1148 (XII) (November 14, 1957). http://daccessdds.un.org/doc/RESOLUTION/GEN/NR0/119/31/IMG/NR011931.pdf?OpenElement

[81] Lyndon B. Johnson, "Annual Message to the Congress on the State of the Union," (January 8, 1964). http://www.presidency.ucsb.edu/ws/index.php?pid=26787

[82] United Nations General Assembly, Resolution 48/75 (December 16, 1993). http://www.un.org/documents/ga/res/48/a48r075.htm

[83] For instance, China has linked FMCT negotiations to prevention of an arms race in outer space negotiations, which the US and UK oppose. See Sharon Squassoni, "Banning Fissile Material Production for Nuclear Weapons: Prospects for a Treaty (FMCT)," (Congressional Research Service report, 2006). http://www.fas.org/sgp/crs/nuke/RS22474.pdf

[84] US Mission to the United Nations in Geneva, "Treaty on the Cessation of Production of Fissile Material for Use in Nuclear Weapons or Other Nuclear Explosive Devices (Draft Text)," (May 18, 2006). http://geneva.usmission.gov/Press2006/0518DraftFMCT.html

[85] Sharon Squassoni, *op. cit.,* page 5.

[86] George P. Shultz, William J. Perry, Henry A. Kissinger and Sam Nunn, "A World Free of Nuclear Weapons," *Wall Street Journal,* (January 4, 2007), page A15; George P. Shultz, William J. Perry, Henry A. Kissinger and Sam Nunn, "Toward a Nuclear-Free World," *Wall Street Journal* (January 15, 2008), page A13.

[87] Douglas Hurd, Malcolm Rifkind, David Owen, and George Robertson, "Start Worrying and Learn to Ditch the Bomb," *The Times Online,* (June 30, 2008). http://www.timesonline.co.uk/tol/comment/columnists/guest_contributors/article4237387.ece

[88] Helmut Schmidt, Richard von Weizsäcker, Egon Bahr, Hans-Dietrich Genscher, "Für eine atomwaffenfrei Welt*" Frankfurter Allgemeine Zeitung* (January 9, 2008). English translation available from the German Foreign Ministry. https://www.diplomatie.diplo.de/index.php?option=com_content&task=view&id=145&Itemid=42 3

[89] K. Subrahmanyan, "When Hawks Turn Moral," *Indian Express* (January 21, 2008).

[90] Gordon Corera, BBC News, "Group seeks nuclear weapons ban," (December 10, 2008). http://news.bbc.co.uk/2/hi/europe/7774584.stm

[91] Russian Prime Minister Vladimir Putin, Valdai Debating Club (September 11, 2008), Quoted on Global Zero Website. http://www.globalzero.org/en/who/governments

[92] State Council Information Office of the People's Republic of China, "China's National Defense in 2006" (December 2006), page 3. http://www.chinadaily.cn/china/2006-12/29/content_5425025.htm

[93] Barack Obama, "Statement on Call for World Without Nuclear Weapons" (January 17, 2008). http://www.barackobama.com/2008/01/17/statement_on_call_for_world_wi.php

[94] John McCain, "McCain's Speech on Nuclear Security" (May 27, 2008). http://www.cfr.org/publication/16349/

[95] Barack Obama, speech at Hradčany Square, Prague, Czech Republic, *op.cit.*

[96] Federation of American Scientists and Natural Resources Defense Council, "Status of World Nuclear Forces," *The Nuclear Information Project* (January 3, 2008). http://www.nukestrat.com/nukestatus.htm

[97] Bruno Tertrais, "French Perspectives on Nuclear Weapons and Nuclear Disarmament," in *Unblocking the Road to Zero: Perspectives of Advanced Nuclear Nations, op.cit.*; Lawrence Freedman, "British Perspectives on Nuclear Weapons and Nuclear Disarmament," in *Unblocking the Road to Zero: Perspectives of Advanced Nuclear Nations, op.cit.*; Rajesh M. Basrur, "Indian Perspectives on the Global Elimination of Nuclear Weapons," in *Unblocking the Road to Zero: Perspectives of Advanced Nuclear Nations, op.cit*; Pan Zhenqiang, "China's Nuclear Strategy in a Changing World Strategic Situation," in *Unblocking the Road to Zero: Perspectives of Advanced Nuclear Nations, op.cit.*; Feroz Hassan Khan, "Pakistan's Perspective on the Global Elimination of Nuclear Weapons," in *Unblocking the Road to Zero: Perspectives of Advanced Nuclear Nations, op.cit.*; Shlomo Brom, "Israeli Perspectives on the Global Elimination of Nuclear Weapons," in *Unblocking the Road to Zero: Perspectives of Advanced Nuclear Nations, op.cit.*

[98] Dmitri Trenin, "Russian Perspectives on the Global Elimination of Nuclear Weapons," in *Unblocking the Road to Zero: Perspectives of Advanced Nuclear Nations*, *op.cit.*

[99] "Joint Statement by President Obama and President Medvedev," London (April 1, 2009). http://www.america.gov/st/texttrans-english/2009/April/20090401125216xjsnommis0.8078381.html

[100] Robert Gates, "Nuclear Weapons and Deterrence in the 21st Century" Carnegie Endowment, (October 28, 2008). http://www.carnegieendowment.org/files/1028_transcrip_gates_checked.pdf

[101] Congressional Commission on the Strategic Posture of the United States, *op.cit.*

ABOUT THE AUTHORS

BRAZIL

AMBASSADOR MARCOS C. de AZAMBUJA is the vice president of the Brazilian Center for International Relations. Previously, he was Brazil's Permanent Representative to the United Nations and the Conference on Disarmament and also held the position of Secretary-General of the Ministry of Foreign Relations in Brazil.

CHINA

MAJOR GENERAL PAN ZHENQIANG is retired from the People's Liberation Army. He is a member of the Executive Council of the Pugwash Conferences on Science and World Affairs.

FRANCE

DR. BRUNO TERTRAIS is a Senior Research Fellow at the Fondation pour la Recherche Stratégique (FRS), as well as an Associate Researcher at the Centre d'études et de recherches internationales (CERI). In 2007-2008, he was a member of the Presidential Commission on the White paper on Defense and National Security and a member of the Ministerial Commission on the White Paper on Foreign and European Policy. Bruno Tertrais is also a member of the International Institute for Strategic Studies (IISS), and a member of the editorial board of the Washington Quarterly. His latest book in English is *War Without End*.

INDIA

DR. RAJESH M. BASRUR is Associate Professor at the S. Rajaratnam School of International Studies, Nanyang Technological University, Singapore. He taught history and politics at the University of Mumbai from 1978 to 2000, and then served as director of the Center for Global Studies in Mumbai, India until 2007. His work focuses on global nuclear politics, nuclear terrorism, South Asian security, international relations theory, and human security. He is the author of *South Asia's Cold War: Nuclear Weapons and Conflict in Comparative Perspective, Minimum Deterrence and India's Nuclear Security*, and *India's External Relations: A Theoretical Analysis*.

IRAN

PROFESSOR ANOUSH EHTESHAMI is Professor of International Relations and also Dean of Internationalisation at Durham University. He was Head of the School of Government and International Affairs at Durham

University (2004-2009) and has also been a Fellow of the World Economic Forum. He was Vice-President and Chair of Council of the British Society for Middle Eastern Studies (BRISMES) from 2000-2003. His current research includes five central themes: The Asian balance of power in the post-Cold War era; the 'Asianisation' of the international system; foreign and security policies of Middle East states since the end of the Cold War; the impact of globalization on the Middle east; and good governance and democratization efforts in the Middle East.

ISRAEL

BRIGADIER GENERAL (ret.) SHLOMO BROM has been a Senior Research Associate at The Institute for National Security Studies in Tel Aviv since 1999. In 2005-2006 he was a guest scholar at USIP (United States Institute of Peace), where his research focused on Israeli national security thinking about Palestinian statehood and the future of Israel's relations with neighboring Arab states. General Brom has also served as Deputy of the national Security Adviser in Israel (2000-2001); Director of the Strategic Planning Division in the IDF's General Staff (1996-1998); and Israeli Defense Attaché in the Republic of South Africa (1988-1990). Throughout the 1990s, general Brom participated in peace negotiations with Syria, Jordan, and the Palestinians. He also represented Israel in multilateral talks on Arms Control and Regional Security. He is the author of numerous articles about strategic and diplomatic issues.

JAPAN

PROFESSOR MATAKE KAMIYA teaches international relations at the Japanese National Defense Academy. His English-language publications have included chapters in edited volumes on Japanese national security policy and articles in The Washington Quarterly and Arms Control Today, among others.

NORTH KOREA

JOEL S. WIT is a Visiting Fellow at the US-Korea Institute, Johns Hopkins School of Advanced International Studies and a Senior Adjunct Research Fellow at Columbia University's Weatherhead Institute for East Asian Studies. Mr. Wit was a State Department official from 1986 until 2002 focusing on arms control and non-proliferation issues. Much of his career was spent working on US policy towards North Korea, including as the department's coordinator for implementation of the 1994 US-North Korea Agreed Framework. He has been a visiting fellow at the Council on Foreign Relations, the Stimson Center and the Brookings Institution as well as a Senior Fellow at the Center for Strategic and International Studies. Mr. Wit is the co-author, along with Robert Gallucci and Dan Poneman, of *Going Critical: The First North Korean Nuclear Crisis* published by the Brookings Institution Press in 2004.

DR. LEON V. SIGAL is director of the Northeast Asia Cooperative Security Project at the Social Science Research Council in New York. Sigal was a member of the editorial board of the *New York Times* from 1989 to 1995. He served in the Bureau of Political-Military Affairs at the US Department of State, in 1979 as International Affairs Fellow and in 1980 as Special Assistant to the Director. His book, *Disarming Strangers: Nuclear Diplomacy with North Korea*, published by Princeton University Press, was one of five nominees for the Lionel Gelber Prize as the most outstanding book in international relations for 1997-1998 and was named the 1998 book of distinction by the American Academy of Diplomacy. His most recent book, *Negotiating Minefields: The Landmines Ban in American Politics*, was published by Routledge in 2006.

PAKISTAN

BRIGADIER GENERAL (ret.) FEROZ KHAN served with the Pakistani Army for 30 years with numerous assignments in the United States, Europe, and South Asia. He has experienced combat action and command on active fronts on the line of control in Siachin Glacier and Kashmir. Most recently he held the post of Director, Arms Control and Disarmament Affairs, within the Strategic Plans Division, Joint Services Headquarters. General Khan has held a series of visiting fellowships at Stanford University's Center for International Studies and Arms Control; the Woodrow Wilson International Center for Scholars; the Brookings Institution; the Center for Non-Proliferation Studies at the Monterey Institute of International Studies; and the Cooperative Monitoring Center, Sandia National Laboratory. General Khan is now a Visiting Professor of National Security Affairs at the Naval Postgraduate School.

RUSSIA

DR. DMITRI TRENIN is a Senior Associate of the Carnegie Endowment for International Peace and Director of its Moscow Center. A graduate of the present Defense University in Moscow, he served in the Soviet/Russian army from 1972 until his retirement in 1993. His assignments included Iraq (military assistance group, 1975-76), Easy Germany/West Berlin (Group of Soviet Forces Germany external relations branch, 1978-83), Switzerland (1985-91, US-Soviet START/INF/Defense and Space talks), and Italy (NATO Defense College, 1993). Trenin taught at the Defense University in Moscow (1983-93) and the Free University of Brussels (1993-94). He received his Ph.D. from the USSR Academy of Sciences' Institute of the USA and Canada in 1994. Trenin's recent books (in English) include: *Getting Russia Right* (2007) and *Central Asia: Views* *from Washington, Moscow and Beijing* (2007). He is a frequent contributor to the world media on international politics and security issues.

TURKEY

DR. HENRI J. BARKEY is a visiting scholar in the Carnegie Endowment for International Peace's Middle Easy Program and the Bernard L. and Bertha F. Cohen Professor at Lehigh University. He previously served as a member of the US State Department Policy Planning Staff working primarily on issues related to the Middle East, the Eastern Mediterranean, and intelligence.

UK

PROFESSOR SIR LAWRENCE FREEDMAN has been Professor of War Studies at King's College London since 1982. He became Vice-Principal at King's in 2003. His most recent books include an Adelphi Paper on *The Revolution in Strategic Affairs*, an edited book on *Strategic Coercion*, an illustrated book on *The Cold War*, a collection of essays on British defence policy and *Kennedy's Wars*, which covers the major crises of the early 1960s over Berlin, Cuba and Vietnam. In addition, the books *Deterrence* and the *Official History of the Falklands Campaign* came out in 2004 and 2005, respectively. His most recent book, *A Choice of Enemies: America confronts the Middle East* was published in May 2008 in the United States.

UNITED STATES

DR. BARRY M. BLECHMAN is the co-founder of the Stimson Center and a Stimson Distinguished Fellow. Dr. Blechman has more than forty years of distinguished service in the national security field. An expert on political/military policies, military strategy, and defense budgets and industries, he has worked in the Departments of State and Defense and at the Office of Management and Budget, and is a frequent consultant to the US Government on a wide range of subjects. A Georgetown Ph.D. in international relations, Dr. Blechman has written extensively on national security issues and has taught at several universities. Alex Bollfrass, a former Scoville Fellow with the Arms Control Association, and Frank Valliere contributed to *US Perspectives on the Global Elimination of Nuclear Weapons*.

ALEXANDER BOLLFRASS is a Research Associate for the International Security and Nuclear Weapons program. Prior to joining the Stimson Center, Alex held a Herbert Scoville, Jr. Peace Fellowship at the Arms Control Association and reported for *Arms Control Today* magazine. He is a graduate of the University of California, Berkeley.

FRANK VALLIERE has interned with the Stimson Center and its International Security and Nuclear Weapons program as well as the Center for Strategic and International Studies and its Homeland Security Program. He holds a BS in Psychology from the University of Florida and a Master's Degree in Forensic Psychology from the City University of New York's John Jay College of Criminal Justice, where he focused on US foreign policy as it relates to terrorism, non-proliferation and national and international security issues, and the application of psychological theory to these areas.